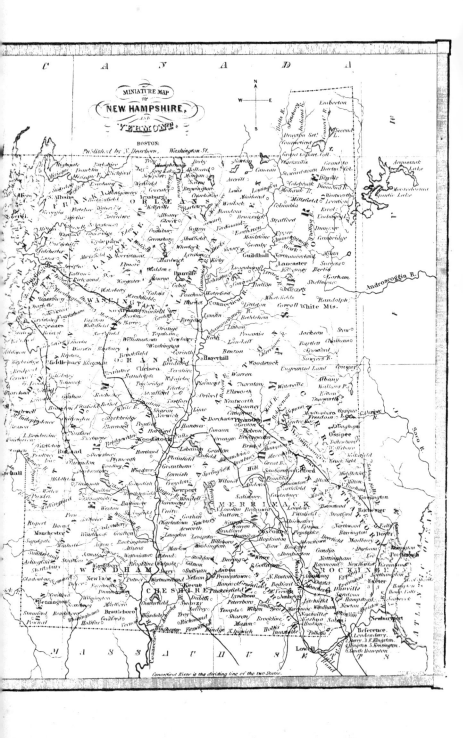

MINIATURE MAP
OF
NEW HAMPSHIRE,
AND
VERMONT

BOSTON:
Published by N. Dearborn, Washington St.

A

GAZETTEER OF VERMONT:

CONTAINING

DESCRIPTIONS OF ALL THE

COUNTIES, TOWNS, AND DISTRICTS

IN THE STATE,

AND OF ITS

PRINCIPAL MOUNTAINS, RIVERS, WATERFALLS, HARBORS, ISLANDS,

AND

CURIOUS PLACES.

TO WHICH ARE ADDED,

STATISTICAL ACCOUNTS OF ITS

AGRICULTURE, COMMERCE AND MANUFACTURES;

WITH A GREAT VARIETY OF OTHER

USEFUL INFORMATION.

BY JOHN HAYWARD,

Author of "The New England Gazetteer," "Book of Religions," &c.

BOSTON:

TAPPAN, WHITTEMORE, AND MASON,

114 WASHINGTON STREET.

1849.

- Notice -

.The foxing, or discoloration with age, characteristic of old books, sometimes shows through to some extent in reprints such as this, especially when the foxing is very severe in the original book. We feel that the contents of this book warrant its reissue despite these blemishes, and hope you will agree and read it with pleasure.

Index by Marlene Towle

Entered according to Act of Congress, in the year 1849, by
JOHN HAYWARD,
In the Clerk's Office of the District Court of Massachusetts.

Facsimile Reprint

Published 1990 By
HERITAGE BOOKS, INC.
1540E Pointer Ridge Place, Bowie, Maryland 20716
(301)-390-7709

ISBN 1-55613-290-5

ANDOVER:
J. D. FLAGG AND W. H. WARDWELL,
STEREOTYPERS AND PRINTERS.

PREFACE.

GAZETTEERS, and other works descriptive of any part of New England, have become so necessary to travellers and men of business, that it behooves those who prepare them, if they value their reputation, to guard, with all their might, against errors; and to use every proper effort to procure, from time to time, such corrections and additions as that favored country requires in its rapid advances in all the moral and physical improvements known to civilized man.

In that respect, the editor of this volume can only say, that he has devoted his whole time and talents, for some years, to this his favorite pursuit; that his means of acquiring information are constantly increasing, so as to enable him to perform his labors with greater ease and fidelity; and that, while he enjoys the good will and confidence of an intelligent community, he shall feel no disposition to relinquish it.

The Rev. Zadock Thompson, of Burlington, Vermont, has recently published a History of that State, Natural, Civil, and Statistical. This is a work of great merit, and valuable to every American citizen; but of peculiar interest to all those, at home and abroad, who claim any alliance to that band of patriots, THE GREEN MOUNTAIN BOYS, whose fame is celebrated in story, and is intimately connected with our country's reputation.

From that work the editor has been permitted to take much of what is valuable in this volume; and for this favor he shall consider Mr. Thompson one of the greatest contributors to his series of NEW ENGLAND Gazetteers, which will soon be completed, and which, with the kind assistance of many friends, he flatters himself will be found worthy of a place in the libraries of many of the sons and daughters of that land, whose green hills and blooming vales exhibit the united power of industry and skill; and on the borders of whose beautiful streams the arts and sciences have erected monuments of renown as enduring as its granite mountains; — a land from whose ports and harbors American commerce first spread its canvas to the breeze, and which now whitens every sea; — a land where Liberty first unfurled her banner, and on which her first battle was fought.

To his learned friend, the Rev. Dr. Jenks, of Boston, for his estimable introductory remarks to this volume; — to the Hon. James McM. Shafter, of Burlington, Secretary of the State of Vermont, for important documents; — to Henry Stevens, Esq., of Barnet, for much valuable antiquarian and historical lore, and to many others who have favored the editor in his complicated task, he tenders the homage of a grateful heart.

INDEX.

Page.

Academies, 30, 46, 52, 54, 90, 103, 110
Agriculture and Manufactures, . 190
Allen, Ethan, ... 171
Asylum for the Insane, . . 188
Banks, ... 190
Bays, Harbors, Capes, Points of
Land, &c., ... 167
Bennington, Battle of, . . 211
Bidwell, George, . . . 118
Bloody Brook, ... 94
Boring for Salt Water, . . 88
Boundaries.— See *Descriptions of*
Towns.
Boundaries and Extent, . . 184
Brave Fellow, . . . 102
Cannon heard at a great distance, 23
——— taken at Bennington, . 216
Cascades, ... 69
Cattle, number of, . . . 169
Caverns and Caves, 21, 30, 48, 49,
53, 55, 69, 80, 83, 87, 100, 131,
141, 163, 199
Censuses, from 1791 to 1840, 145, &c.
Chittenden, Thomas, . . 198
Chief Justices, Succession of, . 186
Climate and Indian Summer, 198
Colburn, Zera, . . . 39
Colleges, ... 194
Commerce and Navigation, . 193
Common Schools, . . 194
Congressional Districts, . . 187
Constitution of Vermont, . 200
Copperas, Manufacture of, . . 119
Counties, area of, . . . 170
County Table, . . 169, &c.
Courts.—See *Counties.*
Crown Point, ... 34
Curious Dwelling-place, . . 112
——— Meeting-house, . . 104
——— Way of Naming a Town, 24
——— Places, 43, 70, 87, 90, 94,
111, 122, 163

Page

Dairies, Large, ... 53
Destructive Worms, . . 102
Distances.—See *Descriptions of*
Towns.
Dutchman's Point, . . . 94
Education, ... 19
Elevated Ponds, . . 81, 87
Farm of a Revolutionary Hero, 77
Fidelity of a dog, . . . 44
Finances, ... 193
First Bridge across Connecticut
River, ... 105
First Ministers.—See *Description of*
Towns.
First Settlers.—See *Description of*
Towns.
Fish, Transferring, . . . 135
Floating Land, ... 137
Four Boys at a birth, . . 68
Frog, old, ... 33
Gallantry and Female Spirit, . 40
Galusha, Jonas, ... 113
General Wait, a brave soldier, 12
Gores of Land, ... 169
Government and Judiciary, . 185
Governors, Succession of, . . 186
Grand List for 1848, . . 170
Grain, bushels of, . . . 170
Great Girl of her age, . . 99
——— Distance to go to mill, . 92
——— Oxbow, . . . 91
Gulf Road, ... 138
Hay, tons of, ... 170
Hardships of the First Settlers, 51,
63, 67, 68, 71, 73, 83, 92, 97, 101,
112, 126, 131
Horses, number of, . . . 169
Ice beds, ... 99, 129
Incorporation of Counties, date of, 169
Indian Captives, . . 32, 77
——— Depredations, . . 77, 102
——— Relics, . . 85, 94, 117

1*

Industry and Bravery rewarded, 124
Introduction, ... 7
Lakes and Ponds, . . . 164
Land Slides, ... 97
Large Families, . . . 137
Light Houses, ... 193
Longevity, . . 84, 122, 124, 137
Loss of a toe, by frost, in June, . 98
Lyon, Matthew, Colonel, . 60
Militia, ... 196
Manufactures, &c., p. 190. — See
    Description of Towns.
Minerals, 24, 32, 33, 42, 47, 48,
    50, 52, 53, 56, 70, 76, 81, 83, 85,
    87, 96, 99, 107, 108, 116, 121,
                            122, 125, 140
Mineral Springs, 36, 37, 48, 68,
    70, 74, 91, 96, 99, 100, 137, 138
Mountains, ... 151
Mutual Fire Insurance Companies, 190
Name of the State, . . . 184
Natural Bridges, 63, 78, 81, 86,
                            131, 163
Note, ... 211
Oath of Allegiance, . . . 123
Paper from bass wood bark, . 60
Personal Estate, value of.—See
    Grand List.
Plot against the Indians, . . 155
Polls, number of.—See Grand List.
Ponds and Lakes, . . . 164
Population Table, . . . 145
Porcelain earth, ... 87
Post Villages, ... 183
Potatoes, bushels of, . . . 170
Probate Courts, . . . 195
Productions of the Soil.—See De-
    scription of Towns.
Public Buildings, . . 88, 141, 187

Quail John, ... 123
Railroads, ... 196
Real Estate, value of.—See Grand
    List.
Rivers, Creeks, and Brooks, . 153
Rogers Rangers, . . . 24, 161
Runaway Pond, ... 64
Scotch Far..iers, and good fare, 109
Sheep, number of, . . . 170
Stark, General, . . . 213
State House, ... 187
—— Prison, . . , . 188
—— Senatorial Districts, . . 187
Statistical Tables, . . . 169
Stockbridge Indians, . . 84
Successful Female Midwife, . 84
Sugar, pounds of, . . . 170
Swine, number of, . . . 170
Taxable Property, amount of.—
    See Grand List.
Tornadoes, . . . 73, 100, 102
Towns, number of, . . . 169
—— Shire, distance of from
    Boston, ... 169
Towns, Shire, Latitude and Lon-
    gitude of, ... 169
Travelling on Connecticut River,
    in 1763, ... 71
Wait, General, . . . 127
Warner, General, . . . 213
Water-cure Establishment, . 32
Waterfalls and Cataracts, 44, 59,
    72, 78, 82, 86, 90, 105, 117, 125,
                            126, 167
Windmill Point, . . . 20
Wool, pounds of, . . . 170
Wreck of Arnold's Fleet, . . 97
Yankee Enterprise, . . . 111

VERMONT.

THE territory which is now included in the State of VERMONT, and which lies between Lower Canada, New Hampshire, Massachusetts, and New York, was, for a long time after the surrounding settlements were made, in great measure unexplored by Europeans. In its vicinity, Canada was the first known and peopled by them, and a settlement was then made by the Dutch at Aurania, now Albany, and at the mouth of the Hudson. Then followed the settlements along the New England shores; but a considerable period elapsed before they penetrated the interior, and, consequently, that interior was hardly marked but by marauding parties of Indians, and the footsteps of their unfortunate captives.

It is not found that any large body of the natives was cantoned within the present limits of the State. There was, indeed, a tribe bearing the name of Coossucks in the north-east part of it; * but these were inconsiderable in number, and hardly known in the records of warfare, being surrounded, although at no little distance, by larger tribes. These tribes consisted, in the first place, of the Five or Six Confederated Nations, at the head of whom figured the Mohawks. Among the French they bore the name of Iroquois, and had at an early period become their enemies, connecting themselves successively with the Dutch and English of New York, and adhering to their interests with great fidelity for more than a century and a half. The territory

* See a description of this tribe of Indians in Mr. *Thompson's* very valuable "History of Vermont, Natural, Civil, and Statistical," from which, with his obliging permission, several items of information are derived in the following pages.

occupied by them, although denominated Canadian by COLDEN, in 1747, was included within the present boundaries of New York, being south of the St. Lawrence and the Lakes, although their conquests extended far to the north and north-west. They were the terror of other tribes, yet seem never to have settled to the eastward .f the Hudson, and the beautiful lake which was once denominated from there, but now has the name of CHAMPLAIN.*

The Indians who were in alliance with the French of Canada were principally the Algonkins, otherwise called Adirondacks, a tribe between whom and the Iroquois there were frequent wars, the result of hostilities previous to the arrival of Europeans.† Whether or not the tribe denominated of St. Francis, as residing on the banks of that river, were of Algonkin or more eastern derivation, or whether connected with the Coossucks or not, is not clear. CHARLEVOIX describes them as Abenakis, who had left their brethren of the east, and migrated to Canada for the benefit of an alliance with the French.

On the south-east and south, the Indians of the other New England States, New Hampshire, Massachusetts, Rhode Island, and Connecticut, inhabited mostly the sea coast, and appear to have greatly dreaded the warlike character and prowess of the Mohawks. On the east were the Abenakis, Etechemins, and Micmacs, attracted also to the sea shore, doubtless by the facility of procuring thence a portion of their provisions.

Thus it would seem, that the interior country which now forms VERMONT was, as it were, a thoroughfare between powerful contending Indian nations or tribes, without being conspicuous as the seat of any considerable body of natives. It was traversed, rather than settled by them; its water conveyances north and south admitting also an easy navigation by their canoes; and hence in the remote periods of native history has little that requires or can repay research. This is an observable peculiarity.

Another circumstance which still more strikingly characterizes the country, is the history of the claims made on its territory, by the States with which it is environed. To enter minutely into this history, is no aim of the present Introduction. But without adverting to it, our account would be exceedingly incomplete, as it tended not a little to mould the character of the inhabitants. For, in the process of settling the country, the lamentable conflicting of claims, as will be seen, imposed severe hardships on the enterprising men who ventured to leave the older settlements, and form in the wilderness homes for their growing families. Many a town contains in its rural burying place the remains of

> " Some village HAMPDEN, who, with dauntless breast,
>   The little tyrant of his fields withstood ; "

since, as successive claimants pressed their demands, the inhabitants were compelled to re-purchase their farms, or leave them; suffering over again the

---

* *Holmes's* Annals, Vol. I., p. 141. This name was given in 1611, three years after *Champlain* had founded Quebec. See also *Dunlap's* Hist. of N. Y., Vol. I., p. 19.

† See *Colden*, Hist. of the Five Nations, Part I., and the excellent " Synopsis of the Indian Tribes," by the Hon. Mr. *Gallatin*, published in the Coll. of the Amer. Antiq. Soc., Vol. II., where the Adirondacks are characterized as of the " family " of Algonkin-Lenape.

grievances which disgraced the government of ANDROS, and ended in his seizure and confinement by the injured and enraged people.* His arbitrary cupidity, in which he but too faithfully imitated his worthless master, the bigoted and tyrannical JAMES II., set an unhappy example, which yet was followed, and produced a hardihood of opposition that nerved the men of Vermont to daring actions.

When the country which forms the sea coast of New England began to be settled from Europe, the claim of Massachusetts to territory was extended to "three miles north of the River Merrimac." Casting one's eye on the map, it is easy to perceive, that a line drawn due west from this northern boundary, as it is formed by the bend of the river toward the north, not far from its mouth, would cut off a considerable portion of the southern part of what now constitutes Vermont. The Massachusetts government, therefore, when it extended its cares to the security of the northern frontiers against the Indians of Canada, without any hesitation or doubt, as it seems, formed in 1723 a lodgement in what is now Brattleborough, on the western bank of Connecticut River. There, during the distressing war with the natives, aided by the French, their instigators, which spread such terror and desolation along the borders of the settlements of Maine and New Hampshire, as well as Massachusetts, a fort was constructed by Lieutenant-Governor DUMMER, of the latter State, which received his name; and the next year a settlement followed. This was the first English settlement within the limits of Vermont.†

But although the frontier toward Canada was thus extended, and, under the shelter of a fort, the labors of clearing and cultivating the land appeared practicable, yet the country was by no means in a state of security. We must never forget that American colonists were from different nations. Spaniards, we know, peopled the southern part of the continent, or overran it with their merciless troops, at an early period after its discovery by COLUMBUS. And, jealous as they ever were of any encroachment on their power, wealth, or influence, they would not have left " the bleak, inhospitable north " to France, or England, each of which nations took a portion of it, had they discovered in it any *gold*, which, as the commodity most available for immediate use, and soonest adapted to the gratification of eager avarice, they chiefly sought. By papal permission and decree, they claimed all America. But France resisted this claim, and labored to form there an empire of her own; and CHARLEVOIX, the historian of it, boasts its extent as "greater than all Europe,"‡ although the proud Spaniard termed it "of nothing worth." § This empire she exerted herself to establish and enlarge, by all practicable means. Among these was the employment of a religious influence over the minds of the natives. Hence, in no inconsiderable degree, the efforts of her able, sagacious, indefatigable missionaries, most if not all of whom were Jesuits, bound to an implicit obedience to their head, eager to extend to heathen nations the papal sway, which had suffered so much from LUTHER and the Reformation, and expecting to

* See *Hutchinson's* Hist. Mass., &c.   † *Holmes's* Amer. Annals, I., p. 531.
‡ Hist. de la Nouv. France, t. I., p. 1.   § The import of the name " Canada."

merit everlasting life by their exertions and sacrifices in spreading the triumphs of their faith; at the same time looking on the English as heretics, beyond the pale of *the church,* and so doomed to everlasting perdition. Religious bigotry, and hatred, and contempt, were all combined in their almost unmitigated hostility; the full spirit of which seemed imparted to their native converts, in addition to their own savage propensities and habits. Can we wonder, then, at the dread of Indian warfare that pervaded the frontier settlements of New England on the north?

It must, however, be observed, that if treachery and cunning marked the Indian, as sensible of his disadvantages in open warfare with his foes of European origin; and breach of promise, and cruelty, and revenge, too often distinguished the Romanist, and led him also to connive at and permit in his Indian subjects and allies atrocities at which Christian civilization shudders; there was yet no disposition in the puritans of New England to view with favor the character or conduct of a papist. The very name was odious.

VERMONT, then, as a "thoroughfare" between nations of different origin, pursuits, and interests, attractive as it was from its fertility and adaptedness to the purposes of agriculture and grazing, could not be occupied by peaceful farmers while the surrounding populations were struggling for mastery. Nor did the impediments end even here.

The French, in 1731, erected a fort on the eastern side of Lake Champlain, towards its southern extremity; but they soon demolished it, and chose a position on the western side, where they built the celebrated fortress generally called Crown Point, although named by themselves Fort St. Frederic. Their object was, to facilitate their way to the Six Nations, whether for war or proselytism, and to their own possessions on the Mississippi beyond them; in order to environ ultimately the English colonists, and confine them to the Atlantic coast. The lake and its water communications were familiar to them, therefore, and highly valued. But on the land it would seem, they had not leisure to make permanent settlements; nor, perhaps, any present inducement, at such distance from their capital, and under other circumstances of the case. Meanwhile, as the lands of Connecticut and Massachusetts became occupied by the posterity of the first settlers, new fields of labor were sought. Applications were therefore made to the government of the latter State, by several of its inhabitants who associated for the purpose, and a grant was made them to the northward of Fort Dummer, and on the eastern side of Connecticut River. This was in 1735, and the settlement took the name of No. 4, afterwards called Charlestown. But not ten years elapsed before war was again rife between England and France; and in 1746 this settlement was attacked by Canadian Indians,* and, for the time, ruined. Nevertheless the spirit of the early settlers was unbroken. They returned, builded again, cultivated their lands afresh, although with their weapons beside them; were again and again attacked, waylaid, several of them made captives and sold in Canada; and thus persevered, with unabated zeal and bravery, through all their severe trials,

* See its interesting history in the Collections made by *Farmer* and *Moore*, &c.

until their efforts were, in the good providence of the GOD of their fathers, crowned with success.

It is almost impracticable, in these times of ease and security, to appreciate justly the hardships undergone by those who " made the wilderness to smile and blossom." Especially may this remark be made in reference to Vermont, although applicable far more extensively.

But, added to the hardships attending the subduing of the soil, and to " the sword of the wilderness," in the " peril " of which they often " gat their bread," the disputes concerning titles to the land itself, to which we have before alluded, occasioned peculiar trouble. The boundary line between Massachusetts and New Hampshire was not settled until March 5, 1740, when it was established by GEORGE II., to whom applications had been made for that purpose, in the manner in which it has since been preserved, and now exists.*
On the establishment of this line, it appeared but reasonable to all parties that New Hampshire should extend on the west as Massachusetts extended in that quarter; and hence her claim to the lands west of the Connecticut, and north of the Massachusetts line. Grants were therefore made by the governor of New Hampshire without scruple, and as the courage or necessities of settlers might prompt their applications. In this manner the territory of Bennington † was granted, in 1749, and other grants followed.

Again, however, war intervened ; and, from 1754 until the final conquest of Canada by the British arms, in 1760, it raged with various success, but with great sacrifices and sufferings on the part of frontier settlers, exposed as they necessarily were, and furnishing no small number of the provincial troops.

The return of peace brought with its blessing still another trouble, in the claims that arose from a new quarter. The State of New York, settled, as we have seen, by the Dutch, a few years after ‡ the French had planted themselves in Canada, had indeed long since passed under the dominion of England, being finally subdued in 1664. But the Dutch had made a small establishment for trading with the nations on the Connecticut ; and, for a considerable period, stoutly disputed the possession with the settlers from the jurisdictions of both Plymouth and Massachusetts.§ Indeed they seem to have honestly purchased from the natives a right to the soil, with as much scrupulousness as the very puritans at the east of them. Their claim, of a nature like that of the English, was made to extend, says DUNLAP,‖ "from Cape Cod to Delaware Bay, on the Atlantic, including the islands of the sea coast; the River St. Lawrence seems to have bounded it on the north ; on the south, some un-

* See *Belknap's* N. H., *Hutchinson's* Mass., and *Williams's* Hist. Vermont, 2d ed.

† See the article in the following Gazetteer.

‡ That is, in 1609, at the commencement of their twelve years' truce with Spain, which opened again the way to foreign enterprise. The year 1604 is fixed, by *Charlevoix* and others, as the time when the Sieur *de Monts* and *Samuel Champlain* completed the discovery of Canada, and took possession of the country for *Henry* IV. of France, almost a century after the first knowledge of it claimed by the French.

§ See *Trumbull's* Connecticut, and *Dunlap's* Hist. N. Y., for particulars, with the authorities quoted in note last but two.

‖ Hist. of N. Y., Vol. I., p. 9.

defined line beyond Delaware Bay ; and west, it was boundless." Afterward, however, it was narrowed down to the territory west of the Fresh River, as they termed the Connecticut. Mention is made of their purchasing of the Indians the territory between this and the North River, and " twenty-one miles inland ; " and DE LAET, one of their early historians,* dwells on the pleasant-ness and fertility of the country, visited, after HUDSON, by ADRIAN BLOCK, in 1614. Until recently, however, we have had little knowledge concerning the voyages of the Dutch navigators. Honor is at length given, and justice done them in the Collections of the New York Historical Society.

Without entering too minutely into details, in this place, it may be suffi-cient to remark that, notwithstanding it has been asserted by some, that as early as 1623 the Dutch built a fortresss at the present site of Hartford ; yet TRUMBULL † states it to have been as late as 1633, only three years before Governor HAYNES and Mr. HOOKER led their little colony thither. Disputes there were, sharp and long continued, with respect to boundaries. The Eng-lish confided in their royal charter, and the ability of their king to sustain it ; the Dutch in the liberty granted them by their High Mightinesses the States General of Holland ; and nothing but the superiority of British power, which effected the conquest of New York, and gave to the " Colony of New Nether-lands " a character, laws, alliances, and interests wholly English, prevented the establishment of a Dutch republic on these western shores. And it admits of question, whether true candor has in this country been shown to the claims of the noble spirited people, who authorized and forwarded the founding of New Amsterdam, " at a time," said a worthy descendant from them, " when that nation [Holland] had just sprung into political existence, after a long, bloody, and most glorious struggle against civil and religious tyranny, during which all the energies of patriotism, courage, and talents had been suddenly and splendidly developed." ‡

To be brief in this rapid review, a long period of silence on the subject of the Dutch claims, or the claims of New York, in reference to territory north of Massachusetts and west of Connecticut River, seems to have been main-tained. This, perhaps, was owing to two considerations : the one, that already more land was claimed and possessed than the inhabitants could occupy and cultivate ; and the other, that the northern frontier beyond Massachusetts, open as it was to the invasion of the French and their Indian allies or sub-jects, presented no attractions to settlers.

When, however, the establishment of peace removed the fears of savage out-rage, and rendered the subduing of the wilderness no longer a perilous enter-prise, " the unsettled lands of the country acquired a new value, and were everywhere explored and sought after by speculators and adventurers. None appeared more inviting than the tract between Lake Champlain and Connecti-cut River. The soil was rich and fertile, favorable in many places to the pro-duction of grain, and in all to grazing and the raising of cattle. It was plenti-

---

* See N. Y. Hist. Coll. Vol. I., pp. 92, 295.　　　　† Hist. of Connect., Vol. I., p. 21.
‡ See *Verplanck's* Anniversary Discourse before the N. Y. Hist. Soc., 1818.

fully watered by streams and rivers, and abounded with necessary and useful timber. In such a soil and situation, the labor and hardships of a few years could scarcely fail of producing rich and valuable farms; with all the ease and independence naturally annexed to industry in the rural economy of life."*

Application being made, as we have seen above, to the governor of New Hampshire, within whose territory this region was supposed to lie, he proceeded so far to issue grants, that in 1761 not less than sixty townships, of six miles square, were granted on the west of Connecticut River. In one or two years more, they amounted to one hundred and thirty-eight; keeping twenty miles east of the Hudson, so far as that extended northward, and then advancing to the eastern shore of Lake Champlain: thus enriching the governor, who, beside the fees and donations attending the business, reserved five hundred acres in each township for himself. This aroused New York. On the 28th of December, 1763, the lieutenant governor, COLDEN, issued a proclamation, in which he recited the grants made to the Duke of York by his brother, CHARLES II., asserted their validity, claimed the jurisdiction as far east as Connecticut River, and commanded the sheriff of Albany County to return the names of all persons who under color of the New Hampshire grants had taken possession of any lands west of the river.

This proclamation governor WENTWORTH met by another, dated March 13, 1764, in which he declared the grant to the Duke of York to be obsolete, and asserted, that New Hampshire extended as far west as did Massachusetts and Connecticut, and that the grants made by New Hampshire would be confirmed, even should the jurisdiction be altered. He exhorted the settlers not to be intimidated, but to cultivate their lands with diligence; and required the civil officers to exercise jurisdiction as far westward as grants had been made, and to punish all disturbers of the peace.

Two authorities were now up, and a contest between them might be anticipated. The assurances of the New Hampshire governor tended to quiet the minds of the settlers; but, on the part of New York, an express application was made to the crown. This stated, on what authority is, however, disputed, that the people were desirous to be included in that government; and that, as the course of business must ever lie toward New York, it would be for the convenience and advantage of the people, who, however, publicly disowned the application afterwards, to be united to that province. Nevertheless, it prevailed; and the king, on the 20th of July, 1764, ordered and declared "the western banks of the River Connecticut, from where it enters the province of the Massachusetts Bay, as far north as the forty-fifth degree of northern latitude, *to be* the boundary line, between the said two provinces of New Hampshire and New York."

Nothing appeared in this decision to alarm the people. Concluding that their title to the lands they had settled would be but confirmed by it, they had no idea of disputing the jurisdiction of New York, or opposing its government. They supposed the words "to be" were designed to express the future, and

---

* Dr. *Williams*, from whose account much of what immediately follows is abridged.

not to refer to the past. But not so did the New York government. They construed it, says the historian, "as a declaration not only of what was to be, for the time to come, but of what was, and always *had been*, the eastern limit of New York: and, of consequence, that the grants which had been made by the governor of New Hampshire were grants of what had always belonged to New York, and were therefore illegal, and of no authority." Letters had indeed passed between the governors of New Hampshire and New York, WENT-WORTH and CLINTON, concerning their respective boundaries, as early as 1750,* notwithstanding which the grants had still been issued; and it is surprising to see the confidence with which, on both sides, the claims were pressed. The late eminent chancellor KENT,† writing of the dispute, as it was in 1777, says, "the inhabitants of *the north-east part of the State* (now Vermont) which had been represented in the convention under the names of the counties of Cumberland and Gloucester, renounced their allegiance, and set up for an independent State. On the 30th of June, in that year, they were knocking at the door of congress for a recognition of their independence, and an admission into the Union." On the other hand, Dr. WILLIAMS, speaking of the New York claim under the grant to king JAMES, says, "there were no principles, which apply to human affairs, by which this grant would bear a strict examination." He terms it "a blundering transaction;" and says that the geographical "bounds of it were contradictory, indefinite, and impossible."

The time, however, came for enforcing authority; and the government of New York required the settlers to surrender the charters they had received from New Hampshire, and take out new grants from New York, attended with great fees and expense. Some settlers complied, and bought their lands a second time; while others absolutely refused. Actions of ejectment followed, commenced in the courts of the new counties which had been formed; and these were decided there in favor of New York. Great profits accrued to its rulers from these measures, for the amount of them was far higher than the original cost of the titles from New Hampshire.

But opposition was made in cases where ejectment by official authority was attempted; and the settlers, "instead of being depressed into submission, seemed to derive new powers from oppression; and the people," says Dr. WIL-LIAMS, "soon began to associate, to defend one another, in their opposition to the courts and officers of New York." Ten years of litigation and of occasional violence followed, of which it is remarked by BELKNAP, "that although [the dispute] was carried on with a degree of virulence, unfriendly to the progress of civilization and humanity within the disputed territory; yet it called into action a spirit of vigorous self-defence, and hardy enterprise, which prepared the nerves of that people for encountering the dangers of a revolution more extensive and beneficial."

Among the hardy, resolute and brave men whom these difficulties were now nurturing, few became more distinguished than SETH WARNER and ETHAN

---

* *Belknap's* Hist. N. H., p. 323, F. and M.'s ed.

† Address to the N. Y. Hist. Soc., 1828. See also *Dunlap*, Hist. N. Y.

ALLEN. Scenes of the revolutionary struggle were fast developing the character of our countrymen. One and another aggression of the British ministry, intent on carrying their favorite point, the civil subjection of the colonies, was provoking the opposition, not of the New England colonies alone, but others along the Atlantic border. The successful resistance to the Stamp Act of 1765, and which produced its welcome repeal, became an encouragement to the friends of liberty; who, in various ways, evinced their determination to make their value and consequence known and felt by the mother country. Of these a better appreciation was indeed made in that quarter, than had heretofore been entertained. But still the progress of events conducted to an open rupture, on the special history of which it is no object of this Introduction to enlarge. Suffice it to say, that the territory now included in Vermont was very peculiarly exposed, and the situation of its inhabitants in many respects very singular.

It would, in fact, be difficult to produce a parallel to the anomalous state of these settlers. Their *improvements*, made on the lands they had purchased, were effected at imminent peril. Their titles to the lands themselves had been honestly acquired on their part, but were disputed by contending governments, which yet exercised over them no effectual authority,* and the total loss of them hazarded. To neither of these governments could they appeal without slighting the other; nor, consistently with their own interest, and duty to their families, submit to either. They felt, therefore, constrained to temporise; and while, with the rest of their brethren, they entered, as individually called by an imperious sense of duty, into the scenes of the Revolution, they were nevertheless not unmindful of the peculiarities of their own case.

But it is not to be supposed, as it surely will not be by any true "Green Mountain boy," or New Englander, that frontier settlers, coming out from such a state of society as had been constituted originally by the pilgrim fathers, and handed down from them, could consent to live without law, order, or those social institutions on which order and law depend. No! The towns, small and exposed as they might be, and struggling, as inevitably they must, with the hardships incident to settlements in the wilderness, cannot thrive without government—and they who are, at least for a season, beyond reach of the laws that govern the larger communities, from which they are providentially separated, become "a law unto themselves." They have their town meetings; they decide on the qualifications of voters in them; they choose their moderator, their town clerk, their selectmen, to manage the affairs of their little, but, to themselves and their families, all-important community. The school and the school committee, the church and its pastor, the constable and the justice of the peace, must all be included.† The citizen of New England, place him where you will, whether in the Old Colony or California, in Vermont or Iowa, cannot feel

* Although four counties had been nominally organized by New York, two on each side of the Green Mountains.

† These were, in fact, the principles on which the original grants from the New Hampshire government were constructed. See the copy of one in *Thompson's* Hist. of Vermont, 2d part, p. 224, and the articles Bennington, Guilford, &c.

contented or happy, until these are all provided for the civic association of
which GOD, in His providence, has made him a member; and thanks be to
GOD, that a clear, sober view of the real wants and true interest of society
forces this just appreciation on so many energetic minds!

Still there were many, doubtless, who entered the wilderness of Vermont, as
they have other regions of frontier exposure and peril, without having previously imbibed a "love of things that are excellent"—men of rude passions,
uneasy temperaments, reckless of rule or resolved to resist it, lawless, selfish
and overbearing. Such are found in all ages and countries. But the progress
to social order either shakes them off, or humanizes them, or neutralizes in
time their baleful influence.

The state of society and the emergency of their times have often in our
country produced individuals of that class which we are early led to admire in
the histories of ancient Greece and Rome: men who become eminent, not for
the possession and cultivation of a single talent only, but for the development
of the various powers bestowed on human nature, in their several fair proportions, as the necessities of their condition may demand. Such in New Hampshire was MESHECH WEARE; in Massachusetts, ELISHA WILLIAMS, characterized so justly and beautifully by DODDRIDGE;* ASHMUN also, of whom
one of the "favored of the Muses"† writes, that he was

> "A leader, when the blast of ruthless war swept by,
> A teacher, when the storm was past, and guide to worlds on high."

And the circumstances which called forth the vigor and courage of WARNER
and ALLEN, whose names only have been mentioned here, but on whose history we cannot dwell, brought into active and beneficial exercise the talents
and virtues of THOMAS CHITTENDEN, who, though enjoying in early life but
few advantages of education, shone nevertheless under the requirements of his
trying times and high office; and has left a name which posterity cannot but
honor, as his cotemporaries revered and loved it.

The anomalous condition of the settlers, to which allusion has been made,
requires a further description. They had represented their case to the throne
as early as 1764; and in 1767 an inhibition was issued to the governor of New
York, who was required to desist from making any further grants until the
royal will should be made known, "upon pain of his Majesty's highest dis-
pleasure." This notwithstanding, grants were made, and resisted; and a series of altercations excited so greatly the animosity of the opposite parties, that
a civil war must have been the issue, had not the events which occurred at
Lexington and Concord, in 1775, arrested the attention of all, and fixed it on
the interests of the whole country.

The seizure of Ticonderoga by Col. ALLEN and his associates; of Crown
Point by Col. WARNER, and of Fort St. John by ARNOLD, soon gave to the
American forces the command of Lake Champlain in its whole extent: while
the subsequent capture of BURGOYNE, after the partial engagements of Hub-

* Quoted by Dr. *Allen*, in his Am. Biogr. and Hist. Dict.   † Mrs. *Sigourney*, Id.

bardton and Bennington, prevented any further fears, at least for a season, respecting the northern frontier.

In the mean time, great want was felt of some well-defined government over the population formed on the " Grants." A Congress had been constituted of delegates from the greater part of the colonies, and held its first session in 1774. At its second meeting the next year, a committee was sent on to Philadelphia to consult with its members. On their return, this committee, by issuing circulars, and reporting the result of their mission, prepared the way for a convention of delegates from the several towns, which had now become accustomed for some time to act together for mutual defence. This convention met on the 16th of January, 1776, and presented its petition to congress; but this was subsequently withdrawn, in consequence of a recommendation to submit for the present to New York; and finally, after other preparatory steps, the territory was declared, January 15th, 1777, a free and independent State, assuming the picturesque name of VERMONT.

This important measure was taken with great firmness, moderation and unanimity. Yet it was followed, as under existing circumstances might have been anticipated, by opposition on the part of New York, petitioning the congress not to acknowledge the act; and on the part of New Hampshire, claiming several of the towns which had embodied themselves in the new State. Nor was it until after a variety of changes, and much negotiation, of which the details might fill a volume,* that these external concerns were adjusted, and VERMONT became an integral part of the NEW AMERICAN UNION. That happy event took place, after a satisfactory settlement of all disputes with the States both of New Hampshire and New York, March 4th, 1791. The general history of the State since is blended with that of the nation.

Under all their difficulties and embarrassments, in the adjustment of land titles, the subduing of the wilderness, the arrangement of their political concerns, and the horrors of warfare, the inhabitants had not neglected the claims of religion and good learning. The settlement of the ministry in the small towns, as they were successively formed and grew able to sustain it, was followed up with a good degree of zeal and perseverance. The condition of society seemed to require and effectually obtained a free toleration of religious sentiments, with no distinction in the claims of sect or denomination. An entire sundering of bonds between the Church and the State was accomplished—and the result has seemed to show, that then the religion of the Gospel flourished best, when left to its own heavenly resources, and the zealous love and efforts of its sincere friends; human laws being only then appealed to, when infractions of special civil compacts rendered such appeal needful. Hence absolute contracts for the support of the ministry can be exacted by law, but the law does not compel any to form such contracts.† Revivals of the power of religion have not been unusual. Nearly 20,000 communicants were found in June,

---

* See, however, for the particulars, either Dr. *Williams's* History, or the clear though brief exhibition of all these transactions, consecutively, in *Thompson's* Vermont, Part II.

† See *Graham's* Sketches.

1848, connected with the 189 churches embodied in the "General Convention of Congregational Ministers and Churches," which then held its session at Brandon.* And the statistics of other denominations, which are found in this State, as in the rest of New England, bear comparison with this result.

For the cause of Education VERMONT has done nobly; and she deserves the high honor of being ranked among the few governments that have wisely discerned and followed out with energy the permanent welfare of those who sustain them. At the last census, when the number of inhabitants was found to be 291,860, the district schools were 2,402, and the children and youth of suitable age to attend them, perhaps from 4 to 18 years, was 97,578. In 1844, the pupils in actual attendance were 52,665. The School Fund was reported to be, in 1841, $164,292,28; and, beside these schools, the State had incorporated, in the course of sixty years, 53 academies—several of which, however, Mr. THOMPSON informs us, "had ceased to exist," while a few among them are sustained by different religious denominations and private benefactions.

To crown this system, VERMONT has a "State University" at Burlington, now in a flourishing condition; and a College at Middlebury, possessing at least equal advantages. Both are high in public favor; the latter having graduated 785 pupils, and the former, 651, in 1841. There is also a Medical College.

Medical societies, and societies for benevolent purposes have been greatly multiplied in the State. Its agriculture, manufactures, and, by means of Lake Champlain, its navigation also, have been encouraged, developed and become greatly successful.† As yet, no State Survey of its Geology has been completed; but the progress of its railroads, so vigorously prosecuted, and promising such advantages, in bringing the riches of the West to the sea coast, will, doubtless, make apparent also at an early period the worth of such a measure.

In 1842, began the celebration of Forefathers' Day :‡ and that whatever was commendable in their character and spirit may, under the blessing of their and our GOD, flourish in this now thriving State, is our hearty wish and prayer.

---

* See the Minutes of that Convention, printed at Windsor, where is established its Religious Journal. The first newspaper in the State was published in 1781.

† For particulars, consult the GAZETTEER, under the several localities.

‡ Boston Recorder of Jan. 12, 1849.

A

DESCRIPTION

OF

COUNTIES AND TOWNS

IN

VERMONT.

ADDISON COUNTY.

MIDDLEBURY is the chief town. This county is bounded on the north by Chittenden County, east by Washington and Orange Counties, and a part of Windsor County, south by Rutland County, and west by Lake Champlain.

Large quantities of white and beautifully variegated marble, which receives a fine polish, are found in this county, and large quantities of it are quarried and transported to various markets. This county is admirably well watered by Otter Creek, which rises near its southern boundary, and extends nearly through its centre; by Mad and White Rivers; and by Lake Champlain, which affords it many navigable privileges. The soil is good, particularly in those towns below the mountains, and bordering the lake and rivers. The scenery on the western borders of this county, lying, as it does, on Lake Champlain, is exceedingly variegated and beautiful.—See *Tables*.

COURTS IN ADDISON COUNTY.

The *Supreme Court* sits at Middlebury, annually, on the first Tuesday in January, and the *County Court* on the second Tuesday in June and December.

ADDISON.

ADDISON Co. This is supposed to be the first place settled by the whites, in this State, west of the mountains. The town is pleasantly located on the east side of Lake Champlain, and nearly opposite to Crown Point, in the State of New York. At this place the lake is about three miles broad. The French, it is said, commenced a settlement here in 1731; the same year that they erected a fort at Crown Point. The English came here about 1770. Otter Creek passes into the town, but affords no important mill sites. The surface of the town is low and level. Mill and Pike Rivers, are small streams, which fall into the lake opposite to Crown Point.

Boundaries. North by Panton, east by Weybridge and Waltham, south by Bridport, and west by Lake Champlain.

First Settlers. The first settlement made by the English was in the year 1769 or 1770, by a Mr. Ward, the Hon. John Strong and Zadock Everest, Esq., with their families. This settlement was broken up and the settlers retired to the south, upon the advance of the British up the lake in the fall of 1776, and none of them returned with their families till the month of May, 1783. During their seven years' absence, every building which they had erected was destroyed by the enemy, who were masters of the lake till the close of the war. From its renewal at the close of the war, the settlement advanced with considerable rapidity, and Messrs. Strong, Everest and some others of the first settlers who had been driven off and returned, lived to see the township nearly all under improvement and themselves in possession of all the rational enjoyments of life.

First Minister. A church was organized here by the Rev. Job Swift, in 1803; who died in 1804.

Productions of the Soil. Wheat, 1,722 bushels; Indian corn, 6,250 bushels; potatoes, 19,750 bushels; hay, 10,800 tons; maple sugar, 865 pounds; wool, 82,900 pounds.

Distances. Forty miles west south-west from Montpelier, and twelve miles west north-west from Middlebury.

ALBANY.

ORLEANS CO. This town was granted in the year 1781, by the name of Lutterloh; in 1815 it was changed to its present name. The town is not mountainous, but in some parts the surface is uneven.

Albany is watered by Black River, which is formed in Craftsbury, and passes through it in a north-easterly direction, and by several of its branches. There are likewise several considerable ponds, the most important of which, Great Hosmer's Pond, is partly in Craftsbury. The soil is generally sandy or gravelly. Along the river is some fine intervale.

Boundaries. North-easterly by Irasburgh, south-east by Glover, south-west by Craftsbury, and north-west by Lowell and Eden.

First Settlers. The town was organized March 27, 1806, and Benjamin Neal was the town clerk.

Productions of the Soil. Wheat, 2,618 bushels; Indian corn, 1,597 bushels; potatoes, 43,389 bushels; hay, 2,685 tons; maple sugar, 42,298 pounds; wool, 6,121 pounds.

Distances. Six miles south from Irasburgh, and thirty-seven north-east from Montpelier.

ALBURGH.

GRAND ISLE CO. Settlements commenced here by emigrants from Canada, in 1782. This town lies at the north-west corner of the State and of New England; ten miles north from North Hero, and seventy-nine miles north-west from Montpelier. It is bounded by the waters of Lake Champlain, except on the north, where it meets the Canada line, in north latitude 45°. The soil is good and finely timbered. It has a mineral spring, of some repute in scrofulous cases.

The French made a small settlement here more than 100 years ago and erected a stone wind-mill upon a point, which has in consequence, received the name of Wind-mill Point. The settlement of this township, by the English, was commenced by emigrants from St. Johns in Lower Canada about the year 1782. The settlers were originally from the States, but, being loyalists, they found it necessary, during the revolutionary war, to shelter themselves in Canada. For some years after the settlement was commenced, they were much harrassed and perplexed by the diversity of claimants to the lands.

Boundaries. East by Missisco Bay, west by Lake Champlain, and runs to a point at the south, being of a triangular form.

First Ministers. There are various denominations of Christians in this town but no settled ministers.

Productions of the Soil. Wheat, 9,237 bushels; Indian corn, 3,786 bushels; wool, 11,191 pounds.

Distances. Ten miles north from North Hero, and seventy-nine miles north-west from Montpelier.

ANDOVER.

WINDSOR Co. Emigrants from Enfield, Ct., first made a permanent settlement in this town, in 1776. It was organized, as a town, in 1781.

Markhum and Terrible Mountains lie in the western part. The land is uneven, the soil is hard, and the town possesses but few water privileges.

Boundaries. North by Ludlow, east by Chester, south by Windham, and west by Weston.

First Minister. A Baptist Church was organized Aug. 31, 1803. The Rev. Joel Manning was ordained over this church, Oct. 2, 1806.

Productions of the Soil. Wheat, 1,159 bushels; Indian corn, 982 bushels; potatoes, 5,050 bushels; hay, 988 tons; maple sugar, 1,255 pounds; wool, 9,000 pounds.

Distances. Twenty miles south-west from Windsor, sixty-eight south from Montpelier, and thirty-seven north-east from Bennington.

ARLINGTON.

BENNINGTON Co. This town was chartered in 1761. The time of its organization is not known. as one Bisco, a tory, the town clerk in 1777. destroyed the records. It is finely watered by Green River, Mill and Warm Brooks, and Roaring Branch, which fall into the Battenkill, at the north part of the town. These streams afford excellent mill sites, and on their banks are large bodies of superior meadow land.

West and Red Mountains extend through the west part of the town, and supply a great variety of good timber. Excellent marble is found here; considerable quantities of which are wrought and transported.

Here is a medicinal spring, and a cavern of large dimensions. The spring is not of much note, but the cavern is a great curiosity.

This is a flourishing town in both its agricultural and manufacturing pursuits.

Boundaries. North by Landgate, east by Sunderland, south by Shaftsbury, and west by Salem.

First Settlers. The first settlement was made in the year 1763, by Dr. Simon Burton, William Searls, and Ebenezer Wallis. In 1764, Jehiel Hawley, Josiah Hawley, Remember Baker, and Thomas Peck, removed into this town. The former was a principal land owner, and has left in this place a numerous and respectable posterity.

First Minister. An Episcopal Society was organized here some years before the Revolution, which has existed ever since. The records of this church, which is called Saint James Church, go back to Aug. 16th, 1784. The first rector of this church was the Rev. James Nichols, settled in 1786.

Productions of the Soil. Wheat, 743 bushels; Indian corn, 5,145 bushels; potatoes. 211,212 bushels; hay, 4,631 tons; maple sugar, 7,420 pounds; wool, 27,750 pounds.

Distances. Fifteen miles north from Bennington, and 106 south-west from Montpelier.

ATHENS.

WINDHAM Co. This town was first settled in 1780. by people from Rindge, N. H., and Winchendon, Mass. They encountered great hardships. "The snow was four feet deep when they came into town; and they had to beat their own path for eight miles through the woods. A small yoke of oxen were the only domestic animals that they took with them."

This is a good township of land, particularly for grazing. Here are productive orchards, pine timber, and a small mill stream.

Boundaries. North by Grafton, east by Westminster and Rockingham, south by Brookline and Townshend, and west by Townshend.

First Settlers. The first beginnings towards a settlement in this town were made in the fall of 1779, by Jonathan Perham, Seth Oakes, Joseph Basier, James Shafter, and Jonathan Foster.

Productions of the Soil. Wheat, 501 bushels ; Indian corn, 1,885 bushels ; potatoes, 10,035 bushels ; hay, 966 tons ; maple sugar, 6,470 pounds ; wool, 5,387 pounds.

Distances. Forty miles north-east from Bennington, ninety-eight south from Montpelier, fourteen north from Newfane, and ten miles from Bellows Falls.

AVERILL.

ESSEX Co. This town lies on the Canada line, about thirty miles north of Guildhall. It has several large ponds and a branch of Nulhegan River. Some of these waters pass to the Connecticut, and some to the River St. Francis. The soil of Averill is cold and broken, with few cultivators.

Boundaries. North-east by Canaan, south-east by Lemington, south-west by Lewis, and north-west by Norton.

First Settlers. This town was chartered in 1762.

Productions of the Soil. Potatoes, 400 bushels ; hay, 20 tons ; maple sugar, 600 pounds.

Distances. Thirty miles north from Guildhall, and sixty miles north-east from Montpelier.

BAKERSFIELD.

FRANKLIN Co. This township is somewhat broken, but not mountainous. It is timbered principally with hard wood, and the soil is in general warm and productive. It is watered by Black Creek, which crosses the south-west corner, and several other branches of the Missisco River. The streams are, however, small, and the mill privileges not numerous.

Boundaries. North by Enosburgh, east by Avery's Gore and Waterville, south by Waterville and Fletcher, and west by Fairfield.

First Settlers. The settlement of this town was commenced in 1789, by Joseph Baker, from whom the town derives its name. He emigrated from Westborough, Mass. Joel Brigham and Abijah Pratt settled in Bakersfield about the same time.

Productions of the Soil. Wheat, 3,000 bushels ; Indian corn, 2,450 bushels ; potatoes, 62,000 bushels ; hay, 3,570 tons ; maple sugar, 33,305 pounds ; wool, 10,876 pounds.

Distances. Thirty miles north-east from Burlington, thirty-eight north north-west from Montpelier, and fifteen miles east from St. Albans.

BALTIMORE.

WINDSOR Co. This town was taken from Cavendish, in 1793. Hawk's Mountain is the division line. The soil is warm, but stony. An abundance of gneiss and granite is found here.

Boundaries. East by Weathersfield and Springfield, south by Chester, and north-west by Cavendish.

First Settlers. The town was organized in 1794, and Joseph Atherton was first town clerk.

Productions of the Soil. Wheat, 2,922 bushels ; Indian corn, 905 bushels ; potatoes, 6,566 bushels ; hay, 519 tons ; maple sugar, 1,650 pounds ; wool, 2,855 pounds.

Distances. Ten miles north-west from Windsor, and about sixty-five south from Montpelier. A railroad passes near this town.

BARNARD.

WINDSOR Co. Barnard is watered by Broad Brook, which empties into White River in Sharon ; and by Locust Creek, which also empties into White River in Bethel. On this creek, during the revolutionary war, there was erected a fort, where the militia of this and other towns were stationed, as a defence against Indian depredations—they having surprised and carried to Canada a number of its first settlers, in 1780.

In the centre of this town is the village, and a beautiful pond, from which issues a stream on which there are mills. On this creek is an establishment for the manufacture of starch from potatoes. This stream joins its waters with the creek one mile from the pond.

The surface of this town is hilly. The soil is well adapted to grazing; and there are but few towns that turn off yearly more cattle, butter and cheese, sheep and wool.

It is stated as a singular fact, that the firing on Bunker Hill, on the 17th of June, 1775, was distinctly heard in this town, 130 miles north-west from Charlestown.

Boundaries. North by Royalton and Bethel, east by Pomfret, south by Bridgewater, west by Stockbridge.

First Settlers. The settlement was commenced in March, 1775, by Thos. Freeman, his son William, and John Newton. The same season Lot Whitcomb, Nathaniel Paige, Wm. Cheedle, and Asa Whitcomb, moved their families into town.

First Minister. The Rev. Joseph Bowman was installed over the Congregational Church, in 1784, and continued their pastor till his death, which happened April 27th, 1806.

Productions of the Soil. Wheat, 2,279 bushels; Indian corn, 1,266 bushels; potatoes, 50,286 bushels; hay, 4,913 tons; maple sugar, 36,360 pounds; wool, 18,027 pounds.

Distances. Twenty-one miles north-west from Windsor, and thirty-seven south from Montpelier.

BARNET.

CALEDONIA Co. This town lies on Connecticut River, at the Fifteen Mile Falls, and opposite to Lyman, N. H. It has a good soil, and is an excellent farming town, with slate and iron ore. Many of the inhabitants are of Scotch descent. This town has a great water power on Passumpsic and Stevens' Rivers. On the latter are falls of 100

feet, in the distance of ten rods. This water power is improved by a number of flannel and other manufactories. There are a number of pleasant and fertile islands in the river, between this place and Lyman, and some beautiful ponds in Barnet, which afford fish of various kinds. This is quite a romantic place, and lies at the head of navigation on the Connecticut River.

There are three natural ponds in this town, viz., Harvey's Pond, covering about 300 acres, Ross' Pond, about 100, Morse's Pond, about fifteen acres. The present head of boat navigation on Connecticut River is at the lower village in this town at McIndoe's Falls. The principal places of business are at this village, at the village at Stevens' Mills, and the village at Randal's Mills, on the Passumpsic River.

This is the birth-place and residence of Henry Stevens, Esq., a celebrated antiquarian. Mr. Stevens is performing great service to the State, by rescuing from oblivion large claims against the general government.

Boundaries. North by Waterford, east by Connecticut River, south by Ryegate, west by Peacham and Danville.

First Settlers. The charter of Barnet is dated September 15, 1763. The principal proprietors were Enos, Samuel, and Willard Stevens, sons of Capt. Phineas Stevens, who so nobly defended the fort at Charlestown, New Hampshire, April 4, 1747, against a large party of French and Indians, under the command of M. Debeline. The first settlement was commenced in this town by Jacob, Elijah, and Daniel Hall, and Jonathan Fowler. Sarah, daughter of Elijah Hall, was the first child, and Barnet, son of Jonathan Fowler, was the first male child born in the town. The latter was presented by Enos Stevens, Esq., with 100 acres of land. The town was subsequently settled mostly by emigrants from Scotland. A part of the township was purchased, in 1774, by the late Alexander Harvey, Esq., and another gentleman, for a company in Scotland. A considerable proportion of the people are of Scotch descent.

In the summer of 1772, Enos Stevens, Esq., erected a grist mill on Stevens' River, about 150 rods from its junction with the Connecticut. The first town meeting was held, and the town organized, March 18, 1783. Walter Brock, Esq., was first town clerk, and Colonel Alexander Harvey the first representative. Major Rogers, on his return from an expedition against the St. Francis Indians, in 1759, encamped near the mouth of the Passumpsic River, in this town, where he expected to meet a supply of provisions to be sent on from Charlestown, New Hampshire, by order of General Amherst. The order of the general was complied with. Samuel Stevens and three others proceeded up Connecticut River with two canoes, to Round Island opposite the mouth of the Passumpsic, where they encamped for the night. In the morning, hearing the report of guns, they were so terrified that they reloaded their provisions and hastened back to Charlestown, leaving Rogers and his famished rangers to their fate.

First Minister. The Rev. David Goodwillie was settled over the Presbyterian Church in 1791, and remained their minister many years.

Productions of the Soil. Wheat, 4,652 bushels; Indian corn, 6,780 bushels; potatoes, 66,410 bushels; hay, 4,815 tons; maple sugar, 19,670 pounds; wool, 12,221 pounds.

Distances. Eleven miles south from Danville, and thirty-six east from Montpelier.

The Connecticut River Railroad passes through this town, and greatly facilitates its business.

BARRE.

WASHINGTON Co. Barre is a pleasant and flourishing town. It is considered one of the best farming towns in the State. Large quantities of pot and pearl ashes, beef, pork, butter, and cheese, are annually taken from this place to Boston market. It is well watered by Stevens' and Jail branches of Winose River, which afford good mill privileges. Inexhaustible quantities of granite are found here, of the excellent quality with which the capitol at Montpelier is built.

Boundaries. North by Montpelier and Plainfield, east by Orange, south by Williamstown, and west by Berlin.

First Settlers. This township was granted November 6, 1780, to William Williams and his associates, and chartered by the name of Wildersburgh. This name being unpopular with the inhabitants of the town, in the year 1793, a town meeting was called, to be holden at the house of Calvin Smith, for the purpose of agreeing on some other name, to be presented to the legislature for their sanction and approval. The meeting being opened, freedom was given for any one to present the name he chose, and the choice among the number presented was to be decided by vote of the town. Several names were proposed, such as Paris, Newburn, &c. Two of the voters present, Capt. Joseph Thompson and Mr. Jonathan Sherman, the first from Holden, the other from Barre, Mass., each in their turn strenuously contended for the name of the town from which he came; and as the matter seemed to lie chiefly between these two, it was proposed that it should be decided between them *by boxing*, to which they readily agreed. The terms were, that they should fight across a pole, but if one should knock the other down, they might then choose their own mode of warfare. The meeting then adjourned to a new barn shed, erected by said Smith, over which a floor of rough hemlock plank had just been laid, and on this the issue was to be decided. Agreeably to this arrangement, the combatants advanced upon each other, and soon Thompson, by a well directed blow, brought his antagonist to the floor, and, springing upon him at full length, began to aim his heavy blows at his head and face; but Sherman, being more supple, avoided them, and they generally fell harmless on the floor, except peeling his own knuckles. During this process, Sherman was dexterously plying his ribs from beneath, when Thompson was soon heard to groan, and his blows became palsied and without effect. Sherman then rolled him off, and, springing upon his feet, exultingly exclaimed, " *There, the name is Barre, by* —*!*" Accordingly a petition for the name of Barre was presented, and sanctioned by the legislature the same year. The day following this encounter, Sherman called on Dr. Robert Paddock, the physician of the town, who was an eye witness of the transaction, and who related these particulars to the writer, and requested him to extract from his back and posteriors the hemlock splinters he had received, while writhing on the plank floor. In 1788, Samuel Rogers and John Goldsbury, one from Bradford, the other from Hartland, Vt., with their families, moved into this town, and began converting the wilderness into farms. The next year a number of other families came in, and from this time the town settled rapidly by emigrants from Worcester county, Mass, and from New Hampshire and Connecticut. The town was organized, March 11, 1793, and Joseph Dwight was first town clerk.

First Ministers. The Rev. Aaron Palmer was ordained to the pastoral care of the Congregational Chr.ch in 1807; he died in 1821. The Rev. Justus W. French was ordained in 1822, and dismissed in 1832.

Productions of the Soil. Wheat, 3,560 bushels; Indian corn, 9,170 bushels; potatoes, 120,337 bushels; hay, 6,938 tons; maple sugar, 62,159 pounds; wool, 26,621 pounds.

Distances. Six miles south-east from Montpelier. The great Northern Railroad passes through the town.

BARTON.

ORLEANS Co. This town is well watered by Barton River, which rises in Glover, and empties into Memphremagog Lake. Here are several ponds containing good fish. Barton is a thriving town, with a good hydraulic power.

The pond in Glover which broke its northern bound and run entirely out on the 6th of June, 1810, passed down Barton River, making very destructive rav-

ages; the traces of which are still to be seen.

At the outlet of Belle Pond is a flourishing village, containing a number of handsome buildings. This place will doubtless become an important site for manufactures; and should the Monarch Carrier come this way, no one need marvel.

Boundaries. North by Barrington, east by Westmore and Sheffield, south by Glover, and west by Irasburgh and Albany.

First Settlers. The town was chartered October 20, 1789, and then took the name of Barton, in honor of the principal proprietor. The settlement of this town was commenced about the year 1796, by Jonathan Allyne, Asa Kimball, James May, and John Kimball. The first settlers were from Rhode Island and New Hampshire. The town was organized March 20, 1798, and Abner Allyne was first town clerk. At the time of its organization there were nineteen legal voters in town.

First Ministers. A Congregational Church was erected here in 1820.

Productions of the Soil. Wheat, 1,177 bushels; Indian corn, 1,952 bushels; potatoes, 34,632 bushels; hay, 2,821 tons; maple sugar, 26,040 pounds; wool, 10,695 pounds.

Distances. Six miles east from Irasburgh, forty-two north-east from Montpelier.

BELVIDERE.

LAMOILLE Co. A considerable part of this township is mountainous, and unfit for cultivation. The settlement was commenced about the year 1800. The township is watered by two branches of the River Lamoille.

Boundaries. North by Avery's Gore and Lowell, east by Eden, south by Johnson, and west by Waterville.

Productions of the Soil. Wheat, 332 bushels; Indian corn, 294 bushels; potatoes, 9.310 bushels; hay, 553 tons; maple sugar, 3,440 pounds; wool, 1,187 pounds.

Distances. Eighteen miles north-west from Hydepark, and forty-five miles north-west from Montpelier.

BENNINGTON COUNTY.

BENNINGTON and MANCHESTER are the chief towns. This is the oldest county in Vermont, on the west side of the Green Mountains. It is bounded on the north by Rutland County, on the east by Windham County, on the south by Berkshire County, Mass., and on the west by the State of New York. The low lands are excellent, and produce good crops, but the largest portion of the county is mountainous, and fit only for grazing. Many streams rise in the mountains and descend to the ocean, some by the Hudson and some by the Connecticut, affording a great hydraulic power. Lead and iron ores of good quality are found in this county, and large quarries of beautiful white marble.

This county is memorable for many revolutionary scenes ; and no county in the State, and perhaps no section of country of its siz: in the United States, presents a greater variety of bold and beautiful scenery.—See *Tables.*

COURTS IN BENNINGTON COUNTY.

The *Supreme Court* sits alternately at Bennington and Manchester, on the second Tuesday after the fourth Tuesday in January.

The *County Court* sits at Manchester, on the second Tuesday in June; and at Bennington, on the 1st Tuesday in December.

BENNINGTON.

BENNINGTON Co. One of the chief towns in the county. It is situated high above the great rivers and the ocean, yet we find it of good alluvial soil, delightfully encircled by evergreen mountains. It abounds in iron ore, manganese, ochre, and marble. The streams are numerous, and afford excellent mill sites. The products of the soil consist of all the varieties common to New England. Great attention is paid to the rearing of sheep.

There are in Bennington a great number of cotton and woollen factories, a very extensive iron foundry, two furnaces, a paper mill, flouring mills, &c. The public schools justly sustain an elevated rank. Bennington is finely located for the muses.

On the borders of this town, about six miles west of the court-house, the gallant Stark, with a small band of " Northern Yeomen," celebrated for their bravery, gained an important victory over the British, August 16, 1777. The fame of that battle is as imperishable as ·the mountains which overshadow the ground. Shame to the country :—there is not a stone to mark the spot !—See *Note.*

Walloomscoik Mill Co. in this town was incorporated in 1847.

Boundaries. North by Shaftsbury, east by Woodford, south by Pownal, and west by Hoosic, in Rensselaer County, New York.

First Settlers. This township was chartered by Benning Wentworth, governor of New Hampshire, January 3, 1749, and was called Bennington. in allusion to his name.

The first settlers were purchasers under the original proprietors, and came from Massachusetts. Samuel

Robinson, of Hardwick, Mass., who had been a captain during the French war, on his return from Lake George to Hoosic Forts, while proceeding up Hoosic River, mistook the *Walloomsoik* for that stream, and followed it up to the tract of country now Bennington. Here he and his companions, finding they had lost their way, encamped over night, and in the morning changed their course, and pursued their way to the forts. Captain Robinson was much pleased with the country, and returned to his family with a determination to begin a settlement upon it. He accordingly repaired to New Hampshire, made purchases of a considerable portion of the rights, and then sought for settlers. The first emigration to the town consisted of the families of Peter Harwood, Eleazar Harwood, Leonard Robinson, and Samuel Robinson, Jr., from Hardwick, and of Samuel Pratt and Timothy Pratt, from Amherst. The party, including women and children, numbered about twenty. They came on horseback across the mountain, by the Hoosic Forts and through Pownal, bringing on their horses all their household goods, and arrived in town the 18th of June, 1761.

First Minister. Rev. Jedediah Dewey, of Westfield, Mass., removed to this town, and became pastor of the church in 1763, and continued so until his death, in 1778.

Productions of the Soil. Wheat, 2,185 bushels; Indian corn, 16,000 bushels; potatoes, 56,475 bushels; hay, 564 tons; maple sugar, 7,828 pounds; wool, 26,327 pounds.

Distances. One hundred and twenty miles south-west by south from Montpelier, twenty-five south from Manchester, and thirty east from Troy, New York.

BENSON.

RUTLAND Co. This town, on Lake Champlain, was first settled in 1783. The lake at this place is about a mile in width. The town has some streams affording mill sites, but none of great importance. The waters are generally brackish and unpleasant. A stream issues from a swamp in this town, and after running a short distance, passes through the base of a high hill, a distance of more than half a mile. Benson has good pine, maple, walnut, oak and beach timber, and a bog of marl resembling fuller's earth. A part of this town was annexed to Orwell in 1847.

Boundaries. North by Orwell, east by Hubbardton, and a small part of Sudbury and Castleton, south by Fair Haven and West Haven, and west by Lake Champlain.

First Settlers. The settlement of the town was commenced 1783, by Barber, Durfee, and Noble. Mr. Durfee came into town and made some improvements before the Revolution, but was driven off. The town was organized about the year 1786, and Allen Goodrich was the first town clerk.

First Minister. A Congregational Church was organized here in 1790, over which the Rev. Dan Kent was ordained in 1792.

Productions of the Soil. Wheat, 2,578 bushels; Indian corn, 5,353 bushels: potatoes, 15,700 bushels; hay, 5,502 tons; maple sugar, 6,285 pounds; wool, 49,048 pounds.

Distances. Seventy-five miles south-west from Montpelier, and twenty-five miles north-west from Rutland.

BERKSHIRE.

FRANKLIN Co. Missisco River runs through the south-east corner of the town, and receives Trout River near the line of Enosburgh. On these streams is some fine intervale. Pike River enters the township from Canada, and, after taking a circuit of several miles, and affording here some of the finest mill sites in the country, returns again into Canada. On Pike River, in this town, are several mills. The soil is various, but generally good. Its surface is diversified with gentle swells and vales, but does not rise into mountains. It is well watered with brooks.

Boundaries. North by St. Armand, in Canada, east by Richford, south by Enosburgh, and west by Franklin.

First Settlers. This township was granted to William Goodrich, Barzilla Hudson, Charles Dibble, and their associates, March 13, 1780, and was chartered by the name of Berkshire, June 22, 1781. The settlement of this town was commenced in 1792 by Job Barber. Stephen Royce, Daniel Adams, Jonathan Carpenter, and Phinehas Heath, moved their families here in 1793, and from this time the settlement advanced with considerable rapidity. Elihu M., son of Stephen Royce, was born in 1793, and was the first child born in town. The town was organized in 1794, and David Nutting was first town clerk.

First Ministers. There are two Congregational Churches, one in East, the other in West Berkshire. The former was organized Oct. 8, 1820; the other many years earlier. The Episcopal Church, called Calvary Church, is in East Berkshire, and was organized about 1820. The names of the clergy of these churches are not given.

Productions of the Soil. Wheat, 3,884 bushels; Indian corn, 2,876 bushels; potatoes, 67,995 bushels; hay, 3,818 tons; maple sugar, 34,785 pounds; wool, 9,457 pounds.

Distances. Fifty miles north-west from Montpelier, twenty-two north-east by east from St. Albans, and forty-five north-east by north from Burlington.

BERLIN.

WASHINGTON CO. This is a pleasant town, watered by Winooski and Dog Rivers, Stevens' Branch, and a number of ponds, furnishing good mill sites, and excellent fishing. The land is somewhat broken, but of strong soil and good for tillage. Considerable manufactures are produced in this town.

There is a mineral spring here of little note.

There is considerable intervale on Winooski and Dog River and Stevens' Branch. The timber, west of Dog River, is a mixture of spruce, hemlock, maple, beach, birch, basswood, and ash; east of that, principally hard wood, excepting in the vicinity of the pond and streams. On a ridge of land south of the centre, is some butternut, and east of the pond, considerable cedar and fir. Iron ore has recently been discovered a little east of Dog River, near which place *terre de sena* has been found of good quality. The town has been generally very healthy.

Boundaries. North by Montpelier, east by Barre, south by Northfield and a small part of Williamstown, and west by Moretown.

First Settlers. A settlement was commenced here in 1785, near the mouth of Dog River, by Ebenezer Sanburne from Corinth, and Joseph Thurber from New Hampshire. The next year Jacob Fowler removed here, and was the first permanent settler.

First Minister. Rev. James Hobart was settled over the Congregationalist Society in 1798, and dismissed in 1829.

Productions of the Soil. Wheat, 2,510 bushels; Indian corn, 7,182 bushels; potatoes, 83,734 bushels; hay, 1,232 tons; maple sugar, 29,175 pounds; wool, 14,647 pounds.

Distances. Four miles south from Montpelier. A railroad passes near the town.

BETHEL.

WINDSOR CO. Bethel is watered by branches of White River, and possesses good mill sites. Soap stone is found here in great quantities and of good quality; much of it is sawed and transported. Garnet in small, but perfect crystals, is also common. The surface of Bethel is broken and mountainous, but the soil is warm and good for grazing. Considerable business is done at both villages, *East* and *West;* the latter is the largest.

Boundaries. North by Randolph, east by Royalton, south by Stockbridge, and a small part of Barnard, and west by Rochester.

First Settlers. This township was chartered to John Payne, John House, Dudley Chase, and others, Dec. 23, 1779, containing thirty-six square miles, The first township chartered by the government. The settlement of this town commenced in the fall of 1779, by Benjamin Smith. A small stockade fort was built here at the commencement of the settlement. The town was organized in 1782.

First Ministers. The Rev. Thomas Russell was settled by the Congregational Society in 1790; dismissed in 1794. From that time no minister was settled over that society till 1837. An Episcopal Church was organized by the Rev. John C. Ogden in 1792.

Productions of the Soil. Wheat, 2,646 bushels; Indian corn, 242 bushels; potatoes, 6,640 bushels; hay, 450 tons; maple sugar, 7,060 pounds; wool, 642 pounds.

Distances. Thirty-one miles south by west from Montpelier, and thirty north-west from Windsor. The great Northern Railroad passes through this town.

BLOOMFIELD.

Essex Co. Bloomfield was chartered, June 29, 1762, by the name of Minehead, and contains 23,040 acres. The settlement of the township was commenced before the year 1800, but the progress of the settlement has been slow. The western and south parts are watered by Nulhegan River. The north-eastern parts are watered by two or three small streams, which fall into the Connecticut.

Boundaries. North-easterly by Lemington, south-easterly by Connecticut River, which separates it from Columbia, N. H., south-westerly by Brunswick, and north-westerly by Lewis.

Productions of the Soil. Wheat, 315 bushels; Indian corn, 242 bushels; potatoes, 6,640 bushels; hay, 450 tons; maple sugar, 7,060 pounds; wool, 642 pounds.

Distances. Eighteen miles north from Guildhall, and eighty-six north-east from Montpelier.

BOLTON.

Chittenden Co. This town was chartered June 7, 1763, and originally contained thirty-six square miles. On the 27th of Oct. 1794, the north-east part of Huntington was annexed to it. The first settlers were Noah Dewey, Peter Dilse, James Moore, Thomas

Palmer, Robert Stinson, and John and Robert Kenedy. The township was first regularly surveyed in 1800 by John Johnson, Esq. It lies midway between Montpelier and Burlington, its post office being eighteen miles from each. The town is very mountainous and broken, and but a small part of it capable of being settled. Winooski River runs through the town from east to west, and along the banks of this stream nearly all the inhabitants reside. The river receives several branches in this town, both from the north and south. The township lies on the western range of the Green Mountains.

Boundaries. North by Mansfield, east by Waterbury, south by Huntington, and west by Richmond and Jericho.

Productions of the Soil. Wheat, 961 bushels; Indian corn, 2,174 bushels; potatoes, 13,400 bushels; hay, 1,116 tons; maple sugar, 13,215 pounds; wool, 6,081 pounds.

Distances. Nineteen miles south-east from Burlington, and nineteen north-west from Montpelier. The great Northern Railroad from Boston to Burlington passes through the town.

BRADFORD.

Orange Co. Wait's River, the principal stream in the town, enters it from the west in two branches, and passing through, in an easterly direction, empties into Connecticut River, affording a number of valuable mill privileges. Hall's Brook and Roaring Brook, are considerable streams, which enter the town from Newbury and pass through the corner of it into the Connecticut. Smaller streams are numerous, and several medicinal springs have been discovered, but are of little note. The surface of the town is somewhat broken. A handsome and fertile strip of intervale skirts Connecticut River, and there is much good land in other parts. There is no waste land with the exception of thirty or forty acres on Wright's Mountain. In the north-west part of the town is situated Wright's Mountain, sometimes, erroneously called Virgin Mountain. In this mountain

3*

is a cavern called the *Devil's Den*, which has several apartments, and is thought to have been the abode of human beings. In the east part of the town is a considerable precipice called Rowell's Ledge. The timber is principally pine, sugar maple, oak, beech, and hemlock. Bradford Academy was incorporated and the building erected in 1820. It has a male and female department, with permanent teachers. The school is in a flourishing condition. The yearly attendance is about 200.

Boundaries. North by Newbury, east by Connecticut River, which separates it from Piermont, N. H., south by Fairlee, and west by Fairlee.

First Settlers. Three thousand acres of this town, lying on Connecticut River, were granted by New York to Sir Harry Moore, and by him conveyed to thirty settlers. The rest of the land was taken up by pitches. The town was first called Moretown, but was altered to Bradford, by an act of the legislature passed Oct. 23, 1788. The settlement of the town was commenced by John Hosmer in 1765, near the mouth of Wait's River. He was joined the next year by Samuel Sleeper and Benoni Wright, and in 1771 the number of families in town amounted to ten. The first grist mill was erected by John Peters in 1772 at the falls near the mouth of Wait's River, and the first saw mill by Benjamin Baldwin in 1774.

First Ministers. The first meeting-house in town was built in 1791, by the Baptists under Elder Rice. A meeting-house was built by the Congregationalists in 1793, who settled the Rev. Gardner Kellogg in 1795.

Manufactures. At the falls in Wait's River, which afford some of the best mill privileges in the State, is a furnace for casting ploughs, stoves, &c., whetstone factories, machine shops, and an extensive paper mill. On Wait's River, about two miles above the village, are manufactures of woollens and other goods. The first artificial globes ever manufactured in the United States, were made here about the year 1812, by Mr. James Wilson.

Productions of the Soil. Wheat, 3,464 bushels; Indian corn, 8,455 bushels; potatoes, 48,178 bushels; hay, 3,932 tons; maple sugar, 9,387 pounds; wool, 16,424 pounds.

Distances. Thirty miles south south-east from Montpelier, and eleven south south-east from Chelsea.

BRADLEYVALE.

Bradleyvale, an unorganized township in the eastern part of Caledonia County, having Victory on the north-east, Concord on the south-east, and Kirby on the west. It was chartered to Thomas Pearsall, Jan. 27, 1791, and contains 3,936 acres, and was incorporated with all the rights and privileges of a town, excepting that of representation, Oct. 29, 1803. It is watered by Moose River, which passes through it near the centre, from north-east to south-west, and joins the Passumpsic at St. Johnsbury. This territory possesses a fine water power and much good land, which will, doubtless, soon be improved.

Productions of the Soil. Wheat, 31 bushels; Indian corn, 63 bushels; potatoes, 1,155 bushels; hay, 83 tons; maple sugar, 1,700 pounds; wool, 197 pounds.

Distances. This town lies about twelve miles easterly from St. Johnsbury.

BRAINTREE.

ORANGE Co. This town is watered by the third branch of White River, and Ayers' and Mill Brook, its tributaries. They are all sufficient for mills. Ayers' Brook rises in Roxbury and Brookfield, waters the north-east part of the town, and after receiving Mill Brook from the west, unites with the third branch of White River, just below the west village in Randolph. Between Ayers' Brook and the third branch, is a large swell of land, and when Mr. Ebenezer Waters was surveying the township he said to those with him, " We will sit down here and dine with our hats on and call it *Quaker Hill*," and it has ever since been known by that name. Between the third branch and the head of White River, is a considerable mountain, which renders that part of the township incapable of settlement. According to tradition, Ayers' Brook derives its name from a person by the name of Ayers, who, having run away from New England, became a guide to the French and Indians in their expeditions against the English, but who was taken and executed near this stream, about the year 1755.

Boundaries. Northerly by Roxbury and Bloomfield, easterly by Randolph, southerly by Bethel, and westerly by Granville.

First Settlers. The settlement of the town was commenced about the year 1783, by Silas Flint, Samuel Bass, Jacob and Samuel Spear, and others, emigrants from Braintree and Sutton, Mass. S. Flint's wife was the first woman who came into the town and received in consequence a present of 100 acres of land from the proprietors. Hiram, son of Samuel Bass, was the first child born in town. The first proprietors' meeting held within the town was at the house of Jacob Spear, September 19, 1786. The town was organized March 7, 1788, and Elijah French was first town clerk. It was first represented by Isaac Nichols in 1791.

First Ministers. The Rev. Aaron Cleveland was settled over the Congregational Church in 1801, and dismissed in 1807 The Rev. Ammi Nichols was settled in 1807.

Productions of the Soil. Wheat, 3,680 bushels; Indian corn, 4,880 bushels; potatoes, 42,010 bushels; hay, 3,581 tons; maple sugar, 18,800 pounds; wool, 12,860 pounds.

Distances. Twenty-one miles south from Montpelier, and fourteen west by south from Chelsea. The Northern Railroad passes through this town.

BRANDON.

RUTLAND Co. Brandon is a flourishing town. It is finely watered by Otter Creek, Mill River, and Spring Pond; on which streams are good mill sites. Some of the land is level, with rather a light soil, but that on Otter Creek is the best alluvial. Bog iron ore, of an excellent quality, is found here; copperas and marble are also found.

There are two curious caverns in this town. The largest contains two apartments, each from sixteen to twenty feet square. It is entered by descending from the surface about twenty feet. They are formed of limestone.

Boundaries. North by Leicester, east by Goshen and Chittenden, south by Pittsford, and west by Sudbury and a small part of Whiting.

First Settlers. The settlement of the town was commenced in the year 1775 by John Whelan, Noah Strong, David June, Jedediah Winslow, Amos Cutler, and others. Mr. Cutler was, however, the only person who remained in town during the following winter. He lived the whole winter here entirely alone, without being visited by a human being. In 1777, the town was visited by a party of Indians, who killed two men, George and Aaron Robins, made prisoners of most of the other inhabitants, and set fire to their dwellings and to a saw mill which they had erected. Joseph Barker, his wife, and a child eighteen months old, were among the prisoners. Mrs. Barker, not being in a condition to traverse the wilderness, was set at liberty with her child. The next night, with no other shelter than the trees of the forest and the canopy of heaven, and with no other company than the infant above named, she had another child. She was found the following day and removed with her children to Pittsford. Mr. Barker was carried to Middlebury, where, feigning himself sick, he succeeded in the night in making his escape, and arrived safely at Pittsford. The town was organized about the year 1784.

First Ministers. The Congregational Church was organized in 1785, but had no settled minister till 1792, when they settled the Rev. Enos Bliss.

Manufactures. The hydraulic power of this town is so great and valuable, that manufactures commenced here at an early period. Bar iron, small cannon, and various other articles of iron ware, are manufactured here. There are other articles manufactured in the town, but to what extent, we regret to say, we are unable to state.

Productions of the Soil. Wheat, 1,498 bushels; Indian corn, 10,222 bushels; potatoes, 26,052 bushels; hay, 5,172 tons; maple sugar, 13,586 pounds; wool, 32,758 pounds.

Distances. Forty miles north-west from Windsor, and forty south-west from Montpelier. The Vermont Southern Railroad passes through this town.

BRATTLEBOROUGH.

WINDHAM CO. The surface of the town is considerably broken. A little west of the centre are two elevations called *Great* and *Little* Round Mountain. They are both accessible, and most of the land capable of cultivation. The soil is similar to that generally found along the Connecticut, consisting of intervale, sand, loam and gravel, with such timber as is naturally adapted to them. The principal streams are West River and Whetstone Brook. The former runs but a short distance in town, entering it from Dummerston and falling into Connecticut River near the north-east corner. Whetstone Brook rises in Marlborough and runs through Brattleborough very near the centre. This affords many excellent water privileges, which are already occupied by a great variety of mills and other machinery.

Connecticut River forms the eastern boundary for about six miles. It runs in several places with a strong current, denominated "The swift water," by the boatmen. The river is crossed at the lower part of the east village, by a handsome bridge, built in 1804, and connecting this town with Hinsdale, N. H. A few rods above the bridge is the general landing place for merchandise, which is brought into town by boats.

There are few minerals worthy of notice. Actynolite is found here in steatite. It is in very perfect capillary crystals which are grouped together in different forms and sometimes radicated. Argillaceous slate is very abundant, and is quarried to considerable extent. Mica is found of rose red col-

or with schorl in quartz, and abundance of schorl in beautiful crystals, and also the red oxyde of titanium.

There are two considerable villages, one standing at the mouth of Whetstone Brook, called the *East Village,* and the other near the centre of the town, called the *West Village.* The east village is one of the most active business places in the State.

In this town is one of the most extensive *Water Cure Establishments* in the United States; for a particular account of which, see *Hayward's Gazetteer of Massachusetts,* p. 168.

Boundaries. North by Dummerston, east by Connecticut River, which separates it from Chesterfield, N. H., south by Vernon and Guilford, and west by Marlborough.

First Settlers. This town derives its name from Colonel Brattle, of Massachusetts, one of the principal proprietors. Fort Dummer, the first civilized establishment within the present limits of Vermont, was built in 1724, in the south-east corner of the town, on what is now called "*Dummer Meadows.*" Nathan Willard, David Sargeant, David Sargeant, Jr., John and Thomas Sargeant, John Alexander, Fairbank Moore and son, Samuel Wells and John Arms were among the first settlers, and were all from Massachusetts, except John and Thomas Sargeant, and John Alexander, who were born at Fort Dummer. John Sargeant is believed to have been the first white person born within the present limits of Vermont. His father and brother David were ambushed by the Indians; the former killed and scalped, and the other carried into captivity, where he adopted the Indian habits and manners, but afterwards returned to his friends. Fairbank Moore and his son were killed by Indians at West River Meadows, two miles north of Fort Dummer, and the wife and daughter of the latter, carried into captivity. In 1771, Stephen Greenleaf, from Boston, having purchased what was called the *Governor's Farm,* situated where the east village now is, opened a store here, which was supposed to be the first store within the limits of Vermont.

First Ministers. The first Congregational minister was the Rev. Abner Reed; he was settled in 1770, and was succeeded by the Rev. Wm. Wells.

Productions of the Soil. Wheat, 1,235 bushels; Indian corn, 6,490 bushels; potatoes, 27,480 bushels; hay, 3,358 tons; maple sugar, 12,250 pounds; wool, 4,058 pounds.

Distances. One hundred miles south from Montpelier, twelve miles south-east from Newfane, and thirty east from Bennington. The "Iron Horse," on his way up and down the river, passes through this beautiful town several times a day, carrying life and prosperity to the business community.

BRIDGEWATER.

WINDSOR Co. The surface of this town is uneven and some parts rough and stony. Along the river, are tracts of valuable intervale, and there are many good farms in other parts. The summits of the hills are, in general, covered with spruce and hemlock; the timber, on other parts, is mostly maple, beech, and birch. The rocks are mica, and talco-argillaceous slate, gneiss, limestone, quartz, &c. There is an inexhaustible quarry of steatite, situated nearly in the centre of the town. It has been manufactured to some extent, and makes excellent jambs, hearths, &c. In the vicinity of the steatite, are large quantities of beautiful green talc. Iron ore is found in several places. Garnets in perfect dodechedral crystals are common, and several handsome specimens of rock crystal, crystals of hornblend and schorl, have been found.

There is a small village, on the river, near the south-east corner of the town, in which are a meeting-house, several mills, factories, stores, and mechanic's shops.

In August, 1822, Mr. Aaron Lamb, while sinking a well about eighty rods north of Ottà Quechee River, dug up a living frog, at the depth of twenty-six feet below the surface of the ground. It was in a state of torpor when taken up, but revived after being exposed a short time to the atmosphere. This town is watered by Ottà Quechee River, which runs through the south part, and by several considerable branches. These streams afford numerous mill privileges.

The Ottà Quechee Mill Company in this town was incorporated in 1847.

Boundaries. North by Barnard, east by Woodstock, south by Plymouth, and west by Sherburne.

First Settlers. Dea. Asa Jones surveyed a lot of land in Bridgewater, in September, 1779, and the next winter, removed his family into this town from Woodstock, a distance of three miles, on hand-sleds. This was the first family in town. Mr. Amos Mendall came in the spring following, May, 1780, and was married to a daughter of Deacon Jones. This was the first couple married, and was the second family in town. Their daughter, Lucy, was the first child born. In 1783, Messrs. Isaiah Shaw and Cephas Sheldon moved their families into the north part of the town, they having commenced improvements the year before. Capt. James Fletcher came in with his family about the same time. In 1784, settlements were commenced along the river in the south part of the town, by the Messrs. Southgates, Hawkins and Topliff, and from this time the settlement proceeded rapidly for a number of years.

First Minister. A Congregational Church was organized here in 1793. The Rev. John Ransom was ordained over it in 1795, and remained its pastor till 1802.

Productions of the Soil. Wheat, 3,165 bushels; Indian corn, 5,815 bushels; potatoes, 47,215 bushels; hay, 4,541 tons; maple sugar, 34,725 pounds; wool, 21,426 pounds.

Distances. Forty-five miles south from Montpelier, and seventeen north-west from Windsor.

BRIDPORT.

ADDISON Co. The surface of this town is very level, and the soil, generally, is a brittle marl, or clay. The hills are a loam and red slaty sandstone. A range of shelly blue slate extends through the town, lying, generally, a little below the surface. The prevailing timber, in the west part of the town, is oak, with white and some Norway pine, along the lake shore. In the eastern part it is, principally, maple and beech. The raising of sheep has been the chief occupation of the people for several years past, which accounts for the decrease of population. This town is poorly watered, there being no durable mill streams, and the springs and ground, generally, being impregnated with epsom salts, or sulphate of magnesia. For family use, rain water is, generally, employed. It is preserved in large reservoirs, or cisterns set in the ground. Of the brackish water, in this town, cattle are extremely fond, and it serves, in a manner, as a substitute for salt. Some of the springs are so strongly impregnated, that, in time of low water, a pailful will yield a pound of the salts. The discovery of these salts as an ingredient in the waters here, was made by the Rev. Sylvanus Chapin, and they were manufactured in considerable quantities, as early as 1790, but the cheapness of the imported salts has prevented much being done at the business for some years past. There is a small but neat and pleasantly located village, consisting of about twenty-five dwelling houses. The prospect, from the "common," of the mountain and lake scenery is very fine. This town has its medicinal spring impregnated with sulphurated hydrogen, similar to those which are so common in the eastern part of the State. There are several landing places of goods on the lake shore.

Across the lake to Crown Point is about two miles. A visit to the ruins of this ancient fortress, so renowned in the annals of the revolutionary war, and elevated forty-seven feet above the level of the lake, is a great treat to the contemplative traveller, or the lover of splendid scenery. From these warlike ruins to those of Ticonderoga, is fourteen miles, south.

Boundaries. North by Addison, east by Weybridge and Cornwall, south by Shoreham, and west by Lake Champlain, which separates it from Crown Point, N. Y.

First Settlers. The first attempt to settle the town, was made in 1768, but was abandoned at that time on account of the urgency of the New York claims. The first permanent settler was Philip Stone, who was also the first colonel in the county. In 1768, being twenty-one years of age, he came from Groton, Mass., to this place, purchased a lot of land, and commenced clearing it. Two families, by the name of Richardson and Smith, settled under New York titles about the same time, and three others, by the name of Towner, Chipman and Plumer, under New Hampshire titles. The settlers mostly retired before Burgoyne and his army in 1776 and '7. During the controversy with New York, no skirmishing happened in this town between the New York and New Hampshire claimants, but the inhabitants, frequently, aided their neighbors in the adjoining towns, in inflicting the customary punishment of whipping upon the Yorkers, who refused to retire after the usual warning. In 1772, Ethan Allen, having been declared an outlaw by the New York government, and a bounty offered for his apprehension, called in company with Eli Roberts, of Vergennes, at the house of Mr. Richards of this town. In the evening, six soldiers from Crown Point garrison, all armed, as were Allen and Roberts, stopped for the night. Mrs. Richards overheard them making their arrangement to take Allen and get the bounty. All was quiet till bed time, when Mrs. Richards, on lighting Allen and Roberts into another room, raised a window, at which they silently escaped. When the soldiers discovered that they were gone, they reprimanded Mrs. Richards severely for favoring their escape. But she replied that "it was for the safety of her house, for had they been taken here, the Hampshire men would have torn it down over their heads."

First Ministers. A Congregational Church was organized here in 1790, and the Rev. Increase Graves was installed over it in 1794. The Rev. James F. McEwen was settled as colleague of the Rev. Mr. Graves in 1827, and in 1829 both were dismissed. In

1831, the Rev. Dana Lamb was settled.

Productions of the Soil. Wheat, 2,920 bushels; Indian corn, 2,988 bushels; potatoes, 15.820 bushels; hay, 11,475 tons; maple sugar, 484 pounds; wool, 69,164 pounds.

Distances. Twelve miles west by south from Middlebury, and forty-five south-west from Montpelier.

BRIGHTON.

Essex Co. This town was named Random by the Hon. Joseph Brown, it being a random purchase from an agent sent to Providence, from Vermont. The name was altered to Brighton, November 3, 1832. The settlement was commenced in 1823, by Enos Bishop; and John Stevens moved his family into the town in 1825. The settlement is mostly in the westerly part of the town. The town was organized in March, 1832.

The township is watered chiefly by Ferren's River, and other head branches of Clyde River, but some of the head branches of the Passumpsic and Nulhegan Rivers originate here. Pitkin's Pond and Knowlton Lake discharge their waters through Clyde River. This is considered a very good township of land, and contains much excellent white pine timber, with several fine mill sites.

Boundaries. Northerly by Wenlock, easterly by Ferdinand, southerly by Newark and a part of Westmore and East Haven, and westerly by Charleston.

Productions of the Soil. Wheat, 358 bushels; Indian corn, 54 bushels; potatoes, 4,700 bushels; hay, 246 tons; maple sugar, 6,050 pounds; wool, 348 pounds.

Distances. Thirty-two miles northwest from Guildhall, and seventy northeast from Montpelier.

BRISTOL.

Addison Co. About one third of this town lies entirely west of the Green Mountains, and is very level, rich, and productive The remainder of the town

is broken, and a considerable part incapable of cultivation. A considerable mountain extends through the town, from north to south. That part of it north of the Great Notch, through which New Haven River passes, is called the Hog Back, and that on the south is called South Mountain. A part of the latter was formerly much infested with rattle snakes. New Haven River enters this town from the south-east, and, before it reaches the centre of the town, receives Baldwin Creek from the north. After passing the Notch and Bristol village, it runs some distance nearly south, and then turns to the west into New Haven. There are three natural ponds here; the largest, called Bristol Pond, is a mile and a half long and three fourths of a mile wide. In the west part of the town is a spring which is slightly medicinal, and is sometimes visited. There is a bed of iron ore in the part of the town next to Monkton, and there have been several forges here. Most of the ore which is used here is brought from Monkton, and from a bed in Moriah, N. York, west of Lake Champlain. This town furnishes large quantities of sawed lumber, which are sent to market.

The *village* is near the centre of the town, upon New Haven River, immediately after it passes the Notch in the mountain. It is very pleasantly located. The greater part of it is watered by an aqueduct nearly 400 rods in length, laid in water lime.

Boundaries. North by Monkton and Starksboro', east by Lincoln and Starksboro', south by Middlebury and Avery's Gore, and west by New Haven.

First Settlers. The settlement of this town was commenced immediately after the revolutionary war, by Samuel Stewart and Eden Johnson. These were soon joined by Benjamin Griswold, Cyprian, Calvin, and Jonathan Eastman, Justus Allen, and others.

First Minister. The first ordained minister was the Rev. Amos Stearns.

Productions of the Soil. Wheat, 1,524 bushels; Indian corn, 6,300 bushels; potatoes, 25,150 bushels; hay, 2,252

tons; maple sugar, 9,500 pounds; wool, 11,800 pounds.

Distances. Twenty-five miles southwest from Montpelier, and eleven north from Middlebury. The Northern Railroad passes near this town.

BROOKFIELD.

ORANGE CO. This township lies nearly on the height of land between White and Winooski Rivers, and parts of it are broken; but it is mostly fit for cultivation and is very productive, particularly in grass. It is well watered with springs and brooks, but has no very good mill privileges. The principal stream is the second branch of White River, which originates in Williamstown, in conjunction with Stevens' branch of Winooski River, and runs through the eastern part of this town into Randolph. There are several considerable ponds, some of which afford streams, a considerable part of the year, sufficient for mills and other machinery. Colt's Pond, near the north village, is crossed by a floating bridge twenty-five rods long. Around and at the bottom of a small pond, in the west part of the town, is an inexhaustible quantity of marl, from which very good lime is manufactured.

Boundaries. North by Williamstown, east by Chelsea, south by Randolph and a part of Braintree, and west by Roxbury.

First Settlers. The first settlement of this town was begun in 1779, by Shubal Cross and family. Mrs. Cross was the first woman who came into town, and on that account was presented by the proprietors with 100 acres of land. Mr. Howard's family came in about the same time, and Caleb Martin, John Lyman, Jonathan Pierce, John and Noah Payne, and several others, came in soon after. The early settlers were principally from Connecticut. Capt. Cross built the first grist and saw mill.

First Ministers. A Congregational Church was organized here in 1787, and the Rev. Elijah Lyman was ordained over it in 1789, and continued

pastor till his death, which took place in 1828.

Productions of the Soil. Wheat, 6,127 bushels; Indian corn, 7,042 bushels; potatoes, 70,686 bushels; hay, 1,419 tons; maple sugar, 26,486 pounds; wool, 25,757 pounds.

Distances. Forty miles north by west from Windsor, and sixteen south from Montpelier.

BROOKLINE.

WINDHAM CO. This town is about eight miles in length and from one and a half to two and a half miles in width. It was set off from Putney and Athens and incorporated into a township, October 30, 1794, and derives its name from *Grassy Brook*, which runs through the whole length of the town, from north to south, and empties into West River, on the south-western boundary.

A deep valley runs through the whole length of the township, from north to south, at the bottom of which runs *Grassy Brook*, which rises in Athens and falls into West River, near the south-west corner of Brookline. Along the whole of the east line of the town is a considerable elevation. West River forms, for a short distance, the western boundary. During a violent freshet, some years since, a bed of kaolin, or porcelain clay, was laid open in this town. The soil is better adapted to the production of grass than grain. There is a medicinal spring in the south part of the town, which is considered efficacious in cutaneous affections. The town has always been remarkably healthy.

Boundaries. North by Athens, east by Westminster and Putney, south by Putney and Dummerston, and west by Townshend and Newfane.

First Settlers. The first settlement was made in this township by Cyrus Whitcomb, Jr., David Ayres, Samuel Skinner, and Jonah Moore, about the year 1777. The first settlers had many hardships to endure, but nothing more than is common in new settlements generally.

First Minister. A Baptist Society was organized here in 1798; the first minister was Rev. Amos Beckwith, settled in 1802.

Productions of the Soil. Wheat, 294 bushels; Indian corn, 2,815 bushels; potatoes, 9,929 bushels; hay, 937 tons; maple sugar, 3,530 pounds; wool, 2,331 pounds.

Distances. Thirty-five miles south from Windsor, ten north-east from Newfane, and eighteen north from Brattleborough.

BROWNINGTON.

ORLEANS CO. This town is watered by Willoughby River. The soil in many parts of the town is good, but is generally better for grazing than tillage. Brownington was formerly the shire town of the county.

It is a place of some business, and has a neat village. The settlement of the township was commenced about the year 1800.

Boundaries. North-easterly by Salem and Charleston, south-easterly by Westmore, south-westerly by Barton, and west by north by Orleans and a small part of Irasburgh.

Productions of the Soil. Wheat, 1,549 bushels; Indian corn, 426 bushels; potatoes, 22,600 bushels; hay, 1,391 tons; maple sugar, 18,395 pounds; wool, 4,711 pounds.

Distances. Six miles east from Irasburgh, and forty-eight north-east from Montpelier.

BRUNSWICK.

ESSEX CO. Brunswick lies on the west side of Connecticut River, and has some excellent mill sites on the waters of Nulhegan River, and Wheeler and Paul's Streams. There are some beautiful ponds in town, and a mineral spring said to contain medicinal virtues.

Boundaries. North by Minehead, east by Connecticut River, south by Maidstone, and west by Wenlock.

First Settlers. The first settlement was commenced in the spring of 1780, by Joseph and Nathaniel Wait. John Merrill removed here the succeeding autumn.

Productions of the Soil. Wheat, 253 bushels; Indian corn, 435 bushels; potatoes, 8,200 bushels; hay, 460 tons; maple sugar, 3,370 pounds; wool, 1,385 pounds.

Distances. Fifteen miles north from Guildhall, and eighty-three north-east from Montpelier.

BURKE.

CALEDONIA CO. A mountain 3,500 feet in height divides this town from Victory, on the east. Branches of Passumpsic River pass through it, and afford a good water power. This is a place of some manufactures, particularly of oil stones. This stone (*novaculite*) is found in an island in Memphremagog Lake. The stones are brought in their rough state, and their quality is said to equal those from Turkey. The soil of the town is good, and abounds with hard wood and evergreens.

Boundaries. North-east by Newark and East Haven, south-east by Victory, south by Langdon and Kirby, and west by Sutton.

First Settlers. The settlement of this town was commenced about the year 1790, by Lemuel and Ira Walter, Seth Spencer, and others, from Connecticut and the south part of this State. The town was organized Dec. 5, 1796.

Productions of the Soil. Wheat, 2,358 bushels; Indian corn, 2,891 bushels; potatoes, 49,620 bushels; hay, 2,931 tons; maple sugar, 42,050 pounds; wool, 7,475 pounds.

Distances. Twenty miles north-east from Danville, and fifty north-east from Montpelier.

BURLINGTON.

CHITTENDEN CO. This is the chief town in the county. It is delightfully situated upon the tongue of land formed by the confluence of the Winooski River with Lake Champlain. This is the most important town in Vermont. It lies in lat. 44° 27′ N., and in lon. 73° 15′ W.

The surface of the township is agreeably diversified, and is so much eleva-

4

ted above the lake that the air is pure and wholesome.

This town is not surpassed in beauty of location by any one in New England. It lies on the east shore of Burlington Bay, and occupies a gentle declivity, descending towards the west, and terminated by the waters of the lake. The principal streets, running east and west, are one mile in length, and these are intersected at right angles, by streets running north and south, and cutting the whole village into regular squares. A large share of the business on Lake Champlain centres at this place, and the town is rapidly increasing in wealth and consequence.

There are regular daily lines of steamboats between this place and Whitehall, between this and St. Johns, and between this and Plattsburgh, besides numerous arrivals of irregular boats, sloops, &c. Three extensive wharves, with store-houses, have been constructed, and most of the merchandize designed for the north-eastern section of Vermont is landed here. The trade is principally with the city of New York, although Montreal and Troy have a share. For the safety of the navigation, a light-house has been erected on Juniper Island, at the entrance of Burlington Bay; and for the security of the harbor, a breakwater has been commenced here, at the expense of the general government. There are four lines of mail stages, which arrive and depart daily, besides three or four others, which come in and go out twice or thrice a week.

The public buildings are six churches, the University of Vermont, the Episcopal Institute, the court house, two banks, the Academy, and two female seminaries. The University consists of four spacious edifices, located upon the summit at the eastern extremity of the village, more than 250 feet above the level of the lake, and commands one of the finest prospects in the United States. The village, the lake, with its bays and islands—its steamboats and sloops—the Winooski River, dashing through frightful chasms and then winding among the beautiful meadows, and the distant and lofty mountains, which form the great outline, render the view from the dome of the University one of the most variegated and interesting to be met with in our country.

As a part of Burlington may be mentioned the village called "Winooski City." It is situated on both sides of the Winooski River, partly in Burlington and partly in Colchester, and is about two miles from the village of Burlington. The water power here is sufficient for propelling almost any amount of machinery.

A substantial covered bridge connects the two sides of the river; a handsome church and several stores have been erected; and "Winooski City" bids fair to become a place of business and importance.

Manufactures. The manufactures of this place consist of two woollen mills, one cotton mill, one foundry and machine shop, two saw mills, one grist and an extensive flour mill.

The principal manufacturing establishment is the Burlington Company, at "Winooski City." They commenced operations in 1836–7. It continued to manufacture on a small scale till 1845, when the company was newly organized and much enlarged. The company now runs sixteen setts of woollen machinery, on fine, fancy, and plain cassimeres and coatings. It employs 450 hands; it uses annually 600,000 pounds of wool, and consumes 4,000 cords of wood. It uses, also, 12,000 gallons olive and 3,000 gallons sperm oil; 140,-000 pounds of soap, 25,000 pounds of glue, 150 tons of dye-woods, &c.

The railroads between Burlington and Boston will greatly enhance the value of the commerce of this place; and at no distant day Burlington will become an important depot for the commerce of Boston as well as of New York.

Boundaries. North by Colchester, from which it is separated by Winooski River, east by Williston, south by Shelburne, and west by Lake Champlain.

First Settlers. The first that was

done in this town, with a view to its settlement, was in 1774. During the summer of 1775 some clearings were made on the intervale north of the village, and in the neighborhood of the falls, and two or three log huts erected. But the revolution commencing this year, the settlers in this and neighboring towns, either retreated to the south in the fall, or took shelter in the blockhouse in Colchester for the winter, and abandoned the country the succeeding spring. During the war no attempt was made to renew the settlement in these parts; but on the return of peace in 1783, many of those who had been compelled to leave the country, returned and others with them, and a permanent settlement was effected. The first man who brought his family into Burlington in the spring of 1783, was Mr. Stephen Lawrence. A number of other families came into Burlington the same season, among whom were Frederick Saxton, Simon Tubbs, and John Collins, and from that time to the present the population has been constantly on the increase.

First Ministers. A Congregational Church was organized here in 1805, and was the only religious society for several years. This church was divided in sentiment in 1810, in which year the Rev. Daniel Haskell was ordained over the Trinitarian Society, and the Rev. Samuel Clark was ordained over the Unitarian part of the congregation.

Productions of the Soil. Wheat, 2,462 bushels; Indian corn, 11,450 bushels; potatoes, 4,598 bushels; hay, 4,241 tons; maple sugar, 340 pounds; wool, 10,660 pounds.

Distances. Thirty-eight miles west north-west from Montpelier, sixty-two south by east from St. Johns, Canada, eighty-five south-east from Montreal, seventy north from Whitehall, twenty-two south-east from Plattsburg, ten miles across to Fort Kent, N. Y., and four hundred and forty from Washington.

CABOT.

CALEDONIA Co. This town lies on the height of land between Winooski and Connecticut Rivers. "The Plain" is delightfully situated, having the Green and White Mountains in prospect. Several branches of the Winooski River water this town, and afford it some water power. Here is *Jo and Molly's* Pond, and a sulphur spring. The surface is broken and hard, but good for sheep. This is the birth place of the late *Zerah Colburn,* the celebrated mathematician.

Boundaries. North by Walden, east by Danville and Peacham, south by Marshfield, and west by Monroe.

First Settlers. The settlement of this town was commenced on what is called *Cabot Plain,* in April, 1785, by James Bruce, Edmund Chapman, Jonathan Heath and Benjamin Webster, with their families. The females came into the town on snowshoes, and were obliged to suffer many privations and hardships.

Productions of the Soil. Wheat, 3,383 bushels; Indian corn, 1,768 bushels; potatoes, 70,487 bushels; hay, 4,489 tons; maple sugar, 34,715 pounds; wool, 13,316 pounds.

Distances. Ten miles south-west from Danville, and twenty north-east from Montpelier.

CALAIS.

WASHINGTON Co. This township is watered by two branches of Winooski River, one entering it near the north-east, the other near the north-west corner. They unite near the south line of the town, affording, in their course, a great number of valuable privileges for mills and other machinery. It is also well watered with springs and brooks. The soil is a warm loam, easily cultivated, well adapted to the production of all kinds of grain, and is not inferior to other towns in its vicinity for grazing. The surface of the township is somewhat uneven, but very little of it so broken as to be incapable of cultivation. The timber on the streams is mostly hemlock, spruce, and pine; on the higher lands, maple, beech, &c. The lowest lands here are in general driest and the most feasible soil. The north line of the township intersects two considerable ponds. There are several other small, but beautiful ponds lying within the township, and which abound with trout and other fish. Long Pond lies in the north-west part of the town. In one autumn, 2,000 pounds of trout were taken from this pond with a hook, which sold for $8 per cwt. In the spring of some years, at the inlet of this pond, more than two tons of fish have been thrown out of the channel with the hands and with baskets. There are several springs in town, whose waters are quite brackish; their medicinal qualities, however, have never been thoroughly tested.

Boundaries. North by Woodbury, east by Marshfield, south by Montpelier, and west by Worcester.

First Settlers. The settlement of this town was commenced in the spring of 1787, by Francis West, from Plymouth County, Mass., who commenced felling timber on a lot adjoining Montpelier. The first permanent settlers, however, were Abijah, Asa and P. Wheelock, who started from Charlestown, June 5th, 1787, with a wagon, two yoke of oxen, provisions, tools, &c. and arrived at Williamstown, within twenty-one miles of Calais, the 19th. They had hitherto found the roads almost impassible, and here they were obliged to leave their wagon, and, taking a few necessary articles upon a sled, they proceeded towards this town, cutting their way and building causeways as they passed along. After a journey of two days and encamping two nights in the woods, they arrived at Winooski River, where Montpelier village is now situated. Here Col. Jacob Davis had commenced clearing land and had erected a small log hut, where they left their oxen to graze upon the wild grass, leaks and shrubbery, with which the woods abounded—proceeded to Calais and commenced a resolute attack upon the forest. They returned to Charlestown in October. Francis West also left town, and returned the following spring, as did also Abijah and Peter Wheelock, accompanied by Moses Stone. They this year erected log houses, the Wheelocks and

Stone returning to Massachusetts to spend the following winter, and West to Middlesex. In this year, also, Gen. Parley Davis, then a new settler, cut and put up two or three stacks of hay upon a beaver meadow, in Montpelier, upon a lot adjoining Calais, a part of which hay was drawn to Col. Davis in Montpelier in the following winter, which served partially to break a road from Montpelier to Calais line. In February or March, 1789, Francis West moved his family on to his farm, where he lived several years. Also, in March of this year, Abijah Wheelock, with his family, Moses Stone, Samuel Twiss with his new married lady, accompanied by Gen. Davis, from Charlestown, arrived at Col. Davis' house in Montpelier, with several teams. His house was a mere rude hut, constructed of logs twenty feet in length, with but one apartment, a back built at one end for a fire place, and covered with bark, with a hole left in the roof for the smoke to escape; and this on their arrival they found to be pre-occupied by several families, emigrants from Peterboro', N. H.; and in that mansion of felicity there dwelt for about a fortnight three families with children in each, one man and his wife, recently married, three gentlemen then enjoying a state of single blessedness, and a young lady; and among the happy group were some of the first settlers of Calais. On the 13th of April, racket paths having been previously broken, Messrs. Wheelock, Twiss and Stone prepared handsleds, loaded thereon their beds and some light articles of furniture, accompanied by Mrs. Wheelock and Mrs. Twiss, and Gen. Davis, proceeded to this town over snow three feet in depth, Mrs. Wheelock travelling the whole distance on foot and carrying in her arms an infant four months' old, while their son about two years of age, was drawn upon the handsled. Mrs. Twiss, the recently married lady, also performed the same journey on foot, making use of her broom for a walking cane. During the day the snow became soft and in crossing a marshy piece of ground, Mrs. Twiss slumped with one foot, and sank to considerable depth and was unable to rise; Gen. Davis, with all the gallantry of a young woodsman, pawed away the snow with his hands, seized her below the knee and extricated her. This incident was a source of no small merriment to the party generally, of mortification to the amiable sufferer, and of gratification to Mrs. Wheelock, who felt herself secretly piqued that Mrs. Twiss did not at least offer to bear her precious burthen some part of the distance. They arrived in safety the same day, and commenced the permanent settlement of the town. A large rock, now in the orchard on the farm owned by Dea. Joshua Bliss, once formed the end and fire place to the *Log Cabin* of the first settlers of Calais. In September of this same year, 1789, Peter Wheelock moved his family, consisting of a wife and six children, to this town. In 1790, James Jennings arrived with a family. Lucinda, daughter of Peter Wheelock, was born this year, and was the first child born in town. On this occasion it is said one woman travelled four miles, on foot, through the woods, in a very dark night.

Productions of the Soil. Wheat, 3,630 bushels; Indian corn, 5,089 bushels, potatoes, 24,246 bushels; hay, 5,899 tons; maple sugar, 24,420 pounds; wool, 14,160 pounds.

Distances. Eight miles north from Montpelier.

CALEDONIA COUNTY.

DANVILLE is the chief town. This county is bounded east by Connecticut River and Essex County, south by Orange County, west by Washington County, and north by the county of Orleans. The eastern range of the Green Mountains extends through the western part of the county. It is watered by many fine streams, but the Connecticut and Passumpsic are its chief rivers. A large part of the county is high and good land; that along the rivers is excellent. It produces wheat and other grain, beef cattle, horses, and sheep. There are some sulphur springs in this county; limestone and granite are abundant.—See *Tables.*

COURTS IN CALEDONIA COUNTY.

The *Supreme Court* sits at Danville, on the 8th Tuesday after the 4th Tuesday in December; and the *County Court*, on the 1st Tuesday in June and December, annually.

CAMBRIDGE.

LAMOILLE Co. The river Lamoille enters this town on the east side one mile from the north-east corner, and after running a serpentine course of twelve miles, in which it receives North Branch from the north, and Brewster's River and Seymour's Brook from the south, passes the west line of the town, one mile from the south-west corner. These streams afford numerous mill privileges. The surface of the town is uneven, and, in some places rough. The land is, however, generally good, and on the river are about 5000 acres of valuable intervale. A branch of Dead Creek, which is a branch of Missisco River, rises in this town, and another branch of said creek issues from Metcalf Pond in Fletcher and

4*

runs across the north-west corner of the town. The town is well watered, and the timber of various kinds.

There are three small villages. The village called the *Borough*, is on the south side of the river Lamoille, in the south-west corner of the town, on the post road. The *centre village* is on the south side of the Lamoille near the centre of the town, west of Brewster's River.

Boundaries. North-easterly by Waterville and a part of Fletcher, easterly by Sterling and a part of Johnson, south by Underhill, and westerly by Fletcher.

First Settlers. The first settler of this town was John Spafford. He came into town May 8, 1783, planted two acres of corn, which was overflowed with water in the fall, and nearly all destroyed. He moved his family, consisting of a wife and two children, into town from Piermont, N. H., in November. The town was surveyed, this year, by Amos Fasset. In 1784, Amos Fasset, Stephen Kinsley, John Fasset, Jr., and Samuel Montague moved their families here from Bennington, and Noah Chittenden his from Arlington.

First Ministers. The Rev. Elijah Woolage was settled over the Congregational Church in 1805, and dismissed in 1812.

Productions of the Soil. Wheat, 3,531 bushels; Indian corn, 6,435 bushels; potatoes, 73,100 bushels; hay, 5,329 tons; maple sugar, 64,111 pounds; wool, 19,091 pounds.

Distances. Fifteen miles west from Hydepark, and forty north-west from Montpelier.

CANAAN.

Essex Co. Canaan lies opposite Stewartstown, N. H. The north-east corner of the town is the most easterly land in Vermont. February 26, 1782, it received a new charter, and October 23, 1801, the town of Norfolk was annexed to it. Canaan being a frontier town, was subject to considerable disturbance during the last war with Great Britain. Willard's Brook, &c., afford good mill privileges. The former is two rods

wide at its junction with the Connecticut, Leeds Pond from which it issues is partly in Canada. There is some fine intervale on the Connecticut, and much good land in other parts. This town affords a fine field for fowling and angling.

Boundaries. North by Hereford, Canada, east by Connecticut River, and south-west by Lemington and Averill.

First Settlers. John Hugh, Hubbard Spencer, and Silas Sargeant in 1791.

Productions of the Soil. Wheat, 692 bushels; Indian corn, 285 bushels; potatoes, 26,400 bushels; hay, 1,451 tons; maple sugar, 11,450 pounds; wool, 2,711 pounds.

Distances. Thirty-five miles north from Guildhall, and one hundred and three north-east from Montpelier.

CASTLETON.

Rutland Co. This is a flourishing town, watered by a river of the same name. The surface of the town is rough and hilly, but there is some rich land. Mill streams abound in Castleton, on which are a woollen and other manufacturing establishments. Lake Bombazine, seven miles in length and two in breadth, is chiefly in this town. It is stored with fish, and has an island near its centre of exquisite beauty. The village of Castleton is elevated, neatly built, and presents a great variety of rich and beautiful scenery.

There is considerable variety in the soil and surface of Castleton. The rocks are chiefly argillaceous, occasionally traversed by veins of quartz, and occasionally alternating with, or enclosing large masses of the latter rock; small quantities of secondary limestone are found in a few localities. Specimens of oxide of manganese are found in the vicinity of Bird's Mountain, in the south-east part of the town. The rocks are disposed in elevated ridges, in the eastern and northern sections, and are in some places abrupt and precipitous; but for the most part covered with fertile arable soil. The south-west part is a pine plain, in some places intersected by slate rock and ridges of slate gravel. The larger streams are generally bordered by rich alluvial intervales, which, in some instances, are broad and extensive. The soil of the plains is sandy and light; on the hills it is slaty gravel, loam, and vegetable mould; these soils are rendered much more productive by the use of plaster of Paris; that of the intervales is strong and productive, in many places however requiring drainage.

The outlet of the lake, at its southern extremity, has sufficient declivity and volume of water to propel a large amount of machinery. Castleton River, which arises in Pittsford, traverses a part of Rutland, Ira, and Castleton, from east to west, where it receives the waters of Lake Bombazine. It afterwards unites with Poultney River, in Fair Haven, and enters Lake Champlain at East Bay. This river and its tributary brooks furnish considerable water power, which is improved in propelling various kinds of machinery. Being increased by many abundant springs along its bed, its waters are very pure and cool in summer, and seldom frozen in winter.

The village of Castleton was incorporated in 1847, and contains some very handsome public and private buildings.

Boundaries. South by Poultney, east by Ira, north by Hubbardton, west by Fair Haven.

First Settlers. The first dwelling-house was erected in August, 1769, of which Col. Lee and his servant were the sole inhabitants the following winter. In 1770, Ephraim Buel, Eleazer, Bartholomew, and Zadock Remington, with their families, settled in this town, and were soon followed by Cols. Bird and Lee. The first inhabitants were chiefly emigrants from Connecticut. The enterprise and worth of Cols. Bird and Lee, entitle them to a prominent place in the early history of Castleton; the former died in the midst of active benevolent exertions for the infant settlement, September 16, 1762. His solitary monument on the banks of Castleton River, and an isolated mountain in the south-east corner of the town, are memorials of his name, still

associated with the remembrance of his worth. Col. Lee was vigilant and active amidst the hardships and dangers which were encountered by the first settlers, under the government of New Hampshire and the *council of safety*, and the vexatious embarrassments consequent to the claims of jurisdiction by the State of New York.

First Ministers. A Congregational Church was organized here in 1784. Rev. Mathias Cazier was settled in 1789, and dismissed in 1792. Rev. Elisha Smith was installed in 1804; dismissed in 1826.

Manufactures. Castleton affords numerous and valuable sites for manufacturing purposes. Operations have already commenced, and many articles are manufactured.

Productions of the Soil. Wheat, 1,752 bushels; Indian corn, 10,185 bushels; potatoes, 23,915 bushels; hay, 4,479 tons; maple sugar, 8,660 pounds; wool, 27,631 pounds.

Distances. Eleven miles west from Rutland, seventy-two south-west from Montpelier, and thirteen east from Whitehall. The great Southern Railroad passes near this town.

CAVENDISH.

WINDSOR CO. The soil of this town is easy, and generally fertile. Black River, which runs from west to east, and Twenty-mile Stream, which runs in a southerly direction and unites with it near White's Mills, are the principal streams. Along these streams are some small tracts of fine intervale.

The greatest curiosity in the town, and perhaps the greatest of the kind in the State, is at the falls on Black River, which are situated between Dutton's Village and White's Mills. "Here the channel of the river has been worn down 100 feet, and rocks of very large dimensions have been undermined and thrown down, one upon another. Holes are worn into the rocks, of various dimensions and forms. Some of them are cylindrical, from one to eight feet in diameter, and from one to fifteen feet in depth; others are of a spherical form, from six to twenty feet in diameter, worn almost perfectly smooth into the solid body of the rock."

Hawk's Mountain, which separates Baltimore from this town, derives its name from Col. Hawks, who, during the French and Indian wars, encamped thereon for the night with a small regular force, among whom was General (then Captain) John Stark. Some traces of their route are still to be seen.

There are two villages, viz., Duttonsville and Proctorsville. The former is a place of considerable business.

Proctorsville is a busy place, and has considerable manufactures of woollen and other goods. Near this village are large quarries of soapstone and serpentine, both of which are manufactured here in large quantities, and transported to the Atlantic cities. Specimens of the latter beautiful stone may be seen at the Tremont House and Merchant's Exchange, in Boston.

The Rutland and Burlington Railroad, which passes through the village, greatly facilitates the trade and manufactures of the place.

Boundaries. North by Reading, east by Weathersfield, south by Chester, and west by Ludlow.

First Settlers. The settlement of this township was commenced in the north part by Captain John Coffein, in June, 1769, at whose hospitable dwelling thousands of our revolutionary soldiers received refreshment, while passing from Charlestown, then No. 4, to the military posts on Lake Champlain, nearly the whole distance being at that time a wilderness. On the farm, now the residence of James Smith, Esq., in the north-westerly part of the town, twenty miles from Charlestown, was another stopping-place, called "The Twenty Miles Encampment," giving name to a small river, near the head of which the encampment was situated. In 1771, Noadiah Russell and Thomas Gilbert joined Captain Coffein in the settlement, and shared with him in his wants and privations. For several years they struggled hard for a scanty and precarious subsistence. The grinding of a single grist of corn was known

to have cost sixty miles travel. Such was the situation of the roads and the scarcity of mills at this early period. Many interesting anecdotes are related of Captain Coffein, which our limits will not permit us to insert. At one time he owed his life to the sagacity of his faithful dog. He was returning from Otter Creek, in March, 1771, while the country was perfectly new, and on account of the depth of the snow was compelled to travel on snow shoes. While crossing one of the ponds in Plymouth the ice broke, and he was suddenly plunged into the water. Encumbered with a large pair of snow shoes and a great coat which he had on, he strove, but in vain, to extricate himself. He struggled about half an hour, and, in despair, was about yielding himself to a watery grave, when, at this critical moment, his large and faithful dog beholding his situation came forward to the rescue of his master. He seized the cuff of his great coat, and, aided by the almost expiring efforts of Captain Coffein, succeeded in dragging him from the watery chasm to a place of safety. Captain Coffein lived to see the town settled and organized, and to take an active part in its public concerns.

Productions of the Soil. Wheat, 1,101 bushels; Indian corn, 3,750 bushels; potatoes, 30,680 bushels; hay, 3,620 tons; maple sugar, 7,545 pounds; wool, 14,279 pounds.

Distances. Ten miles south-west from Windsor, and sixty south from Montpelier.

CHARLESTON.

ORLEANS Co. The principal stream in this town is Clyde River, which enters the township in Brighton, and runs north-westerly nearly through its centre, into Salem. There are some falls of consequence on this stream, particularly the Great Falls, where the descent is more than 100 feet in forty rods, but its current is generally slow. The alluvial flats along this stream are extensive, but generally too low and wet for cultivation. In the south-east part of the township are 1,000 acres of bog meadow, in a body, upon this river. There are several considerable ponds. *Echo* Pond, the most important, is in the northern part, and was named by Gen. J. Whitelaw, on account of the succession of echoes which are usually heard, when any sound is produced in its vicinity. It is one and a half miles long and half a mile wide. The stream which discharges the waters of Seymour's Lake, in Morgan, into Clyde River, passes through this pond. On the outlet mills are erected. The other pond of most consequence is called *Pension* Pond, and lies in the course of Clyde River. These ponds abound in fish, and large quantities are annually caught. There are two small villages situated upon Clyde River, about six miles apart, designated as East Charleston and West Charleston. The soil of the township is a rich loam, and produces good crops, and the roads and business of the town are rapidly improving.

Boundaries. North-east by Morgan, south-east by Brighton, south-west by a part of Westmore and Brownington, and north-west by Salem.

First Settlers. The settlement of this township was commenced in 1803, by Andrew McGaffey, who this year moved his family here from Lyndon. Mrs. McGaffey died Oct. 30, of this year, which was the first death in town. In July, Abner Allyn also moved his family here, and his was the second family in town. In 1804 Joseph Seavey moved his family here; Orin Percival, his in 1805; and from this time the settlement proceeded more rapidly.

First Ministers. The dates of the settlement of the first ministers in this town are not given. The Freewill Baptists are the most numerous denomination of Christians. There are, however, other denominations, all of which are generally supplied by itinerant preachers.

Productions of the Soil. Wheat, 1,431 bushels; Indian corn, 467 bushels; potatoes, 26,279 bushels; hay, 1,499 tons; maple sugar, 23,965 pounds; wool, 2,861 pounds.

Distances. Twelve miles east from Irasburgh, and fifty-four north-east from Montpelier.

CHARLOTTE.

CHITTENDEN Co. This township is pleasantly situated on the lake shore, and is watered by the river Laplott, which runs through the north-east corner, and Lewis Creek, which runs through the southern corner. The western part of the town was originally timbered with hard wood, and the soil is excellent, producing in abundance. The eastern part was principally timbered with pine, hemlock, &c.. There are no elevations which deserve the names of mountains, but a range of considerable hills running through the centre of the town from north to south. From many parts of this ridge the scenery to the west is peculiarly picturesque. The lake with its islands, may be seen at a great distance. Add to this the extensive range of lofty mountains with their broken summits which lie beyond it, and it is believed that, particularly at some seasons of the year, the beauty and sublimity of the prospect is not excelled by any part of our country.

Boundaries. North by Shelburne, east by Hinesburgh, south by Ferrisburg and a part of Monkton, and west by Lake Champlain.

First Settlers. The first attempt to settle this town was made by Derick Webb. He first began in March, 1776, but soon left. He came in again, in March, 1777, and left in May, following; but no permanent settlement was made till 1784, when Derick Webb and Elijah Woolcut moved into the town, and were followed by others, so that the town was soon after organized. John McNeil was one of the early settlers.

First Ministers. There is a small village a little west of the centre, called the four corners, with a meeting-house and parsonage, belonging to the Methodist Society, built with brick in the year 1841, and well finished in modern style. Also, a female seminary, built in 1836, which is now under the superintendence of the Methodist Society. At about the same distance north of the centre, there is a village of still smaller size, and also two miles east of the centre, where there is a Baptist Meeting-house, built with brick and well finished, in the year 1841. The Congregational Meeting-house stands near the centre of the town, and was erected in the year 1808. The church was organized January 3, 1792, and on the next day the Rev. Daniel C. Gillet was ordained over it. He was dismissed in 1799, and the church was vacant till Nov. 4, 1807, when the Rev. Truman Baldwin was ordained over it, who was dismissed March 21, 1815.

Productions of the Soil. Wheat, 2,195 bushels; Indian corn, 26,885 bushels; potatoes, 52,985 bushels; hay, 9,175 tons; maple sugar, 6,000 pounds; wool, 31,348 pounds.

Distances. Forty-nine miles west of Montpelier, eleven south of Burlington, and twenty-one north-west of Middlebury. The Northern Railroad passes through this town.

CHELSEA.

ORANGE Co. This is the shire town of the county, and is a township of good land, with a pleasant village in the centre. It is watered by the head branches of White River and has a good hydraulic power. Chelsea produces all the various commodities common to the climate, and is a beautiful place of residence. The Chelsea Academy was incorporated in 1848.

Boundaries. North by Washington and Williamstown, east by Vershire, south by Tunbridge, and west by Brookfield.

First Settlers. This town was formerly called Turnersburgh. Improvements were commenced in this township in the spring of 1784, by Thomas and Samuel Moore, and Asa Bond. who, the next spring, brought in their families from Winchester, N. H. They were soon joined by others from different quarters, who settled in different parts of the town. Those who first came in brought all their furniture and provisions on their backs from Tun-

bridge, nine miles distant, where were their nearest neighbors. The first house in town was erected in the present burying ground by Thomas Moore, and was burned to the ground with all its contents, in September, 1785, but four or five months after his family had entered it. The first child born in town was Thomas Porter Moore, son of Thomas Moore, born Oct. 16, 1785.

First Ministers. A Congregational Church was early organized here, over which Rev. Lathrop Thompson was settled in November, 1799. He was dismissed in April, 1805, and Rev. Calvin Noble was ordained over the church in September, 1807, and continued in its charge till his death in April, 1834.

Productions of the Soil. Wheat, 3,177 bushels; Indian corn, 4,427 bushels; potatoes, 47,090 bushels; hay, 4,124 tons; maple sugar, 18,782 pounds; wool, 11,122 pounds.

Distances. Twenty miles south by east from Montpelier, and from this town to Northfield, through which the great Northern Railroad passes, is about thirteen miles.

CHESTER.

WINDSOR Co. William's River is formed in this township by the union of three considerable branches. These branches unite, nearly in the same place, and about one and a half miles south-east of the two villages; they constitute the principal waters, heading in the towns of Andover, Ludlow, and Windham. No natural pond, cave, or Indian name or relic was ever known or recorded in this town The surface is considerably diversified with hills and valleys, but the soil is generally good; the uplands yield excellent pasturage, and when newly cleared, produce abundance of grain. The intervales are rich and fertile, producing good crops of rye, corn, barley, oats, peas, beans, potatoes, &c. The roads are now all free, remarkably well laid, level and well wrought for such an uneven township, mainly following streams. Timber, mostly hard wood, with some hemlock, spruce, and pine

Minerals, granite, actynolite, augite chlorite, common and potter's clay, cyanite, epidote, feldspar, garnet, hornblend, iron, magnetic, oxyde of sulphuret, quartz, serpentine, talc, and mica. There are two villages, called the north and south village; the north village is situated near the centre of the township, on the northerly side of the north branch of William's River. The south village is situate in a pleasant valley on the north side of the middle branch of William's River, three fourths of a mile south of the north village, and one and a half mile south-easterly of the centre of the town.

Boundaries. North by Cavendish and Baltimore, east by Springfield, south by Grafton and a small part of Rockingham, and west by Andover and part of Ludlow.

First Settlers. The settlement was commenced in 1764, by Thomas Chandler and his two sons, John and Thomas Chandler, Jr., Jabez Sargeant, Edward Johnson, Isaiah Johnson, Charles Man, William Warner, Ichabod Ide, and Ebenezer Hotton, from Woodstock, Ct., and Worcester and Malden, Mass.

First Ministers. A Congregational Church was organized in 1773, and Rev. Samuel Whiting was settled by this town and Rockingham for five years; he officiating one third of the time at Chester, the remainder at Rockingham; after which they had no settled minister for thirty-six years.

Productions of the Soil. Wheat, 1,477 bushels; Indian corn, 8,627 bushels; potatoes, 35,255 bushels; hay, 4,490 tons; maple sugar, 18,987 pounds; wool, 30,263 pounds.

Distances. Sixteen miles south-west from Windsor, and seventy-nine south from Montpelier. The great Southern Railroad between Boston and Burlington, passes through this handsome town, which will greatly facilitate the business of this fertile region.

CHITTENDEN COUNTY.

Burlington is the chief town. This county is bounded north by Franklin County, east by Washington County, south by Addison County, and west by Champlain Lake. A few settlements commenced in this county before the revolution, but they were all abandoned during the war. Its soil varies from rich alluvial meadows to light and sandy plains. The beautiful Champlain, washing its western boundary, gives it great facilities for trade. Its agricultural and manufacturing products are considerable. Lamoille River passes through its north-west corner, and Winooski River pierces its centre. These streams, with several others of smaller size, afford the county a good water power.

The railroads which intersect this county in various directions; its fine mill privileges, and good soil, renders this a highly interesting section of the State. —See *Tables.*

COURTS IN CHITTENDEN COUNTY.

The *Supreme Court* sits at Burlington, on the Monday preceding the first Tuesday of January.

The *County Court* on the fourth Tuesday of May and November.

CHITTENDEN.

RUTLAND Co. The north-west part of this town is watered by Philadelphia River, which falls into Otter Creek at Pittsford. Tweed River rises in the eastern part, and falls into White River. The south-western part is watered by East Creek. Near Philadelphia River is a mineral spring, and among the mountains are some caverns, but they are little known. The town is interesting on account of its minerals. Iron ore of good quality is found here in abundance, and also manganese. Large quantities of iron ore are raised annually, much of which is smelted at the works in Pittsford. The manganese is found at unequal depths below the surface.

Boundaries. Northerly by Goshen, easterly by Pittsfield, southerly by Mendon, and west by Pittsford and a part of Brandon.

First Settlers. The settlement of this township was commenced about the close of the revolutionary war, but much of it being mountainous remains unsettled.

The most distinguished man who resided here was Aaron Beach. He fought under Wolf on the Heights of Abraham, served his country through the war of the revolution, and was prevented only by the solicitations of friends from being with the Green Mountain Boys in the battle of Plattsburg.

First Ministers. The Methodists erected a house of worship in 1832, and the Congregationalists in 1833.

Productions of the Soil. Wheat, 1,115 bushels; Indian corn, 2,379 bushels; potatoes, 16,830 bushels; hay, 1,970 tons; maple sugar, 11,790 pounds; wool, 9,202 pounds.

Distances. Twelve miles north by east from Rutland, and forty south west from Montpelier.

The great Southern Railroad passes through the vicinity of this town.

CLARENDON.

RUTLAND Co. Otter Creek runs through this town from south to north, a little east of the centre, and receives here Mill River and Cold River from the east, which affords numerous sites for Mills and other machinery. *Mill River* rises in Mount Holly, runs nearly on the line between this town and Wallingford, receiving from the latter the waters of a considerable pond, crosses the south-west corner of Shrewsbury, and falls into Otter Creek near the south part of Clarendon. *Cold River* rises in Parkerstown, crosses the north-west corner of Shrewsbury, and enters Otter Creek near the north part of Clarendon. *Furnace Brook*, called also Little West River, rises from a small pond in the south part of Tinmouth, and runs north, parallel to Otter Creek, through the west part of the town, and falls into Otter Creek near the Centre of Rutland. Near the north line of Clarendon it receives Ira Brook, from Ira. Near Furnace Brook are situated *Clarendon Springs.*

The east part of the town borders on the Green Mountains, but the principal elevations are the range of hills between Otter Creek and Furnace Brook, and between the latter and Ira Brook, on the west line of the town. The alluvial flats on Otter Creek are from half to a mile wide through the town, and are very productive. The uplands are a gravelly loam. Very good marble is found here, and is wrought to some extent. There are two small villages, one in the eastern and the other in the western part.

Clarendon Springs. These springs are situated in a picturesque and beautiful region, seven miles south-west from Rutland, and have, in their immediate vicinity, good accommodations for 500 visitors. The waters are found to be highly efficacious in affections of the liver, dyspepsia, urinary, and all cutaneous complaints, rheumatism, inveterate sore eyes, and many others, and they promise fair to go on increasing in notoriety and usefulness. These waters differ in their composition from any heretofore known, but resemble most nearly the German Spa water. For their curative properties they are believed to be indebted wholly to the gases they contain.

Clarendon Cave. This cave is situated on the south-easterly side of a mountain in the westerly part of that town. The descent into it is through a passage two and a half feet in diameter and thirty-one feet in length, and which makes an angle of 35° or 40° with the horizon. It then opens into a room twenty feet long, twelve and a half wide, and eighteen or twenty feet high. The floor, sides, and roof of this room are all of solid rock, but very rough and uneven. From the north part of this room is a passage about three feet in diameter and twenty-four feet in length, but very rough and irregular, which leads to another room twenty feet wide, thirty feet long, and eighteen feet high. This room, being situated much lower than the first, is usually filled with water in the spring of the year, and water stands in the lowest part of it at all seasons.

Boundaries. North by Rutland, east by Shrewsbury, south by Tinmouth and Wallingford, and west by Ira.

First Settlers. The settlement was commenced in 1768, by Elkanah Cook, who was joined the same year by Randal Rice, Benjamin Johns, and others. The first settlers were mostly from Rhode Island, and purchased their lands of Colonel Lideus, who claimed them under a title derived from the Indians. This title was, however, never confirmed by either of the colonial governments, and the diversity of claimants occasioned much litigation, which continued till 1785, when the legislature passed what was called the quieting act:- By it the settlers were put in peaceable possession of their land, and the New Hampshire title to the lands not settled was confirmed.

First Ministers. Elder Isaac Beals, of the Baptist order, was the first settled minister. The Congregational Church was gathered here February, 1822, by the Rev. Henry Hunter, who was installed over the same on the 6th of November following, and continued six years.

Productions of the Soil. Wheat, 1,663 bushels; Indian corn, 10,936 bushels; potatoes, 44,601 bushels; hay, 5,415 tons; maple sugar, 24,950 pounds; wool, 4,980 pounds.

Distances. Fifty-five miles south west from Montpelier, and seven south from Rutland.

The great Southern Railroad, between Boston and Burlington, passes through this town.

COLCHESTER.

CHITTENDEN Co. There are two small ponds in this town. The largest contains about sixty acres. On the outlet to this pond are still seen the remains of beavers' works. The principal streams of this town are, the River Lamoille, which runs from Milton through the north-west corner into Lake Champlain; Mallet's Creek, which also comes from Milton, and empties into Mallet's Bay; Indian Creek, which runs into Mallet's Creek; and Winooski River, on the south. The soil in the north and north-western parts is a variety of gravel and loam, and is well adapted to grazing, though Indian corn, the English grains, and the common culinary roots, are successfully cultivated. The timber in these parts is principally white pine, beech, maple, birch, basswood, ash, elm, oak, walnut, butternut, and some chestnut. In the middle part of the town is a large tract of pine plain, mostly covered with pitch pine and small oaks, and seems more particularly adapted to the raising of rye and corn. On the bank of the Winooski River are large tracts of intervale. Besides the ordinary methods of enriching the soil, plaster of Paris has been used in this town with great success. The rocks in the northern and eastern parts are mostly composed of lime and slate, with occasional boulders of granite; red sand stone is found in abundance near Mallet's Bay. Iron ore has been found in small quantities in the western part of the town, and sulphate of iron is found in the north-eastern part.

Boundaries. North by Milton, east by Essex, south by Winooski River, which separates it from Burlington and Williston, and west by Lake Champlain.

5

First Settlers. The settlement of this town was commenced in 1774, at the Lower Falls on Winooski or Onion River, by Ira Allen and Remember Baker. Baker's family, consisting of a wife and three children, was the first in town. In 1775, Joshua Staunton began improvements on the intervale above the Narrows in that river, and there was a small clearing made at Mallet's Bay before the revolution. From the spring of 1776, the town was abandoned by the settlers till after the close of the war, in 1783, when Messrs. McLain, Low, and Boardman, settled on Colchester Point, and Gen. Allen returned and renewed the settlement at the Falls. Allen erected mills, a forge and a shop for fabricating anchors, and the place soon assumed the appearance of a considerable village. The town was organized about the year 1791, and Ira Allen was first town clerk.

First Ministers. A Congregational Church was gathered here in 1805, but during a great portion of the time were destitute of regular preaching. A Baptist Church was organized in 1816.

Productions of the Soil. Wheat, 1,903 bushels; Indian corn, 10,343 bushels; potatoes, 36,324 bushels; hay, 3,401 tons; maple sugar, 1,900 pounds; wool, 11,375 pounds.

Distances. Thirty-six miles north-west from Montpelier, and six north from Burlington.

Winooski Village lies in Burlington and Colchester.

CONCORD.

Essex Co. *Hall's Pond*, lying near the centre of the town, is about a mile long, and on an average 100 rods wide. *Miles' Pond* is about the same size, and lies near the north-east corner of the town. This town is watered by Moose River, which passes through the north-west part, by Connecticut River on the south, and by several small streams. The surface of the town is uneven, and in the north-eastern parts very stony. It is an excellent grazing township, and has some good tillage land.

A manufacturing company in this town was incorporated in 1847.

Boundaries. North-westerly by Kirby and Bradley Vale, north-easterly by Lunenburg, south-easterly by Connecticut River, and south-westerly by Waterford.

First Settlers. The first settlement of Concord was commenced in 1788, by Joseph Ball. Among the settlers who came into town previous to the year 1794, may be mentioned Amos Underwood, Solomon Babcock, Daniel Gregory, Benjamin Streeter, Jonathan and Jesse Woodbury, and Levi Ball. In 1795, when John Fry came into town, there were seventeen families here. The first settlers were principally from Westboro' and Royalston, Mass.

First Ministers. A Congregational Church was organized here in 1807, and the Rev. Samuel Godard was ordained over it in 1809; dismissed in 1821. The Rev. Samuel K. Hall was ordained in 1823.

Productions of the Soil. Wheat, 3,579 bushels; Indian corn, 1,906 bushels; potatoes, 48,885 bushels; hay, 3,699 tons; maple sugar, 19,090 pounds; wool, 6,218 pounds.

Distances. Twenty-four miles south-west from Guildhall, and forty-four north east by east from Montpelier.

CORINTH.

Orange Co. The surface of this township is generally very uneven and broken, and the elevations abrupt, yet the land is, in almost every part, susceptible of cultivation. The soil consists of a dark loam, mixed with a small portion of sand, is easily cultivated, and is very productive. The land was originally timbered with hard wood except on the streams, where there was a mixture of hemlock, spruce and fir. Small but handsome specimens of feldspar, garnet, serpentine, hornblend, mica and rock crystal have been found. The rocks are principally granite and mica slate. This township is well watered by Wait's River, which runs through the north-east part, and by several of its branches.

On North Branch, from Topsham, in the north-east corner of the town, is *East village*. Another branch rises in Washington, passes through the south part of this town, and unites with Wait's River in the western part of Bradford. There are some other streams on which mills and other machinery are erected.

Boundaries. Northerly by Topsham, easterly by Bradford, southerly by Vershire, and westerly by Washington.

First Settlers. In the spring of 1777, previous to the settlement of the town, Ezekiel Colby, John Nutting and John Armand, spent several weeks here in manufacturing maple sugar. They started together from Newbury, with each a five pail kettle on his head, and with this load they travelled, by a pocket compass, twelve miles through the wilderness to the place of destination near the centre of the township. This year, Mr. Colby moved his family into Corinth, which was the first family in town. The next year, 1778, Mr. Nutting moved his family here, and Mrs. Colby was delivered of a son, Henry, the first child born in town. In 1779, Messrs. Edmund Brown, Samuel Norris, Jacob Fowler and Bracket Towle, moved their families here, and the same year, Mr. John Aiken, of Wentworth, N. H., erected the first grist mill, which went into operation the year following. Previous to this, the settlers had to go to Newbury, twelve miles, for their grinding. In 1780, several other families came in, and the town was organized.

First Ministers. A Freewill Baptist Church was organized in the north part of the town in 1805, and one in the south part in 1807. A Congregational Church was organized in 1820, and in 1821 they settled the Rev. Calvin Y. Chase, who died here in 1831.

Productions of the Soil. Wheat, 6,745 bushels; Indian corn, 10,506 bushels; potatoes, 71,845 bushels; hay, 6,240 tons; maple sugar, 33,585 pounds; wool, 20,343 pounds.

Distances. Twenty miles south-east from Montpelier, and ten north-east from Chelsea. The Connecticut River Railroad passes near this town.

CORNWALL.

ADDISON Co. This is a very handsome township of land, and the surface is generally level. Lemonfair River crosses the north-west corner, and Otter Creek washes a part of the eastern boundary. This township, by charter, comprehended that part of Middlebury, which lies west of Otter Creek, including the mill privileges on the west side of the creek at Middlebury Falls.

In the south part of the town is a quarry of excellent dark blue limestone, from which the material for the front of the new college in Middlebury was obtained, and near the centre of the town is a bed of hydraulic cement, or water lime. Calcareous spar, in very beautiful, transparent, rhomboidal crystals, is found in the western part of this township. Along Otter Creek, in the south-east part, is a large swamp covering several thousand acres.

Boundaries. North by Weybridge, east by Middlebury and Salisbury, south by Whiting, and west by Bridport and Shoreham.

First Settlers. The settlement was commenced in 1774, by Asa Blodget, Eldad Andrus, Aaron Scott, Nathan Foot, William Douglass, James Bentley, Jr., Ebenezer Stebbins, Thomas Bentley, Samuel Blodget, and Joseph Troup. When Ticonderoga was abandoned to the British in 1777, the settlers all fled to the south, and did not return till after the war. In the winter of 1784, about thirty families came into the township from Connecticut.

First Ministers. The Congregational Church, in this town, was organized July 15, 1785, and September 26, 1787, they settled the Rev. Thomas Tolman, who was dismissed November 11, 1790. The Rev. Benjamin Wooster was ordained over this church February 23, 1797, and dismissed January 7, 1802.

Productions of the Soil. Wheat, 2,436 bushels; Indian corn, 7,288 bushels; potatoes, 24,307 bushels; hay, 8,751 tons; maple sugar, 11,000 pounds; wool, 60,897 pounds.

Distances. Seventy-five miles south-west from Montpelier, and thirty-six south from Burlington. The Southern Railroad passes near this town.

COVENTRY.

ORLEANS Co. Barton and Black Rivers run northerly through this town into Memphremagog Lake. These streams are from four to eight rods wide, and very deep near their mouths. There are good mill privileges in this town on Black River, and likewise on some of the smaller streams. The other waters are *South Bay* of Lake Memphremagog, and two small ponds. The soil is generally good. Near the lake it is, in some places, clayey, and on Black River it is somewhat sandy, but the township, generally, consists of a deep, rich loam. Its timber is mostly maple and beech, with some elm, basswood, birch, hemlock, spruce, fir, cedar, &c. The western part of the town is somewhat broken, but not mountainous.

The village of Coventry was commenced in the fall of 1821, by Calvin and Daniel W. Harmon, when all that part of the town was a dense forest. It is situated at the falls in Black River in the south-west part of the town, and is in a flourishing state. This town received the name of Orleans in 1841, but it resumed its former name a few years after.

Boundaries. North and west by Newport, east by Brownington, and south by Irasburgh.

First Settlers. The first settlement of the town was begun about the year 1800, and it appears from the census of this year that there were, at this time, seven persons in town. The first settlers were S. and T. Cobb, Samuel Wells, John Farnsworth, Jotham Pierce, Joseph Marsh, John Ide, and others.

First Ministers. The Rev. John Ide was ordained over the Baptist Church in 1814, and the Rev. Lyman Case was settled over the Congregational Church in 1823.

Productions of the Soil. Wheat, 2,364 bushels; Indian corn, 1,892 bushels; potatoes, 39,901 bushels; hay, 2,832 tons; maple sugar, 38,445 pounds; wool, 7,706 pounds.

Distances. Four miles north from Irasburgh, and forty-six north-east from Montpelier. The railroad from Boston to Montreal passes near this town.

CRAFTSBURY.

ORLEANS Co. This township is well watered by Black River which is formed here, and by its several branches, which afford numerous mill privileges. Black River was known to the natives, who occasionally resided in this part of Vermont, by the name of *Elligo-sigo.* Its current is in general slow, the whole descent from Elligo Pond to Memphremagog Lake, including the falls at Irasburgh and Coventry, being by actual survey only 190 feet. Wild Branch, a tributary of Lamoille, rises in Eden and passes through the western part of this township.

There are five natural ponds, viz. Elligo, which lies partly in Greensborough, Great Hosmer, lying partly in Albany, Little Hosmer, and two smaller ponds.

The geology of this town is in many respects interesting, and, in some, peculiar. Few areas of the same space, in a region of primary rocks, furnish so many varieties *in situ.*

Near the centre of the township, on an elevated plain, affording an extensive prospect, is situated the centre village. This village is principally situated round an open square, forty rods north and south, by twenty-four rods east and west. Craftsbury Academy is located here; was incorporated in October, 1829, and has the avails of one half of the grammar school lands in Orleans County, being about two thousand six hundred acres, about half of which is leased. The building is of brick, two stories high, and is pleasantly situated on the west side of the common. It is the object of the trustees and instructors to render it a place of thorough education to those who resort to it.

Boundaries. North by Albany, east by Greensboro', south by Walcott, and west by Eden.

First Settlers. The first settlement in the town was commenced in the summer of 1788, by Col. Ebenezer Crafts, who during that summer opened a road from Cabot, eighteen miles, cleared ten or twelve acres of land, built a house and saw mill, and made considerable preparation for a grist mill. In the spring of 1789, Nathan Cutler and Robert Trumbell moved their families into this township. In the ensuing fall Mr. Trumbell, by reason of the sickness of his family, spent the ensuing winter in Barnet, but Mr. Cutler's family remained through the winter. Their nearest neighbors were Ashbel Shepard's family, in Greensborough, distant six miles; there were at that time no other settlements within the present bounds of Orleans County.

First Minister. In 1797, a Congregational Church was organized, and the Rev. Samuel Collins was installed, and continued to preach in this town until 1804, when he died.

Productions of the Soil. Wheat, 1,730 bushels; Indian corn, 1,928 bushels; potatoes, 47,906 bushels; hay, 3,171 tons; maple sugar, 35,412 pounds; wool, 7,880 pounds.

Distances. Twelve miles south from Irasburgh, and thirty-one north-east from Montpelier.

DANBY.

RUTLAND Co. Otter Creek runs nearly on the line between this township and Mount Tabor, but there are no streams of much consequence within the township. The most considerable are, Mill River which rises in the north-western part, and falls into Otter Creek in Mount Tabor, and Flower Branch which rises in the north-west part, and falls into Pawlet River in Pawlet. These and a branch of Otter Creek, in the north-eastern part, are all sufficient for mills. The surface of the township is uneven, and some parts of it mountainous. South Mountain and Spruce mountain are the principal elevations. The soil is well adapted to the production of grass, and there are here some of the largest dairies in the State. No less than 300,000 pounds of cheese, and butter in proportion, have been carried from this town to market in one year.

There are several caverns in this township, which are considerable curiosities, but they have never been thoroughly explored. One of them, in the south-eastern part, descends like a well into the solid rock. It is said that a person was let down by a rope 150 feet perpendicularly into this cavern without discovering any bottom.

Specimens of galena, or sulphuret of lead, have been found here. In the western part of the township is a spring, which is nearly sufficient to carry a mill, where it issues from the foot of the mountain. There are several marble quarries in the south-east part, and in the east village are mills for sawing marble. A part of this town was annexed to Mount Tabor in 1848.

Boundaries. North by Tinmouth, east by Mount Tabor, south by Dorset, and west by Pawlet.

First Settlers. The settlement of this township was commenced in 1765, by Joseph Soper, Joseph Earl, Crispin Bull, Luther Calvin, and Micah Vail.

First Ministers. Among other denominations of Christians, there are in this town two societies of Friends. These societies are somewhat opposed to each other in sentiment.

Productions of the Soil. Wheat, 2,217 bushels; Indian corn, 4,267 bushels; potatoes, 47,563 bushels; hay, 5,378 tons; maple sugar, 35,715 pounds; wool, 25,433 pounds.

Distances. Seventeen miles south from Rutland, and sixty-eight south south-west from Montpelier. The Southern Railroad passes near this town.

DANVILLE.

CALEDONIA Co. The eastern part of this township is elevated about 200 and the western about 800 feet above Connecticut River. The soil is free from stone, is easily cultivated, and is perhaps equal, in richness and adaptation to agriculture, to any in the State. It is watered by numerous streams of pure water, which arise in the higher lands of Wheelock, Walden, and Cabot. Joe's Pond lies mostly in the western part of the township and covers about

5*

1000 acres. It discharges its waters into the Passumpsic by Merritt's River or Joe's Brook. At its outlet a large never failing sheet of water falls over a limestone ledge, seventy-five feet in twelve rods. In the north part of the town are Sleeper's River and the Branch. Large quantities of butter, pork and wool, are here produced for market. This is the shire town.

Danville village is very pleasantly situated nearly in the centre of the township, on elevated land, and in the midst of a beautiful farming country. The public buildings are, a Congregational, a Methodist, and a Baptist Meeting-house, a Court House and Jail, and an Academy, all in a neat and modest style. The village encloses an open square of several acres. The academy was incorporated in 1840, and named Philips Academy, in honor of Paul D. Philips, who endowed it with $4,000. The building was erected by the inhabitants and cost $4,000.

Boundaries. North by Wheelock, north-east by St. Johnsbury, south-east by Barnet, south by Peacham, west by Walden, Goshen, and a part of Cabot.

First Settlers. In 1785, or '6, the settlement was commenced by about fifty emigrants from New Hampshire and Massachusetts, who entered on the lands as "squatters." In October, 1786, the legislature granted the township, as above stated, reserving to the settlers the lands on which they had located, not exceeding 320 acres each. In the following winter forty families more joined the settlement, and for two or three years the settlement was so rapid that, in 1789, the number of families was estimated to be 200. The consequence of such an influx, was an extreme scarcity, and much suffering for the want of provisions.

First Minister. A Congregational Church was organized in 1792, and the Rev. John Fitch was its pastor from 1793 to 1816.

Productions of the Soil. Wheat, 6,355 bushels; Indian corn, 5,883 bushels; potatoes, 160,662 bushels; hay, 8,311 tons; maple sugar, 62,467 pounds; wool, 26,834 pounds.

Distances. Thirty miles north-east from Montpelier. The Boston and Montreal Railroad passes in this vicinity.

DERBY.

ORLEANS Co. The surface of this township is very level, more so than any other in the county. There are some plains of several hundred acres extent; and, where the land rises, the elevations are gradual and moderate and hardly deserve the name of hills. The land is well timbered, principally with rock maple and other hard wood.

Cedar swamps of from one to ten acres are found in various parts. The soil is fertile and abundantly productive. The River Clyde passes through the south part of the township in a north-westerly direction, affording numerous mill sites. Salem Pond, through which Clyde River passes, lies partly in this town, and is four miles long and three broad. Hinman's Pond, near the centre of the town, is one and a half miles long and three quarters broad, and empties into Salem Pond.

Boundaries. North by Stanstead in Canada, east by Holland, south by Salem, and west by Memphremagog Lake, which separates it from Newport.

First Settlers. The first settlement was made here in 1795, by Alexander Mogoon, Henry Burrel, and the Hon. Timothy Hinman. Emigrants from Connecticut and other places soon made it a flourishing town.

First Ministers. In 1808, Elder Samuel Smith was settled over the Baptist Church and Society in this town, and died in 1810. The Rev. Luther Leland was settled over the Congregational Church in 1810, and died in November, 1822.

Productions of the Soil. Wheat, 5,176 bushels; Indian corn, 3,080 bushels, potatoes, 9,306 bushels; hay, 3,896 tons; maple sugar, 47,633 pounds; wool, 10,446 pounds.

Distances. Twelve miles north-east from Irasburgh, and fifty-two north-east from Montpelier. This is the celebrated *Derby Line* over which the brazen steed will soon pass, to smoke a pipe with the Canadians.

For the distances from the mouth of Connecticut River to this place, see *Hayward's Book of Reference.*

DORSET.

BENNINGTON Co. There are no considerable streams in this township. Otter Creek heads in Mount Tabor, runs south-westerly two or three miles, into Peru, then west three-fourths of a mile into this township, when it takes a northerly direction through a considerable natural pond, and leaves the township near the north-east corner. The Battenkill heads in this township, on the flat about twenty-five rods south of the bend in Otter Creek, and runs off to the south. Another branch of this stream rises in the south-western part, and unites with it in Manchester. Pawlet River, rises in the north-western part, and passes off into Rupert. These streams afford a number of mill privileges.

This township is considerably mountainous. Dorset Mountain lies in the north part, and extends into Danby, where it is called South Mountain. Equinox Mountain lies partly in the south-west corner. In this township are several remarkable caverns.

One in the south part, is entered by an aperture nearly ten feet square, "which opens into a spacious room nine rods in length and four wide. At the further end of this apartment are two openings, which are about thirty feet apart. The one on the right is three feet from the floor, and is about twenty inches by six feet in length. It leads to an apartment twenty feet long, twelve wide, and twelve high. From this room there is an opening sufficient to admit a man to pass through sideways about twenty feet, when it opens into a large hall eighty feet long and thirty wide. The other aperture from the first room is about as large as a common door, and leads to an apartment twelve feet square, out of which is a passage to another considerable room, in which is a spring of water. This cavern is said to have been ex-

plored forty or fifty rods without arriving at the end." Considerable quantities of marble are wrought here.

Boundaries. North by Danby, east by Peru, south by Manchester, and west by Rupert.

First Settlers. The first settlement was made in 1768, by Felex Powell, from Massachusetts, Isaac Lacy, from Connecticut, and Benjamin Baldwin, Abraham Underhill, John Manley, and George Gage, from New York.

First Ministers. The Rev. Elijah Sill was settled over the Congregational Church in 1781, and in 1796 the Rev. William Jackson was settled over this church. The first minister of the Baptist Society was Elder Cyrus M. Fuller, settled in 1818.

Productions of the Soil. Wheat, 1,321 bushels; Indian corn, 5,595 bushels; potatoes, 31,018 bushels; hay, 4,080 tons; maple sugar, 17,560 pounds; wool, 18,030 pounds.

Distances. Twenty-six miles north from Bennington, and ninety-one south south-west from Montpelier.

DOVER.

WINDHAM Co. This town was a part of Wardsborough until 1810. The land in Dover is high and uneven;—more fit for pasturage than tillage. It is the source of several branches of West, and a branch of Deerfield River. Serpentine and chlorite slate are found here.

Although this township is quite mountainous, yet the soil is warm, sweet, and productive.

Boundaries. North by Wardsborough, east by Newfane, south by Wilmington and a part of Marlboro', and west by Somerset.

First Settlers.—See *Wardsborough.*

Productions of the Soil. Wheat, 1,194 bushels; Indian corn, 17,715 bushels; potatoes, 35,986 bushels; hay, 3,140 tons; maple sugar, 22,678 pounds; wool, 4,104 pounds.

Distances. Twelve miles north-west from Brattleborough, eighteen north-east from Bennington, and one hundred and twenty south by west from Montpelier.

DUMMERSTON.

WINDHAM Co. This township is watered by West River, which enters it from Newfane, and passes through it in a south-easterly direction into Brattleborough, and by several small streams, some of which fall into this river and others into the Connecticut, affording a considerable number of good sites for mills. The surface of Dummerston is broken. The rocks, which constitute Black Mountain, near the centre of the town are an immense body of granite. A range of argillaceous slate passes through it from south to north, and is considerably quarried for roof slate and grave stones. Primitive limestone occurs in beds. Specimens of tremolite, limpid quartz, and galena, or the sulphuret of lead, are also found here. This is one of the oldest towns in the State.

Boundaries. North by Putney and Brookline, east by Connecticut River, which separates it from Westmoreland, N. H., south by Brattleborough, and west by a part of Marlborough and Newfane.

First Ministers. A Congregational Church was early formed here, over which the Rev. Thomas Farrer was settled in 1779 ; and in 1784 the Rev. Aaron Crosby was settled, and continued twenty years.

Productions of the Soil. Wheat, 907 bushels ; Indian corn, 8,270 bushels ; potatoes, 27,950 bushels ; hay, 3,090 tons ; maple sugar, 7,220 pounds ; wool, 5,713 pounds.

Distances. Ninety miles south from Montpelier, and eight south-east from Newfane. The Connecticut River Railroad passes through this town.

DUXBURY.

WASHINGTON Co. The south and western parts of this township are mountainous, and incapable of settlement. Nearly all the inhabitants are confined to the margin of Winooski River, and the north-eastern parts of the township. This township is watered by Winooski River, which forms the northern boundary, by Duxbury branch, on which is a considerable settlement, and several small branches of Mad River. The natural bridge over Winooski River is between this town and Waterbury, and near it are some curious caverns.

Boundaries. North by Waterbury and a part of Bolton, from which it is separated by Winooski River, east by Moretown, south by Fayston, and west by Huntington and a part of Bolton.

First Settlers. The settlement of this township was commenced about the year 1786.

Productions of the Soil. Wheat, 1,293 bushels ; Indian corn, 2,714 bushels ; potatoes, 27,910 bushels ; hay, 2,289 tons ; maple sugar, 26,374 pounds ; wool, 4,837 pounds.

Distances. Eleven miles west from Montpelier. The Northern Railroad passes through Waterbury, on the opposite side of the Winooski.

EAST HAVEN.

ESSEX Co. The land in this township is high, but much of it very suitable for grazing. Passumpsic River crosses the west corner, and the head of Moose River waters the eastern part, each being about two rods wide, and affording good mill sites.

Boundaries. North-westerly by Newark, north-easterly by Brighton and Ferdinand, south-east by Granby, and south-west by Victory and Burke.

First Settlers. There were five or six families in this town as early as 1814 ; but the settlement has advanced very slowly, and it is still unorganized.

Productions of the Soil. Wheat, 99 bushels ; Indian corn, 69 bushels ; potatoes, 3,280 bushels ; hay, 136 tons ; maple sugar, 3,330 pounds ; wool, 370 pounds.

Distances. Twenty-four miles northwest from Guildhall, and sixty-nine north-east from Montpelier.

EAST MONTPELIER.

WASHINGTON Co. This town was incorporated November 9th, 1848, and comprises the northern and eastern part of the fertile and pleasant town of MONTPELIER.

The Act is in common form for the division of towns.

We hope, ere long, to see an act passed by the legislature of Vermont, prohibiting any reference to the points of compass, in the choice of names for their new towns; particularly when some beautiful Indian name meets the ear on the banks of almost every stream.

EDEN.

LAMOILLE CO. The streams in this township are numerous. *Wild Branch* and *Green River* rise in the eastern part. The former runs through the corner of Craftsbury, and the latter through the corner of Hydepark, and both fall into the River Lamoille in Wolcott. They are both considerable mill streams. The *Branch*, which is the outlet of North Pond, runs across the north-west corner of Hydepark, and falls into the Lamoille in Johnson. North Pond is two miles long, and of very unequal width. A tongue of land extends into it from the south, three quarters of a mile, which is, in some places, no more than two rods wide, and on which grow large quantities of blue and black whortleberries. These berries are found nowhere else in this part of the county. The township is considerably mountainous. Mount Norris and Hadley Mountain lie on the north line of the township, and partly in Lowell. Belvidere Mountain lies partly in the north-west corner of the township, and its summit is probably the highest land in the county, excepting, perhaps, Jay Peak. In the western part of Eden is some good tillage land. The eastern part, being the dividing ridge between the waters of Lakes Champlain and Memphremagog, is moist and cold, but good for grazing. No town in the vicinity furnishes, in proportion to its wealth and number of inhabitants, so many and so good beef cattle as this, for market. Rocks, principally mica and chlorite slate.

Boundaries. Northerly by Lowell, easterly by Craftsbury, southerly by Hydepark and Johnson, and westerly by Belvidere.

First Settlers. The settlement was commenced in 1800, by Thomas H. Parker, Isaac Brown, and Moses Wentworth.

First Minister. The Rev. Joseph Farrar was settled over the Congregational Church in 1811, and dismissed in 1815.

Productions of the Soil. Wheat, 1,318 bushels; Indian corn, 828 bushels; potatoes, 38,250 bushels; hay, 2,050 tons; maple sugar, 18,290 pounds; wool, 3,958 pounds.

Distances. Ten miles north-east from Hydepark, and thirty miles north from Montpelier.

ELMORE.

LAMOILLE CO. Fordway, or Elmore Mountain, lies in the north-west part of the township, and is a considerable elevation. The remaining part of the surface is accessible and not very uneven. It is mostly timbered with hard wood, and the soil is of a middling quality. A part of the waters of this township pass off to the north into the River Lamoille, and a part to the south into Winooski River. Mead's Pond lies in the north-western part, and covers about 300 acres. There are three other small ponds within the township. Iron ore is found here in abundance.

Boundaries. North by Wolcott, east by Woodbury, south by Worcester, and west by Morristown.

First Settlers. The settlement of this township was commenced in July, 1790, by Martin and Jesse Elmore, James and Seth Olmstead, and Aaron Keeler, from Sharon and Norwalk, Connecticut. The Congregationalists and Methodists are the most numerous denominations of Christians.

Productions of the Soil. Wheat, 831 bushels; Indian corn, 266 bushels; potatoes, 2,170 bushels; hay, 1,310 tons; maple sugar, 9,790 pounds; wool, 3,958 pounds.

Distances. Eight miles south from Hydepark, and thirty-seven miles north from Montpelier.

ENOSBURGH.

FRANKLIN Co The surface of this township is pleasantly diversified with hills and valleys ; but the soil is better adapted to the production of grass than grain. It is well watered by Missisco River, which runs through the north part, by Trout River, which runs across the north-east corner, and by two considerable streams, which run through the south part. These streams afford numerous and excellent mill privileges.

Boundaries. North by Berkshire, east by Montgomery and a part of Richford, south by Bakersfield, and west by Sheldon.

First Settlers. The settlement of this township was commenced in the spring of 1797, by Amos Fassett, Stephen House, Martin D. Follett, and others, mostly emigrants from other townships in this State.

First Ministers. A Congregational Church was formed here in 1811, and in 1814 the Rev. James Parker took charge of it, and it continued under his pastoral care till 1821.

Productions of the Soil. Wheat, 3,613 bushels ; Indian corn, 2,928 bushels ; potatoes, 78,015 bushels ; hay, 8,830 tons ; maple sugar, 41,730 pounds ; wool, 11,262 pounds.

Distances. Fifty-five miles north by west from Montpelier, twenty north-east from St. Albans, and about thirty-seven north-east from Burlington.

ESSEX COUNTY.

GUILDHALL is the chief town. This county is bounded north by Canada, east and south by Connecticut River, which separates it from Coos County, New Hampshire, south-west by Caledonia County, and west by Orleans County. It is about forty-five miles long from north to south, and twenty-three broad from east to west.

This county is the least populous in the State, with the exception of Grand Isle County. There are some towns which are entirely destitute of inhabitants. The settlements are mostly confined to the towns lying along Connecticut River. The county is in general very uneven and the soil rocky and unproductive. It comprehends that part of the county called Upper Coos, which lies on the west side of Connecticut River. Nulhegan River is the principal stream, which is wholly within the county. This and several smaller tributaries, of the Connecticut, water all the eastern parts. Passumpsic and Moose River, rise in the south-western part, and Clyde River and several streams, which run off to the north into Canada, water the north-western parts. Essex County presents a great variety of magnificent scenery.—See *Tables.*

COURTS IN ESSEX COUNTY.

The *Supreme Court* sits at Guildhall on the 19th Tuesday after the 4th Tuesday in December, and the *County Court* on the last Tuesday in May and the third in December.

ESSEX.

CHITTENDEN Co. There are no mountains, and but few hills in this township. The south and western parts are timbered principally with pine, the soil is dry and sandy, but produces good rye and corn. The remaining part of the township is timbered with hard wood, and is more natural to grass. Winooski River washes the southern boundary. In this river are two falls. The lower, called Hubbell's Falls, afford several valuable mill privileges. Brown's River rises in Underhill and Jericho, enters this township from the latter, and, after running across the north-east corner, and through Westford, falls into the River Lamoille in Fairfax. Indian River, called here Steven's Brook, Alder Brook, and Crooked Brook, are considerable streams. On Winooski River are beautiful tracks of intervale.

Boundaries. North by Westford, east by Jericho, south by Williston and Burlington, from which it is separated by Winooski River, and west by Colchester.

First Settlers. The first permanent settlement was made in this township, in 1783, by Messrs. Smiths, Winchels, and Willard. The first settlers were principally from Salisbury, Ct. In 1789, there was a very great scarcity of provisions in this part of the country, and the settlers suffered extremely on that account.

First Ministers. A Congregational Church was organized here in 1790, and the Rev. Asaph Morgan was ordained over it in 1804. A Baptist Church was formed about the year 1800.

Productions of the Soil. Wheat, 2,246 bushels; Indian corn, 7,934 bushels; potatoes, 43,328 bushels; hay, 4,532 tons; maple sugar, 10,955 pounds; wool, 10,223 pounds.

Distances. Seven miles north-east from Burlington. The great Northern Railroad passes through the town.

FAIRFAX.

FRANKLIN Co. The surface of this township is somewhat uneven, and the soil light and easily cultivated, producing good corn and rye. Its principal streams are the River Lamoille, which runs through the south part, and Brown's River and Parmelee's and Stone's Brook, its tributaries, all of which afford good mill privileges. The great falls, on the Lamoille, eighty-eight feet in thirty rods, are situated in the south-east part of the town, and afford some of the best water privileges in the State. In this town are two pleasant villages.

Boundaries. North by Fairfield, east by Fletcher, south by Westford, and west by Georgia.

First Settlers. Broadstreet Spafford and his two sons, Nathan and Asa, came into this township from Piermont, N. H., in 1783, and began improvements. They soon after removed their families here. A Mr. Eastman started from New Hampshire with them, with his family, but died on the road, and was buried in a trough on the flats in Johnson. His family came to Fletcher.

First Ministers. The first settled minister was the Rev. Amos Tuttle. He was settled over the Baptist Church in 1806; dismissed in 1811. A Congregational Church was organized here in 1814, when the Rev. Eben H. Dorman was settled.

Productions of the Soil. Wheat, 3,188 bushels; Indian corn, 9,191 bushels; potatoes, 42,730 bushels; hay, 4,105 tons; maple sugar, 38,330 pounds; wool, 20,315 pounds.

Distances. Thirty-seven miles north-west from Montpelier, and twelve south-east from St. Albans.

FAIRFIELD.

FRANKLIN Co. Black Creek is a considerable stream, which issues from Metcalf Pond in Fletcher, and runs through this township, affording an excellent stand for mills. Fairfield River is a small stream, which, also, takes its rise in Fletcher, and passes through the town near its centre, affording several good mill privileges. These streams unite and fall into Missisco River in Sheldon. Smithfield Pond, lying in the westerly part of the town, is about three miles long and one and a half broad. At the outlet is an excellent stand for mills, and another on the same stream about two miles below. The township was originally covered principally with hard wood. The surface is uneven, but very little of it so broken as to be unfit for cultivation. The soil is generally good.

Boundaries. North by Sheldon, east by Bakersfield, south by Fletcher and Fairfax, and west by St. Albans and Swanton.

First Settlers. The first settler of this town was Mr. Joseph Wheeler. He moved into it with his family in March, 1788. In 1789, Hubbard Barlow and Andrew Bradley, with several others, moved into the town. Smithfield Beadeu, was the first child born here, in the part called Smithfield. The proprietors made him a present of 100 acres of land.

First Minister. The Rev. Benjamin Wooster was settled over the Congregational Church in 1805; died in 1840, aged seventy-seven.

Productions of the Soil. Wheat, 4,270 bushels; Indian corn, 5,685 bushels; potatoes, 76,920 bushels; hay, 7,765 tons; maple sugar, 71,765 pounds; wool, 24,663 pounds.

Distances. Forty-five miles northwest from Montpelier, and twenty-seven north north-east from Burlington.

FAIR HAVEN.

RUTLAND Co. The surface of the township consists of swells and vales, but there is nothing which deserves the name of a mountain. The soil is various, consisting of gravel, sand. and marl. Along the rivers, the soil is alluvial and very productive. The timber is pine, hemlock, beech, maple, walnut, butternut, button wood, &c. The principal streams are Poultney and Castleton Rivers. The former rises among the mountains in the south-east, and divides this township from New York. The latter originates principally from a large spring in the west part of Rutland. About one mile above Fair Haven village it receives the waters of Lake Bombazine, and

one mile west of the village it joins Poultney River, and, after running three miles further, falls into the lake. Between the junction of these streams and the lake are two considerable falls.

Boundaries. North by Benson, east by Castleton, and a part of Poultney, south by Poultney River, which separates it from Hampton, N. Y., and west by West Haven.

First Settlers. The settlement was commenced in 1779, by John and William Meacham, Oliver Cleveland, Joseph Ballard, and Joseph Haskins, with their families. In 1783, Col. Mathew Lyon, Silas Safford and others moved into town, and the former commenced erecting mills. Col. Lyon had in operation at Fair Haven before 1796, one furnace, two forges, one slitting mill, one printing office, one paper mill, one saw mill, and one grist mill, and he did printing on paper manufactured by himself from basswood bark. The first settlers were from Connecticut and Massachusetts. The town was organized in 1783.

Col. Lyon, who has figured in the political world, was a native of Ireland. He emigrated to this country when sixteen years old, and was sold in Connecticut for his passage.

First Minister. The Rev. Rufus Cushman was ordained over the Congregational Church in 1807; died in 1829.

Productions of the Soil. Wheat, 1,055 bushels; Indian corn, 3,050 bushels; potatoes, 18,100 bushels; hay, 1,690 tons; maple sugar, 1,845 pounds; wool, 5,655 pounds.

Manufactures. Manufactures, particularly of iron, commenced here at an early period. The water power at this place is so good, that manufactures will doubtless annually increase.

Distances. Sixteen miles west from Rutland, and nine north-east from Whitehall, N. Y.

FAIRLEE.

ORANGE Co. This is a rough and mountainous township, with very little productive land, on the west side of

Connecticut River, and connected with Orford, N. H., by a bridge across that river.

Fairlee pond is two miles in length and about three fourths of a mile wide. It formerly had no fish. Some years ago a gentleman placed some pickerel in it, and the legislature passed a law protecting the fish from molestation for two years. Since that time the pond has had an abundance of pickerel, of good size and quality.

Boundaries. North by Bradford, east by Connecticut River, which separates it from Orford, N. H., south by Thetford, and west by West Fairlee.

First Settlers. The settlement was commenced in 1766, by a Mr. Baldwin, who had settled the year before in Thetford. In 1768, Mr. Samuel Miller, Samuel Bentley, and William and David Thompson, Noah Dewey, and Joel White, settled here.

First Minister. A Congregational meeting-house was erected here, in 1806.

Productions of the Soil. Wheat, 599 bushels; Indian corn, 3,205 bushels; potatoes, 8,085 bushels; hay, 1,449 tons; maple sugar, 620 pounds; wool, 8,242 pounds.

Distances. Seventeen miles east south-east from Chelsea, and thirty-one south-east from Montpelier. The Connecticut River Railroad passes through this town.

FAYSTON.

WASHINGTON Co. Fayston is generally too mountainous to be much cultivated. Along the borders of some of the branches of Mad River, which rises here, is some arable land. The town was settled in 1798, by Lynde Wait, Esq.

Boundaries. North by Duxbury, east by Waitsfield, south by a part of Warren and Lincoln, and west by Huntington.

Productions of the Soil. Wheat, 1,651 bushels; Indian corn, 1,189 bushels; potatoes, 22,593 bushels; hay, 1,905 tons; maple sugar, 24,134 pounds; wool, 3,833 pounds.

Distances. Sixteen miles west south-

west from Montpelier, and twenty-five south-east from Burlington.

FERDINAND.

Essex Co. This town was chartered in 1761, and contains twenty-three square miles. Paul's Stream affords it a good water power; but the land is so mountainous, rocky, cold, and swampy, that people do not choose to cultivate it.

For the distances from this place see its boundaries.

Boundaries. Northerly by Wenlock, easterly by Maidstone, southerly by Granby and East Haven, and westerly by Brighton.

FERRISBURGH.

ADDISON Co. This township is watered principally by Otter, Little Otter, and Lewis Creeks. Otter Creek enters the township from Vergennes, and after running north-westerly about eight miles, across the south-west part, falls into Lake Champlain about three miles south of the mouth of Little Otter Creek. Little Otter and Lewis Creeks run through the township in a westerly direction; the former through the middle, and the latter through the north part. The mouths by which they are discharged into the lake are within eighty rods of each other. Otter Creek is navigable eight miles to Vergennes, and Little Otter Creek three miles, by the largest vessels on the lake. In Little Otter Creek are four, and in Lewis Creek three commodious falls, on which mills and other machinery are erected. Large quantities of pike, bass, &c., are annually taken in the spring of the year, about the mouths of these streams. About three miles north of the south-west corner of the township is one of the best harbors on the lake, called *Basin Harbor.* Five miles north-west from Vergennes, and a short distance south of the mouth of Little Otter Creek, is a ferry across the lake, which is here something more than two miles wide. This place is known by the name of *Grog Harbor*, taking its name from the landing place in Essex, on the New York side.

The surface of the north-eastern part of this township is somewhat hilly. The remaining parts, especially the western, are remarkably level. No township in the State has afforded more or better timber for market than this. The soil is very various; some parts of it being clayey, while others consist of rich mould, which is easily tilled and very productive. In 1823, one acre here produced 120 bushels of corn, which cost ten days labor and two bushels of plaster of Paris, (*gypsum.*) The same kind of soil has produced fifty bushels of wheat, seventy of oats, &c., per acre. It is a good grazing township, and large numbers of fat cattle are yearly driven from it to market.

A part of this town was annexed to Panton, in 1847.

Boundaries. North by Charlotte, east by Monkton and New Haven, south by Waltham, Vergennes, and Panton, and west by Lake Champlain, which separates it from the State of New York.

First Settlers. The first permanent settlement was made in 1784 and 1785, by Mr. Ward, Abel Thompson, Gideon Hawley, Timothy Rogers, Jos. Chilson, Jona. Saxton, and Zuriel and Absalom Tupper, emigrants from Bennington, in this State, and from Connecticut.

Manufactures. Here is a fine water power, and manufactures on its beautiful streams are rapidly increasing.

Productions of the Soil. Wheat, 2,700 bushels; Indian corn, 8,910 bushels; potatoes, 21,680 bushels; hay, 12,000 tons; maple sugar, 1,400 pounds; wool, 65,690 pounds.

Distances. Sixteen miles north-west from Middlebury, and thirty-four west from Montpelier.

The Northern Railroad passes in the vicinity of this town.

FLETCHER.

FRANKLIN Co. The River Lamoille just touches upon the southern extremity of this township. Metcalf Pond is about one mile long from north to south, and one third of a mile wide from east to west. It discharges its waters at the south end, forming one of the head branches of Black Creek. This stream runs a south-easterly course about two miles into Cambridge, and, after crossing the corner of that township, returns again into Fletcher, and passes off to the north. Fairfield River also rises in Fletcher, and is joined in Fairfield by Black Creek. Stone's Brook waters the western part. The surface of this township is considerably broken.

Boundaries. North by Bakersfield and Fairfield, east by Waterville, south-east by Cambridge, and south-west by Fairfax.

First Settlers. This town was chartered to Moses Robinson, John Fay, and others, in 1781. The settlement was commenced in 1784.

Productions of the Soil. Wheat, 1,717 bushels; Indian corn, 2,000 bushels; potatoes, 36,200 bushels; hay, 2,680 tons; maple sugar, 38,650 pounds; wool, 6,558 pounds.

Distances. Twenty-two miles north north-west from Montpelier, and about eighteen south-east from St. Albans.

FRANKLIN COUNTY.

ST. ALBANS is the county town. This county is bounded north by Lower Canada, east by Orleans County, south-east and south by Lamoille County, south by Chittenden County, and west by Lake Champlain. The Missisco River passes through the northern part of the county, and the Lamoille its most southern section. The principal part of the trade of this county goes to Canada, by Lake Champlain, which affords it many facilities of transportation. Although the surface is somewhat broken, and in some parts mountainous, yet the soil is productive of wheat and grass. Many cattle are annually taken from this county to market. In this county marble and iron ore, of excellent qualities, are found.—See *Tables.*

COURTS IN FRANKLIN COUNTY.

The *Supreme Court* sits here on the second Tuesday in January, and the *County Court* on the second Tuesday of April and September.

FRANKLIN.

FRANKLIN CO. The River Rocher, or Rock River, rises in this township, and falls into Missisco Bay in Highgate. It is also watered by several small branches of Missisco and Pike Rivers. A large pond lies near the centre. This pond is three miles long, and about one mile wide.

Boundaries. North by St. Armand, in Canada, east by Berkshire, south by Sheldon, and west by Highgate.

First Settlers. The settlement was commenced in 1789, by Samuel Hubbard, Samuel Peckham, David Sanders, and John Bridgman, mostly emigrants from Massachusetts.

Productions of the Soil. Wheat, 3,256 bushels; Indian corn, 2,940 bushels; potatoes, 57,870 bushels; hay, 3,438 tons; maple sugar, 25,720 pounds; wool, 11,635 pounds.

Distances. Sixty miles north-west from Montpelier, and seventeen north north-east from St. Albans.

GEORGIA.

FRANKLIN CO. The River Lamoille, which runs through the south-east corner of the township, is the principal stream. In the north-east part is a pond, covering thirty or forty acres. It is surrounded by high lands, except a narrow outlet to the north, and is bordered by a grove of alders. The mill privileges are numerous; there being no less than twelve. The soil is sandy in the south part, and the timber principally pine. In the north part it is a gravelly loam and the timber mostly hard wood. The rocks, in the western part, are limestone; in the eastern part, slate. The soil is, in general, rich and productive. There are some tracts timbered with hemlock, and some cedar swamps near the lake.

Over what is called *Stone Bridge Brook,* in the south-western part of the township, is a natural bridge twelve or fourteen feet wide, and the top of it seven or eight feet above the surface of the water. The width of the arch is forty or fifty feet, and its height but a few inches above the surface of the stream.

Boundaries. North by St. Albans, east by Fairfax, south by Milton, and west by Lake Champlain.

First Settlers. The settlement was commenced in 1784 and 1785, by Andrew Guilder, from Agremont, Mass., and William Farrand, from Bennington, Vt., with their families. During the two following years a great number of families, mostly from Bennington and the western parts of Massachusetts, moved into the town, and a considerable number of young men without families. The first settlers of Georgia had their share of those privations and hardships which are incident to the settlers of new townships. They at first had to go to Burlington and

Plattsburgh for their grinding, but the population increased so rapidly, that mills were soon erected.

First Minister. The Rev. Publius Virgil Bogue was settled over the Congregational Church in 1803 ; dismissed in 1813.

Productions of the Soil. Wheat, 3,897 bushels ; Indian corn, 7,875 bushels ; potatoes, 34,616 bushels ; hay, 4,476 tons ; maple sugar, 17,957 pounds ; wool, 26,467 pounds.

Distances. Fifty miles north-west from Montpelier, and eight south from St. Albans. Georgia is on the route of the Burlington and Montreal Railroad.

GLASTENBURY.

BENNINGTON Co. This is a township of forty square miles of mountainous land, more fit for the residence of wild beasts than human beings. Its waters flow both into Deerfield River and Walloomscoik. The town was chartered in 1761.

Boundaries. North by Sunderland, east by Somerset, south by Woodford, and west by Shaftsbury.

Productions of the Soil. Wheat, 18 bushels ; Indian corn, 25 bushels ; potatoes, 880 bushels ; hay, 162 tons ; maple sugar, 575 pounds ; wool, 127 pounds.

Distances. Nine miles north-east from Bennington, and twenty-five north-west from Brattleborough.

GLOVER.

ORLEANS Co. This town is hilly, and the soil is more fit for grazing than tillage. There are in the town branches of Barton's, Passumpsic, Lamoille, and Black Rivers, and several ponds. On these streams are some manufactures.

We copy an account of the *running off* of Long Pond, from Thompson's valuable Gazetteer of Vermont :

" Long Pond was situated partly in this township, and partly in Greensborough. This pond was one and a half miles long and about half a mile wide, and discharged its waters to the south, forming one of the head branches of the River Lamoille. On the 6th of June, 1810, about sixty persons went to this pond, for the purpose of opening an outlet to the north into Barton River, that the mills on that stream might receive an occasional supply of water. A small channel was excavated, and the water commenced running in a northerly direction. It happened that the northern barrier of the pond consisted entirely of quicksand, except an encrusting of clay next the water. The sand was immediately removed by the current, and a large channel formed. The basin formed by the encrusting of the clay was incapable of sustaining the incumbent mass of waters, and it brake. The whole pond immediately took a northerly course, and, in fifteen minutes from this time, its bed was left entirely bare. It was discharged so suddenly, that the country below was instantly inundated. The deluge advanced like a wall of waters, sixty or seventy feet in height and twenty rods in width, levelling the forests and the hills, and filling up the valleys, and sweeping off mills, houses, barns, fences, cattle, horses, and sheep, as it passed, for the distance of more than ten miles, and barely giving the inhabitants sufficient notice of its approach, to escape with their lives into the mountains. A rock, supposed to weigh more than 100 tons, was removed half a mile from its bed. The waters removed so rapidly as to reach Memphremagog Lake, distance twenty-seven miles, in about six hours from the time they left the pond. Nothing now remains of the pond but its bed, a part of which is cultivated and a part overgrown with bushes and wild grass, with a small brook running through it, which is now the head branch of Barton River. The channel through which the waters escaped is 127 feet in depth and several rods in width. A pond, some distance below, was at first entirely filled with sand, which has since settled down, and it is now about one half its former dimensions. Marks of the ravages are still to be seen through nearly the whole course of Barton River."

Boundaries. North by Barton, east by Sheffield, south by Greensborough, and west by Albany.

First Settlers. The settlement of this township was commenced about the year 1797, by Ralph Parker, James Vance, Samuel Cook, and Samuel Conant.

Productions of the Soil. Wheat, 3,129 bushels; Indian corn, 1,947 bushels; potatoes, 54.708 bushels; hay, 3,448 tons; maple sugar, 61,430 pounds; wool, 15,718 tons.

Distances. Ten miles south-east from Irasburgh, and thirty-eight north-east from Montpelier.

GOSHEN.

ADDISON Co. Leicester and Philadelphia Rivers supply this town with mill privileges. The lands along the rivers are very good, but in general they are too mountainous for profitable cultivation. Some minerals are found in this town. A part of Goshen was annexed to Rochester in 1847.

No permanent settlement was commenced here till 1800.

Boundaries. North by Ripton and Hancock, south-east by Pittsfield and Chittenden, south-west by Brandon and Leicester, and north-west by Salisbury.

Productions of the Soil. Wheat, 1,040 bushels; Indian corn, 516 bushels; potatoes, 18,600 bushels; hay, 1,360 tons; maple sugar, 5,230 pounds; wool, 5,116 pounds.

Distances. Thirty-one miles south-west from Montpelier, and eighteen miles south-east from Middlebury. The Southern Railroad passes through a neighboring town.

GRAFTON.

WINDHAM Co. Grafton is finely watered by Sexton's River, which is formed in the town by the union of several streams; and by a branch of Williams' River. On these streams are manufactures of woolen and other goods. Soapstone of an excellent quality is very abundant in this place. It is manufactured by water power for

various uses to a great extent; it is bored for aqueducts and sold at a very low price. This town contains two pleasant and flourishing villages, and a great variety of mineral treasure. Its surface is uneven with a strong and productive soil. A manufacturing company in this town was incorporated in 1848.

Boundaries. North by Chester, east by Rockingham, south by Athens and Acton, and west by Windham.

First Settlers. A Mr. Hinkley and two other families came into this township about the year 1768, and began a settlement on what is called Hinkley Brook. They, however, soon abandoned it, and no permanent settlement was made till 1780. In the spring of this year, Amos Fisher, Samuel Spring, Benjamin Latherbee, and Edward Putnam moved into the township from Winchester, Mass.

First Minister. A Congregational Church was organized June 28, 1785; settled the Rev. William Hall, Nov. 7, 1788, who was dismissed in 1810.

Productions of the Soil. Wheat, 1,386 bushels; Indian corn, 4,859 bushels; potatoes, 31,646 bushels; hay, 3,363 tons; maple sugar, 16,185 pounds; wool, 20,164 pounds.

Distances. Ninety miles south from Montpelier, and eighteen north from Newfane. The Southern Railroad passes through this town.

GRANBY.

ESSEX Co. Granby is nearly allied to *Ferdinand*, both in location and the character of the soil; it lies the next town south of it. This town was settled a few years previous to 1800.

Boundaries. North-east by Ferdinand and Maidstone, south-east by Guildhall, south-west by Victory, and north-west by East Haven.

Productions of the Soil. Buckwheat, 94 bushels; Indian corn, 14 bushels; potatoes, 3,680 bushels; hay, 257 tons; maple sugar, 1,925 pounds; wool, 325 pounds.

Distances. Twelve miles west from Guildhall, and sixty-eight north-east from Montpelier.

6*

GRAND ISLE COUNTY.

NORTH HERO is the county town. This county comprises a group of islands in Lake Champlain, and a point of land jutting into the north part of that lake on the south side of the Canada line, on which Alburgh is situated. This county contains about eighty square miles; most of the land is level and excellent for grazing and tillage. Grand Isle has no considerable streams, but its navigable facilities are very great. It was first settled about the close of the revolutionary war.—See *Tables.*

COURTS IN GRAND ISLE COUNTY.

The *Supreme Court* sits at North Hero on the third Tuesday in January, and the *County Court* on the last Tuesday in February, and the last Tuesday in August, in each year.

———

GRAND ISLE.

GRAND ISLE CO. The soil of the town is very fertile; it produces fine crops of grain, and an abundance of fruit and cider. Marble, limestone, rock crystals, &c., are found here, and Grand Isle contains the only water mill in the county. This is a fine place for fishing and fowling.

Boundaries. It is bounded on all sides by Lake Champlain, except the south, where it is bounded by South Hero.

First Settlers. The settlement of the township was commenced about the year 1783, by Alexander Gordon, William Hazen, and Lamberton Allen, emigrants from New Hampshire, and the southern parts of this State. For some years after the settlement commenced, many circumstances tended to prevent its progress.

First Minister. The Rev. Asa Lyon, a Congregationalist, preached here many years previous to his death, which occurred in 1840.

Productions of the Soil. Wheat, 2,953 bushels; Indian corn, 2,187 bushels; potatoes, 19,968 bushels; hay, 2,061 tons; maple sugar, 9,893 pounds; wool, 12,504 pounds.

Distances. Fifty miles north-west from Montpelier, and eighteen north by west from Burlington.

GRANVILLE.

ADDISON CO. White River is formed here by the union of several considerable branches. One of these has a fall of 100 feet. Fifty feet of the lower part of it is perpendicular, and at the bottom is a hole worn into the rock ten feet deep. A considerable part of the surface of the township is mountainous.

Boundaries. Northerly by Warren, and a part of Roxbury, easterly by Braintree, southerly by Hancock, and a part of Rochester, and west by Ripton.

First Settlers. The settlement of this township commenced soon after the close of the Revolution, by Reuben King and others.

Productions of the Soil. Wheat, 1,006 bushels; Indian corn, 560 bushels; potatoes, 19,200 bushels; hay, 1,390 tons; maple sugar, 15,900 pounds; wool, 5,900 pounds.

Distances. Twenty-two miles southwest from Montpelier, and about sixteen south-east from Middlebury. The Northern Railroad passes near this town.

GREENSBOROUGH.

ORLEANS Co. The surface of this town is uneven, but the elevations are not generally abrupt. The land is well timbered, mostly with hard wood, except on the river and about its head waters, where it is almost entirely hemlock, spruce, cedar, and fir. The soil is of a middling quality. The River Lamoille is formed by the union of several streams in this town. *Caspian Lake* or Lake Beautiful, lies in the south part of this town, and discharges its waters to the east into the Lamoille, affording a number of valuable mill privileges, around which has grown up a beautiful little village. This pond is about three miles long, and one and a half broad. *Elligo Pond*, lying mostly in the western part of Greensboro', is about a mile long, and forms the head waters of Black River. These ponds produce abundance of fine trout. *Runaway Pond* (*see Glover*) was partly in this town, and was formerly the source of the Lamoille. There are several other small ponds in the north part of the town, which, at present, form the head waters of the Lamoille.

Boundaries. Northerly by Glover, easterly by Wheelock and Goshen Gore, southerly by Hardwick, and westerly by Craftsbury, and a small part of Wolcott.

First Settlers. The first settlement was begun in the spring of 1789, when Messrs. Ashbel and Aaron Shepard removed, with their families, from Newbury to this place. The hardships which the first settlers of this town had to endure, were very considerable. In coming into the town, the women had to proceed on foot, and all the furniture, belonging to the two families, was drawn upon three hand-sleds, on the crust. Both families consisted of five persons, Mr. Ashbel Shepard and his wife, and Mr. Aaron Shepard, his wife and one child. Mr. Aaron Shepard removed his family to Coos in August, and did not return till March, when his brother, Horace Shepard and family, returned with him. Thus were Mr. Ashbel Shepard and his wife, left from August till March, with no other human being in the town. Their nearest neighbors were Mr. Cutler's family, in Craftsbury, which had removed there the preceding autumn, and Mr. Webster's family, in Cabot. Mr. Shepard brought all his grain from Newbury, a distance of more than forty miles, of which he drew it sixteen miles upon a hand-sled, with the snow between four and five feet deep. In the same manner, he drew hay for the support of a cow, from a meadow of wild grass, three miles distant. On the 25th of March, Mrs. Shepard was delivered of a son, William Scott, the first child born in this town. The proprietors voted him a present of 100 acres of land.

First Minister. The Rev. Salmon King was settled over the Congregational Church in 1803, and continued a few years.

Productions of the Soil. Wheat, 2,074 bushels; Indian corn, 557 bushels; potatoes, 42,423 bushels; hay, 3,215 tons; maple sugar, 43,920 pounds; wool, 11,820 pounds.

Distances. Fifteen miles south from Irasburgh, and twenty-seven north-east from Montpelier.

GROTON.

CALEDONIA Co. The surface of this township is generally uneven, rough and stony. There is, however, some very good land, both in the north-east and south-western parts. The timber is mostly spruce and hemlock, interspersed with maple, beech and birch. This township is watered by Wells River and some of its branches, which afford several good mill privileges. There are also several natural ponds. Wells River Pond, through which Wells River passes, is in the north part, and is three miles long and three quarters of a mile wide. Little Pond, in the south-eastern part, covers about 100 acres, and lies in the course of Wells River. Kettle Pond, so called on account of Mr. Hosmer, a hunter, having lost a small kettle in its vicinity, lies in the north-west corner, and covers about forty acres. The south branch rises in Harris' Gore, and running nearly east through the south part of the town, joins Wells River just below Little Pond. In the south part of the township is an extensive bank of white clay or marl, which is a very good substitute for chalk, and which has been used instead of lime in plastering, and is said to answer a very good purpose.

Boundaries. North by Peacham, east by Ryegate, south by Topsham, and west by Harris' Gore.

First Settlers. The settlement of the township was commenced in 1787, by Messrs. James, Abbott, Morse, and Osmore. John James was the first male child born in town. The wife of a Mr. Page, in this town, was, in 1819, delivered of four male children at a birth.

Productions of the Soil. Wheat, 2,185 bushels; Indian corn, 2,967 bushels; potatoes, 31,095 bushels; hay, 2,009 tons; maple sugar, 20,530 pounds; wool, 4,001 pounds.

Distances. Fifteen miles south-west from Danville, and thirty-five south-east from Montpelier. The Connecticut River Railroad passes near this town.

GUILDHALL.

Essex Co. Guildhall is the county town, and is situated on the west side of Connecticut River, and is united to Lancaster, N. H., by two bridges across the river. The town is watered by several small streams, and the surface is quite uneven and stony, except a tract of intervale on the river. Cow and Burnside Mountains are considerable elevations, and afford excellent views of the meanderings of the Connecticut.

There is a pleasant village in the north-east part of the town, where the county buildings are situated.

Boundaries. North by Maidstone, east by Connecticut River, south by Lunenburgh, and west by Granby, and lies opposite to Lancaster, N. H.

First Settlers. The settlement was commenced in the lower part of this town, which was then thought to be a part of Lunenburgh, in 1764, by David Page, Timothy Nash, and George

Wheeler. In 1775, Enoch Hall, Micah Amy and James Rosbrook joined the settlement; Eleazar Rosbrook and Samuel Page, in 1778, and David Hopkinson, and Reuben and Simeon Howe, in 1779. The first settlers suffered severe privations and hardships for a number of years. They brought their grain and provisions, in canoes, from Northfield in Massachusetts, a distance of more than 150 miles. During the revolutionary war, they were in continual alarm, and frequently annoyed by the Indians and tories, who killed their cattle, plundered their houses, and carried a number of the inhabitants into captivity.

First Minister. A Congregational Church was formed in 1799, and settled the Rev. Caleb Burge in 1808; dismissed in 1814.

Productions of the Soil. Wheat, 957 bushels; Indian corn, 905 bushels; potatoes, 25,025 bushels; hay, 1,415 tons; maple sugar, 11,800 pounds; wool, 2,081 pounds.

Distances. Sixty-eight miles north-east from Montpelier. The Connecticut River Railroad will doubtless be extended through this place on the route to Canada.

GUILFORD.

Windham Co. The people of this town took an active part in defending the rights of Vermont against the claims of jurisdiction set up by the State of New York, about the years 1783-4. Guilford produced a number of patriots in this as also in the revolutionary cause. The soil of the town is warm and fertile, exceedingly productive of grain, fruits, maple sugar, butter, cheese, pork, sheep, horses, and beef cattle. It has good mill sites on Green River and branches of Broad Brook, a number of manufactories, a medicinal spring, and various kinds of minerals.

Boundaries. North by Brattleborough, east by Vernon, south by Leyden, Mass., and west by Halifax.

First Settlers. This town was chartered April 2, 1754, to fifty-four proprietors, principally of Massachusetts, and contained 23,040 acres. When granted, the town was a perfect wilderness. The first settlement was made by Micah Rice and family, in September, 1761.

First Ministers. The Rev. Royal Girley was the first settled minister in Guilford. He was of the Congregational order, and received the right of land reserved and located for that purpose. He was settled in the year 1775, and died soon after. He was a young man of science, and much respected for his pious and amiable deportment. The second of the same order was the Rev. Henry Williams, who was settled in 1779. Rev. Bunker Gay, of Hinsdale, preached his ordination sermon. His text was "*Death in the pot.*" He was a violent Yorker, and when the town submitted to the state authority he left with his political brethren. The third, the Rev. Elijah Wollage, was settled in 1794, and dismissed in 1799. The next of that order was the Rev. Jason Chamberlain. He was settled in 1807.

Productions of the Soil. Wheat, 920 bushels; Indian corn, 9,028 bushels; potatoes, 31,795 bushels; hay, 3,438 tons; maple sugar, 21,555 pounds; wool, 6,472 pounds.

Distances. Fifty miles south from Windsor, and thirty-one south east from Bennington.

HALIFAX.

WINDHAM Co. This township is watered by North and Green River. The former runs through the western and southern part, and the latter through the north-eastern. They are both large and commodious mill streams, and the mill privileges are numerous. In the branch of North River, on the farm of Henry Niles, is a succession of cascades extending about 100 rods. The falls are from fifteen to twenty feet each, and are overlooked by the projecting rocks on the right in ascending the stream. The place is visited by the curious, and the scene, which presents itself, is rugged, wild, and romantic.

The surface of the township is un-even, but there are no mountains worthy of notice.

On the margin of North River is a cavern, called *Woodard's Cave* or *Dun's Den.* It is twenty-five feet in length, five in width, and the same in height. The sides and top are of solid rock. This is also a place of resort for the curious. The soil is generally of a good quality, well adapted to the production of grass, and much attention is devoted to the raising of cattle and the keeping of dairies. The people are mostly industrious and wealthy.

Boundaries. North by Marlborough, east by Guilford, south by Colerain, Mass., and west by Whitingham.

First Settlers. The settlement was commenced in 1761, by Abner Rice, from Worcester County, Mass. He was joined by others from Colerain and Pelham, Mass., in 1763.

First Ministers. The first settled minister was the Rev. David Goodall of the Congregational order. He was settled in 1781; dismissed in 1796. The Rev. Jesse Edson was ordained over the same church November 23, 1796; died December 14, 1805.

Productions of the Soil. Wheat, 1,335 bushels; Indian corn, 5,420 bushels; potatoes, 52,825 bushels; hay, 4,149 tons; maple sugar, 46,660 pounds; wool, 9,875 pounds.

Distances. One hundred and twenty-five miles south from Montpelier, and fifteen south from Newfane.

HANCOCK.

ADDISON Co. Emerson's Branch of White River, the sixth branch of the same, and Leicester River, all rise near the south-west corner of this township. Emerson's Branch runs south-easterly and joins White River in Rochester, the sixth branch runs north-easterly and falls into White River, near the north-east corner of this town, and Leicester River runs westerly into Otter Creek. Middlebury River also heads in the western part of the township. These streams afford several very good mill privileges. The whole of the township lies upon the Green Mountains, but the principal ridge is on the western side. The surface of Hancock is high and broken, and but a small portion of it suitable for tillage; it, however, produces good grass.

Boundaries. North by Granville, and a part of Ripton, easterly by Rochester, southerly by Goshen, and westerly by Goshen and Ripton.

First Settlers. The settlement was commenced in the year 1788, by Joseph Butts, from Canterbury, Ct., Daniel Claflin, from New Salem, and John Bellows, from Dalton, Mass., with their families. Several young men also began improvements the same year, among whom were Zenas Robbins, and Levi Darling. Ebenezer, son of Daniel Claflin, was the first child born here.

First Minister. A Congregational Church was organized here in 1804.

Productions of the Soil. Wheat, 567 bushels; Indian corn, 396 bushels; potatoes, 16,960 bushels; hay, 1,090 tons; maple sugar, 10,600 pounds; wool, 4,890 pounds.

Distances. Fifteen miles south-east from Middlebury, and thirty south-west from Montpelier.

HARDWICK.

CALEDONIA CO. Hardwick is finely watered by Lamoille River, which gives the town valuable mill sites, and which are well improved for manufacturing purposes. The soil of the town is generally very good, and produces a variety of exports.

There are in this town three small villages. The oldest, called the Street, or Hazen's Road, is situated on high land near the north line of the town; the second, called Stevensville, is on the River Lamoille, in the eastern part; and the third and largest, called Lamoilleville, on the same river in the south-west part of the town. Each of these villages contains a number of mechanics' shops, stores, &c., and the two latter possess excellent water privileges, on which mills and other machinery are erected.

There is a mineral spring in the south part of the town, which is a place of considerable resort, and is found to be very efficacious, particularly in cutaneous affections.

Boundaries. North-east by Greensborough, south-east by Walden, south-west by Woodbury, and north-west by Wolcott.

First Settlers. About the year 1790, the first permanent settlement was made by several families of the name of Norris from New Hampshire. Mr. Porter Page came in about the same time, and also a number of families, by the name of Sabin, soon after, among whom was Mr. Gideon Sabin, whose wife was the mother of twenty-six children.

First Ministers. The Baptists formed the first religious society soon after the settlement commenced, and settled Elder Amos Tuttle, who continued their minister several years. In 1804, a Congregational Church was organized.

Productions of the Soil. Wheat, 2,053 bushels; Indian corn, 1,803 bushels; potatoes, 67,265 bushels; hay, 4,931 tons; maple sugar, 60,843 pounds; wool, 17,714 pounds.

Distances. Twelve miles north-west from Danville, and twenty-eight north-east from Montpelier.

HARTFORD.

WINDSOR CO. Hartford is watered by White and Quechee Rivers, which are the only streams of consequence. White River enters the township near the north-west corner, and falls into the Connecticut about the middle of the eastern boundary, and Quechee River runs through the south part. They both afford very valuable privileges for mills, and other machinery driven by water, particularly at the places called White River Village and Quechee Village.

The surface of the town is broken, but the soil is rich and warm, and produces good grass and grain.

The gulf formed by the passage of Quechee River through a considerable hill, is a curiosity, and is about one mile below Quechee Village. There are evident appearances of there having been a considerable pond here, which was emptied by the wearing down of the channel. The timber is principally white pine, beech, maple, and birch.

There are several villages in town; the largest are White River Village and Quechee Village. White River Village is pleasantly situated on the banks of White River, about one mile from its mouth. The river is here crossed by a handsome bridge.

Quechee Village is situated around a considerable fall in Ottá-Quechee River, about five miles from its mouth.

The passage of the great Northern and Connecticut River Railroads through this beautiful town, and the hydraulic power it possesses, bid fair to render them important places for manufacturing operations and depots of a large inland trade of the fertile country which surrounds them. The White River Iron Co. in this town was incorporated in 1844.

The railroad bridge across the Connecticut is a fine structure.

Boundaries. North by Norwich, east by Connecticut River, which separates it from Lebanon, N. H., south by Hartland, and west by Pomfret.

First Settlers. The first settlers were Elijah, Solomon, and Benajah Strong. They emigrated from Lebanon, Ct., and came into this township with their families in 1764. The next year they were joined in the settlement by twelve other families.

First Minister. The Rev. Thomas Gross was the first settled minister. He was settled over the Congregational Church June 7, 1786, and dismissed in Feb. 1808.

Productions of the Soil. Wheat, 4,507 bushels; Indian corn, 19,753 bushels; potatoes, 59,050 bushels; hay, 5,687 tons; maple sugar, 11,400 pounds; wool, 39,915 pounds.

Distances. Forty-two miles south south-east from Montpelier, and fourteen north from Windsor.

The great Northern Railroad between Boston and Burlington, and the Connecticut River Railroad, pass through the town.

HARTLAND.

WINDSOR Co. This is a rich farming township, and its surface is pleasantly diversified with hills and valleys. Connecticut River washes the eastern boundary, and at Quechee Falls, on this stream, are several mills, situated on the Hartland side. Quechee River runs across the north-east corner, and Lull's Brook through the southern part of the town, and afford some of the best mill privileges in the State. On the lands of David H. Sumner, Esq., has recently been discovered a valuable bed of paint. It is abundant, and of an excellent quality.

Boundaries. North by Hartford, east by Plainfield, N. H., from which it is separated by Connecticut River, south by Windsor, and west by Woodstock.

First Settlers. The settlement of the township was commenced in May, 1763, by Timothy Lull, from Dummerston, in this State. At this time there were no inhabitants on Connecticut River, between Charlestown, then No. 4, and Hartland. A few families had, however, settled in Newbury, about forty miles to the north of this place. Mr. Lull moved into the town in the following manner. Having purchased a log canoe, he proceeded in that up Connecticut River, with his furniture and family, consisting of a wife and four children. He arrived at the mouth of a considerable brook in Hartland, where he landed his family, tied his canoe, and, breaking a junk bottle in the presence of his little family, named the stream *Lull's Brook*, by which name it has ever since been known. He proceeded up the brook about a mile, to a log hut which had been previously erected, near the place now called Sumner's Village. Here he spent his days, and died at the advanced age of eighty-one years. His son Timothy, lately deceased, was the first child born in town. He was born in December, 1764, on which occasion the midwife was drawn by the father from Charlestown, upon the ice, a distance of twenty-three miles, upon a hand-sled. Mr. Lull had to suffer many privations and hardships for several years; but possessing a strong constitution and a vigorous mind, he overcame all obstacles, accumulated a handsome property, lived respected, and died generally lamented.

First Ministers. There are in this town four houses of public worship: one erected in 1788, another in 1822, and two others have since been erected.

Productions of the Soil. Wheat, 4.403 bushels; Indian corn, 9.127 bushels; potatoes, 79.395 bushels; hay, 7.211 tons; maple sugar, 25,280 pounds; wool, 48,575 pounds.

Distances. Fifty miles south southeast from Montpelier, and nine north from Windsor.

The Connecticut River Railroad passes through the town, and the great Northern Railroad passes through the neighboring town of Hartford.

HIGHGATE.

FRANKLIN Co. The Missisco River enters this township from Sheldon, and after running some distance in the south part of it, passes into Swanton, and then taking a circuitous course of several miles, returns into Highgate, and pursuing a north-westerly course falls into Missisco Bay. About six miles above Swanton Falls is a fall in the river of about forty feet, affording some excellent mill privileges. Rock River is in the north part of the township, and has on it one saw mill. The soil is mostly sandy, and covered with pine, except along the course of the Missisco River, where the timber is hemlock, ash, &c., and in the southeast corner, which constitutes a part of what is called *Hog Island*, and is marshy. Bog iron ore is found in this town in great abundance, and has been worked to some extent.

Boundaries. North by Dun's Patent, in Canada, east by Franklin, south by Swanton and Sheldon, and west by Missisco Bay, which separates it from the township of Alburgh.

First Settlers. The first settlers in this town were Germans, mostly soldiers who had served in the British army during the revolution, but the time of their settlement is not known. The town was chartered in 1763.

First Minister. A Congregational Church was erected in 1812, and the Rev. Phinehas Kingsley settled over it in 1819; dismissed in 1829.

Productions of the Soil. Wheat, 5.032 bushels; Indian corn, 6.762 bushels; potatoes, 39,845 bushels; hay, 4.347 tons; maple sugar, 12,108 pounds; wool, 18,874 pounds.

Distances. Seventy miles north-west from Montpelier, and twelve north from St. Albans.

Although the "Iron Horse" is very fantastic in his course, he understands his business too well not to pay proper respect to his worthy neighbors. He is about passing through this town, on a visit to the Canadians, and in the most respectful manner to solicit of them a portion of the carrying trade of their great and increasing commerce, between Montreal and the Atlantic shores of New England. We feel assured that Johnny Bull and Brother Jonathan are too fond of a good bargain, not to put their *horses together* to effect a union of interest so desirable.

HINESBURGH.

CHITTENDEN Co. There is in the north part of the town a high ridge of rough land, called Prichard Mountain. The west part has generally a level surface, interspersed with small hillocks. In the eastern part the land is hilly and broken, containing, however, a good share of feasible, fertile, and valuable land. The forest consisted of hard timber generally. There were some beaver meadows, one of which contained between 100 and 200 acres, from which the first settlers derived much benefit.

The principal streams are Lewis Creek, Laplot River, and Pond Brook. Lewis Creek enters the town from Monkton, and takes a westerly course through the south-west part of the town. On this stream, in the year 1790, Mr. Nathan Leavenworth, one of the early settlers, built a saw mill and a grist mill. This mill is in the bounds of Charlotte. Before it was built, the inhabitants were obliged to go to Winooski Falls, at Burlington, or to Vergennes, for their grinding.

Hinesburgh affords an abundant water power, and manufactures of iron, wool, and various other articles, are rapidly increasing on the banks of its beautiful streams. A manufacturing company was established in 1847.

Boundaries. North by Shelburne, St. George, and Richmond, east by Huntington and Starksborough, south by Starksborough and Monkton, and west by Charlotte.

First Settlers. The first inhabitants were a Mr. Isaac Lawrence and family, from Canaan, Connecticut, whose wife said that she lived ten months without seeing the face of any other woman, and that at one time the family lived for some time on dried pumpkins, without any other food whatever. This family came here before the revolutionary war, and also Mr. Daniel Chaffey, who was here for a short time; they both left when the war commenced. Mr. Lawrence returned in 1783. Messrs. Jacob Meacham, Amos Andrews, and Hezekiah Tuttle, came in 1784. In 1785, Mr. George McEwen with his family, Mr. Eliphaz and George Steele came without families, and spent the summer. The first child born in town was a son of Jacob Meacham, on the first day of April, 1785; he was named Hine, in reference to the name of the town.

First Ministers. The Congregational Church was formed in the year 1789, with twelve members; the Rev. Reuben Parmelee was ordained as pastor, in 1791, and dismissed in 1795. From this time until 1818 the church was destitute of a stated pastor.

Productions of the Soil. Wheat, 2,020 bushels; Indian corn, 6,888 bushels; potatoes, 27,605 bushels; hay, 4,639 tons; maple sugar, 14,170 pounds; wool, 16,336 pounds.

Distances. Twelve miles south southeast from Burlington, and thirty-six west from Montpelier. The Southern Railroad passes through this town, and facilitates the business of the place.

HOLLAND.

ORLEANS Co. This is an excellent township of land, producing in great abundance all the varieties common to the climate.

There is a large pond situated in the north-east part of the town, and several small ponds. The streams are small; part flowing north into Canada, and part south into Clyde River.

On the 2d of July, 1833, Holland was visited by a violent tornado. It commenced on Salem Pond in Salem, and passed over the town in a north-easterly direction. It was from half to three quarters of a mile wide, and it prostrated and scattered nearly all the trees, fences, and buildings, in its course. It crossed the outlet of Norton Pond, and passed into Canada, and its course could be traced through the forests nearly to Connecticut River.

Boundaries. North by Barnston and Stanstead, Canada, east by Norton, south by Morgan, and west by Derby.

First Settlers. The settlement was commenced in 1800, by Edmund Eliot and Joseph Cowal.

Productions of the Soil. Wheat, 1,844 bushels; Indian corn, 151 bushels; potatoes, 14,510 bushels; hay, 1,281 tons; maple sugar, 20,685 pounds; wool, 2,400 pounds.

Distances. Eighteen miles north-east from Irasburgh, and fifty-eight north-east from Montpelier.

HUBBARDTON.

RUTLAND Co. The surface of the township is uneven, and somewhat mountainous. The most noted summit is Mount Zion, so named by Ethan Allen. There are several natural ponds, the largest of which is Gregory's Pond, which is about three miles long and one broad, and lies partly in Sudbury. At its outlet are excellent mill privileges, surrounded by a pleasant little village.

Berbe's Pond, situated a mile northwest of the centre of the town, is one and a half miles long and a mile wide, and discharges south into Lake Bombazine. Round Pond, Marsh Pond,

7

Keeler's Pond, Black's Pond, and Howland's Pond, are smaller. The latter discharges into Otter Creek.

The town is well timbered with hard wood and hemlock. Pine was formerly plenty, but is now become scarce. The soil is various. The eastern part is hard pan, and is very good for grass and grain. In other parts the soil is slaty loam, and better suited to the production of winter grain. Plaster, ashes, and lime, are here found to be very beneficial for manures. Springs of good water are common, and in the south-west part of the town is a spring, said to possess precisely the same properties as the celebrated springs in Clarendon. The geological character of the township is very interesting.

Boundaries. North by Sudbury, east by Pittsford, south by Castleton, and west by Benson.

First Settlers. The settlement was commenced in the spring of 1774, by Uriah Hickok and William Trowbridge, with their families, from Norfolk, Ct. Elizabeth, daughter of Mrs. Hickok, was born August 1st of this year, and died in September, 1776. This was the first birth and first death in town. The first barn was built in 1785, and the first house in 1787. The first settlers of this town suffered very severely by the Indians and tories.

First Ministers. The Baptist Church was formed Sept. 24, 1787. Elder Nathaniel Culver was their minister from 1787 to 1792. Elder Nathan Dana was settled in 1798, and was regarded as their first settled minister.

Productions of the Soil. Wheat, 1,849 bushels; Indian corn, 2,957 bushels; potatoes, 12,800 bushels; hay, 3,138 tons; maple sugar, 5,557 pounds; wool, 29,862 pounds.

Distances. Fifty miles south-west from Montpelier, and ten north-west from Rutland. The great Northern Railroad passes in the vicinity of this town.

HUNTINGTON.

CHITTENDEN Co. That celebrated summit of the Green Mountains, called

Camel's Hump, is in the east part of this township. There are some farms which produce tolerable crops, but the soil is, in most parts, rocky and poor. Timber, such as is common to the mountain towns.

Boundaries. North by Bolton, and a part of Richmond, east by Duxbury and Fayston, south by Avery's and Buel's Gores, and west by Starkborough, and Hinesburgh.

First Settlers. The settlement of this township was commenced in March, 1786, by Jehiel Johns and Elisha Bradley, emigrants from Manchester and Sunderland in this State.

First Ministers. The Freewill Baptists and Methodists built a meeting-house here in 1836.

Productions of the Soil. Wheat, 1,423 bushels; Indian corn, 3,615 bushels; potatoes, 24,987 bushels; hay, 2,596 tons; maple sugar, 19,480 pounds; wool, 7,738 pounds.

Distances. Twenty miles west from Montpelier, and fifteen south-east from Burlington.

HYDEPARK.

LAMOILLE Co. Hydepark is the county town. The Lamoille, Green, and other rivers give this town a great water power, some of which is advantageously improved. The soil is generally of a good quality and easily cultivated.

There are in the north-east part of the town twelve ponds, containing from one half to fifty acres, beside several smaller ones. Trout have been abundant in most of them, but are becoming more scarce. Some of them have names, such as Great Pond, Clear Pond, George's Pond, Zack's Pond, Mud Pond, &c.

Hydepark village is situated in the south-west part of the town, on a beautiful elevated plain; it contains a court house, jail, and jail house, built in 1836, by the inhabitants of the town, at which time it became the seat of justice for Lamoille County.

This town, having so valuable a water power, and being surrounded by a country rich in agricultural and mineral productions, and rapidly increasing in its manufacturing interest, it would not surprise the natives, if the "Iron Horse" should soon take a trip this way, to assist them in their laudable pursuits.

Boundaries. Northerly by Eden, easterly by Wolcott, and a small part of Craftsbury, southerly by Morristown, and westerly by Johnson, and a part of Belvidere.

First Settlers. The settlement of this township was commenced by John McDaniel, Esq., who removed his family here July 4, 1787. He emigrated from Northfield, N. H. At this time the nearest settlements were at Johnson on the west, and at Cabot on the east; the former distant eight miles and the latter about twenty-six. The intervening country was a perfect wilderness, with no road or guide except marked trees. Through this wilderness Mr. McDaniel conveyed his family from Cabot to Hydepark. He was joined the same season by William Norton, from New York; and those two families were the first and only families who wintered in town that year. The next spring they were joined by Capt. Jedediah Hyde, Peter Martin, Jabez Fitch, Esq., and sons, and Ephraim Garvin. These pioneers were followed in a few years by Aaron Keeler, Truman Sawyer, Oliver Noyes, and Hon. N. P. Sawyer and others. The first settlers experienced all the privations usual in a wilderness. They were under the necessity of getting their milling done at Cambridge, eighteen miles distant. The town was named Hyde's Park in the charter, as a compliment to Capt. Jedediah Hyde, the first named in that instrument.

Productions of the Soil. Wheat, 2,185 bushels; Indian corn, 3,533 bushels; potatoes, 47,816 bushels; hay, 2,501 tons; maple sugar, 32,570 pounds; wool, 7,132 pounds.

Distances. Twenty-seven miles north from Montpelier.

IRA.

RUTLAND Co. This township is elevated; it contains good land for rearing cattle. Castleton River and Ira Brook wash a part of the town, but afford no valuable mill privileges.

Boundaries. East by Rutland and Clarendon, south by Tinmouth, southwest by Middletown, and west by Poultney and Castleton.

First Settlers. The town was organized in 1779. Isaac Clark was the first town clerk and representative.

First Minister. A Baptist Church was organized in 1783, and Elder Thomas Skeels was settled over it the same year.

Productions of the Soil. Wheat, 580 bushels; Indian corn, 2,305 bushels; potatoes, 11,510 bushels; hay, 1,167 tons; maple sugar, 10,962 pounds; wool, 17,247 pounds.

Distances. Forty miles south-west from Montpelier, and eight south-west from Rutland. The Southern Railroad passes in this neighborhood.

IRASBURGH.

ORLEANS Co. Irasburgh is somewhat diversified with gentle hills and valleys. The soil is easy to cultivate, and, in general, produces good crops. Black River passes through the township in a north-easterly direction, receiving a number of small streams, but its current is generally moderate, and it affords but few mill privileges. Barton River just touches upon the eastern corner. Nearly in the centre of the township is a small village.

Boundaries. Northerly by Orleans, easterly by Barton, and a small part of Brownington, southerly by Albany, and westerly by Lowell, Coventry Gore, and a part of Newport.

First Settlers. The settlement of this township was commenced a little previous to the year 1800.

Productions of the Soil. Wheat, 2,129 bushels; Indian corn, 1,529 bushels; potatoes, 39,808 bushels; hay, 2,847 tons; maple sugar, 25,961 pounds; wool, 7,847 pounds.

Distances. Forty-two miles northeast from Montpelier. The Monarch Carrier will soon pass in the vicinity of Irasburgh, on his way to Montreal.

ISLE LA MOTTE.

GRAND ISLE CO. An island in the western part of the county. It was chartered by this name to Benjamin Wait and others, October 27, 1789, containing 4,620 acres. The name was altered to Vineyard, November 1, 1802, and again altered to Isle la Motte, Nov. 6, 1830. The settlement of this town was commenced about the year 1785. Among the early settlers were Ebenezer Hyde, Enoch Hall, William Blanchard, and Ichabod Fitch. The town was organized about the year 1790. There are no streams on the island. A marsh extends across it from east to west, which abounds with excellent cedar. The rocks are limestone, and are extensively quarried for building, for which purpose they answer well.

Boundaries. On all sides by Lake Champlain.

Productions of the Soil. Wheat, 3,318 bushels; Indian corn, 1,717 bushels; potatoes, 6,788 bushels; hay, 505 tons; maple sugar, 3,141 pounds; wool, 2,763 pounds.

Distances. Twenty-eight miles northwest from Burlington, and thirteen nearly west from St. Albans.

JAMAICA.

WINDHAM CO. West River passes through this township, and, together with its tributaries, affords numerous and excellent mill privileges. The surface of Jamaica is broken and mountainous, and the elevations rocky, but the soil is, in general, warm and productive. A range of primitive limestone passes through the township, from which lime is manufactured in the eastern part, where there is a fine locality of dolomite. It is granular, flexible, and of a snow white color. In a vein of the dolomite is found the micaceous oxyde of iron. It is brilliant, fine grained, and the particles are separated by rubbing between the fingers. There is a pleasant and flourishing village near the centre of the town, in which are several stores and manufacturing establishments. The Ball Moun-

tain Manufacturing Company in this town was incorporated in 1848.

Boundaries. North by Windham and Londonderry, east by Townshend, south by Wardsborough, and west by a part of Stratton, and a part of Winhall.

First Settlers. This settlement was commenced in 1780, by William, Benjamin, and Caleb Howard, and others, from Mendon, Mass., and its vicinity.

First Minister. The Rev. John Stoddard was the first settled minister. He was settled over the Congregational Church in 1795; dismissed in 1798.

Productions of the Soil. Wheat, 1,226 bushels; Indian corn, 5,152 bushels; potatoes, 44,680 bushels; hay, 3,531 tons; maple sugar, 13,531 pounds; wool, 8,111 pounds.

Distances. Ninety miles south from Montpelier, and fourteen north-west from Newfane.

JAY.

ORLEANS CO. A part of this town is very mountainous—Jay's Peak lying in the south-west part; the other part is good arable land, and would produce good crops if well cultivated. A number of streams issue from the mountain and produce an ample water power.

Boundaries. North by Sutton, Canada, east by Troy, south by Westfield, and west by Richford.

First Settlers. Previous to the late war with Great Britain, five or six families had settled in this township, but during the war they nearly all left it. A few families have since returned, and the settlement has been advancing.

Productions of the Soil. Wheat, 885 bushels; Indian corn, 268 bushels; potatoes, 10,680 bushels; hay, 650 tons; maple sugar, 8,015 pounds; wool, 1,112 pounds.

Distances. Sixteen miles north west from Irasburgh, and fifty north from Montpelier.

JERICHO.

CHITTENDEN COUNTY. Jericho is watered with springs and brooks. Winooski River washes the south-western boundary. Brown's River enters the town at the north-east, from Underhill, and runs into Essex. Little River, or Lee's Brook, so called, takes its rise in the east, and, running near the centre of the town, unites with Brown's River at the village, in the west part of the town. Mill Brook enters the township from Bolton, and runs into the Winooski about half way from Richmond to Essex. On all these streams are good alluvial flats, and the mill privileges are good, but the best and most numerous are on Brown's River, near the west village. The soil and timber is various in different parts. It is a good farming town, and well adapted to raising most kinds of grain and grass.

There is a village at the centre of the town, containing a good brick church, owned by the First Congregational Society, an academy, together with a number of buildings scattered around a handsome common, given by Lewis Chapin, one of the early settlers, for that purpose. There is another flourishing village at the *corners*, in the westerly part of the town.

Boundaries. Northerly by Underhill, east by Bolton, south by Richmond, south-west by Williston, from which it is separated by Winooski River, and westerly by Essex.

First Settlers. The settlement of Jericho was commenced in 1774, by Messrs. Messenger, Rood and Brown, with their families, from the western part of Massachusetts; but the settlement was mostly abandoned during the revolution. Mr. Brown settled on the flats near Underhill, on what is now called Brown's River. He, with his family, consisting of a wife, a daughter, and two sons, remained unmolested during the fore part of the revolutionary war, and had made such improvement on his land as to raise most of the necessaries of life. In the autumn of 1780 the family was surprised and made prisoners by a party of Indians. At the time, a young man by the name of Olds was in the house, and made his escape to the Block house on the Winooski River, in the west part of the town. The Indians, after securing

their prisoners, killed the cattle, sheep, and hogs belonging to Mr. Brown, set the house on fire, and started for Montreal. The prisoners suffered much on their journey through the woods, from fatigue and hunger, the most of their food being raw bear's meat. On their arrival at St. Johns, they were sold to British officers at $8 per head, and by them retained as prisoners nearly three years, during which time they were compelled to labor for their masters, and allowed but miserable fare. On their return they were enabled to keep a part of their land in Jericho, and by industry and perseverance accumulated a handsome property. The two sons settled, lived, and died on the same land where they were made prisoners, and were among the most respectable families in town. Their children still own and live on a share of the same land. Mr. Messenger settled on the Winooski River, and remained there until June, 1776, when Gen. Ira Allen called on him to leave for his own safety. Mr. Messenger, with his family and a small share of their effects, in a canoe belonging to Gen. Allen, proceeded down the river to what is called Hubbell's Falls, in Essex, where they unloaded. Mr. Messenger went over the falls in the canoe without injury, except breaking in the bow of the canoe. He changed ends, reloaded, and proceeded to what has since been called the Lawrence farm, where they stayed for the night. At the falls in Colchester they carried their load around, let the boat drift over, and arrived safe at the lake, where an open boat was waiting to receive them, with others, when they were transported in safety to Skenesboro', (now Whitehall,) and from thence to Bennington, and were there at the battle. On the return of peace, Mr. Messenger, with his family, returned to Jericho and settled on his old place, where he lived to an advanced age, an industrious and respectable farmer.

First Minister. The Rev. Ebenezer Kingsbury was settled over the Congregational Church in 1791; dismissed in 1808.

Productions of the Soil. Wheat, 2,412

bushels; Indian corn, 4,566 bushels; potatoes, 32,322 bushels; hay, 3,222 tons; maple sugar, 11,300 pounds; wool, 13,915 pounds.

Distances. Twenty-five miles north-west from Montpelier, and twelve east from Burlington. The great Northern Railroad passes in this vicinity.

JOHNSON.

LAMOILLE Co. The River Lamoille enters this township, near the south-east corner, and running wester-ly about two miles, through a rich tract of intervale, falls over a ledge of rocks about fifteen feet in height into a basin below. This is called *M'Connel's Falls.* Thence it runs north-westerly over a bed of rocks, about 100 rods, narrow-ing its channel and increasing its velo-city, when it forms a whirlpool and sinks under a barrier of rocks, which extends across the river. The arch is of solid rock, is about eight feet wide, and at low water is passed over by footmen with safety. The water rises below through numerous aper-tures, exhibiting the appearance of the boiling of a pot.

The surface of this township is un-even, being thrown into ridges, which are covered with hemlock, spruce, and hard wood. The soil is a dark or yel-low loam, mixed with a light sand, is easily tilled, and very productive. The alluvial flats are considerably exten-sive, but back from the river the lands are in some parts rather stony. In the north-eastern part has been discovered a quantity of soapstone.

The village in Johnson is very pleasant, and contains a number of mills, for the manufacture of various articles.

Boundaries. Northerly by Belvidere, easterly by Hydepark, southerly by Sterling, and westerly by a part of Cambridge and a part of Belvidere.

First Settlers. Johnson was first set-tled in 1784, by a revolutionary hero of the name of Samuel Eaton. Mr Eaton frequently passed through this township, while scouting between Con-necticut River and Lake Champlain; and several times encamped on the same flat which he afterwards occupied as a farm, it being a beautiful tract of intervale. Like many other settlers of this State, he had many difficulties to encounter. In indigent circumstan-ces, and with a numerous family, he loaded his little all upon an old horse, and set out in search of that favorite spot, which he had selected in his more youthful days. He had to travel nearly seventy miles through the wilderness, guided by the trees which had been marked by the scouts, and opening a path as he passed along. He depend-ed, for some time after he arrived at Johnson, entirely upon hunting and fishing, for the support of himself and family.

Productions of the Soil. Wheat, 3,144 bushels; Indian corn, 2,402 bushels; potatoes, 66,405 bushels; hay, 3,487 tons; maple sugar, 31,460 lbs.; wool, 10,585 pounds.

Distances. Five miles north-west from Hydepark, and thirty-two north-west from Montpelier.

KIRBY.

CALEDONIA Co. There are some tracts of good land in Kirby, but the township is generally either wet and cold, or too mountainous for cultiva-tion. It has a number of springs, brooks, and a good fish pond.

Boundaries. North by Burke, north-east and south-east by Bradleyvale, south-west by St. Johnsbury, and west by Lyndon.

First Settlers. The settlement of this township was commenced about the year 1799, by Phinehas Page and Theophilus Grout, who were soon after joined by Josiah Joslin, Jude White, Jonathan Leach, Ebenezer Damon, Antipas Harrington, Asahel Burt, Jon-athan Lewis, and others, principally from New Hampshire and Massachu-setts.

First Ministers. A Congregational Church was formed here in 1812.

Productions of the Soil. Wheat, 2,370 bushels; Indian corn, 1,020 bushels; potatoes, 29,435 bushels; hay, 1,887 tons; maple sugar, 8,142 pounds; wool, 4,547 pounds.

Distances. Fifteen miles north-east from Danville, six north-east from St. Johnsbury, and forty-five north-east from Montpelier. The Boston and Montreal Railroad passes in this vicinity.

LAMOILLE COUNTY.

HYDEPARK is the shire town. This county was established in 1836. It is bounded north by Franklin and Orleans Counties, east by Orleans and Caledonia Counties, south by Washington County, and west by Chittenden and a part of Franklin Counties. This county lies on the Green Mountain range, and is the source of many streams. The River Lamoille passes nearly through its centre, and, with its tributaries, gives the county a great hydraulic power. The elevation of the county renders the soil more adapted for grazing than for tillage, yet there are large tracts of excellent meadow bordering its streams. Manufactures flourish, and the exports of beef cattle and the products of the dairy are valuable, and annually increasing.—See *Tables.*

COURTS IN LAMOILLE COUNTY.

The *Supreme Court* sits at Hydepark, in this county, on the sixteenth Tuesday after the fourth Tuesday of December, and the *County Court* on the second Tuesday in June and December.

LANDGROVE.

BENNINGTON Co. This town is on elevated land, at the north-east corner of the county. Some of the head branches of West River have their sources here. The lands are too rough and high for much improvement.

Boundaries. North by Weston, east by Weston and Londonderry, south by a part of Londonderry, and west by Peru.

First Settlers. The settlement was commenced by William Utley and family, consisting of a wife and six children. in June, 1769, emigrants from Ashford, Ct.

Productions of the Soil. Wheat, 320 bushels; Indian corn, 716 bushels; potatoes, 13,550 bushels; hay, 1,204 tons; maple sugar, 6,780 pounds; wool, 2,350 pounds.

Distances. Thirty-three miles north-east from Bennington, and seventy south from Montpelier.

LEICESTER.

ADDISON Co. Leicester is watered by a river of its own name, by Otter Creek, and by a part of Lake Dunmore. These waters are too sluggish to afford the town much water power. The soil is of a sandy loam, interspersed with some flats of clay. Along the rivers the soil is rich and productive. The highlands are hard and fit for grazing.

There are in this town several beautiful ponds, which abound in trout and other fish.

Boundaries. North by Salisbury, east by Goshen, south by Brandon, and west by Whiting.

First Settlers. The first settlement was commenced in 1773, by Jeremiah Parker, from Massachusetts. The settlement, however, made but little progress till after the revolution.

Productions of the Soil. Wheat, 772 bushels; Indian corn, 3,321 bushels; potatoes, 10,960 bushels; hay, 4,600 tons; maple sugar, 820 pounds; wool, 12,900 pounds.

Distances. Thirty-six miles southwest from Montpelier, and ten south by east from Middlebury.

The great Southern Railroad between Boston and Burlington, passes through this town.

LEMINGTON.

ESSEX Co. This is a mountainous township, on the west side of Connecticut River, with a small portion of intervale. There are several brooks in the town, and a beautiful cascade of fifty feet. There is a mountain in the town called "The Monadnock of Vermont," from which circumstance may be discovered that this town, generally, is not fit for cultivation.

Boundaries. Northerly by Canaan, easterly by Connecticut River, which separates it from Colebrook, N. H., southerly by Bloomfield, and westerly by Averill.

Productions of the Soil. Wheat, 294 bushels; Indian corn, 163 bushels; potatoes, 7,470 bushels; hay, 503 tons; maple sugar, 1,650 pounds; wool, 757 pounds.

Distances. Twenty-five miles north from Guildhall, and sixty-four northeast from Montpelier.

LEWIS.

ESSEX Co. Lewis is an uninhabited township, six miles square, in the northern part of Essex County; bounded north-easterly by Averill, southeasterly by Bloomfield, south-westerly by Wenlock, and north-westerly by Avery's Gore. It was chartered June 29, 1762. It is mountainous, and has no streams of consequence, excepting the north branch of Nulhegan River, which crosses the north-east corner.

LINCOLN.

ADDISON COUNTY. Lincoln is considerably uneven. The western part is watered by New Haven River, which is formed here; and several small branches of Mad River rise in the eastern part. The timber is principally hard wood, with some tracts of spruce.

Boundaries. North by Starksboro' and Fayston, east by Warren, south by Avery's Gore, and west by Bristol.

First Settlers. The settlement of this township was commenced about the year 1790. The first settlers were mostly of the denomination called Friends, or Quakers, There is at present a society of this order, who have a house for public worship.

Productions of the Soil. Wheat, 860 bushels; Indian corn, 1,080 bushels; potatoes, 20,400 bushels; hay, 650 tons; maple sugar, 29,510 pounds; wool, 9,000 pounds.

Distances. Twenty-one miles southwest from Montpelier, and fifteen northeast from Middlebury.

LONDONDERRY.

WINDHAM Co.. West River passes through this town, and receives several tributaries in it. The land on the streams is rich and fertile; the uplands are good for grazing, except those parts that are mountainous.

There are in this town two pleasant villages.

Boundaries. North by Weston and a part of Landgrove, east by Windham, south by Jamaica, and west by Landgrove.

First Settlers. The settlement of this township was commenced in 1774, by James Rogers, S. Thompson, and Jas. Patterson, from Londonderry, New Hampshire.

First Minister. Elder David Sweet was ordained over the Baptist Church in this place in 1820.

Productions of the Soil. Wheat, 1,066 bushels; Indian corn, 2,164 bushels; potatoes, 41,579 bushels; hay, 3,422 tons; maple sugar, 21,076 pounds; wool, 9,197 pounds.

Distances. Twenty-eight miles south-west from Windsor, and thirty north-east from Bennington.

LOWELL.

ORLEANS Co. The Missisco River originates in a small pond, nearly on the line between this township and Eden, and taking a northerly course, and receiving a number of considerable tributaries, enters Westfield near its south-east corner. Several of these tributaries are sufficient for mills, and the river is increased by them to considerable magnitude, forming meadows of considerable extent and fertility before leaving the township. Although encompassed by mountains on all sides, except the north-east, much of the township is handsome land, easy to till, and generally productive. At the grist mill of Asahel Curtis, near the centre of Lowell, the whole river passes through a hole in the solid rock. This natural bridge is situated at the foot of a fall in the river of about ten feet. The top of the bridge is about three feet wide, and the same distance from the surface of the water, and under it the water is fifteen feet deep.

Boundaries. North by Troy, West-field, Coventry Gore, and a part of Montgomery, south-east by Irasburgh and Albany, south-west by Eden and Belvidere, and westerly by Avery's Gore.

First Settler. The first permanent settlement was made here in 1806, by Major Wm. Caldwell.

Productions of the Soil. Wheat, 591 bushels; Indian corn, 397 bushels; potatoes, 22,417 bushels; hay, 1,084 tons; maple sugar, 14,635 pounds; wool, 2,107 pounds.

Distances. Nine miles south-west from Irasburgh, and forty north from Montpelier.

LUDLOW.

WINDSOR Co. Black River passes through the centre of the town, and has many valuable mill sites. In the upper part of its course it widens into four large basins; the largest in Ludlow being nearly circular, and one mile in diameter, known as the Ludlow and Plymouth Ponds. In the north-west corner of the town is the " Tiney Pond," several hundred feet above the level of the river, and nearly half a mile in diameter. No stream supplies it, but a small rivulet passes from it, tumbling from one rock to another in its rugged course, until, after passing half a mile, it empties into the largest Ludlow Pond. The only fish it contains is that commonly called the horn pout. There is another large collection of water in the western part of the town, and several extensive bogs upon both sides of the river, now presenting only a surface of mud, covered many feet deep with moss, but evidently once the bed of mountain ponds. These bogs afford the botanist many rare and curious varieties of shrubs and flowers. The soil upon the river is alluvial, and throughout the town is fertile, and well adapted for grazing and cultivation.

The prevailing rock is mica slate, and, imbedded in masses, or forming independent boulders, are found the white, ferruginous, and smoky quartz, black and green hornblende, and steatite, with localities of ligniform asbestos, its strands from twelve to twenty-four inches in length, plumbago, galena, and garnet.

In the western part of the town are quarries of the carbonate mingled with the sulphate of lime, and containing beautiful specimens of calcareous spar. In the eastern border is a lofty range of serpentine, containing the harder varieties of asbestos, talc, and hornstone, and forming, near the line of Cavendish, that most beautiful variety of marble known by the name of *verd antique*. Limestone and serpentine mingle, and produce every possible shade of green, from the lightest grass to an almost perfect black, and these shades running into each other in a most pleasing and apparently never ending variety.

Boundaries. North by Plymouth, east by Cavendish and Chester, south by Andover and Weston, and its western line passes, for about nine miles, along the ridge of highlands which separate Windsor and Rutland Counties, and form the boundary between Ludlow and Mount Holly.

First Settlers. No attempt was made at commencing a settlement until 1784-5, when Josiah and Jesse Fletcher, Simeon Reed, and James Whitney, emigrants from Massachusetts, removed within the limits of the township, and began their clearings upon the alluvial flats bordering upon Black River.

First Minister. A Congregational Church was organized here in 1806, but had no settled minister until 1810, when the Rev. Peter Kead became their pastor.

Productions of the Soil. Wheat, 1,385 bushels; Indian corn, 3,060 bushels; potatoes, 23,626 bushels; hay, 3,600 tons; maple sugar, 5,154 pounds; wool, 9,069 pounds.

Distances. Sixty-one miles south from Montpelier, and eighteen southwest from Windsor.

LUNENBURG.

ESSEX Co. This town is on the west side of Connecticut River, and watered by Neal's Branch and Pond, and Catbow Branch, good mill streams. Some of the land is very good, but the most of it is stony, apparently of diluvial formation, consisting of rounded masses of granite, embedded in clay and gravel. This is a good grazing town, and produces some cattle, and butter and cheese for market.

Boundaries. North-west by Victory, north-east by Guildhall, south-east by Connecticut River, south-west by Concord, and is opposite Dalton, in New Hampshire.

First Settlers. This town was probably settled as early as 1770.

First Minister. A Congregational Church was organized here in 1802, and the next year they settled the Rev. John Willard for their pastor.

Productions of the Soil. Wheat, 3,308 bushels; Indian corn, 1,628 bushels; potatoes, 81,630 bushels; hay, 3558

tons; maple sugar, 18,210 pounds; wool, 6,147 pounds.

Distances. Thirteen miles south from Guildhall, and fifty-five miles north-east by east from Montpelier

LYNDON.

CALEDONIA Co. Lyndon is one of the best townships in the State; its surface is undulating, with a soil of rich loam, free from stone, easy to cultivate, and very productive of wool, cattle, pork, butter, and cheese. It is well watered by the Passumpsic and some of its tributaries. Two important falls of that river are in the town: one of sixty-five feet in the distance of thirty rods; the other of eighteen feet. These are called *Great* and *Little Falls*, and afford a water power of great extent. Agaric mineral, used for chalk, and a good substitute for Spanish white, is found here. The principal village is very pleasant, and the seat of considerable business. The scenery about the town is picturesque and interesting. There is probably no interior town in the State that contains more valuable water privileges than Lyndon.

Boundaries. North by Sutton and Burke, east by Kirby, south by St. Johnsbury, and west by Wheelock.

First Settler. The settlement of the town was commenced by Daniel Cahoon, Jr., in 1788.

First Minister. A Congregational Church was organized in 1817, and settled the Rev. Samuel G. Tenney in 1825.

Productions of the Soil. Wheat, 3,370 bushels; Indian corn, 7,277 bushels; potatoes, 113,934 bushels; hay, 6,015 tons; maple sugar, 68,364 pounds; wool, 15,850 pounds.

Distances. Fourteen miles north-east from Danville, forty-four north-east from Montpelier, and about ten miles north from St. Johnsbury. The Railroad to Montreal passes through this town

MAIDSTONE.

ESSEX Co. This township is watered by Paul's Stream, which runs through the north part, and by Maidstone Lake, which is three miles long and half a mile wide, lying in the western part, and discharging its waters into Paul's Stream. The settlement here is mostly confined to the margin of Connecticut River, along which a road passes through the township.

The settlement of this township was probably commenced about the year 1770.

Boundaries. Northerly by Brunswick, easterly by Connecticut River, which separates it from Northumberland, N. H., southerly by Guildhall and a part of Granby, and westerly by Ferdinand.

Productions of the Soil. Wheat, 853 bushels; Indian corn, 962 bushels; potatoes, 15,310 bushels; hay, 863 tons; maple sugar, 11,200 pounds; wool, 3,356 pounds.

Distances. Three miles north from Guildhall, and seventy-one north-east from Montpelier.

MANCHESTER.

BENNINGTON Co. One of the county towns. Situated between the Green Mountains on the east, and Equinox Mountain on the west. The latter is 3,706 feet above the sea. There are two neat villages in this valley; the county buildings are in the south village. The scenery here is very beautiful. The town is watered by the Battenkill and its branches, and affords good mill sites.

The soil along the water courses is good, but the principal part of the town is better for grazing than tillage. Here are large quarries of beautiful marble, some manufactures, and a curious cavern.

There are a variety of minerals in Manchester.

Boundaries. North by Dorset, east by Winhall, south by Sunderland, and west by Sandgate.

First Settlers. The settlement of Manchester was commenced in 1764, by Samuel Rose and others, from Dutchess County, N. Y.

Productions of the Soil. Wheat, 1,481

bushels; Indian corn, 5,764 bushels; potatoes, 30,576 bushels; hay, 3,553 tons; maple sugar, 34,950 pounds; wool, 23,010 pounds.

Distances. Twenty-five miles north by east from Bennington, and about forty west from Bellows Falls across the mountains.

MANSFIELD.

LAMOILLE Co. This rough and mountainous township was annexed to *Stowe* in 1848.

MARLBOROUGH.

WINDHAM Co. The town is well watered by the west branch of West River, Whetstone Brook, and Green River. It has a good soil, and is very productive in wheat, rye, and other grain, fruit and potatoes.

Here are a pleasant village, several fine trout ponds, various kinds of minerals and medicinal springs. Marlborough suffered some by the Indians, and did much for the cause of independence.

Boundaries. North by Newfane, and a part of Dover, east by Brattleborough, and a part of Dummerston, south by Halifax, and west by Wilmington.

First Settlers. The settlement was commenced as early as the spring of 1763, by Abel Stockwell, from West Springfield, Mass., and Thomas Whitmore, from Middletown, Ct. Whitmore came in by the way of Halifax, and settled in the south part of the town, and Stockwell by the way of Brattleborough, and settled in the eastern border. These families spent nearly a year in town, and endured many hardships, without any knowledge of each other, each considering his own the only family in town. Whitmore brought his provisions from Deerfield, Mass., on his back, distance from twenty to thirty miles. Mrs. Whitmore spent most of the winter of 1765 alone, her husband being absent in the pursuit of his calling, as a tinker. Mrs. Whitmore was very useful to the settlers, both as a nurse and a midwife. She possessed a vigorous constitution, and frequently travelled through the woods on snow shoes, from one part of the town to another, both by night and day, to relieve the distressed. She lived to the advanced age of eighty-seven years, officiated as midwife at more than 2,000 births, and never lost a patient.

First Ministers. A Congregational Church was organized in this town by Rev. Joseph Lyman, of Hatfield, Mass., in 1776, and in 1778 the Rev. Gershom C. Lyman was settled over it.

Productions of the Soil. Wheat, 857 bushels; Indian corn, 2,982 bushels; potatoes, 51,648 bushels; hay, 3,695 tons; maple sugar, 23,545 pounds; wool, 8,439 pounds.

Distances. Eight miles south from Newfane, and twenty-four east from Bennington.

MARSHFIELD.

WASHINGTON Co. The surface of this township is very uneven. That part of it west of the river is timbered with hard wood, and the soil is good. East of the river the timber consists principally of evergreens, and the surface is broken, wet and stony. The town is watered principally by Winooski River. Here, in this stream, is a fall, said to be 500 feet in the distance of thirty rods. A good view of it may be had from the road leading from Marshfield to Cabot, and it is worthy the attention of the traveller. In the north-east part of the town is a considerable natural pond. The rocks are principally slate and granite. In the north part of the town is a pleasant village.

Boundaries. Northerly by Cabot, easterly by Peacham, and Harris' Gore, southerly by Plainfield, and westerly by Calais and part of Montpelier.

First Settlers. The town was granted to the Stockbridge tribe of Indians, October 16, 1782, and chartered to them June 22, 1790, containing 23,040 acres. The township was purchased of the Indians by Isaac Marsh, Esq., of Stockbridge, Mass., from whom the town derives its name, for 140*l.* lawful money, and was deeded to him,

July 29, 1789. The deed was signed by eighteen Indians, who were then residents of New Stockbridge, in Montgomery County, N. Y. The improvements were commenced here in the spring of 1790, by Martin and Calvin Pitkin from East Hartford, Ct. They left the town in the fall, and returned again the succeeding spring, accompanied by Gideon Spencer. Thus, they continued to spend the summer here, and abandon the township in the winter till 1794. This year, Caleb Pitkin, Gideon Spencer, and Aaron Elmore moved their families here in the winter, while the snow was more than four feet deep. In the summer they were joined by Ebenezer Dodge and family. John Preston Davis, son of Ebenezer Dodge, was born September 17, of this year, and was the first child born in town.

Productions of the Soil. Wheat, 2,351 bushels; Indian corn, 3,202 bushels; potatoes, 50,256 bushels; hay, 3,966 tons; maple sugar, 14,790 pounds; wool, 6,731 pounds.

Distances. Fifteen miles north-east from Montpelier.

MENDON.

RUTLAND Co. There is some good land in the town, but it is generally too high up the Green Mountains for cultivation.

Boundaries. Northerly by Chittenden, easterly by Sherburne, southerly by Shrewsbury, and west by Rutland.

First Settlers. Mendon was chartered to Joseph Banker and others, Feb. 23, 1781, by the name of Medway. Parker's Gore was annexed to it, and the whole incorporated into a township by the name of Parkerstown, Nov. 7, 1804; and Nov. 6, 1827, the name was altered to Mendon.

Productions of the Soil. Wheat, 385 bushels; Indian corn, 1,658 bushels; potatoes, 7,897 bushels; hay, 1,013 tons; maple sugar, 11,961 pounds; wool, 4,533 pounds.

Distances. Forty-seven miles south south-west from Montpelier. The great Southern Railroad passes through the neighboring town of Rutland.

MIDDLEBURY.

ADDISON Co. Chief town. This is a large and flourishing town on both sides of Otter Creek. The surface of the town is generally level. Chipman's Hill, 439 feet above Otter Creek, is the highest elevation.

The soil is fertile and productive, and furnishes large quantities of wool, beef, pork, butter, and cheese. The town is admirably watered by Otter Creek and Middlebury River. At the falls on Otter Creek, the site of the flourishing village, are extensive manufacturing establishments; and large quantities of white and variegated marble, with which the town abounds, are sawed and polished for various uses and transported to market. Middlebury is a very beautiful town, and the mart of a large inland trade.

Nearly on the line between this township and Salisbury, is a bed of the sulphuret of iron, connected with the carbonate of lime. It is thought to exist in large quantities and has a powerful effect upon the magnetic needle.

Middlebury is a delightful place of residence, and has long been the site of considerable manufactures. The advantages of a great hydraulic power, united with a speedy conveyance, by railroad, cannot fail of rendering Middlebury one of the most important marts of trade and manufactures in the State. This is the site of a flourishing college.—See *Colleges.*

Boundaries. North by New Haven and Bristol, east by Ripton, south by Salisbury, and west by Cornwall and Weybridge.

First Settlers. The first clearing was commenced by Col. John Chipman, in 1766, on the north bank of Middlebury River, where the west and centre road from Salisbury now unite. At this time there was no dwelling-house in the State, on the west side of the mountains, north of Manchester, distant sixty miles from Middlebury. The prospects were so discouraging that Mr. C. soon returned to Connecticut, and did not visit the township during the seven succeeding years. In 1773, Col. Chipman and the Hon. Gamaliel Painter,

from Salisbury, Ct., determined to risk their all in effecting a settlement of this township. They came into the town in May of this year with their families, and threw up a small log hut for a shelter from the weather. Benjamin Smalley had previously commenced and built a log house, which was the first house built here. Chipman located himself on the lot which he had commenced clearing seven years before, and Painter erected his habitation near the road leading to Salisbury, on the west bank of Middlebury River, near a spot of alluvial land, which had been an Indian encampment. On this spot are found numerous articles of Indian manufacture, such as arrows, hammers, &c., some being made of flint, others of jasper. A pot composed of sand and clay, of curious workmanship and holding about twenty quarts, was dug up here nearly entire in 1820.

First Ministers. A Congregational Church was organized in 1790. It was placed the same year under the pastoral care of the Rev. John Barnet, who was dismissed in 1795. The Rev. T. A. Merrill was settled in 1805. The Episcopal Church was organized in 1810.

Productions of the Soil. Wheat, 2,310 bushels; Indian corn, 7,500 bushels; potatoes, 23,023 bushels; hay, 8,900 tons; maple sugar, 1,200 pounds; wool, 52,300 pounds.

Distances. Thirty five miles southwest from Montpelier, and thirty-three south south-east from Burlington. The great Southern Railroad between Boston and Burlington passes through the town.

MIDDLESEX.

WASHINGTON Co. The south part of Middlesex is watered by Winooski River, which furnishes here one of the best stands for mills in the county. The north branch of this river runs across the north-east corner of the town.

Middlesex is uneven, but the only mountain of consequence lies along the line between the town and Water-

8

bury, and is called the Hogback. The timber is such as is common to the mountain towns, and the soil generally good. There are some fine intervales along the river, but the flats are not extensive.

The channel worn through the rocks by Winooski River, between this township and Moretown, is a considerable curiosity. It is about thirty feet in depth, sixty in width, and eighty rods in length, the rocks appearing like a wall upon each side. Over this chasm a bridge is thrown, which is perfectly secure from floods. But little is yet known of the mineralogy. Some fine specimens of rock crystal have been picked up.

On the bank of the Winooski River at the falls, near the middle of the south line of Middlesex is a flourishing village.

Boundaries. Northerly by Worcester, easterly by Montpelier, southerly by Moretown, from which it is separated by Winooski River, and westerly by Waterbury.

First Settlers. Mr. Thomas Mead was the first settler of this township, and also the first settler of Washington County. He began improvements in Middlesex in 1781 or '82, and the next year moved his family here from Chelmsford, Mass. Mr. Harrington moved his family into town the year following, and two Messrs. Putnams the year after. The town was organized about the year 1788.

Productions of the Soil. Wheat, 2,182 bushels; Indian corn, 3,708 bushels; potatoes, 32,395 bushels; hay, 3,206 tons; maple sugar, 18,117 pounds; wool, 5,045 pounds.

Distances. Six miles north-west from Montpelier. The great Northern Railroad passes through the town.

MIDDLETOWN.

RUTLAND Co. This town lies between two mountains, is watered by Poultney River, and has a good soil for grazing. It has a neat and flourishing village, with some manufacturing establishments.

Boundaries. North-west by Poult-ney, north-east by Ira, south-east by Tinmouth, and south-west by Wells.

First Settlers. A settlement was commenced here and mills erected a short time before the Revolution, by Thomas Morgan and others.

First Minister. A Congregational Church was organized about 1784, and the Rev. Henry Bigelow was settled over it in 1805 till his death in 1832.

Productions of the Soil. Wheat, 1,108 bushels; Indian corn, 3,057 bushels; potatoes, 18,040 bushels; hay, 2,947 tons; maple sugar, 9,820 pounds; wool, 17,640 pounds.

Distances. Fourteen miles south-west from Rutland, and forty-five north from Bennington.

MILTON.

CHITTENDEN Co. Milton is bounded on the west by Lake Champlain, and is finely watered by the River Lamoille. The soil of the town is generally good. There are some places in Milton worthy of the traveller's notice. A little distance from the neat and flourishing village are the Great Falls, on the Lamoille. In the course of fifty rods the whole river falls 150 feet. About the middle of the rapid is a small island, by which the water passes on each side, with great violence and loud roaring. The scenery on the banks of the river is wild and beautiful. There are some mills on the river, and considerable trade on the lake.

There is another pleasant village two miles west of the falls, called Checker-Berry. The water power of this town is so immense, and the facilities afforded it by Lake Champlain for an extensive commerce, together with the improved power of steam which it will shortly possess, and seated in a fertile and healthy region, will, doubtless, render this place a site of important business. A bridge is now constructing (1849) called the Sand Bar Bridge, connecting this town with South Hero.

Boundaries. North by Georgia, east by Westford, south by Colchester, and west by Lake Champlain.

First Settlers. The settlement of

Milton was commenced Feb. 15, 1782, by William Irish, Leonard Owen, Amos Mansfield, Absalom Taylor, and Thos. Dewey; and they were soon after joined by Gideon Hoxsie, Zebadiah Dewey, Enoch and Elisha Ashley, and others. The first settlers suffered many privations and hardships, but there is nothing in the early history which is peculiarly interesting.

First Minister. Rev. Joseph Cheney was ordained over the Congregational Church in 1807; dismissed in 1817.

Productions of the Soil. Wheat, 4,425 bushels; Indian corn, 16,603 bushels; potatoes, 49,791 bushels; hay, 5,978 tons; maple sugar, 19,204 pounds; wool, 31,686 pounds.

Distances. Twelve miles north from Burlington, and forty north-west from Montpelier. The Burlington and Montreal Railroad passes through the town.

MONKTON.

ADDISON Co. The western part of the town is watered by Little Otter Creek, and the eastern part by Pond Brook, which rises from a considerable pond nearly on the line between Monkton and Bristol, and runs north through the township into Lewis Creek in Hinesburgh. Lewis Creek also runs a short distance in the north-eastern part. These streams afford but few mill privileges. Monkton Pond lies in the north part of the town, and is about a mile in length and half a mile wide. A mountain called the Hogback, extends along the eastern boundary of Monkton, and there are several other considerable elevations. "Iron ore is found in the south part of this township in large quantities. The color of the surface of this ore is a velvet black, and that of the interior a brownish black. Its structure is fibrous and commonly radiated. This ore makes excellent iron, and is extensively manufactured at Bristol and other places. Connected with the iron ore, is found the black oxyde of manganese.

"About a mile north of the iron ore bed, on the east side of a ridge of land running north and south, is an extensive bed of kaolin, or porcelain earth. It is white, sometimes grayish white; dry to the touch, and absorbs water with rapidity. It is evidently decomposed feldspar, or rather, graphic granite, as these substances are found in the bed, in all stages of decomposition, from the almost entire stone, down to the finest and purest porcelain earth. It might be manufactured into the best China ware. The quantity is immense, sufficient to supply the world with this ware for centuries. By mixing this earth with common clay in different proportions, various kinds of pottery are produced." "In the south part of this township is a pond, curiously located on the summit of a considerable hill. In the north-western part is a remarkable cavern. The orifice, by which it is entered, is at the bottom of a large chasm in the rocks on the side of a small hill. After descending about sixteen feet, you arrive at a room thirty feet long and sixteen wide. From this is a passage leading to a second apartment, which is not quite so large but more pleasant."

Boundaries. North by Hinesburgh and Charlotte, east by Starksborough, south by Bristol, and west by Ferrisburgh.

First Settlers. Monkton was settled in 1774, by John and Ebenezer Stearns, Barnabas Burnham, and John Bishop. They left during the war, but returned in 1784.

Productions of the Soil. Wheat, 1,840 bushels; Indian corn, 7,430 bushels; potatoes, 39,340 bushels; hay, 5,708 tons; maple sugar, 9,340 pounds; wool, 18,940 pounds.

Distances. Twenty-seven miles west from Montpelier, and sixteen north from Middlebury. The great Northern Railroad passes through the town.

MONTGOMERY.

FRANKLIN Co. This town lies in a mountainous country, but it has a valuable tract of land on Trout River, a good mill stream, a branch of the Missisco.

Boundaries. North by Richford, east

by Westfield, south by Lowell and
Avery's Gore, and west by Enosburgh.

First Settlers. Montgomery was
granted March 13, 1780, and chartered
October 8, 1789, to Stephen R. Bradley and others. Capt. Joshua Clap, a
respectable revolutionary officer, removed his family from Worcester
County, Mass., into this town, in March,
1793, and this was for two years the
only family in town. Hon. Samuel
Barnard, Reuben Clap, and James Upham, Esq., all from Mass., were among
the earliest settlers.

First Minister. A Congregational
Church was organized in 1802, over
which the Rev. Avery Ware was settled in 1825.

Productions of the Soil. Wheat, 1,110
bushels; Indian corn, 1,344 bushels;
potatoes, 26,425 bushels; hay, 1,498
tons; maple sugar, 23,875 pounds;
wool, 3,797 pounds.

Distances. Fifty miles north from
Montpelier, and twenty-seven east
north-east from St. Albans.

MONTPELIER.

Washington Co. **Montpelier** is
the county town, and capital of the
State. The township is watered by the
Winooski River, which runs through
the south-east corner, and along the
southern boundary by the Little North
Branch, which crosses the south-west
corner, by Kingsbury Branch, which
crosses the north-east corner, and by
several smaller streams. The mill
privileges are both good and numerous.

The surface of the town is uneven,
but the soil is very warm, is uncom-
monly fine, and there is scarcely an
acre of waste land in Montpelier,—the
most of it richly, and all of it fairly
rewarding the labors of the industrious
farmer. The prevailing character of
the rocks is slate and lime, sometimes
distinct, but more generally combined.
Rare minerals have not been found
here, unless the sulphurets of iron,
copper, and talc, which are common
in the slate rocks, be reckoned. Some

years ago there was a company formed and a charter obtained, for boring
for salt; and, by the aid of machinery,
a hole was perforated to the depth of
800 feet, through a solid rock, below
the falls on Winooski River, but no
salt water obtained. From the sedi-
ment drawn up, it appeared that the
rock, the slate limestone, preserved its
character, with an occasional layer of
flint or sand stone, through the whole
of that depth; and one or two
springs, impregnated with iron, which
were come across in the course of the
drilling, were the only discoveries
made, till the project was relinquished.

Montpelier Village, incorporated in
1818, embracing a square mile, and in
the south-west corner of the township,
on the bank of Winooski River, and
on both sides of the Little North
Branch. It is about ten miles north-
easterly from the geographical centre
of the State, and, besides being the
point of intersection of the roads from
all parts, is the great thoroughfare between the ocean and Canada; the travel
going through not only in this, but in
all directions. The situation is low,
but the streets and building ground
have been raised so much, that it is
now as dry as other places of the like
soil. The whole site of this village
bears unequivocal evidence of having
been the bed of a lake about forty feet
deep, the original surface of the water
being indicated by the strata of earth
and rocks on all the surrounding hills,
and the whole having been drained,
probably, by the deepening of the
channel at Middlesex Narrows. The
place has had a rapid growth, and is
now one of the most flourishing interior villages in New England.

The public buildings are, the beautiful
and durable State House, built under
the superintendence of A. B. Young,
architect, in 1836-7, which is superior,
perhaps, to any State House in the
Union, unless we except the recent
one in North Carolina,—a court house,
jail, a brick academy, a spacious brick
meeting house, and two handsome
wooden ones. The academy, or county
grammar school, was incorporated Nov.
7, 1800, and is now a flourishing institu-

tion, with a library, philosophical apparatus, &c.

Montpelier has already become a place of considerable manufacture and trade, by the laudable enterprize of its citizens; but the passage of a railroad within its borders, uniting a large and fertile country with the Atlantic shores, is a new era in the history of the town, and will be found to accomplish very important services, both to the town and its enterprising projectors.—See *Public Buildings.*

A manufacturing company was incorporated at Montpelier in 1847.

Boundaries. Northerly by Calais, easterly by Plainfield and a small part of Marshfield, southerly by Berlin, from which it is separated by Winooski River, and a part of Barre, and westerly by Middlesex.

First Settlers. The first attempt to settle in this town was made in the spring of 1786, when Joel Frizzle, a hunter and trapper, felled a few trees, planted a little corn among the logs, after the Indian fashion, and erected a very small log cabin on the bank of Winooski River, in the south-west corner of this township, and moved his family, himself and wife, a little French woman, into it. from Canada, the same season. But the first permanent clearing and settlement was not made till the spring after. On the 4th of May, 1787, Col. Jacob Davis and Gen. Parly Davis, from Charlton, Worcester Co., Mass., with one hired man and one horse, each loaded with pork, flour, beans, and other necessaries, came and settled.

First Ministers. The religious denominations in this town are two societies of Congregationalists, and one each of Methodists, Universalists, and Friends.

Productions of the Soil. Wheat, 3,652 bushels; Indian corn, 7,630 bushels; potatoes, 66,860 bushels; hay, 7,205 tons; maple sugar, 67,070 pounds; wool, 12,941 pounds.

Distances. It is one hundred and eighty-two miles west from Augusta, Me; ninety-seven north north-west from Concord, N. H.; one hundred and sixty north-west by north from Boston, Mass.; two hundred north by

west from Providence, R. I.; two hundred and five north from Hartford, Ct., one hundred and forty-eight north-east from Albany, N. Y.; and five hundred and twenty four miles from Washington.

The above distances are by the old mail routes, and vary some by the new mode of travelling by railroads.

The Iron Horse paid his first visit to this beautiful mountain town in the autumn of 1848, and is determined to press his course northward in the most amicable manner, to induce the Canadians to make the Atlantic shores of New England the deposit of a large share of their great and increasing commerce.

MORETOWN.

WASHINGTON Co. Mad River, a branch of the Winooski, waters this town, and gives it good mill sites. The surface is mountainous, and a great part of the soil unfit for cultivation.

Boundaries. Northerly by Middlesex and a part of Waterbury, from which it is separated by Winooski River, easterly by Berlin, southerly by Waitsfield, and westerly by Duxbury.

First Settlers. The settlement of this township was commenced about the year 1790, and the town was organized three or four years after.

Productions of the Soil. Wheat, 1,735 bushels; Indian corn, 4,104 bushels; potatoes, 38,848 bushels; hay, 3,171 tons; maple sugar, 28,791 pounds; wool, 6,570 pounds.

Distances. Thirteen miles south-west from Montpelier. The great Northern Railroad passes in this vicinity.

MORGAN.

ORLEANS Co. The surface of the town consists of swells and valleys, and is mostly susceptible of cultivation. Timber generally hard wood. Soil good. A head branch of Clyde River, called Farrand's River, passes through the east part of Morgan; and Seymour's Lake, which is about four miles long and nearly two wide, lies in the central part. It discharges its waters

to the south, through Echo Pond, into Clyde River.

Boundaries. North by Holland and a part of Derby, easterly by Wenlock and Warner's Gore, and south-west by Charleston and Salem.

First Settler. The settlement of this township was commenced about the the year 1800 by Nathan Wilcox.

First Minister. A Congregational Church was organized here in 1823.

Productions of the Soil. Wheat, 1,617 bushels; Indian corn, 303 bushels; potatoes, 17,675 bushels; hay, 1,037 tons; maple sugar, 16,102 pounds; wool, 1,889 pounds.

Distances. Eighteen miles north-east from Irasburgh, and sixty-north-east from Montpelier.

MORRISTOWN.

LAMOILLE Co.   The soil of this town is of a good quality, and easily cultivated.   Morristown is, in point of agricultural products, the second in the county.   The timber is maple, beech, birch, hemlock, &c.   The Lamoille River enters the town near the north-east corner, passing by Morrisville and Cadysville, and after running four miles in the north part of the town, returns into Hydepark.   Along this river, in Morristown, are some fine tracts of intervale, and on it are two excellent mill sites.   There are several other streams in town on which mills are erected.

Morrisville is a pleasant, flourishing village, situated near the Great Falls. Here is one of the finest situations for manufacturing establishments which the State affords.   At the falls a few rods west of the village, may be found curious specimens of the wonder working power of water, in wearing holes into the solid rock, some of which are nearly eight feet deep and four feet broad.   The river at this place pours itself into a channel cut directly across the stream, twenty feet deep and thirty broad.   This channel the early settlers denominated the *pulpit*, from the resemblance of the rocks at the north end to that structure.   On the west side of this chasm the rocks rise per-pendicularly to the height of thirty feet; and the beholder, while standing on the edge of this precipice, sees the whole body of the river plunged down at his feet into this boiling cauldron, from which it escapes through a channel at the south end, and immediately spreading itself out, encircles numerous islands, whose high, jagged points are covered with a thick growth of cedar and fir, and altogether presenting a scene of grandeur and beauty seldom found surpassed.   Cadysville is situated two miles below Morrisville, and bids fair to become a place of considerable business.   At the centre of the town is a small village, pleasantly located, and wanting only the facilities of water power, to make it the principal place of business.   In the south-east corner of the town is a pond called *Joe's* Pond, from an old Indian pensioner who lived by the side of it.

The People's Academy, in this town, was incorporated in 1847.

Boundaries. Northerly by Hydepark, easterly by Elmore, southerly by Stowe, and westerly by Sterling.

First Settlers. This settlement was commenced in the spring of 1790, by Mr. Jacob Walker, who came from Bennington.

First Minister. The first sermon preached in town was by the Rev. Mr. Bogue, a missionary, in the summer of 1798.

Productions of the Soil. Wheat, 3,454 bushels; Indian corn, 5,614 bushels; potatoes, 66,720 bushels; hay, 5,095 tons; maple sugar, 44,120 pounds; wool, 8,342 pounds.

Distances. Three miles south from Hydepark, and thirty miles north from Montpelier.

MOUNT HOLLY.

RUTLAND Co.   Mill River, which rises in the south part of this township, and runs through the north-east corner of Wallingford and the south-west corner of Shrewsbury, and unites with Otter Creek in Clarendon, is the only stream of consequence.   In the north-eastern part is a considerable pond, called *Palches Pond.*   In soil and timber it is similar to the mountain towns generally, being much better adapted to the production of grass than grain. On the summit of the Green Mountains is found amianthus, common and ligniform asbestos, and fossil leather. Its color is a grayish white, and it is very abundant. Ludlow mountain is a considerable elevation, lying along the line between Mount Holly and Ludlow.

Boundaries. North by Plymouth and Shrewsbury, east by Ludlow, south by Weston, and west by Wallingford and a part of Mount Tabor.

First Settlers. The settlement of Mount Holly was commenced in 1781, by Ichabod G., Stephen, and John Clark, Jonah, Amos, and Ebenezer Ives, from Connecticut, Jacob Wilcox, from Rhode Island, and Joseph Green, David Bent, Abraham Crowly, and Nathaniel Pingrey, from Massachusetts.

First Minister. Elder Parker was settled over the Baptist Church, in 1811.

Productions of the Soil. Wheat, 1,832 bushels; Indian corn, 836 bushels; potatoes, 65,930 bushels; hay, 5.317 tons; maple sugar, 44,120 pounds; wool, 8,342 pounds.

Distances. Sixty miles south-west from Montpelier, and seventeen south-east from Rutland.

MOUNT TABOR.

RUTLAND Co. Otter Creek rises in this town, by a branch on each side of a mountain. Most of the land is unfit for cultivation, it being so high on the Green Mountain range.

Although the surface of the town is elevated and uneven, it affords good pasturage for cattle. The town was chartered in 1761. A part of Danby was annexed to it in 1848.

Boundaries. North by Wallingford, east by Weston and a part of Mount Holly, south by Peru, and west by Danby.

Productions of the Soil. Wheat, 329 bushels; Indian corn, 390 bushels; potatoes, 6,000 bushels; hay, 550 tons;

maple sugar, 3,585 pounds; wool, 1,760 pounds.

Distances. Sixty-six miles south by west from Montpelier, and nineteen south by east from Rutland.

NEWARK.

CALEDONIA Co. The Passumpsic River is formed in this town by a collection of streams issuing principally from ponds. The town is not mountainous, but the soil is cold and generally unproductive. The settlement of this town commenced about the year 1800.

Boundaries. North-easterly by Brighton, south-easterly by East Haven, south-westerly by Burke and Sutton, and north-westerly by Westmore.

Productions of the Soil. Wheat, 1,756 bushels; Indian corn, 315 bushels; potatoes, 18,260 bushels; hay, 801 tons; maple sugar, 21,813 pounds; wool, 1,679 pounds.

Distances. Twenty-six miles northeast from Danville, and fifty-six northeast from Montpelier.

NEWBURY.

ORANGE Co. This is a beautiful town on the west side of Connecticut River, and supplied with mill privileges by Wells River, and Hariman's and Hill's Brooks. These brooks have their sources in ponds of considerable size.

Newbury comprises the tract commonly called the Great Oxbow, on a bend in Connecticut River. This tract is of great extent, and celebrated for its luxuriance and beauty. The agricultural productions of the town are very valuable, consisting of beef cattle, wool, and all the varieties of the dairy. The town contains a number of mineral springs, of some celebrity in scrofulous and cutaneous complaints.

The villages of *Newbury and Wells River* are very pleasant; they command a flourishing trade, and contain manufacturing establishments of various kinds. Some of the buildings are very handsome. The scenery of the windings of the river through this fine tract of alluvial meadow, contrasted with the abrupt acclivities in the north part of the town, is very striking and beautiful.

The town is connected with Haverhill, N. H. by two bridges.

Newbury village is the site of a well conducted seminary, under the patronage of the Methodist Episcopal Church; but it is open to all denominations.

The Newbury Steam Manufacturing Company was incorporated in 1848.

Boundaries. North by Ryegate, east by Connecticut River, which separates it from Haverhill, N. H., south by Bradford, and west by Topsham.

First Settlers. The settlement of this township was commenced in the spring of 1762. The first family was that of Samuel Sleeper. The next were the families of Thomas and Richard Chamberlain. John Hazleton also moved his family to Newbury in 1762, and his daughter Betsey, born in 1763, was the first child born in town. Jacob Bailey Chamberlain, son of Thomas C., born the same year, was the first male child. The parents of the latter received a bounty of 100 acres of land, agreeably to a promise of the proprietors of the township. Among the first settlers, in addition to the above, may be mentioned Gen. Jacob Bayley, Col. Jacob Kent, Col. Thomas Johnson, John Taplin, Noah and Ebenezer White, Frye Bayley, and James Abbott. The early inhabitants were mostly emigrants from the south-eastern parts of New Hampshire, and from Newbury, Mass. They had peculiar hardships to endure, there being no inhabitants on Connecticut River, at this time, north of No. 4, now Charlestown, N. H., or between this place and Concord. Nor were there any roads through the wilderness, or anything, but marked trees, to facilitate the communication between this and the civilized settlements. The nearest mill was at Charlestown, distant more than sixty miles. To that they went for their grinding, carrying their grain down the river in canoes during the summer, and drawing it upon the ice in the winter. The crank, for the first saw mill built in Newbury, was drawn from

Concord, N. H., distant nearly eighty miles, upon a hand-sled. Gen. Bayley was very active in forwarding the settlement of this part of the country, and distinguished himself as a general officer in the revolutionary war.

First Minister. The Congregational Church of this town was formed at Hollis, Mass., in September, 1764. The Rev. Peter Powers, the first minister of Newbury, was installed over this church Feb. 27, 1765, and he preached his own installation sermon.

Productions of the Soil. Wheat, 6,358 bushels; Indian corn, 11,297 bushels; potatoes, 91,689 bushels; hay, 5,616 tons; maple sugar, 32,755 pounds; wool, 20,758 pounds.

Distances. Twenty-seven miles southeast from Montpelier, and twenty northeast from Chelsea. The Connecticut River Railroad passes through this town.

NEWFANE.

WINDHAM Co. County town. The town is watered by a branch of West River, and several other streams. The surface of the town is diversified by hills and valleys; the soil is good, and produces white oak and walnut in abundance. There is but little waste land in the town; the uplands are inferior to none for grazing, and the intervales afford excellent tillage. Newfane exhibits a great variety of minerals, among which are some of value. Perhaps no town in the State presents a more inviting field for the mineralogist than this.

There are two pleasant villages in the town. The centre village contains the county buildings; it is on elevated land, and commands a very extensive and delightful prospect.

Boundaries. North by Townshend, east by Dummerston, Putney, and Brookline, west by Wardsborough and Dover, and south by Marlborough.

First Settlers. The settlement of this town was commenced in the month of May, 1766, by Dea. Jonathan Park, Nathaniel Stedman, and Ebenezer Dyer, who emigrated from Worcester County, Mass.

First Minister. A Congregational Church was formed in 1774, and Mr. Taylor was ordained over it the same year.

Productions of the Soil. Wheat, 973 bushels; Indian corn, 6,472 bushels; potatoes, 37,564 bushels; hay, 3,584 tons; maple sugar, 14,505 pounds; wool, 9,663 pounds.

Distances. One hundred miles south from Montpelier, and twelve northwest from Brattleborough.

NEW HAVEN.

ADDISON CO. The soil of this town is various, consisting of marl, clay and loam, and is generally productive. The waters of Otter Creek, Middlebury River, and Little Otter Creek give the town a good water power. There are some manufactures in the town, but agriculture is the chief pursuit of the inhabitants. Quarries of excellent marble are found in almost every part of this town.

Boundaries. North by Bristol and Ferrisburgh, east by Bristol, south by Middlebury and Weybridge, and west by Addison and Waltham.

First Settlers. The settlement of New Haven was commenced in 1769, by a few emigrants from Salisbury, Ct., on that part which is now set off to Waltham. The settlement was, however, broken up and abandoned in '76, in consequence of the revolutionary war. Near this settlement, and on that part of the township, now constituting a part of the city of Vergennes, a fort was erected and garrisoned by troops, commanded by Capt. Ebenezer Allen, and others, to protect the frontier settlements from the common enemy the "Yorkers." At the close of the war the settlers returned, and in '85 the town was organized.

First Ministers. A Congregational Church was formed here in 1797, over which the Rev. Silas L. Bingham was installed in 1805.

Productions of the Soil. Wheat, 1,964 bushels; Indian corn, 10,368 bushels; potatoes, 59,482 bushels; hay, 9,867 tons; maple sugar, 9,468 pounds; wool, 59,388 pounds.

Distances. Forty miles west southwest from Montpelier, and seven northwest from Middlebury. This town is easily approached by the Southern Railroad, which passes through Middlebury.

NEWPORT.

ORLEANS CO. Newport is separated from Derby by Memphremagog Lake, and is watered by a branch of Missisco River. The settlement of this township was begun before the year 1800.

Boundaries. North by Patton, Canada, east by Orleans and Memphremagog Lake, which separates it from Derby, south by Coventry Gore, and west by Troy.

Productions of the Soil. Wheat, 2,047 bushels; Indian corn, 1,034 bushels; potatoes, 21,080 bushels; hay, 1,224 tons; maple sugar, 33,920 pounds; wool, 2,527 pounds.

Distances. Ten miles north from Irasburgh, and fifty-two north-east from Montpelier.

NORTHFIELD.

WASHINGTON CO. The principal stream in this town is Dog River, which runs through it in a northerly direction, and affords a great number of valuable mill privileges. The timber is hemlock, spruce, maple, beech and birch, intermingled with fir, pine, ash, butternut, &c. The soil is generally good, and in many places, is easily cultivated. A range of argillaceous slate passes through the township from south to north. The surface is uneven, and a range of high lands passes from north to south through the town, both on the eastern and western side of the river. There are four villages in this town, in which are considerable manufacturing operations. The railroad between Boston and Burlington which passes here will greatly enhance the value of real estate in this and the neighboring towns. The Northfield Manufacturing Company was incorporated in 1848.

First Settlers. The first settlement was made here in 1785, by Amos and

Ezekiel Robinson, and Staunton Richardson, from Westminster. The first land was cleared by Hon. Elijah Paine.

First Ministers. There are a number of ordained ministers of various denominations in the town, but the dates of their settlement are not stated.

Productions of the Soil. Wheat, 7,159 bushels; Indian corn, 4,362 bushels; potatoes, 57,367 bushels; hay, 3,862 tons; maple sugar, 24,515 pounds; wool, 15,057 pounds.

Distances. Ten miles south-west from Montpelier. The great Northern Railroad between Boston and Burlington passes through the town.

NORTH HERO.

GRAND ISLE Co. The soil of North Hero is of an excellent quality, and produces grain of all kinds in abundance. It has no streams of any consequence, and no mills or mill privileges. Its public buildings are a stone court house and jail. This is the shire town of Grand Isle County.

First Settlers. The settlement of this township was commenced in 1783, by Enos and Solomon Wood, the former from Bennington, in this State, and the latter from Norwich, Ct. The British erected a block house here, at a place called Dutchman's Point, which was garrisoned, and not given up till 1796, The town was organized in 1789.

Productions of the Soil. Wheat, 4,005 bushels; Indian corn, 3,127 bushels; potatoes, 14,525 bushels; hay, 1,317 tons; maple sugar, 5,185 pounds; wool, 8,044 pounds.

Distances. Fifty-seven miles north-west from Montpelier, and twenty-eight north north-west from Burlington.

NORTON.

ESSEX Co. An uninhabited township in the north-west corner of Essex County. It is twelve miles long from east to west, and four from north to south. The land is said to be good and well timbered, considerable tracts of it with pine. The charter of the township was burnt, and it is difficult getting a valid title to the lands. There are two considerable ponds lying partly in the town. The outlet of Norton Pond is the head branch of Coatacook River, which unites with the Masuippi, in Ascot, and then unites with the St. Francis, at Lenoxville. Farrand's River, also, heads here and runs south.

Boundaries. North by Bradford and Barnston, Canada, east by Averill, south by Avery's, Warner's, and Warren's Gore, and west by Holland.

NORWICH.

WINDSOR Co. The Connecticut River washes the eastern boundary of this township, and is from thirty to forty rods in width. It is fordable in three places at low water. Ompomponoosuc River enters Norwich from Thetford, two miles west of Connecticut River, and, after running three miles across the north-east corner, mingles its waters with those of the Connecticut. It is a rapid stream, with a gravelly bottom, about six rods in width, and affords several eligible mill sites. Bloody Brook arises wholly in this township, and, passing a little westerly of Norwich Plain, falls into the Connecticut just below the bridge leading from Norwich to Dartmouth College. On this stream are several excellent mill sites. It is said to have had its name from a bloody battle fought here during the French war.

The surface of the township is uneven, but nearly all admits of cultivation. It produces all kinds of grain and grass, and some of the finest orchards in the State. Extensive beds of iron ore are found in the north-west corner of the town.

On the bank of Connecticut River, about seventy rods above the mouth of the Ompomponoosuc, is an Indian burying ground, where human bones, stone pots, arrows, &c., are frequently found. Between the Connecticut and the Ompomponoosuc is a high bluff, where explosions were formerly heard, like the report of cannon, to the great terror of the inhabitants.

Norwich village is pleasantly situated on a plain near Connecticut River, and is the site of the Norwich University, now given up. This is a beautiful town and a fine place for residence.

Boundaries. North by Thetford, east by Connecticut River, which separates it from Hanover, N. H., south by Hartford, and west by Sharon.

First Settlers. In 1762, the township was partly lotted, and the next year Jacob Fenton, Ebenezer Smith and John Slafter came here from Mansfield, Ct., built them a camp, and began improvements.

First Minister. The First Congregational Church was organized in 1770, and the Rev. Lyman Potter ordained over it in 1775.

Productions of the Soil. Wheat, 3,801 bushels; Indian corn, 11,119 bushels; potatoes, 53,480 bushels; hay, 5,265 tons; maple sugar, 15,730 pounds; wool, 27,639 pounds.

Distances. Forty miles south-east from Montpelier, and nineteen north from Windsor. The Connecticut River Railroad passes through the town; and the great Northern Railroad between Boston and Burlington passes through the neighboring town of Hartford.

ORANGE COUNTY.

CHELSEA is the chief town. This county is bounded north by Washington and Caledonia Counties, east by Connecticut River, south by Windsor County, and west by Addison and Washington Counties. The eastern range of the Green Mountains extends along the north-western part of the county. The principal rivers, besides the Connecticut, are the Ompomponoosuc, Wait's, branches of the White, and Stevens' branch of the Winooski.

The lands in Orange County are generally good for grazing, and supply many cattle and all the varieties of the dairy, of which a large amount is annually sent to market.

This county contains some excellent tracts of land on the banks of the Connecticut. Iron and lead ores, slate and granite, are abundant.

COURTS IN ORANGE COUNTY.

The *Supreme Court* commences its session at Chelsea on the fifth Tuesday after the fourth Tuesday in January, and the *County Court* on the third Tuesdays of June and December.

ORANGE.

ORANGE Co. Knox Mountain in the north-easterly part of the town is a considerable elevation, and affords inexhaustible quantities of granite for building stone. The timber is chiefly hard wood, except along the streams, where it is spruce, hemlock, cedar, pine and fir. The soil in some parts of the town, particularly on the heights, is rather cold and wet; in other parts and on the streams it is rich and productive.

The principal stream of water is Jail Branch. Coming from Washington, it receives a considerable stream from the north, called Cold Branch, and then passes into Barre. Orange possesses a large and valuable water power.

Boundaries. North by a part of Plainfield, Goshen, Harris' Gore and Groton, east by Topsham, south by a part of Corinth and Washington, and west by Barre.

First Settlers. The first settlement was commenced by Ensign Joseph Williams in 1793 on the south line of the town.

First Minister. The Rev. Enos Bliss was settled over the Congregational Church in 1799.

Productions of the Soil. Wheat, **2,048** bushels; Indian corn, 2,189 bushels; potatoes, 60,316 bushels; hay, **3,412** tons; maple sugar, 22,208 pounds; wool, 11,619 pounds.

Distances. Twelve miles south-east from Montpelier, and twelve north from Chelsea.

ORLEANS COUNTY.

IRASBURGH is the chief town. This county is bounded north by Lower Canada, east by Essex and Caledonia Counties, south by Caledonia County, and west by Franklin and Lamoille Counties. This county lies between the eastern and western ranges of the Green Mountains. The surface is generally handsome, and the soil well adapted for wheat, rye, and grass; the climate is rather too cold for corn, and some parts of the county are low and marshy.

Orleans County is watered by Missisco, Black, Barton, and other rivers. It contains more ponds than any county in the State. Much of its trade goes to Canada by the way of Memphremagog Lake, which lies in this county and Canada.—See *Tables.*

COURTS IN ORLEANS COUNTY.

The *Supreme Court* sits at Irasburgh, on the seventeenth Tuesday after the fourth Tuesday in December; and the *County Court* on the fourth Tuesday in June and December.

ORWELL.

ADDISON Co. Some of the land in this township is broken and hilly; the remaining part is very level, handsome land, and produces abundant crops of all kinds of grain.

The principal streams are East Creek, which rises in Benson and falls into Lake Champlain, on the north side of Mount Independence, and Lemonfair River, which here consists of two branches, running parallel with each other, along the eastern border, and uniting near the north line of the town. On these streams are several mill privileges, which are good during a part of the year. The waters, where the land is clayey, are slightly impregnated with Epsom salts, or the sulphate of magnesia. There is a spring on the lake shore, about 100 rods south from the north-west corner, the waters of which are strongly impregnated; and from these salts have been manufactured in considerable quantities.

In the compact limestone in this town are shells of various kinds. In the compact limestone on Mount Independence, flint is found. Specimens of blende, or the sulphuret of zinc, have also been found.

The width of the lake between Mt. Independence and Ticonderoga is about eighty rods. A mile further south, at a place called Sholes Landing, it is only forty rods wide. The average width of the lake against Orwell is about one mile, and the widest place two miles. May 13, 1820, a piece of land in the town, of more than five acres area, sunk about forty feet, and slid into the lake. The impulse made upon the water was so great, as to raise the lake three feet at the opposite shore, a mile and a half distant. The ground was partly covered with small trees, some of which moved off erect, while others were thrown down. A part of Benson was annexed to Orwell in 1847.

In common with most of the towns on Lake Champlain, the scenery in Orwell and its vicinity is truly delightful.

Boundaries. North by Shoreham, east by Sudbury and a part of Whiting, south by Benson, and west by Lake Champlain, being opposite to Ticonderoga, N. Y.

First Settlers. The first permanent settlement was made in 1783, by Amos Spafford, Shadrach Hathaway, Eber Murray, Ephraim and William Fisher, and John Charter, upon Mount Independence.

First Minister. Elder E. Phelps was settled over the Baptist Church, about the year 1789.

Productions of the Soil. Wheat, 3,702 bushels; Indian corn, 6,456 bushels; potatoes, 16,960 bushels; hay, 7,053 tons; maple sugar, 5,525 pounds; wool, 77,485 pounds.

Distances. Twenty miles north-west from Rutland, and forty-seven south-west from Montpelier.

PANTON.

ADDISON Co. Panton is bounded west by Champlain Lake, and east by Otter Creek. A sluggish stream passes through it; yet, although thus watered, it does not possess a good mill site, the country being exceedingly level.

A part of Ferrisburg was annexed to Panton in 1847.

Boundaries. North by Ferrisburgh,

east by Otter Creek, which separates it from Waltham, and by a part of Vergennes, south by Addison, and west by Lake Champlain.

First Settlers. A settlement was commenced here in 1770, by John Pangborn and Odle Squire, from Cornwall, Ct., who were soon joined by Timothy Spalding and others, from the same place, and by Peter Ferris, from Nine Partners, N. Y. Ferris settled at the bay where Arnold blew up his fleet during the revolution. The wrecks of this fleet are now to be seen here at low water. During the revolution this settlement was broken up. Most of the men were made prisoners, their dwellings burnt, and the women and children driven to the south. The settlers returned after the war, and in 1784 the town was organized.

First Minister. Elder Henry Chambers was ordained over the Baptist Church, in 1800, and dismissed in 1804.

Productions of the Soil. Wheat, 671 bushels; Indian corn, 2,334 bushels; potatoes, 5,722 bushels; hay, 2,971 tons; maple sugar, 22,022 pounds; wool, 24,890 pounds.

Distances. Forty miles west south-west from Montpelier, and thirteen north-west from Middlebury.

PAWLET.

RUTLAND Co. Pawlet River runs south-westerly nearly through the centre of the town, and Indian River, which runs the same course across the south-west corner. The latter rises from a spring of pure water, sufficiently large to carry a grist mill. It abounds in trout, and takes its name from the great number of Indians who formerly resorted here for the purpose of fishing. Pawlet is divided nearly in the centre by a range of mountains, extending through it from south to north. The most remarkable summit is a little north of the centre, and is called Haystack Mountain. The soil is dry and warm, easily cultivated, and produces good crops of grain and grass.

Boundaries. North by Wells, east

by Danby, south by Rupert, and west by Granville, N. Y.

First Settlers. The settlement of the town was commenced in 1761, by Simeon Barton and Wm. Fairfield.

First Ministers. A Congregational Church was organized August 8, 1781. The Rev. Lewis Beebe, the first settled minister, was settled over it from June 14, 1787, to May 6, 1791; the Rev. John Griswold, from Oct. 23, 1793, to Aug. 11, 1830.

Productions of the Soil. Wheat, 2,477 bushels; Indian corn, 10,950 bushels; potatoes, 41,920 bushels; hay, 6,931 tons; maple sugar, 10,300 pounds; wool, 49,422 pounds.

Distances. Twenty-one miles southwest from Rutland, and twenty-seven south-east from Whitehall, N. Y.

PEACHAM.

CALEDONIA CO. *Onion River Pond,* so called from its giving rise to one of the principal branches of Onion or Winooski River, lies in the western part of the town, and covers about 300 acres. There are two considerable streams passing off to the east into Stevens' Branch, which afford numerous mill privileges.

A ridge of land passes through the western part, but there is no very considerable elevation in the town. The western part is a hard soil, but the eastern is rich, and pleasantly diversified with hills and valleys, being inhabited by a great number of respectable and wealthy farmers. There is, in the eastern part of the town, a natural bog meadow, containing an inexhaustible quantity of shell marl, from which lime has been manufactured to a considerable extent. The color of the marl is a bluish white.

There is also plenty of limestone, from which lime is made.

One of the most remarkable occurrences in the town was the loss of a man's great toe, by frost, in the month of June. Mr. Walker, the gentleman who sustained the loss, was eighty-four years old, and was frozen, in consequence of being lost in the woods, and

lying out through the night of the 8th of June, 1816.

There is a pleasant village situated on an elevated spot near the centre of the town, which is a place of considerable business.

Boundaries. Northerly by Danville, easterly by Barnet, southerly by Groton, and westerly by Marshfield and Cabot.

First Settlers. In the spring of 1775 Jonathan Elkins came to Peacham, with several hired men, and began improvements upon the lot he had pitched the year before.

First Minister. A Congregational Church was organized here in 1794, and in 1799 they settled the Rev. Leonard Worcester for their pastor.

Productions of the Soil. Wheat, 5,491 bushels; Indian corn, 2,377 bushels; potatoes, 67,816 bushels; hay, 4,001 tons; maple sugar, 21,180 pounds; wool, 17,786 pounds.

Distances. Six miles south-west from Danville, and thirty east from Montpelier. This town lies in the neighborhood of the Connecticut River Railroad.

PERU.

BENNINGTON CO. This is a Green Mountain township, high and broken. It contains two large fish ponds, from which issue beautiful mountain streams. Here is fine fishing and delightful scenery.

Boundaries. North by Mount Tabor, east by Landgrove, south by Winhall, and west by Dorset.

First Settler. The settlement of this town was commenced about the year 1773, by Wm. Barlow, from Woodstock, Ct.

First Minister. The Rev. Oliver Plympton was ordained over the Congregational Church in 1813, and died the next year.

Productions of the Soil. Wheat, 534 bushels; Indian corn, 320 bushels; potatoes, 23,100 bushels; hay, 1,290 tons; maple sugar, 7,640 pounds; wool, 1,610 pounds.

Distances. Thirty miles north northeast from Bennington, and thirty southwest from Windsor.

PITTSFIELD.

RUTLAND Co. Tweed River is formed in this town by two branches, which afford mill sites ; it empties into White River, which passes through the north-east corner. The surface of the town is mountainous, and the soil hard.

Boundaries. Easterly by Rochester, south-easterly by Stockbridge, and westerly by Chittenden and Goshen.

First Settlers. The settlement was commenced in 1786, by Thomas Hodgkins, Stephen Holt, George Martin, Daniel and Jacob Bowe, and a Mr. Woodard.

First Minister. A Congregational Church was organized in 1793; Rev. Justus Parsons was settled over it from 1814 to 1831.

Productions of the Soil. Wheat, 584 bushels; Indian corn, 1,531 bushels; potatoes, 16,373 bushels; hay, 1,632 tons ; wool, 5,220 pounds.

Distances. Thirty-five miles southwest from Montpelier, and seventeen north-east from Rutland.

PITTSFORD.

RUTLAND Co. Otter Creek, which flows through the middle of Pittsford, from south to north, with a gentle meandering current, is the principal stream, and its width here is from forty to fifty yards. Furnace Brook, a considerable tributary of Otter Creek, is formed by the union of East Creek and Philadelphia River. Along these streams are extensive meadows of the rich alluvial soil. On Furnace Brook and its branches are numerous mill privileges, which are well improved.

There are two ponds in the town : one in the south-eastern part, covering about twenty acres ; and the other in the north-eastern, covering about thirty acres. There are no mountains.

The soil is generally loam, with some tracts which are sandy, and some of clay. The timber is oak, of several kinds.

Pittsford abounds in iron ore, which makes the best of ware and bar iron, and has inexhaustible quarries of ex-

cellent marble. The iron ore yields about twenty-five per cent. of metallic iron. The marble is coarse grained, and somewhat flexible. Much of it is conveyed down Otter Creek to Middlebury, to be sawn and manufactured into jambs, &c. The oxyde of manganese is also found in this town.

In the eastern part of Pittsford is a deep cavern in which ice may commonly be found in the months of July and August.

There are two pleasant and flourishing villages in the town ; one near the centre, the other on Furnace Brook. These villages will be greatly benefitted by the railroad from Rutland, which passes near them.

A female child was born here in 1784, who died at the age of nine years, and weighed 200 pounds.

Boundaries. North by Brandon, east by Chittenden, south by Rutland, and west by Hubbardton and a small part of Ira.

First Settlers. The settlement of the town was commenced in the year 1769, by Messrs. Gideon and Benjamin Cooley, from Greenwich, Mass.; they were soon joined by Roger Stevens, Felix Powell, Ebenezer Hopkins, Stephen Mead, Moses Olmsted, Edward Owen, Joshua Woodward, and others, from Massachusetts and Connecticut.

First Minister. Elder Elisha Rich was ordained over the Baptist Church in 1784.

Productions of the Soil. Wheat, 1,837 bushels; Indian corn, 13,425 bushels ; potatoes, 30,661 bushels; hay, 7,162 tons ; maple sugar, 20,539 pounds ; wool, 54,128 pounds.

Distances. Forty-four miles southwest from Montpelier, and eight north from Rutland.

The great Southern Railroad between Boston and Burlington passes through Pittsford.

PLAINFIELD.

WASHINGTON Co. Plainfield is watered by Winooski River, which passes through the north-west corner, and by Great Brook, which passes through the town in a northwesterly direction into Winooski River. At the junction of these streams is a neat village.

There is a small pond in the eastern part, which is well furnished with excellent trout. There is also a mineral spring, similar to those in Newbury, which is a place of some resort for invalids. It is situated so near the margin of Great Brook, as to be overflowed at high water.

The surface of the town is uneven, but is well timbered.. There is but little waste land, and the soil is generally of a good quality.

Boundaries. North by Marshfield, east by Goshen Gore, south by Barre and Orange, and west by Montpelier.

First Settlers. The settlement was commenced about the year 1794, by Theodore Perkins, Joseph Batchelder, and Seth Freeman. They were joined the next year by Jonathan and Bradford Kinney, Moulton Batchelder, John Moore, and others, from different parts of New England.

First Ministers. A Congregational Church was organized here about the year 1796 or 1797; a Methodist, about the year 1800; and a Universalist Society, about the year 1820. These societies have generally been supplied by itinerant preachers.

Productions of the Soil. Wheat, 4,298 bushels; Indian corn, 1,036 bushels; potatoes, 26,316 bushels; hay, 2,832 tons; maple sugar, 13,980 pounds; wool, 11,201 pounds.

Distances. Nine miles south-east from Montpelier.

PLYMOUTH.

WINDSOR Co. The principal stream in this township is Black River, which is formed here, and runs south-easterly into Ludlow. On this stream are several good mill sites, and a number of natural ponds, which abound in fish. Two considerable branches of Quechee River also rise in this town. A large share of the rocks are primitive limestone, which makes the best of lime. Not less than 2,000 hogsheads are annually manufactured, and transported to different parts of the country. Some of the limestone makes excellent marble; and in 1834 a factory, where 150 saws can be put in operation, was erected on Black River for its manufacture. Some of the marble is white, and some beautifully variegated.

The surface of Plymouth is considerably broken. Two mountains extend through it, parallel to the river, and at no great distance from it. That on the north-eastern side is very abrupt, and is known by the name of Mount Tom. Near the meeting-house is an extensive bed of steatite, or soapstone.

At the foot of the mountain, on the south-western side of the river, and about eighty rods from it, is situated the Plymouth Cave. This cavern was discovered about the 1st of July, 1818. —See *Caves.*

Boundaries. North by Bridgewater, east by Reading, south by Ludlow and a part of Mount Holly, and west by Shrewsbury.

First Settlers. The settlement of Plymouth was commenced in 1777, by John Mudge, who was soon followed by Aaron Hewett and others.

First Ministers. The religious societies are Congregationalists, Baptists, Methodists, Christians, and Freewill Baptists. The Congregational Church was formed in 1806, and the Rev. Prince Jennie settled over it for five or six years.

Productions of the Soil. Wheat, 1,910 bushels; Indian corn, 3,374 bushels; potatoes, 59,840 bushels; hay, 4,127 tons; maple sugar, 13,480 pounds; wool, 17,105 pounds.

Distances. Fifty-two miles south from Montpelier, and fifteen west by north from Windsor.

POMFRET.

WINDSOR Co. The surface of this town is considerably uneven, but the soil is generally good. There are to be seen here the traces of a hurricane, which formerly passed through the township from west to east. The timber was, probably, all laid prostrate, through the distance of seven or eight miles, and about one hundred rods in width.

White River touches upon the north-east corner, and Quechee River touches upon the south-east corner. The other streams are small.

Boundaries. North by Sharon, east by Hartford, south by Woodstock, and west by Barnard.

First Settlers. The settlement of Pomfret was commenced in the spring of 1770, by Bartholomew Durkee, from Pomfret, Ct., who came into it with his family, consisting of a wife and five children, on the 6th day of March. In coming into the town, the family proceeded on foot, upon a snow shoe path, six miles, drawing their furniture upon hand-sleds. In the course of a few days they were joined in the settlement by Mr. John Cheedle and family.

First Ministers. The first settled minister was the Rev. Elisha Hutchinson, of the Congregational order. He was ordained Dec. 14, 1784, and dismissed Jan. 8, 1795. He was succeeded by the Rev. Ignatius Thompson, who was ordained Nov. 20, 1805, and dismissed April 26, 1811.

Productions of the Soil. Wheat, 4,435 bushels; Indian corn, 11,021 bushels; potatoes, 65,135 bushels; hay, 5,947 tons; maple sugar, 39,264 pounds; wool, 32,683 pounds.

Distances. Forty-five miles south from Montpelier, and twenty north north west from Windsor.

The great Northern Railroad passes through this town.

POULTNEY.

RUTLAND Co. This township is watered by Poultney River and its numerous tributaries, which afford a number of valuable mill sites. The soil is generally warm and productive, and the surface pleasantly diversified with hills and valleys. Along Poultney River the alluvial flats are extensive and very productive. The timber is mostly deciduous, there being but few evergreens.

A violent freshet, in July, 1811, swept off a number of mills. There are two pleasant villages in Poultney, called East Poultney and West Poultney. Both of these villages are very flourishing in their trade and manufactures, and contain a number of handsome buildings.

Boundaries. North by Castleton, east by Middletown and Ira, south by Wells, and west by Hampton.

First Settlers. The settlement was commenced in 1771, by Thomas Ashley and Ebenezer Allen. The early settlers were mostly emigrants from Connecticut and the western part of Massachusetts.

First Ministers. Rev. Ithamer Hibbard was settled over the Congregational Church in 1780; dismissed in 1796. His successor was Rev. James Thompson, from 1803 to 1820.

Productions of the Soil. Wheat, 1,613 bushels; Indian corn, 22,082 bushels; potatoes, 28,724 bushels; hay, 5,013 tons; maple sugar, 10,765 pounds, wool, 34,946 pounds.

Distances. Sixty miles south-west from Montpelier, and thirteen south-west from Rutland.

POWNAL.

BENNINGTON Co. The surface of this township is considerably uneven, but the soil is generally good, and produces plentiful crops. It is well adapted to the production of grain and grass, and here are kept some of the finest dairies in the State. The principal stream is Hoosic River, which is formed here and passes off in a north-westerly direction into the town of Hoosic, N. Y. Along this stream are some rich and beautiful tracts of intervale, and on it are several valuable stands for mills.

Some of the head branches of Walloomscoik River rise in the north-eastern part of Pownal, and pass off into Bennington.

Boundaries. North by Bennington, east by Stamford, south by Williamstown, Mass., and west by Hoosic, New York.

First Settlers. The settlement of Pownal, under the New Hampshire charter, was commenced in the spring

9*

of 1762, there being at that time four or five Dutch families within the limits of the township, claiming under the "Hoosic Patent," granted by the government of New York. Among the early settlers of the town were the families of Wright, Gardner, Morgan, Dunham, Noble, Card, Curtis, Watson, and Seelye, but the precise time when they severally came into the town is not ascertained.

Productions of the Soil. Wheat, 1,075 bushels; Indian corn, 11,147 bushels; potatoes, 28,215 bushels; hay, 3,164 tons; maple sugar, 6,087 pounds; wool, 22,367 pounds.

Distances. Thirty miles west by south from Brattleborough, and eight south from Bennington.

PUTNEY.

WINDHAM Co. This town is finely located, on the west side of Connecticut River, and embosoms a large tract of excellent intervale land, called the "Great Meadows." There is also a good tract of intervale on Sacket's Brook, a fine mill stream, with beautiful falls, on which are erected valuable mills for the manufacture of woollen goods, paper, and various other articles.

Sacket's Brook is a large and constant stream; it falls 150 feet in the course of 100 rods. There are various mineral substances in the town worthy of the notice of the geologist. The village is pleasant, and bears the marks of taste and prosperity.

On the 19th of August, 1788, a violent tempest prostrated a great part of the forest trees here. In 1770 the town was overrun by immense swarms of worms, which, like the swarms of Egypt, ate up every green thing; also, to a limited extent, in 1823 and 4.

Boundaries. North by Westminster, east by Connecticut River, which separates it from Westmoreland, N. H., south by Dummerston, and west by Brookline.

First Settlers. A settlement was commenced and a fort built on the "Great Meadow," so called, in the eastern part of the town, a little pre-

vious to the breaking out of the French war, in 1744; but on the commencement of hostilities the fort was evacuated, and the inhabitants, together with those from adjacent towns, retired to Northfield, Mass., which was the frontier post during that war. One circumstance took place, however, previous to the breaking up of the fort, which undoubtedly hastened that event, which was as follows:—"A man by the name of William Phipps was hoeing corn, on the 5th of July, 1745, near the south-west corner of the meadow, when two Indians sprang upon him, and dragged him into the woods near by. Here, after a short parley, one of the Indians departed, leaving the prisoner under the care of his comrade. Phipps, with the hardihood characteristic of the pioneers in these wilds, watching an opportunity, struck his keeper down with his hoe, and, seizing his gun, gave the other, who was returning, a fatal wound. Thus at liberty again, he sought refuge in the fort, but, unfortunately, before he reached it, he fell in with three other Indians, who butchered the brave fellow in cold blood."

First Ministers. A Congregational Church was organized Oct. 17, 1776, at which time they settled the Rev. Josiah Goodhue, who died November 14, 1797. His successors have been Rev. Jairus Remington, from Feb. 12, 1800, to Feb. 15, 1803.

Productions of the Soil. Wheat, 993 bushels; Indian corn, 12,225 bushels; potatoes, 26,390 bushels; hay, 2,849 tons; maple sugar, 8,830 pounds; wool, 13,730 pounds.

Distances. Nine miles east from Newfane, and nine north from Brattleborough. The Connecticut River Railroad passes through the town.

RANDOLPH.

ORANGE COUNTY. Randolph is watered by the second and third branch of White River; the former running through the eastern, and the latter through the western part of the town. These streams and their tributaries afford a number of advantageous situations for mills. The timber is, principally, maple, beech, and birch, with some hemlock, and spruce. The surface of Randolph is considerably elevated, but is less broken than that of the towns generally in this vicinity. The soil is productive, and the farming interest extensive.

There are here three pleasant villages; one in the centre of the town, another in the eastern, and the other in the western part. The *Centre Village* is very handsomely situated on elevated ground. These villages are places of considerable business and some manufactures.

The West Randolph Academy was incorporated in 1847.

Boundaries. North by Brookfield, east by Tunbridge, south by Bethel, and west by Braintree.

First Settlers. This town was chartered in 1781, and was settled three or four years before by Wm. Evans and family, Edward Evans, John Park, and Experience Davis.

First Ministers. The Rev. Elijah Brainard was ordained over the Congregational Church in 1786, and dismissed in 1798. The Rev. Tilton Eastman was settled in 1801, and dismissed in 1830.

Productions of the Soil. Wheat, 5,525 bushels; Indian corn, 18,499 bushels; potatoes, 112,598 bushels; hay, 8,831 tons; maple sugar, 34,660 pounds; wool, 40,782 pounds.

Distances. Twenty-three miles south from Montpelier, and nine south-west from Chelsea.

The great Northern Railroad passes through the town.

READING.

WINDSOR CO The surface of this town is uneven, and the elevations pretty abrupt. Towards the west part is an elevated tract of land, extending through the town from north to south, from which issues its principal streams. It is worthy of remark, that no water runs into this town. In the south-west part, and on the line between Reading and Plymouth, is a natural pond, about

200 rods in length and fifty in breadth. The outlet of this pond is to the south, and leads into Plymouth Pond. From the north-west part of the town the streams take a northerly direction, and fall into Quechee River at Bridgewater. From the middle and north-east parts the streams take an easterly direction, and unite with Connecticut River at Windsor; whilst those in the south-east part take a south-easterly direction, and fall into Black River at Weathersfield. Some small streams, however, rise in the north part, and, taking a north-easterly direction, fall into Quechee River, at Woodstock, North Village. The streams in Reading, though generally small, afford a tolerable supply of water for common mills.

The soil in Reading is of a middling quality, and affords excellent pasturage.

There are three villages in the town; Reading Centre Village, South Reading, and Felchville. These places have considerable trade and manufactures.

Boundaries. North by Woodstock, east by Windsor, south by Cavendish, and west by Plymouth.

First Settlers. The settlement of the township was commenced about the year 1772, by Andrew Spear, who removed his family here from Walpole, N. H. This was for several years the only family in town. About the year 1778, John Weld, Esq., moved his family from Pomfret, Ct.

First Minister. On the 23d of Nov. 1787, the Rev. Nahum Sergeant was ordained to the pastoral care of the Congregational Church in Reading, with a permanent salary for life. A log meeting house was erected about the same time. The church, however, were not long blest with his labors; for in visiting his friends in Chelsea, Mass., he died of the small-pox, in 1792.

Productions of the Soil. Wheat, 2,950 bushels; Indian corn, 3,984 bushels; potatoes, 22,540 bushels; hay, 4,177 tons; maple sugar, 24,215 pounds; wool, 18,379 pounds.

Distances. Fifty-three miles south

from Montpelier, and ten west from Windsor.

READSBOROUGH.

BENNINGTON Co. This is a mountainous township, at the south-east corner of the county, watered by Deerfield River. Much of the land in the town is too elevated to admit of cultivation. When it was first settled is unknown.

Boundaries. North by Searsburgh, east by Whitingham, south by Rowe, Mass., and west by Stamford and a part of Woodford.

Productions of the Soil. Wheat, 249 bushels; Indian corn, 972 bushels; potatoes, 20,952 bushels; hay, 2,146 tons; maple sugar, 27,217 pounds; wool, 5,376 pounds.

Distances. Twelve miles south-east from Bennington, and eighteen west by south from Brattleborough.

RICHFORD.

FRANKLIN Co. This is a mountainous township at the north-east corner of the county, on the line of Canada, and watered by Missisco River and its branches. There is some good land along the river; and the upland, though rough, affords good grazing.

Boundaries. North by Sutton, Canada, east by Jay, south by Montgomery, and west by Berkshire.

First Settlers. The settlement was commenced in 1797; the town was organized in 1799.

Productions of the Soil. Wheat, 2,238 bushels; Indian corn, 2,112 bushels; potatoes, 39,706 bushels; hay, 2,236 tons; maple sugar, 19,505 pounds; wool, 5,168 pounds.

Distances. Fifty miles north by west from Montpelier, and twenty-four northeast from St. Albans.

RICHMOND.

CHITTENDEN Co. The town is finely watered by Winooski and Huntington Rivers, on the banks of which are good mill sites and large tracts of beautiful meadow. The village° is

neat, and the centre of considerable travel. This is a healthy place, and noted for the longevity of its inhabitants.

Boundaries. Northerly by Jericho, easterly by Bolton, southerly by Huntington, and westerly by Williston.

First Settlers. The first attempt to form a settlement here was made in 1775, by Amos Brownson and John Chamberlain, with their families; but they abandoned the town in the fall, and did not return till the close of the revolutionary war. In the spring of 1784 they returned to the farms, on which they had made beginnings, accompanied by Asa and Joel Brownson, Samuel and Joshua Chamberlain, Jas. Holly, Joseph Wilson, and Jesse McFarlain.

First Ministers. The religious denominations are the Congregationalist, Baptist, Freewill Baptist, and Universalist. Elder Ezra Wilmot was ordained over the Baptist Church, and continued several years. He was the first settled minister, and there was no other in town till Sept. 25, 1823, when Elder John Peck was settled over the same church. There is a meetinghouse in the centre of the town having sixteen sides, with a steeple rising from the centre, and owned by the several denominations.

Productions of the Soil. Wheat, 1,941 bushels; Indian corn, 7,864 bushels; potatoes, 38,115 bushels; hay, 3,767 tons; maple sugar, 11,650 pounds; wool, 11,717 pounds.

Distances. Twenty-five miles northwest from Montpelier, and thirteen south-east from Burlington. The Northern Railroad passes in this vicinity.

RIPTON.

ADDISON Co. This is a mountainous township, the surface and soil of which are too broken and cold for much cultivation. Middlebury River and the Turnpike from Royalton to Vergennes pass through it.

This town was granted in 1781, and chartered to Abel Thompson and associates.

Boundaries. North by Avery's Gore

and Bristol, east by Granville, south by Goshen, and west by Middlebury.

Productions of the Soil. Wheat, 170 bushels; Indian corn, 120 bushels; potatoes, 9,360 bushels; hay, 690 tons; maple sugar, 4,200 pounds; wool, 1,796 pounds.

Distances. Twenty-six miles south-west from Montpelier, and nine east from Middlebury.

This town is easily approached from the great Southern Railroad.

ROCHESTER.

WINDSOR Co. The principal stream is White River, which runs through the township from north to south. About half a mile south of the centre, it receives a considerable tributary from the west, which originates in Goshen. On each of these streams are good situations for mills.

Rochester is mountainous and broken, but contains much good land. The intervale along the river is handsome, but not extensive. The timber is mostly hard wood.

There is a pleasant village situated near the centre of the town, on the eastern bank of White River, and is a place of some business.

A part of Goshen was annexed to Rochester, in 1847.

Boundaries. Northerly by Braintree and a small part of Kingston, easterly by Bethel, southerly by Pittsfield, and westerly by Hancock.

First Settlers. The settlement of Rochester was commenced about the close of the revolutionary war.

First Minister. Rev. Salmon Hurlbut was settled over the Congregational Church in 1822.

Productions of the Soil. Wheat, 2,367 bushels; Indian corn, 4,446 bushels; potatoes, 44,945 bushels; hay, 5,250 tons; maple sugar, 39,110 pounds; wool, 29,980 pounds.

Distances. Thirty miles south south-west from Montpelier, and thirty-seven north-west from Windsor. The great Northern Railroad passes in this vicinity, through the town of Bethel, about six miles distant.

ROCKINGHAM.

WINDHAM Co. Connecticut River washes the eastern border of this township. William's River runs through the central part, and unites with the Connecticut about three miles north of Bellows Falls. Saxton's River runs through the south part, and falls into the Connecticut a mile south of Bellows Falls, in the north-east corner of Westminster. These streams afford a great number of valuable sites for mills.

The surface of Rockingham is somewhat broken, but the soil is in general warm and productive.

Bellows Falls are in Connecticut River, near the south-east corner of this town. The breadth of the river above the falls is from sixteen to twenty-two rods. At the falls a large rock divides the stream into two channels, each about ninety feet wide. When the water is low, the eastern appears crossed by a bar of solid rock, and the whole river flows into the western channel, where it is contracted to the breadth of sixteen feet, and flows with astonishing rapidity. There are several pitches, one above another, for the distance of half a mile, the largest of which is that where the rock divides the stream. Notwithstanding the velocity of the current, the salmon formerly passed up this fall, and were taken many miles above, but the shad were never taken above here.

In 1785, Col. Enoch Hale erected a bridge over the Connecticut at these falls. Its length was 365 feet, and it was supported in the middle by the great rock mentioned above. Till 1796 this was the only bridge across the Connecticut. The bridge here is about fifty feet from the water, and from it the traveller has an interesting and sublime view of the falls. The whole descent of the river at these falls is forty-two feet. They are passed by a canal, on the Rockingham side, consisting of nine locks, and are half a mile in length. Around these falls is an interesting locality of minerals. The rocks are principally gneiss.

There are in Rockingham several

pleasant villages. *Bellows Falls Village,* situated on the bank of the Connecticut at Bellows Falls, in the south-eastern part of the town, is the most important. *Rockingham Village* is situated near the centre of the town. *Saxton's River Village* is situated on the stream of that name, in the south part of Rockingham. The village of *Cambridge Port* is in the south-west corner of the town. These villages are very neat, and contain many handsome houses.

Boundaries. North by Springfield, east by Connecticut River, which separates it from Charlestown, N. H., south by Westminster, and west by Grafton.

First Settlers. The settlement of Rockingham was commenced in 1753, by Moses Wright, Joel Bigelow, and Simeon Knight, who emigrated from Massachusetts. The attention of the first settlers was principally directed to fishing for salmon and shad, which were then taken in great abundance at Bellows Falls. For this reason agriculture was, for many years, much neglected.

First Minister. The Congregational Church was organized about 1770. Rev. Samuel Whiting was settled over it from October 27, 1773, to May 18, 1809.

Manufactures. There are large and important manufactures in this town, the statistics of which, we regret to say, we cannot give at present. The immense water power, which this and its neighboring town of Walpole possesses, the salubrity of the climate, the industry of the inhabitants, and located in the heart of a fertile country, are circumstances which give promise of great prosperity to their location. When to these advantages is added the power of steam, to facilitate the transportation of persons and property to and from the Atlantic, no one can doubt that this place stands, for all manufacturing purposes, almost without a rival in New England.

The Phœnix Mill Co. in this town was incorporated in 1847.

Productions of the Soil. Wheat, 2,695 bushels; Indian corn, 1,221 bushels;

potatoes, 25,855 bushels; hay, 2,055 tons; maple sugar, 16,198 lbs.; wool, 32,371 pounds.

Distances. Eighty-five miles south from Montpelier, and eighteen north-east from Newfane.

This place is accommodated by the passage through it of the great Southern Railroad, which runs from Boston to Burlington, by the Connecticut River Railroad, and by the Sullivan Railroad, on the opposite side of the river.

ROXBURY.

WASHINGTON COUNTY. Roxbury is situated on the height of land between Winooski and White Rivers, and has consequently no large streams. The waters in the north part flow through Dog River into Winooski River, and those in the south part through Ayres' Brook, and the third branch into White River.

The surface of Roxbury is uneven, but the soil is well adapted to the production of grass, and in general yields good crops of grain. The timber is mostly hard wood. The rocks in the eastern part are argillaceous slate, and abound with cubical crystals of the sulphuret of iron. Iron ore is found in the south-eastern part.

There is a small village in the north-east corner, on a principal branch of Dog River.

Boundaries. North by Northfield, east by Brookfield, south by Braintree and Granville, and west by Warren.

First Settler. The settlement of Roxbury was commenced in 1789, by Christopher Huntington. He was originally from Mansfield, Ct., but resided a while in Norwich, in this State, previous to his moving into the town. He, like many other settlers of new townships, had to draw his effects several miles upon a hand-sled, and had many hardships to encounter.

First Ministers. The various denominations of Christians in this town generally depend on itinerant preachers.

Productions of the Soil. Wheat, 2.695 bushels; Indian corn, 1,221 bushels;

potatoes, 25,855 bushels; hay, 2,055 tons; maple sugar, 16,198 lbs.; wool, 9,061 pounds.

Distances. Fifteen miles south-west from Montpelier.

This place borders on Northfield, through which the Northern Railroad passes.

ROYALTON.

WINDSOR CO. The surface of this township is somewhat broken and hilly, but the soil is good, particularly along White River and its branches, where it is of a superior quality. White River runs through the town in an easterly direction, and receives here its first and second branches, which are the only streams of much consequence.

Royalton Village is pleasantly situated on the bank of White River, about half way between the mouths of the first and second branches, and near the centre of the town.

Boundaries. North by Tunbridge, east by Sharon, south by Barnard, and west by Bethel.

First Settlers. The first permanent settlement was made in 1771, by Mr. Robert Havens, who this year moved his family into the town. The next year he was joined in the settlement by Mr. Elisha Kent and family, and the inhabitants were so much increased in the course of a few years, that the town was organized.

First Ministers. The Rev. John Searle was the first settled minister. He was ordained over the Congrega-tional Church in 1783, and died in 1787 or 88. In 1789 the Rev. Azel Washburn was ordained in his place, and dismissed in 1792. Rev. Martin Tuller was ordained in 1794, and died in 1813.

Productions of the Soil. Wheat, 2,727 bushels; Indian corn, 11,383 bushels; potatoes, 60,835 bushels; hay, 5,173 tons; maple sugar, 30,470 pounds; wool, 20,828 pounds.

Distances. Thirty miles south from Montpelier, and twenty-five north north-west from Windsor. The Northern Railroad passes through this town.

RUPERT.

BENNINGTON CO. A part of this township is mountainous, but the soil is generally good for grazing. Rupert produces some fine cattle. It is watered by Pawlet River, and a branch of the Battenkill, on which streams are mills of various kinds.

Boundaries. North by Pawlet, east by Dorset, south by Sandgate, and west by Hebron, N. Y.

First Settlers. The settlement of this town was commenced in 1767, by Isaac Blood, Reuben Harmon, Oliver Scott, and a Mr. Eastman.

Productions of the Soil. Wheat, 1,442 bushels; Indian corn, 5,417 bushels; potatoes, 30,920 bushels; hay, 4,804 tons; maple sugar, 5,900 pounds; wool, 26,446 pounds.

Distances. Seventy-eight miles south-west from Montpelier, and twenty-five north from Bennington.

RUTLAND COUNTY.

RUTLAND is the chief town. This county is bounded north by Addison County, east by Windsor County, south by Bennington County, and west by the State of New York. The principal streams are Otter Creek, Black, White, Queechy, and Pawlet Rivers. There is some fine land in this county along Otter Creek, but a large portion of it is elevated, and some parts mountainous. The soil, however, is generally warm, and well suited for grazing. Many cattle are annually taken to market. Excellent iron ore is found at the base of the mountains, and a range of marble quarries extends the whole length of the county, from north to south. This marble is of a fine quality; much of it is wrought and transported.—See *Tables.*

COURTS IN RUTLAND COUNTY.

The *Supreme Court* commences its session at Rutland, on the first Tuesday after the fourth Tuesday of January; and the *County Court* on the second Tuesdays in April and September.

The *United States Circuit Court* sits here annually on the third, and the *District Court* on the sixth day of October.

RUTLAND.

RUTLAND Co. This is a shire town. The principal stream in Rutland is Otter Creek, which enters the town about the middle of the south line, and leaves it about the middle of the north line, cutting it into two nearly equal parallelograms. Tributary to this are West River, rising in Tinmouth, and East Creek, one of whose branches rises in Chittenden, and the other in Mendon, the latter entering Otter Creek one mile above Gookin's Falls, and the former about forty rods below. In addition to these, there are two other streams of less magnitude, flowing in above East Creek, on the right bank; the first of which, near the south line, is Cold River, the other, one mile and a half below, is the confluent stream formed by the union of the Moon and Mussey Brooks, so called. Near the north-west corner of the town, on the north line, another stream, called Castleton River, enters; and, after pursuing a southerly course about three miles, turns to the right, and passes off into Ira. On all of these streams are convenient sites for mills, and other machinery, most of which are already occupied.

The soil of Rutland presents all the varieties from heavy loam to a light sand; the eastern half appearing to be chiefly of *primitive formation,* while that of the western is *transitory.* Among the useful minerals are found considerable quantities of iron, superior clay for bricks, and an abundance of lime in almost all its various forms. In the west part, several quarries of very beautiful white and clouded marble have been opened, and from which fire places, monuments, and other useful and ornamental articles, are manufactured, both for domestic use and for the New York and other markets. The quarry opened within a few years, near Sutherland's Falls, is exceedingly fine and beautiful, and is wrought to great extent.

Rutland is divided into two parishes, denominated *East* and *West* parish. *Rutland Village,* situated in the East Parish, is the most important place. It is handsomely situated, principally on a street running north and south, and contains many beautiful buildings. In the West Parish are two small villages, called *West Rutland* and *Gookin's Falls.*

This town has hitherto possessed all the advantages of soil, climate, and water power, to render it as prosperous as any part of our country; but now, when this site of industry and wealth is brought within a few hours ride of the Atlantic coast, by that magnificent power which sets at defiance all horse teams, stage coaches, baggage wagons, and carryalls, and unites the town and country almost by magic, no one can doubt the fortunate destiny which awaits Rutland and its neighboring towns.

The village of Rutland was incorporated in 1847.

Boundaries. North by Pittsford, east by Mendon, south by Clarendon, and west by Ira.

First Settlers. This town was chartered in 1761. During the war of the revolution, it was, for some time, a frontier town, and was subject to all the commotions and inconveniences incident to its situation. Through it lay the only military road from Charlestown, N. H., to Ticonderoga and Crown Point, on Lake Champlain. During the war, the Vermont troops, or *Green Mountain Boys*, erected here two small picket forts, sufficient to contain about 100 men each. One of them was situated on the ground occupied by the present village, in the East Parish, about twelve rods from the spot where the court house now stands. The other fort was situated at the head of the falls in Otter Creek, then called Mead's Falls. As a means of checking the incursions of the enemy, and of facilitating the communications between the eastern part of the State and Lake Champlain, these forts were found to be very useful.

First Ministers. The first Congregational Church was organized in the West Parish, in 1773, and has had the following settled ministers. Rev. Benajah Root, from 1774 to 1787 ; Rev. Lemuel Haynes, from March, 1788, to 1818.

Productions of the Soil. Wheat, 3,708 bushels; Indian corn, 19,347 bushels; potatoes, 48,193 bushels; hay, 10,025 tons ; maple sugar, 51,833 pounds ; wool, 69,902 pounds.

Distances. Fifty miles south-west from Montpelier.

The great Southern Railroad between Boston and Burlington passes through this town.

RYEGATE.

CALEDONIA Co. This town is situated on the west bank of Connecticut River, opposite to Bath, N. H. Ryegate is watered by Wells River, some smaller streams, and several ponds. There is not much intervale land on the river, in the town, but the soil is generally rich, and very productive of

all kinds of vegetables and grain, but more particularly of grass. The products of the soil annually transported to market are very considerable.

Ryegate was first settled by emigrants from Scotland, in the year 1774. A large part of the present population of Ryegate are of Scotch descent, and are said to follow, in a great degree, the peculiar habits, in regard to diet, which Scotchmen are accustomed to in their own country. They annually prepare large quantities of oatmeal for cakes, and lay in a good stock of hulled barley for broth, soups, and puddings. The people of Ryegate are generally frugal and industrious, good farmers and good livers. They manufacture their own apparel, and some for their neighbors.

Boundaries. North by Barnet, east by Connecticut River, south by Newbury, in the county of Orange, and west by Groton.

First Ministers. The first religious society in this town was the Associate Presbyterian, organized about 1790. From 1791 to 1822, they enjoyed a part of the services of the Rev. David Goodwillie, of Barnet. In September, 1822, they settled the Rev. Thomas Farrier, and, in 1830, the Rev. William Pringle.

Productions of the Soil. Wheat, 3,421 bushels ; Indian corn. 3,389 bushels; potatoes, 47,176 bushels ; hay, 3,959 tons ; maple sugar, 11,308 pounds ; wool, 9,200 pounds.

Distances. Fifteen miles south from Danville, and forty south-east from Montpelier.

The Connecticut River Railroad passes through this town.

ST. ALBANS.

FRANKLIN Co. This is the shire town. The soil of St. Albans is fertile, and, under the management of good farmers, is rendered very productive. The exports of wool, and other productions of the soil, are large and valuable.

The water communications by the lake to New York and Canada, render St. Albans a mart of considerable trade from the surrounding country. The first vessel from Lake Champlain that arrived at New York, by the northern canal, was from, built, and owned at St. Albans.

The *Village of St. Albans* is beautifully situated on elevated ground, and commands a fine prospect. It contains many handsome buildings, and is a busy place in the manufacture of various articles. It lies three miles from the lake, and fifteen from the line of Canada.

Boundaries. North by Swanton, east by Fairfield, south by Georgia, and west by Lake Champlain, a part of which separates it from North Hero.

First Settlers. J. Walden is supposed to have been the first civilized person who settled in this town. He removed here during the revolutionary war, and began improvements at the bay. There was no addition to the settlement till 1785, when Andrew Potter emigrated to the town, and from that time the settlement advanced rapidly, by emigrants from the south part of this State, and from the other States of New England. Among the earliest settlers were the families of Messrs. Potter, Morrill, Gibbs, Green, and Meigs.

First Minister. Rev. Jonathan Nye was settled over the Congregational Church, from 1807 to 1810.

Productions of the Soil. Wheat, 5,250 bushels ; Indian corn, 7,112 bushels ; potatoes, 33,325 bushels; hay, 5,180 tons ; maple sugar, 5,000 pounds ; wool, 39,175 pounds.

Distances. Forty-six miles northwest by north from Montpelier, and twenty-five north from Burlington.

The business of this place will be greatly enhanced, by the passage through it of the Burlington and Montreal Railroad.

ST. GEORGE.

CHITTENDEN Co. The surface of this town is very uneven, with considerable elevations. The timber is principally maple, beech, and birch. There are no streams of consequence, and no mills or mill privileges.

A part of Shelburne was annexed to St. George in 1848.

Boundaries. North and north-east by Williston, south by Hinesburgh, and west by Shelburne.

First Settlers. The settlement was commenced here in the spring of 1784, by Joshua Isham, from Colchester, Ct. The next year several others joined the settlement.

Productions of the Soil. Wheat, 217 bushels ; Indian corn, 616 bushels ; potatoes, 4,635 bushels ; hay, 566 tons ; maple sugar, 1,130 pounds ; wool, 2,368 pounds.

Distances. Twenty-eight miles west by north from Montpelier, and eight south-east from Burlington.

ST. JOHNSBURY.

CALEDONIA Co. The Passumpsic River runs through this town from north to south, and receives, just below the *Plain*, the Moose River, a considerable stream from the north-east, and Sleeper's River, a smaller tributary, from the north-west. The amount of available water power, furnished by these streams within the town, exceeds that of any other town in this part of the State, and affords facilities for manufacturing operations to any desirable amount.

The business of the town centres in three villages. The *Centre Village*, so called, lies upon the Passumpsic River, in the northerly part of the town. It has been of rapid growth, and does a prosperous business.

The *East Village*, situated upon Moose River, in the east part of the town, is the natural centre for the business of parts of St. Johnsbury, Waterford, Concord, Kirby, Victory, and Bradleyvale.

The pleasant village called the *Plain* is situated in the southerly part of the town.

All these villages are important places of business, and contain very handsome public and private buildings. The Village of the Plain is of superior beauty, and contains an excellent academy.

The soil in this town is rich and

productive; the surface uneven, and somewhat hilly, though not broken; and the farms are in a high state of cultivation.

St. Johnsbury presents a fine specimen of Yankee industry and perseverance. Although shut up in a cold region, amid the craggy mountains of the North, and hitherto a three days' toilsome journey to any Atlantic city, this mountain villa has sent forth, throughout our whole country and to foreign lands, articles of manufacture which would vie in workmanship and utility with any of those produced in Europe.

Until the present day, the location of our cities and trading towns have been selected for their proximity to the ocean, or situated on some navigable stream. Now the great considerations are, in the choice of a location. Does the place possess a good hydraulic power? Is it situated in a fertile and healthy country? Does the Monarch Carrier pass that way? These three things attained, St. Johnsbury, like many other places similarly situated, throws into the shade many large towns, whose sites were selected solely for being situated on the banks of some shallow river, or at the head of some navigable creek.

The giant power which unites the business communities of States and distant countries, as it were, by magic, will take the burthen of a ship's cargo and 500 passengers from Boston to St. Johnsbury, 170 miles, in less time than it takes the swiftest steamer to pass from Albany to New York, a distance of 145 miles, and that in any day of any season in the year.

The Monarch Carrier will commence his trips this way in the course of the year 1850. After whistling a tune in honor of the enterprise of the citizens of St. Johnsbury, he will visit the Canadians, to solicit the pleasure of becoming the medium of communication between the Atlantic coast and the largest and most important mart of British commerce in America.

Boundaries. Northerly by Lyndon, north-east by Kirby, south-east by Waterford, and southwest by Danville.

First Settlers. James Adams, and his son Martin Adams, with their families, commenced the settlement on " Benton's Meadow," and Simeon Cole on the " Butler Meadow," in 1786, and the next year Dr. Jona. Arnold, Dr. Jos. Lord, Barnabas Barker, and others, moved into town.

First Ministers. The First Congregational Church was organized Nov. 21, 1809. The Rev. Pearson Thurston was settled over this church from Oct. 25, 1815, to Oct. 13, 1817. The Rev. Josiah Morse was settled Feb. 21, 1833. The Second Congregational Church was organized April 7, 1825. The Rev. James Johnson was settled over it from Feb. 28, 1827, to May 3, 1838. Rev. John H. Worcester was settled Sept. 5, 1839. A third Congregational Church was organized in the East Village, Nov. 25, 1840.

Productions of the Soil. Wheat, 2,478 bushels; Indian corn, 6,950 bushels; potatoes, 74,115 bushels; hay, 4,953 tons; maple sugar, 50,520 pounds; wool, 14,599 pounds.

Manufactures. The establishment of Messrs. E. & T. Fairbanks & Co., for the manufacture of their celebrated Platform Scales, is upon Sleeper's River, near the south end of the *Plain.* From 100 to 150 men are constantly employed in this establishment, while an equal number find, indirectly, employment and support, in connexion with these operations.

These balances are manufactured very extensively, from the small counter scale used by traders and merchants, to the ponderous railroad scale 50 to 100 feet in length for weighing trains of cars.

The improvement has been patented in the United States and in England, and the article now is in extensive use in both countries, possessing the entire confidence of the public.

It is worthy of remark, that the mechanics of this establishment seldom leave the place, and, as a class, are respectable and worthy citizens, in independent circumstances.

Near the north end of the Plain there is a blast furnace, a machine shop, grist mill, saw mill, and sash and

blind factory. In the other villages
are various kinds of mechanical operations.

Distances. Seven miles north-east
from Danville, ten miles from Connecticut River, thirty-seven north-east
from Montpelier, forty-five south of
Canada line at Stanstead, one hundred
and seventy miles north from Boston,
three hundred and twenty-five from
New York, and 140 from Montreal.

SALEM.

ORLEANS Co. Clyde River runs
through this town in a north-westerly
direction, and falls into Salem Pond,
which is partly in Salem and partly in
Derby. There is no other stream of
consequence, and no mills nor mill
privileges. There are two other ponds;
one of which lies in the course of
Clyde River, and the other on the line
between this town and Brownington;
and they are each about one mile in
length and three-fourths of a mile in
breadth. South Bay of Lake Memphremagog lies between Salem and
Newport. The surface of this town is
uneven, but not mountainous.

Boundaries. North by Derby, north-
east by Morgan, south-east by Charleston, and south-west by Brownington
and Orleans.

First Settlers. The settlement of
Salem was commenced by Ephraim
Blake, in March, 1798. Amasa Spen-
cer came into town in 1801, and David
Hopkins, jr., in 1802. The town was
organized April 30, 1822.

Productions of the Soil. Wheat, 791
bushels; Indian corn, 454 bushels;
potatoes, 13,270 bushels; hay, 689
tons; maple sugar, 19,420 pounds;
wool, 1,871 pounds.

Distances. Ten miles north-east
from Irasburgh, and fifty-three north-
east from Montpelier.

SALISBURY.

ADDISON Co. Otter Creek forms
the western boundary of this town.
The other streams are Middlebury River, which touches upon the north part,
and Leicester River, which waters the
southern part. Lake Dunmore is about
four miles long and from half to three
fourths of a mile wide, and lies partly
in Salisbury and partly in Leicester.
On the outlet of this pond, called Leicester River, are several falls, which
afford some fine mill privileges, around
which, near the south line of the town,
is a thriving village.

The surface is somewhat uneven, but
the soil is generally good. The eastern
part extends on to the Green Mountains. In the western part are some
fine tracts of meadow.

In the mountain east of Lake Dunmore is a cavern which consists of a
large room, and is thought to have been
inhabited by the Indians, as their arrows and other instruments have been
found here.

Boundaries. North by Middlebury,
east by Goshen, south by Leicester,
and west by Cornwall and Whiting.

First Settlers. The first person who
came into Salisbury with a view of
settling, was Amos Storey. He built
a log hut which was consumed by fire,
and he himself was killed by the fall
of a tree, before his family moved here.
Thomas Skeeles and Abel Waterhouse
were the two next to make beginnings.
The widow of Mr. Storey, and eight
or ten small children, were the first
family which moved into town, and
Mrs. Storey was consequently entitled
to 100 acres of land, by a vote of the
original proprietors. She came into
the town the 22d day of February,
1775. She endured almost every hard-
ship; laboring in the field, chopping
down timber, and clearing and cultivating the soil. She retreated several
times to Pittsford during the revolution, on account of the danger appre-
hended from the enemy, but at length
she and a Mr. Stevens prepared themselves a safe retreat. This was effected by digging a hole horizontally into
the bank, just above the water of Otter
Creek, barely sufficient to admit one
person at a time. This passage led to
a spacious lodging room, the bottom
of which was covered with straw, and
upon this their beds were laid for the
accommodation of the families. The
entrance was concealed by bushes,

which hung over it from the bank above. They usually retired to their lodgings in the dusk of the evening, and left them before light in the morning, and this was effected by means of a canoe, so that no path or footsteps were to be seen leading to their subterraneous abode.

First Minister. A Congregational Church was organized Feb. 8, 1804, and the same year a meeting-house was built. The Rev. Rufus Pomroy was settled over this church from Sept. 15, 1811, to Nov. 19, 1816.

Productions of the Soil. Wheat, 1,460 bushels; Indian corn, 5,060 bushels; potatoes, 20,240 bushels; hay, 2,150 tons; maple sugar, 5,600 pounds; wool, 15,900 pounds.

Distances. Thirty-four miles south-west from Montpelier, and about six miles south from the Southern Railroad depot in Middlebury.

SANDGATE.

BENNINGTON Co. The people of this town are favored with mountain air, and with crystal streams which even the Bostonians might relish.

Shetterack and Bald Mountains are in the north-west part of the town; Spruce and Equinox are in the north-east; Red Mountain is in the south-east; and Swearing Hill in the south-west. Between these elevations is some good land, which produces grass and grain; and which, with the mountain browse, affords feed for large flocks of sheep.

Boundaries. North by Rupert, east by Manchester, south by Arlington, and west by Salem, N. Y.

First Settler. The settlement of this town was commenced in 1771, by a Mr. Bristol.

The religious denominations are Congregationalists and Methodists.

Productions of the Soil. Wheat, 621 bushels; Indian corn, 3,427 bushels; potatoes, 23,278 bushels; hay, 3,145 tons; maple sugar, 5,725 pounds; wool, 17,020 pounds.

Distances. Twenty miles north from Bennington, and thirty-one south by west from Rutland.

SEARSBURGH.

BENNINGTON Co. Searsburgh is too elevated on the Green Mountains, either for cultivation, population, or wool growing. It presents, from almost every point, wild and beautiful landscapes.

Boundaries. North by Somerset, east by Wilmington, south by Readsborough, and west by Woodford.

Productions of the Soil. Wheat, 8 bushels; potatoes, 2,240 bushels; hay, 158 tons; maple sugar, 5,640 pounds; wool, 234 pounds.

Distances. Eleven miles east from Bennington, and twenty miles west from Brattleborough.

SHAFTSBURY.

BENNINGTON Co. Shaftsbury lies between the Battenkill and Walloomscoik Rivers; it has no large streams. Some tributaries of each of these rivers rise here, which afford several mill privileges. West Mountain lies partly in this town and partly in Arlington. It extends into Shaftsbury about three miles, and is about two miles in width. This mountain is timbered with chestnut, oak, maple, birch, &c.

The soil is generally of a good quality, and, in the south-western part, is probably not exceeded in fertility by any in the State. The timber on the highlands is mostly chestnut and oak. The minerals are iron ore, of an excellent quality, and a beautiful white marble, which has been extensively quarried.

Boundaries. North by Arlington, east by Glastenbury, south by Bennington, and west by Cambridge, New York.

First Settlers. The settlement of this town was commenced about the year 1763. Among the early settlers may be mentioned Messrs. Cole, Willoughby, Clark, Doolittle, Waldo, and several families of Mattisons.

The Hon. Jonas Galusha, late Governor of Vermont, came into this town in the spring of 1775. During the revolutionary war he was made captain of one of the two companies of militia in this town, and the other was commanded by Captain Amos Huntington. Capt. Huntington was taken prisoner at the battle of Hubbardton, and sent to Canada, after which the two companies were united, under the command of Captain Galusha, who fought at their head in Bennington battle.

First Ministers. The Baptists are the most numerous religious denomination, and they have two societies. The town gives name to the Baptist Association in this section of the State, it being called the "Shaftsbury Association," and is one of the first formed in the State. The Rev. Caleb Blood was, for many years, a zealous and successful preacher of the gospel here. He removed to Boston about the year 1807.

Productions of the Soil. Wheat, 1,999 bushels; Indian corn, 12,684 bushels; potatoes, 50,000 bushels; hay, 4,380 tons; maple sugar, 9,527 pounds; wool, 43,682 pounds.

Distances. Ninety-seven miles south-west from Montpelier, and eight north from Bennington.

SHARON.

WINDSOR CO. White River passes through Sharon, and affords it an abundant water power. Here are mills for the manufacture of woollen goods, paper, and other articles. It contains a handsome and flourishing village. The surface of the town is broken, but the soil is warm and productive.

Boundaries. North by Strafford, east by Norwich, south by Pomfret, and west by Royalton.

First Settlers. The settlement of Sharon was commenced about the year 1765, by emigrants from Connecticut. As near as can be ascertained, Robert Havens and family were the first who wintered in the town.

First Ministers. The Congregational was the first church formed, and was organized September 11, 1782. The Rev. Lathrop Thompson was ordained over this church December 3, 1788, and dismissed March 16, 1793. The Rev. Sam'l Bascom was settled Mar.12, 1806.

Productions of the Soil. Wheat, 2,774 bushels; Indian corn, 9,142 bushels; potatoes, 41,735 bushels; hay, 3,813 tons; maple sugar, 8,580 pounds; wool, 20,602 pounds.

Distances. Twenty-two miles north from Windsor, and thirty-four south-east from Montpelier.

The great Northern Railroad passes through Sharon.

SHEFFIELD.

CALEDONIA CO. This town lies on the height of land, between Connecticut River and Memphremagog Lake. Branches of Passumpsic and Barton Rivers both rise here. It is watered by several ponds. The lands are generally broken, and not very productive.

The settlement of this town was commenced about the year 1792.

Boundaries. North-east by Glover and a part of Barton, easterly by Sutton, and south and south-west by Wheelock.

Productions of the Soil. Wheat, 1,396 bushels; Indian corn, 725 bushels; potatoes, 39,200 bushels; hay, 2,292 tons; maple sugar, 25,615 pounds; wool, 4,273 pounds.

Distances. Sixteen miles north from Danville, and forty-six north-east from Montpelier.

SHELBURNE.

CHITTENDEN CO. Shelburne is finely watered by La Platt River, a pond covering 600 acres, and by the waters of Lake Champlain.

Shelburne Bay sets into the town, about four miles from the north-west, and affords the town a good harbor, and a depot of the interior trade on the beautiful Champlain.

The soil of the town is strong, fertile, and generally well improved.

A part of this town was annexed to St. George in 1848.

Boundaries. North by Burlington, east by St. George, south by Charlotte, and west by Lake Champlain.

First Settlers. A small settlement

was made in this town previous to the revolutionary war. The earliest settlers were two Germans, by the name of Logan and Pottier, who commenced upon two points of land extending into Lake Champlain, which still bear the names " Pottier's Point," and " Logan's Point." The first settlers were employed principally in getting out lumber for the Canada market, and tradition says that Pottier and Logan were murdered for their money, near the north end of Lake Champlain, by a party of soldiers sent out from Montreal to protect them from the Indians, on their return after having sold a raft of lumber.

First Ministers. The principal religious denominations are Episcopalians and Methodists. The Methodist Church is the most numerous, and has a neat chapel, built in 1831, and parsonage at the centre of the town. There was a small Episcopal parish here, under the charge of the Rev. Bethuel Chittenden, soon after the town was settled.

Productions of the Soil. Wheat, 1,768 bushels; Indian corn, 5,854 bushels; potatoes, 25,281 bushels; hay, 2,158 tons; maple sugar, 1,220 pounds; wool, 36,677 pounds.

Distances. Thirty-three miles west by north from Montpelier, and seven south from Burlington.

The great Southern Railroad from Boston to Burlington passes this way.

SHELDON.

FRANKLIN Co. This is a good township of land, productive of wool, grain, and other northern commodities. The River Missisco passes through the town, and Black Creek, a branch of that river, gives Sheldon an ample water power. The village is a thriving place, both in its manufactures and trade.

Boundaries. North by Highgate and Franklin, east by Enosburgh, south by Fairfield, and west by Swanton.

First Settlers. The settlement of Sheldon was commenced about the year 1790, by Colonel Elisha Sheldon, and Samuel B. Sheldon, emigrants

from Salisbury, Connecticut. The settlement advanced with considerable rapidity, and the town was soon organized.

First Ministers. A Congregational Church was organized in 1816; and an Episcopal Church, by the name of Grace Church, not far from the same time.

Productions of the Soil. Wheat, 3,850 bushels; Indian corn, 5,000 bushels; potatoes, 66,185 bushels; hay, 4,340 tons; maple sugar, 29,270 pounds; wool, 14,721 pounds.

Distances. Forty-six miles north west from Montpelier, thirty-two north by east from Burlington, and ten north north-east from St. Albans.

SHERBURNE.

RUTLAND Co. Killington Peak, 3,924 feet in height, several ponds, and Thundering Brook, with a handsome fall, lie in this town. Queechy River rises in this town, and along its banks is some good land; but the lands are generally too elevated, even for pasturage.

Boundaries. North by Stockbridge, east by Bridgewater, south and west by Mendon.

First Settlers. The settlement was commenced here in 1785, by Isaiah Washburn. The town was organized in 1794.

First Minister. A Congregational Church was formed here in 1823.

Productions of the Soil. Wheat, 686 bushels; Indian corn, 762 bushels; potatoes, 12,245 bushels; hay, 1,295 tons; maple sugar, 6,970 pounds; wool, 4,257 pounds.

Distances. Ten miles north-east from Rutland.

This town is but a few miles from the Southern Railroad depot at Rutland.

SHOREHAM.

ADDISON Co. Shoreham lies on the east side of Lake Champlain, and is watered by Lemonfair River, a good mill stream. The lake here is about a mile wide. The surface of Shoreham is level, and the soil remarkably good. This is one of the best farming towns in the State. There are some manufactures in the town, and a pleasant and flourishing village on the banks of the lake. Most of the waters here are impregnated with Epsom salts.

This is the site of Newton Academy.

Boundaries. North by Bridport, east by Whiting and Cornwall, south by Orwell, and west by Lake Champlain.

First Settlers. The settlement was commenced about the year 1766, by Col. Ephraim Doolittle, Paul Moore, Marshal Newton, and others. They adopted the Moravian plan, and had all things common, until the settlement was broken up during the revolutionary war. On the return of peace the settlement was recommenced, by some of the former settlers and others from Massachusetts and Connecticut, and the town was soon organized.

First Ministers. Rev. Abel Woods, of the Baptist order, was the first settled minister. The Congregational Church was organized in May, 1792. Rev. Evans Beardsley was settled over it from December 26, 1805, to May 9, 1809.

Productions of the Soil. Wheat, 3,348 bushels; Indian corn, 8,580 bushels; potatoes, 26,180 bushels; hay, 13,560 tons; maple sugar, 2,160 pounds; wool, 95,276 pounds.

Distances. Twelve miles south-west from Middlebury, about forty-two south-west from Montpelier, and twenty-six north from Whitehall, N. Y.

SHREWSBURY.

RUTLAND CO. Shrewsbury lies mostly on the Green Mountains and the eastern part is very much elevated. In the north part is Shrewsbury Peak, which is one of the highest summits of the Green Mountains, and is more than 4100 feet above the tide water. This is often mistaken for Killington Peak. Mill River runs through the south-west part of the township, and Cold River through the north part, both of which are sufficiently large for mills. There are two considerable

ponds in the southerly part called Peal's and Ashley's Pond. Shrewsbury is well adapted to the production of grass, and the timber is such as is common to the mountain towns. The town was chartered in 1763.

Boundaries. North by Mendon, east by Plymouth, south by Mount Holly, and west by Clarendon.

Productions of the Soil. Wheat, 528 bushels; Indian corn, 1,658 bushels; potatoes, 55,005 bushels; hay, 4,788 tons; maple sugar, 38,981 pounds; wool, 11,835 pounds.

Distances. Twenty-two miles west from Windsor, and nine south-east from Rutland. The great Southern Railroad passes near the border of this town.

SOMERSET.

WINDHAM CO. Mount Pisgah and other elevations give to the surface of this township so rough and dreary an aspect, that but few are bold enough to attempt the cultivation of its soil. It is watered by the upper branches of Deerfield River. It would put the neighboring towns into a pretty pickle if it should *turn a Somerset.*

Boundaries. North by Stratton, east by Dover and a part of Wardsborough, south by Searsburgh and a part of Wilmington, and west by Glastenbury.

Productions of the Soil. Wheat, 115 bushels; Indian corn, 151 bushels; potatoes, 9,930 bushels; hay, 777 tons; maple sugar, 5,440 pounds; wool, 993 pounds.

Distances. Fourteen miles north-east from Bennington, and sixteen north-west from Brattleborough.

SOUTH HERO.

GRAND ISLE CO. Lake Champlain bounds this town on all sides. The passage in the lake however, is very narrow between the towns of North and South Hero. The lake is fordable a considerable part of the year on the Vermont side. The town was formerly a part of North Hero, and was separated from it in 1788. It is supposed that all the lands of this island county were once covered by the waters of the lake, as clam shells are found incorporated with the rocks in the highest places. The scenery around these islands is beautiful. This vicinity was a favorite resort for the Indians, as appears from a large number of their implements found on the islands. It seems they manufactured hatchets, spear heads, chisels, arrows, and a variety of other implements at this place, from a flint stone not found in this region, but brought from a distance. This town furnishes a great abundance of food for the inhabitants, and some for exportation. This is a pleasant stopping place for the angler, the painter or the geologist. The Sand Bar Bridge now constructing (1849) will connect this island with the main land at Milton.

Boundaries. North by the township of Grand Isle, and on all other parts by Lake Champlain.

First Settlers. South Hero was chartered together with Grand Isle, North Hero, and Vineyard, to Ethan Allen, Samuel Herrick and others, October 27, 1779.

First Ministers. A Congregational Church was formed here in 1799, and a Methodist Society in 1802.

Productions of the Soil. Wheat, 1,917 bushels; Indian corn, 3,000 bushels; potatoes, 13,076 bushels; hay, 2,182 tons; maple sugar, 6,852 pounds; wool, 23,044 pounds.

Distances. Twelve miles north-west from Burlington, and sixteen south-west from St. Albans.

SPRINGFIELD.

WINDSOR Co. The land in Springfield is generally rich, with a deep soil suitable for grass or tillage; on the rivers are extensive intervales, forming some of the most beautiful farms in the State.

The principal village is situated on Black River Falls, near the centre of the town. These falls are about four miles from the confluence of Black River with the Connecticut; their descent is rapid over a rocky bed, about sixty rods, when the waters are con-

tracted, and precipitated fifty or sixty feet down an abrupt ledge into a narrow channel. This ravine extends about twelve rods; it is sixty or seventy feet deep, and is walled by perpendicular ledges of mica slate. Over this ravine has been erected a bridge, from which may be had a full view of the falls. A mist constantly arises, in which may be seen, in a fair day, all the colors of the rainbow.

This is a very flourishing town, and the scenery around its neat and handsome village is delightful.

Boundaries. North by Weathersfield, east by Connecticut River, which separates it from Charlestown, N. H., south by Rockingham, and west by Chester, and a small part of Baltimore.

First Settlers. It was chartered August 20, 1761, containing 26,400 acres. Among the first settlers were Mr. Simeon Stevens and the Hon. Lewis R. Morris.

First Ministers. There are various denominations of Christians in this town. The Congregationalists built a church in 1792, and settled the Rev. Robinson Smiley in 1801.

Productions of the Soil. Wheat, 2,305 bushels; Indian corn, 3,181 bushels; potatoes, 46,603 bushels; hay, 6,345 tons; maple sugar, 13,247 pounds; wool, 48,412 pounds.

Distances. Seventy miles south from Montpelier, and twenty-four south from Woodstock. The Connecticut River Railroad passes through the town.

STAMFORD.

BENNINGTON Co. A mountain township on the line of Massachusetts. Branches of the Hoosack and Walloomsack rise here. There are several fine fish ponds among the mountains; and some good land; but the lands in Stamford are generally too elevated for culture. The township was chartered in 1753.

Boundaries. North by Woodford, east by Reedsborough, south by Clarksburgh, Mass., and west by Pownal.

Productions of the Soil. Wheat, 267 bushels; Indian corn, 569 bushels; potatoes, 14,755 bushels; hay, 1,652

tons; maple sugar, 21,050 pounds; wool, 3,059 pounds.

Distances. Nine miles south-east from Bennington, and twenty-one west by south from Brattleborough.

STARKSBOROUGH.

ADDISON Co. This town is watered by Lewis Creek and Huntington River, which are good mill streams. There are three springs in the town, not more than twenty rods apart, which unite and form a stream of sufficient power for a number of mills, and is thus improved. The town is rough and mountainous.

Hog's Back Mountain skirts its western border, and East Mountain passes through its centre, and divides the waters of the rivers. There is some good land in the town, but a large portion of the territory is too elevated for cultivation. Here are two pleasant villages, and the manufactures of iron are considerable.

Boundaries. North by Huntington and Hinesburgh, east by Huntington and Buel's Gore, south by Lincoln and Bristol, and west by Monkton.

First Settlers. The settlement was commenced in April, 1788, by George Bidwell and Horace Kellogg with their families. John Ferguson and Thomas V. Ratenburgh came into that part of Monkton which has since been added to this township, about the same time. The first settlers emigrated principally from New York and Connecticut. Mr. Bidwell lived fifty-two years on the place where he settled, endured at first many privations and hardships, but by industry and economy acquired a handsome landed property, and died April 13, 1840, aged eighty-four. He was in his day one of the principal men in the town, and he is still remembered with gratitude and affection.

First Ministers. A Congregational Church was organized here in 1804. There is in this town a society of Friends.

Productions of the Soil. Wheat, 1,478 bushels; Indian corn, 5,800 bushels; potatoes, 30,200 bushels; hay, 3,120

tons; maple sugar, 10,690 pounds; wool, 10,260 pounds.

Distances. Twenty-two miles west by south from Montpelier, and eighteen north by east from Middlebury.

STERLING.

LAMOILLE Co. Sterling Peak, in the south part of this town, ranks among the most elevated summits of the Green Mountain range. Some streams issue from this mountain town. It was first settled in 1799, and contains 23,040 acres of land.

Boundaries. Northerly by Johnson, easterly by Morristown, southerly by Mansfield, and westerly by Cambridge.

Productions of the Soil. Wheat, 536 bushels; Indian corn, 262 bushels; potatoes, 10,870 bushels; hay, 833 tons; maple sugar, 5,400 pounds; wool, 1,806 pounds.

Distances. Five miles south-west from Hydepark, and thirty-two north-west from Montpelier.

STOCKBRIDGE.

WINDSOR Co. White River runs through the northerly part of this town, and in its passage receives the fourth branch, or Tweed River, from the west. The mill privileges are sufficiently numerous, but those at the Great Narrows in White River are the best. The whole river is here compressed into a channel but a few feet in width. Steatite is found here.

Boundaries. Northerly by Bethel, easterly by Barnard, southerly by Sherburne, and westerly by Pittsfield.

First Settlers. The settlement of Stockbridge was commenced in 1784, and 1785 by Asa Whitcomb, Elias Keyes, John Durkee and Joshua Bartlet, with their families.

First Minister. The Rev. Justin Parsons was settled over the Congregational Church in this town and Pittsfield September 15, 1812. He continued till 1827.

Productions of the Soil. Wheat, 1,746 bushels; Indian corn, 4,982 bushels; potatoes, 42,680 bushels; hay, 4,057

tons; maple sugar, 34,320 pounds; wool, 18,005 pounds.

Distances. Thirty-six miles south by west from Montpelier, and twenty-six north-west from Windsor. The great Northern Railroad passes through the neighboring town of Bethel.

STOWE.

LAMOILLE Co. Waterbury River and its branches give this town a good water power, and by which several mills are put into operation.

Stowe is situated between the Mansfield and Hog's Back Mountains, and contains a large tract of level, fertile land, which appears to have been of alluvial formation. This valley contains some very beautiful and productive farms. The exports of agricultural products are valuable. Stowe is a flourishing town, and contains four neat and pleasant mountain valley villages.

All that tract of land formerly called Mansfield was annexed to this town in 1848.

Boundaries. North by Morristown, east by Worcester, south by Waterbury, and west by Mansfield.

First Settlers. The settlement was commenced about the year 1793.

The first meeting-house built in this town was in 1818.

Productions of the Soil. Wheat, 2,636 bushels; Indian corn, 5,337 bushels; potatoes, 75,957 bushels; hay, 4,812 tons; maple sugar, 31,150 pounds; wool, 16,628 pounds.

Distances. Ten miles south from Hydepark, and thirty-seven north from Montpelier. The Northern Railroad passes through a neighboring town.

STRAFFORD.

ORANGE Co. Strafford contains two pleasant villages. The surface is uneven, but the soil is generally good. It is watered by a principal branch of Ompomponoosuc River, which affords several good mill privileges, on which are erected a number of mills and other machinery.

In the north-easterly part is a pond covering about 100 acres, called Podunk Pond, which is a place of considerable resort for amusement and angling.

In the south-east corner of Strafford is an extensive bed of the sulphuret of iron, from which immense quantities of copperas are manufactured.

"*Strafford Copperas Works.* This establishment was formerly styled the Vermont Mineral Factory Company, but is now called the *Vermont Copperas Company;* the owners, residing chiefly in Boston, having united this with a mine they own in Shrewsbury. It is situated in the extreme southeastern corner of the town, on the east side of a hill, which contains an inexhaustible *ridge* of the ore, or, technically, *sulphuret of iron.* This mass of solid rock, in appearance, is usually covered with what miners call the *cap,* a petrifactive soil of various depths, in which roots, leaves, and limbs of trees, beech-nuts, hazle-nuts, and acorns, are often found turned into stone or iron. There are two factories, each about 267 feet in length by ninety-four in width. These contain eight vats made of lead, ten feet by twelve feet, twenty-one inches in depth and three fourths of an inch in thickness, used for boilers. Lead is the only metal that will endure the operation of the copperas liquor, and this requires constant repair. An unlimited quantity can be made; the facilities for manufacturing being, perhaps, unsurpassed in the world. The copperas made here is used by most of the manufactories of New England, and is sent to all parts of the United States. It is supposed to excel for dyeing purposes any copperas offered in market. The process of making is as follows. The ore is blasted from the bed, by means of powder. It is then broken into pieces with sledges, and afterwards the miners assort and break it up still finer with hammers. It is then thrown into large heaps, where it ignites spontaneously, or fire is sometimes set to it to hasten the process. In this condition it generally burns for the space of two months; in that time the sulphur is converted into *sulphuric acid,* and unites itself with the iron, forming *sulphate of iron,* or copperas. The smoke gives to vegetation, and to all surrounding objects, a sterile and sickly appearance, but the health of the workmen is not affected. These heaps of pyrites, being now thoroughly pulverized by fire, are carried to places where water, from a fountain on the summit of a hill, is made to run upon and leach this mass of crude *sulphate of iron.* The lye is now drawn off into large wooden reservoirs, and thence into the leaden vats as fast as wanted. In these vats the lye or liquor is boiled to a certain strength, tested by acidimeters, and then drained off into wooden vats, where it remains to crystalize. Branches of trees were formerly thrown in, for the crystals to adhere to; but Mr. Reynolds made an improvement. Pieces of joist three inches square, six feet long, laid across the top of the vats, with holes bored, and round sticks eighteen inches long by three quarters of an inch in diameter, inserted at intervals of about six inches, are now used with great advantage. This makes a great saving of labor, although it has in some measure destroyed the fanciful shapes which the crystals formerly assumed upon some favorite branch; and the poet, had he been born on copperas hill, would have written, 'as the twig is bent the copperas is inclined.' The crystals are multangular, and of a beautiful transparent green color. These twigs, with specimens varnished, may be seen in the cabinets of many scientific gentlemen in various parts of the country. After crystalization takes place the liquor is drained off, and the copperas is shovelled into the packing rooms. When dry, it is usually put into casks, holding about half a ton each, but frequently into casks of every size.

"The mine was discovered in 1793, by two men who were tapping sap-trees. Tradition says they discovered a spontaneous combustion among the leaves, but it is more probable that they found copperas in some wet spot spontaneously formed. The works were first commenced by Mr. Eastman, but were not successfully prosecuted until within about thirty years, when the stock was taken up in Boston by the Messrs. Reynolds and the late energetic Col. Binney. President Monroe visited the works, in his tour in the summer of 1817. In 1827, the company employed from thirty to forty hands to make about the same quantity of copperas they now make with ten hands. A thousand tons of copperas has been made in a year."

Boundaries. North by Vershire, east by Thetford, south by Sharon, and west by Tunbridge.

First Settlers. The settlement of this town was commenced just before the revolutionary war.

First Ministers. The first meeting-house was built in town by the Baptists, in 1794, and the second in 1799. The Rev. Joab Young was the first settled minister. He was settled by the Universalists in 1799, and died in 1816.

Productions of the Soil. Wheat, 4,382 bushels; Indian corn, 6,640 bushels; potatoes, 51,634 bushels; hay, 4,909 tons; maple sugar, 28,485 pounds; wool, 13,550 pounds.

Distances. Thirty miles south southeast from Montpelier, and eleven southeast from Chelsea.

This town adjoins Thetford, through which the Connecticut River Railroad passes.

STRATTON.

WINDHAM CO. This is a mountainous town in the west part of the county. Branches of Deerfield and Winhall Rivers rise here from two ponds. The soil is cold and generally unprofitable.

Stratton was settled principally by emigrants from Massachusetts. Among the early settlers were families by the name of Morsman and Patch. A meeting-house was built here about the year 1809.

Boundaries. North by Winhall, east by Jamaica and Wardsborough, south by Somerset, and west by Sunderland.

Productions of the Soil. Wheat, 169 bushels; Indian corn, 141 bushels; potatoes, 942 bushels; hay, 837 tons; maple sugar, 2,672 pounds; wool, 1,637 pounds.

Distances. Eighteen miles north-east from Bennington, and twenty-two north-west from Brattleborough.

SUDBURY.

RUTLAND Co. Otter Creek touches upon the eastern border of this town. The other streams are small. Hubbardton Pond extends into the south part, and there are in town several smaller ponds, of which Hinkum Pond is the most considerable. The surface is uneven, and a high ridge of land extends through the town, near the centre, from south to north. The soil is generally a rich loam. The timber is principally pine, beech, and maple. There is a small village in the easterly part of the town.

Boundaries. North by Whiting, east by Brandon, south by Hubbardton, and west by Orwell and a part of Benson.

First Settlers. This town was chartered in 1761; the early settlers were generally from Connecticut.

First Minister. Rev. Silas Parsons was settled over the Congregational Church in 1806.

Productions of the Soil. Wheat, 1,488 bushels; Indian corn, 3,890 bushels; potatoes, 13,315 bushels; hay, 3,009 tons; maple sugar, 550 pounds; wool, 24,718 pounds.

Distances. Forty-three miles south-west from Montpelier, and seventeen north-west from Rutland.

The Southern Railroad passes in this vicinity.

SUNDERLAND.

BENNINGTON Co. The Battenkill River passes through the north-western part of this town, in a south-westerly direction. On this stream are some fine alluvial flats, which are overflowed every spring. Roaring Branch originates in several large ponds in the eastern part of the town, and, running

westerly, unites with the Battenkill in Arlington. On this stream are several excellent situations for mills and other machinery. The soil consists of alluvion, loam, and marl. Near the foot of the Green Mountains, the sulphate of iron is found in considerable quantities. On the side of the mountain a vein of lead ore has been discovered in granular limestone.

Boundaries. North by Manchester, east by Stratton, south by Glastenbury, and west by Arlington.

First Settlers. The settlement of Sunderland was commenced in 1766, by Messrs. Brownson, Bradley, Warrens, Evarts, Chipman, and Webb, emigrants from Connecticut.

First Minister. Rev. Chancey Lee was settled over the Congregational Church in 1786; dismissed in 1795.

Productions of the Soil. Wheat, 125 bushels; Indian corn, 1,861 bushels; potatoes, 7,804 bushels; hay, 1,232 tons; maple sugar, 5,577 pounds: wool, 4,349 pounds.

Distances. Eighty-seven miles south-west from Montpelier, and fifteen north by east from Bennington.

SUTTON.

CALEDONIA Co. Sutton is watered by two considerable branches, which unite near the south line of Burke, and join the Passumpsic River in Lyndon. There are several ponds, of which Fish Pond is the largest, and it lies in the north-west corner. It covers about 200 acres, and discharges its waters into Barton River.

The surface of Sutton is generally even, and considerable tracts of it are so low and wet as to be incapable of cultivation. There are several bogs of marl in this town.

Boundaries. North-easterly by Westmore and a part of Newark, east by Burke, south by Lyndon, and west by Sheffield.

First Settlers. The settlement of Sutton was commenced about the year 1791, by a Mr. Hacket, who was soon after joined by other families from R. Island and Connecticut.

First Minister. Elder Amos Beck-

11

with was settled over the Baptist Church in 1804.

Productions of the Soil. Wheat, 2,876 bushels; Indian corn, 1,372 bushels; potatoes, 61,175 bushels; hay, 3,088 tons; maple sugar, 85,430 pounds; wool, 7,755 pounds.

Distances. Twenty-one miles north from Danville, and fifty-one north-east from Montpelier.

SWANTON.

FRANKLIN Co. This township is situated on the east side of Lake Champlain, opposite to North Hero and Alburgh.

Missisco River passes through Swanton, and fertilizes a considerable portion of its territory. This river is navigable for lake vessels to Swanton Falls, six miles from its mouth. These falls descend twenty feet, and, with other smaller streams, give to Swanton a water power of great value.

Bog iron ore is found in this town, and an abundance of beautiful marble. This marble is of various colors, and large quantities of it are wrought into all desired patterns, polished, and transported.

The surface and soil of Swanton are favorable to agricultural pursuits, with the exception of a part bordering the lake, which is low, wet, and cold; and which is the favorite abode, in summer, of wild geese, ducks, and other water fowls.

The village of Swanton is pleasantly located, and is the site of a number of manufactories, and of an increasing trade.

Swanton may boast of the purity of its air and water, and of *a* Walter Scott, who died in 1815, aged one hundred and ten years.

Boundaries. North by Highgate, east by Sheldon and Fairfield, south by St. Albans, and west by Lake Champlain.

First Settlers. Before the conquest of Canada by the English, the French and Indians had a settlement at Swanton Falls, consisting of about fifty huts, and had cleared some land, on which they raised corn and vegetables.

They had also built a church and a saw mill; and the channel cut through the rocks, to supply water for the latter, still remains. This place was occupied by the Indians till the commencement of the revolution. The first permanent settlers here were John Hilliker and family, about the year 1787. They were soon joined by other settlers.

First Ministers. A Congregational Church was organized in 1800, and in 1825 Rev. Eben H. Dorman was settled. In this town is a society of Friends.

Productions of the Soil. Wheat, 4,290 bushels; Indian corn, 7,184 bushels; potatoes, 46,264 bushels; hay, 4,920 tons; maple sugar, 10,474 pounds; wool, 22,759 pounds.

Distances. Fifty miles north-west from Montpelier, twenty-eight north from Burlington.

The proposed railroad from Burlington to Highgate would add much to the facilities of the trade of this flourishing town.

THETFORD.

ORANGE Co. This town is pleasantly situated on the west side of Connecticut River, opposite to Lyme, N. H. The Ompomponoosuc, and its branches, give the town an excellent water power. There are several ponds in Thetford, one of which is worthy of notice. It covers about nine acres, and is situated on an elevation, the base of which is only four rods from Connecticut River, and 100 feet in height. It is very deep; it has neither inlet or outlet, and contains large quantities of perch and other fish.

The surface of the town is generally rocky and uneven; it has but little intervale, but the soil is strong and productive. There are some manufactures in the town, a rich vein of galena, and three neat villages.

Boundaries. North by Fairlee and west Fairlee, east by Connecticut River, which separates it from Lyme, N. H., south by Norwich, and west by Strafford.

First Settlers. The settlement was

commenced here in 1764, by John Chamberlain, from Hebron, Ct. The next year he was joined by two other families; one by the name of Baldwin, and the other by the name of Hosford. Samuel, the son of John Chamberlain, was the first English child born in town. John Chamberlain was nick-named *Quail John*. Being industrious, and somewhat parsimonious, he accumulated considerable property, and his fame has been perpetuated in the following stanza:

" Old Quail John was the first that came on,
  As poor as a calf in the spring ;
But now he is rich as Governor Fitch,
  And lives like a lord or a king."

First Minister. A Congregational minister, by the name of Clement Sumner, was ordained here in 1773. He became a tory, and went to Swanzey, N. H. Rev. Asa Burton was ordained in 1779. He continued here till his death, 1836, aged eighty-four.

Productions of the Soil. Wheat, 3,635 bushels ; Indian corn, 15,628 bushels; potatoes, 58,957 bushels ; hay, 4,978 tons ; maple sugar, 21,288 pounds; wool, 25,798 pounds.

Distances. Thirty-four miles south south-east from Montpelier, and eighteen south-east from Chelsea.

The Connecticut River Railroad passes through the town.

TINMOUTH.

RUTLAND CO. This town is separated from Wallingford by Otter Creek. Furnace Brook rises from a pond in the south part of the town, and passing through Tinmouth and Clarendon, falls into Otter Creek at Rutland. This stream has been noted for great quantities of fish of an extraordinary size.

The surface of Tinmouth is hilly, in some parts mountainous. There is some good land on the streams, and a large portion of the high land is good for pasturage.

There are several quarries of beautiful marble in town, iron ore in abundance, and several iron works.

Boundaries. North by Clarendon

and Ira, east by Wallingford, south by Danby, and west by Wells and Middletown.

First Settlers. The settlement was commenced here about the year 1770. Among the first settlers were Thomas Peck and John McNeal. This town was organized March 11, 1777. Soon after, the following oath of allegiance was imposed upon the freemen of the town. "You each of you swear, by the living God, that you believe for yourselves that the King of Great Britain hath not any right to command, or authority in or over the States of America, and that you do not hold yourselves bound to yield any allegiance or obedience to him within the same, and that you will, to the utmost of your power, maintain and defend the freedom, independence, and privileges of the United States of America against all open enemies, or traitors, or conspirators whatsoever; so help you God."

First Ministers. A Congregational Church was organized here in 1780, and has had the following settled ministers. Rev. Benjamin Osborn, from 1780 to 1787; Rev. Wm. Boies, from 1804 to 1818.

Productions of the Soil. Wheat, 1,441 bushels ; Indian corn, 2,824 bushels; potatoes, 10,750 bushels; hay, 3,187 tons ; maple sugar, 19,555 pounds ; wool, 10,759 pounds.

Distances. Eight miles south from Rutland, through which the great Southern Railroad passes.

TOPSHAM.

ORANGE CO. Topsham is on elevated ground, with a rocky, strong soil, adapted to grazing. It contains much granite, and is watered by the upper branches of Wait's River, which propel a number of mills.

Boundaries. North by Stratton, east by Newbury, south by Corinth, and west by Orange.

First Settlers. The settlement was commenced about the year 1781, by Thomas Chamberlain, Thomas McKeith, and Samuel Farnum. In 1783 they were joined by Robert Mann,

Samuel Thompson, and John Crown; and, in 1784, by Lemuel Tabor. The first settlers were generally from New Hampshire.

The town house, which has been occupied as a meeting-house, was erected in 1806.

Productions of the Soil. Wheat, 5,576 bushels; Indian corn, 5,653 bushels; potatoes, 63,179 bushels; hay, 4,294 tons; maple sugar, 31,645 pounds; wool, 8,961 pounds.

Distances. Nineteen miles south-east from Montpelier, and fifteen north-east from Chelsea.

The Connecticut River Railroad passes through the neighboring town of Newbury.

TOWNSHEND.

WINDHAM CO. West River passes through this town, with considerable rapidity. Along its banks are some tracts of good intervale; but the surface of the town is generally hilly, and the soil more calculated for grazing than tillage. There are some manufactures in the town, a high school of good reputation, and two pleasant villages.

The West Townshend Manufacturing Co. was incorporated in 1848.

Boundaries. North by Grafton and Athens, east by Athens and Brookline, south by Newfane, and west by Windham, Jamaica, and Wardsborough.

First Settlers. The first settlement was commenced here in 1761, by Joseph Tyler, who was soon joined by John Hazleton, whose mother lived to the age of one hundred and four years.

Among the early and distinguished inhabitants of Townshend may be mentioned the late General Samuel Fletcher. He was born at Grafton, Mass., in 1745. At the age of seventeen he enlisted as a soldier in the contest between the British and French colonies, in which service he continued one year. On his return he learned the trade of a blacksmith, which he followed about four years, when he married a young lady with a handsome property, and, resigning the sledge, removed to Townshend, to wield the axe among the trees of the forest. In 1775 he joined the American standard at Bunker's Hill, with rank of orderly serjeant. He returned to Townshend in January following, where he was made a captain of militia. He was, at this time, principal leader in the county convention, and was ordered, as captain, to raise as many minute men as possible in his vicinity, who were to hold themselves in readiness to march at the beat of the drum. His whole company volunteered, and, in 1777, they marched to Ticonderoga, for the purpose of relieving the American army, which was there besieged. On this expedition, with thirteen volunteers, he attacked a British detachment of forty men, killed one, and took seven prisoners, without sustaining any loss himself. He soon after received a major's commission, and continued in the service till after the capture of Burgoyne. After his return, he rose through the different grades of office to that of Major-General of militia, which office he held six years. He was several years member of the executive council, and, in 1788, was appointed high sheriff of the county of Windham, which office he held eighteen years successively, and he was three years a judge of the county court. He died Sept. 15, 1814, aged about seventy years.

First Minister. Rev. Mr. Dudley was ordained over the Congregational Church in 1777, and dismissed in 1780. This church then became extinct until 1792, when it was re-organized.

Productions of the Soil. Wheat, 2,025 bushels; Indian corn, 7,946 bushels; potatoes, 41,488 bushels; hay, 4,178 tons; maple sugar, 10,460 pounds; wool, 17,276 pounds.

Distances. Twelve miles north-west from Brattleboro', twenty-eight north-east from Bennington, and ninety-five south from Montpelier.

TROY.

ORLEANS CO. This town is well watered by Missisco River, which runs through it near the western border from south to north, and by several of its tributaries.

The falls on the Missisco, in the north part, are a considerable curiosity. Here the river precipitates itself down a ledge of rocks about seventy feet. These falls, and the deep still water below, present a grand and interesting spectacle, when viewed from a rock which projects over them, 120 feet in perpendicular height.

The soil is in general a strong loam, suitable for grass and most kinds of grain. The surface is generally level, and along the river are tracts of intervale, of considerable extent and fertility. The principal rocks are chlorite and mica slate, serpentine, limestone, and steatite.

Some years ago, an immense mass of iron ore, of an excellent quality, was discovered in Troy, a short distance to the eastward of Missisco River. A furnace and forge have been erected, which produce annually large quantities of iron. The quantity of ore is inexhaustible.

The Orleans Iron Company, in this town, was incorporated in 1847.

Boundaries. North by Patton, Canada, east by Newport, south by Lowell, and west by Westfield and Jay.

First Settlers. The settlement was commenced about the year 1800, by emigrants from different towns on Connecticut River. During the late war with Great Britain, most of the inhabitants left the town. A part of them, however, returned after the war, and the settlement has since advanced with considerable rapidity.

Productions of the Soil. Wheat, 923 bushels; Indian corn, 1,880 bushels; potatoes, 30,880 bushels; hay, 2,192 tons; maple sugar, 19,066 pounds; wool, 5,944 pounds.

Distances. Ten miles north from Irasburgh, and forty-seven miles north from Montpelier.

TUNBRIDGE.

ORANGE Co. A branch of White River passes through this town, on which are mills of various kinds. The soil is generally a rich loam; on the stream the intervale land is extensive and valuable. In some parts of the town the surface is elevated.

Tunbridge contains a medicinal spring of some notoriety in cutaneous diseases. Considerable quantities of the products of the farms are sent to market.

There are three pleasant villages situated on the first branch of White River.

Boundaries. North by Chelsea, east by Strafford, south by Royalton, and west by Randolph.

First Settlers. The settlement of the township was commenced about the year 1776, by James Lyon, Moses Ordway, and others, emigrants from New Hampshire.

First Minister. Rev. David H. Williston was ordained over the Congregational Church in 1793, and dismissed in 1802.

Productions of the Soil. Wheat, 3,310 bushels; Indian corn, 7,620 bushels; potatoes, 67,705 bushels; hay, 3,430 tons; maple sugar, 31,670 pounds; wool, 18,905 pounds.

Distances. Twenty-six miles south by east from Montpelier, and seven south from Chelsea.

This town is in the neighborhood of the Northern and Connecticut River Railroads.

UNDERHILL.

CHITTENDEN Co. The head branches of Brown's River water this town. The surface is hilly and broken, and the soil hard, but tolerable for sheep, of which a considerable number are reared.

The settlement of this town was commenced about the year 1786.

A Congregational Church was organized in 1802, and in 1804 the Rev. James Parker was settled.

Boundaries. Northerly by Cambridge, easterly by Mansfield, southerly by Jericho, and westerly by Westford.

Productions of the Soil. Wheat, 1,186 bushels; Indian corn, 1,954 bushels; potatoes, 30,375 bushels; hay, 1,556 tons; maple sugar, 30,827 pounds; wool, 8,010 pounds.

11*

Distances. Fifteen miles north-east from Burlington, and twenty-six north-west from Montpelier.

VERGENNES.

ADDISON Co. This city is beautifully located on Otter Creek, at the falls on that stream, and is seven miles from Lake Champlain. Otter Creek, at this place, is about 500 feet wide, and, at the falls, is separated by two islands, which form three distinct falls of thirty-seven feet. These falls produce a great hydraulic power, rendered more valuable by being situated in the heart of a fertile country, and on the navigable waters of the lake.

The creek, or river, between the city and the lake, is crooked, but navigable for the largest lake vessels. During the late war, this was an important depot on the lake. Here was fitted out the squadron commanded by the gallant McDonough, who met the British fleet off Plattsburgh, N. Y., on the 11th of September, 1814, and made it his.

This is a very favorable position for ship-building; it now possesses important manufactories, and considerable trade. Although the territory of this city is quite small, its peculiarly favorable location, and the enterprise of its people, warrant it a great degree of prosperity.

This place has become a depository for munitions of war.

The railroad between Boston and Burlington passes through this city. No passer through this place can but observe the peculiar advantages of Vergennes. Here are united, in great perfection, the two great powers,—water for mills, and steam for transportation,—which cannot fail to render any place that possesses them an important mart for trade and manufacture.

Boundaries. North-east by Ferrisburgh, south by Waltham, and west by Panton and Ferrisburgh.

First Settlers. The first settlement within the present limits of Vergennes was made in 1766, by Donald M'Intosh, a native of Scotland, who was in the battle of Culloden. He came to this country with Gen. Wolfe's army, during the French war, and died July 14, 1803, aged eighty-four years. The emigrants, who subsequently located themselves here, were principally from Massachusetts, Connecticut, and the south parts of this State.

First Minister. A Congregational Church was formed Sept. 17, 1793. The Rev. Daniel C. Sanders was settled over it from June 12, 1794, to Aug. 24, 1799.

Productions of the Soil. Wheat, 150 bushels; Indian corn, 1,353 bushels; potatoes, 34,200 bushels; hay, 1,284 tons; wool, 9,900 pounds.

Distances. Twelve miles north-west from Middlebury, twenty-one south by east from Burlington.

The great Southern Railroad, between Boston and Burlington, passes through this smart little city.

VERNON.

WINDHAM Co. Vernon lies on the west side of Connecticut River, opposite to Winchester, N. H. That River bends abruptly at this place, but in consequence of its elevated and rocky shore, affords comparatively little intervale.

The surface is generally mountainous and rocky. There are in the town fine forests of oak and chestnut timber, and quarries of slate.

Boundaries. North by Brattleborough, east by Connecticut River, which separates it from Hinsdale, N. H., south by Northfield, Mass., and west by Guilford.

First Settlers. This was one of the first settled towns in the State, but the precise time of its commencement is not known. The earliest inhabitants were emigrants from Northampton and Northfield, Mass. The inhabitants of Vernon encountered all the dangers and solicitudes of Indian wars, and struggled with all those difficulties and hardships which are incident to frontier settlements. Fort Dummer, in Brattleborough, Hinsdale's Fort, in Hinsdale, and Bridgman's Fort, in this town, were all insufficient to shield the inhabitants from the incursions of the Indians.

First Ministers. The Baptists are the most numerous religious sect. A meeting-house was erected here in 1802. Elder David Newman, a Baptist, has officiated a number of years. The Rev. Bunker Gay, a Congregationalist, was ordained over the churches in this town and Hinsdale, N. H., in 1764, and dismissed in 1802.

Productions of the Soil. Wheat, 127 bushels; Indian corn, 5,910 bushels; potatoes, 7,955 bushels; hay, 970 tons; maple sugar, 300 pounds; wool, 1,965 pounds.

Distances. Eighteen miles south-east from Newfane, and about fifty miles south from Windsor.

The Connecticut River Railroad passes through the town.

VERSHIRE.

ORANGE Co. The surface of Vershire is uneven and stony, but furnishes pasturage for a large number of sheep, horses, and neat cattle. Branches of Ompomponoosuc River rise here, but give the town no valuable water power.

The settlement commenced here in 1780. The town was organized in 1783.

The Rev. Stephen Fuller, Congregationalist, and Rev. Ebenezer West, Baptist, were the first settled ministers.

Boundaries. North by Corinth, east by West Fairlee, south by Strafford, and west by Chelsea.

Productions of the Soil. Wheat, 6,303 bushels; Indian corn, 3,533 bushels; potatoes, 65,915 bushels; hay, 3,940 tons; maple sugar, 35,375 pounds; wool, 14,194 pounds.

Distances. Twenty-five miles south-east from Montpelier, and six east by south from Chelsea.

VICTORY.

ESSEX Co. This unorganized town was granted November 6, 1780, and chartered September 6, 1781, to Ebenezer Fisk and others, containing 23,040 acres. It is watered by Moose River, which runs through it from north-east to south-west.

Boundaries. North-westerly by Burke and a part of Kirby, north-easterly by Granby and a part of East Haven, south-east by Lunenburgh and Concord, and south-west by Bradleyvale.

Productions of the Soil. Wheat, 200 bushels; Indian corn, 50 bushels; potatoes, 2,610 bushels; hay, 123 tons; maple sugar, 2,450 pounds; wool, 921 pounds.

Distances. Twenty miles west from Guildhall, and fifty-four north-east from Montpelier.

WAITSFIELD.

WASHINGTON Co. This town is settled with industrious, enterprising, and generally flourishing farmers. The soil is diversified, but generally a mellow loam, deep, and of excellent quality, producing grass in the greatest abundance. Wheat, rye, barley, oats, corn, &c., are raised in such quantities, as amply to reward the hand of industry.

Mad River passes through the town, near the western boundary, in a direction from south-west to north-east, and falls into Winooski River in Moretown, seven miles below Montpelier. It receives here Mill Brook and Shepherd's Brook from the west, and Fay's Brook and Pine Brook from the east, all of which are sufficient for mills. Along this river the intervales are extensive, and, together with the adjacent uplands, make many excellent farms. The high lands, too, are of a good quality, and there can hardly be said to be a poor farm in town. A range of high lands runs through the eastern part of the town, the chief summit of which is called Bald Mountain.

Boundaries. North by Moretown, east by Northfield, south by Warren, and west by Fayston.

First Settlers. Gen. Wait, the first inhabitant of this town, was born at Sudbury, Mass., Feb. 13, 1737. He possessed a firm and vigorous constitution, and early manifested a disposition and talent for military enterprise.

At the age of eighteen he entered the service of his country, under the brave Gen. Amherst. In 1756 he was taken by the French, carried to Quebec, and from thence sent to France as a prisoner. On the coast of France he was retaken by the British, and carried to England. In the spring of 1757 he returned to America, and in 1758 assisted at the capture of Louisburgh. During the two succeeding years, he aided in the reduction of Canada. After the submission of Canada, he was sent, by the commandant at Detroit, to Illinois, to bring in the French garrisons included in the capitulation. He left Detroit Dec. 10, and returned on the 1st of March following, having performed the difficult service with singular perseverance and success. At twenty-five years of age he had been engaged in forty battles and skirmishes; and his clothes were several times perforated with musket balls, but he never received a wound. In 1767 he removed to Windsor, in this State, and constituted the third family in that township. He acted a decided and conspicuous part in favor of Vermont, in the controversy with New York. In 1776 he entered the service of the United States as captain, and fought under the banners of Washington till the close of the war, during which time he had been raised to the rank of colonel. After this he was made a brigadier-general of militia, and was seven years high sheriff of the county of Windsor. Having made a large purchase here, he removed his family to this town in 1789. Here he lived to behold the wilderness converted into fruitful fields, in the enjoyment of competence, and died in 1822, aged eighty-six years.

First Minister. A Congregational Church was organized in 1796, over which Rev. Wm. Salisbury was settled in 1801.

Productions of the Soil. Wheat, 1,615 bushels; Indian corn, 3,550 bushels; potatoes, 47,315 bushels; hay, 2,256 tons; maple sugar, 30,495 pounds; wool, 17,499 pounds.

Distances. Twenty miles south-west from Montpelier.

The Northern Railroad passes through Northfield, one of the boundary towns.

WALDEN.

CALEDONIA Co. This is an elevated town, between the head waters of Winooski and Lamoille Rivers. Cole's Pond, a large sheet of water lying in the town, produces a small stream, called "Joe's Brook." The surface is generally rough; but the soil in some parts of the town produces good crops. Some years ago a stone mortar was found here, supposed to have been made by the Indians.

Boundaries. Northerly by Goshen Gore, easterly by Danville, southerly by Cabot, and westerly by Hardwick.

First Settlers. Nathaniel Perkins, Esq., moved his family into this township, in January, 1789, and his was for three years the only family in Walden.

First Ministers. The religious societies are the Methodist, the Universalist, Baptist, and Freewill Baptist. The first was organized in 1810, the second in 1829, and the last in 1837.

Productions of the Soil. Wheat, 2,812 bushels; Indian corn, 486 bushels; potatoes, 38,833 bushels; hay, 3,466 tons; maple sugar, 40,370 pounds; wool, 4,226 pounds.

Distances. Ten miles north-west from Danville, and twenty-five north-east from Montpelier.

WALLINGFORD.

RUTLAND Co. This town is watered by Otter Creek, Mill River, and by three ponds, one of which, Hiram's Pond, covering an area of 350 acres, lies on very elevated ground, and is one of the principal sources of Otter Creek. The other ponds are of less size, and less elevated. These mountain ponds are very handsome, and contain fish. The soil of the town is generally good; that on the banks of Otter Creek is very fertile and productive. Wallingford produces all the varieties of grain, grass, &c., and feeds a large number of sheep.

A range of primitive limestone passes through the western part of the town, in which have been opened several quarries of excellent marble. Green Hill, situated near the centre, is composed almost entirely of quartz. A part of White Rocks, belonging to the Green Mountain range, appears to be granite, the rest quartz. At the foot of White Rocks are large cavities, formed by the fallen rocks, called the *icebeds*, in which ice is found in abundance through the summer season.

There are some valuable manufacturing establishments in Wallingford, and a flourishing trade. The village is pleasantly located on the banks of Otter Creek, near one of the ponds. It contains some handsome buildings, and presents a variety of picturesque scenery.

Boundaries. North by Clarendon, east by Mount Holly, south by Mount Tabor, and west by Tinmouth.

First Settlers. The settlement was commenced in 1773, by Abraham Jackson and family. The early settlers were mostly emigrants from Connecticut.

First Ministers. The Baptist Church was the first organized in town, and Elder Henry Green was the first settled minister. The Congregational Church was organized about 1802, when they settled the Rev. Benjamin Osborn.

Productions of the Soil. Wheat, 2,614 bushels; Indian corn, 7,384 bushels; potatoes, 38,775 bushels; hay, 5,216 tons; maple sugar, 17,715 pounds; wool, 14,560 pounds.

Distances. Ten miles south by east from Rutland, and forty-two north north-east from Bennington.

The Southern Railroad, between Boston and Burlington, passes through the town.

WALTHAM.

ADDISON Co. Buck Mountain lies near the centre of Waltham, and, as it is the highest land in the county, west of the Green Mountains, its summit exhibits a good view of a delightful section of country.

Waltham lies on the east side of Otter Creek, which it separates from Panton. Otter Creek, at this place, is sluggish in its course, and affords no mill privileges. The soil is generally good; that along the stream is excellent.

Boundaries. North by Ferrisburgh, east and south by New Haven, and west by a part of Vergennes and Otter Creek.

First Settlers. The settlement of Waltham was commenced just before the beginning of the revolutionary war, by a family of Griswolds, and others, from Connecticut.

First Ministers. The religious denominations are Congregationalists and Baptists.

Productions of the Soil. Wheat, 346 bushels; Indian corn, 1,910 bushels; potatoes, 7,600 bushels; hay, 1,730 tons; wool, 12,652 pounds.

Distances. Nine miles north-west from Middlebury, twenty-four south from Burlington, and forty miles southwest from Montpelier.

The Southern Railroad passes through a neighboring town.

WARDSBOROUGH.

WINDHAM Co. The surface of this town is hilly, and in some parts rocky; the soil is hard, but rendered productive by the industry of its people. Wardsborough is watered by West River, and contains a number of minerals, of which tremolite and zoisite are the most important, and of which fine specimens are found. There are some mills in the town, but the water power is not extensive.

Boundaries. North by Jamaica, east by Newfane and Townshend, south by Dover, and west by Stratton and Somerset.

First Settlers. The settlement of Wardsborough was commenced June, 1780, by John Jones, Ithamer Allen, and others, from Milford and Sturbridge, Mass.

First Ministers. The Congregational Church was organized May 1, 1793, over which the Rev. James Tufts was ordained Nov. 4, 1795. The Rev. E.

G. Bradford was settled as his assistant, Oct. 5, 1836.

Productions of the Soil. Wheat, 1,277 bushels; Indian corn, 2,487 bushels; potatoes, 35,538 bushels; hay, 2,833 tons; maple sugar, 15,810 pounds; wool, 5,442 pounds.

Distances. Fifteen miles north-west from Brattleborough, twenty north-east from Bennington, and ten north-west from Newfane.

WARREN.

WASHINGTON COUNTY. Warren is watered by Mad River, and, although between the two Green Mountain ranges, the surface is not much broken. It has some good mill sites, and some mechanical operations by water. Many cattle are reared in the town.

Boundaries. Northerly by Waitsfield and a part of Fayston, easterly by Roxbury, southerly by Granville, and westerly by Lincoln.

First Settlers. The settlement of this town commenced about the year 1797, by Samuel Lord and Seth Leavitt. There are various denominations of Christians in Warren.

Productions of the Soil. Wheat, 1,711 bushels; Indian corn, 1,737 bushels; potatoes, 44,081 bushels; hay, 2,054 tons; maple sugar, 26,934 pounds; wool, 14,667 pounds.

Distances. Twenty-three miles south-west from Montpelier.

WASHINGTON COUNTY.

MONTPELIER is the chief town. This county is nearly in the centre of the State, and the principal part of it lies between the two ranges of the Green Mountains. It is bounded north by Lamoille and parts of Chittenden and Caledonia Counties, east by Caledonia County, south by Orange and Addison Counties, and west by Addison and Chittenden Counties. It was incorporated in 1810, by the name of Jefferson, and took its present name in 1814.

This county is finely watered by its chief river, the Winooski, or Onion, and many of its important branches. These streams afford the county an abundant water power, and manufacturing establishments increase and flourish in this mountainous region.

The surface of the county is uneven, hilly, and in some parts mountainous, but there is much valuable land along the streams, which in many parts are sluggish, and form large tracts of excellent intervale.

The agricultural productions consist of neat cattle, horses, hogs, wool, and of the productions of the dairy. There are large bodies of beautiful granite in the county, and slate of various kinds.—See *Tables.*

COURTS IN WASHINGTON COUNTY.

The *Supreme Court* sits at MONTPELIER, on the sixth Tuesday after the fourth Tuesday in January; and the *County Court* on the second Tuesday in April, and the third Tuesday in November.

WASHINGTON.

ORANGE Co. Branches of Winooski, Wait's, and White Rivers rise in this town, but afford no considerable water power. The two former are called *Jail Branches*, from the circumstance that the proprietors were required by their charter, of 1781, to erect a jail within the limits of the town at an early period.

There is some excellent land along the streams, and the uplands are generally arable, and afford good pasturage.

There is a neat village in the town, some trade, and manufactures.

Boundaries. North by Orange, east by Corinth, south by Chelsea, and west by Williamstown.

First Settlers. The settlement was commenced in 1785, by Daniel Morse, who was soon joined by his brother, John Morse. A son of John Morse was the first child born here, and received, in consequence, fifty acres of land from the proprietors.

There are various denominations of Christians in Washington, with some handsome meeting-houses.

Productions of the Soil. Wheat, 3,647 bushels; Indian corn, 2,838 bushels; potatoes, 70,770 bushels; hay, 4,381 tons; maple sugar, 27,595 pounds; wool, 10,836 pounds.

Distances. Fifteen miles south by east from Montpelier.

WATERBURY.

WASHINGTON Co. The surface of Waterbury is generally level, with some pleasant swells. The soil is warm and fertile; the meadow lands on the rivers, of which there are large tracts, are not excelled in richness by any in the State.

Waterbury is separated from Duxbury by Winooski River, which, with Waterbury River and other streams, afford the town a good water power.

In the south-west corner of the town, the passage of Winooski River through a considerable hill is considered a curiosity. The stream has here worn a channel through the rocks, which, in times past, undoubtedly, formed a cataract below of no ordinary height, and a considerable lake above. The chasm is at present about 100 feet wide, and nearly as deep. On one side, the rocks are nearly perpendicular, some of which have fallen across the bed of the stream in such a manner as to form a bridge, passable, however, only at low water. On the same side, the rocks which appear to have been loosened and moved by the undermining of the water, have again rested, and become fixed in such a posture as to form several caverns, or caves, some of which have the appearance of rooms fitted for the convenience of man. Several musket balls and flints were found in the extreme part of one of them, a few years since, with the appearance of having lain there many years, which makes it evident that they were known to the early hunters.

Waterbury River rises in Morristown, and runs south through the western part of Stowe and Waterbury into Winooski River. In Stowe it receives one considerable tributary, from the east, which rises in Worcester, and two from the west, which rise in Mansfield. It also receives several tributaries from the west, in Waterbury, which originate in Bolton. The whole length of the stream is about sixteen miles, and it affords a number of good mill privileges.

Boundaries. North by Stowe, east by Middlesex, south by Winooski River, which separates it from Duxbury, and a part of Moretown, and west by Bolton.

First Settlers. In June, 1784, Mr. James Marsh moved his family, consisting of a wife and eight children, into Waterbury, from Bath, N. H., and took possession of a surveyor's cabin, which was standing near Winooski River. Mr. Marsh was induced to move his family here, at the time he did, by the promise of the proprietors, that several other families should be procured to move into the town in the following fall. This promise was not fulfilled; and for nearly a year this solitary family scarcely saw a human being but themselves, and, for more than two years, their nearest neighbors were in Bolton, seven miles distant.

First Ministers. About the year 1800 a revival of religion commenced in this town, which continued through that and the following year ; and during that time Congregational, Baptist, and Methodist Churches were organized.

Productions of the Soil. Wheat, 2,329 bushels ; Indian corn, 4,070 bushels ; potatoes, 21,389 bushels ; hay, 3,327 tons ; maple sugar, 25,502 pounds ; wool, 9,001 pounds.

Distances. Twelve miles north-west from Montpelier, and twenty-six east south-east from Burlington.

The great Northern Railroad, from Boston to Burlington, passes through this town.

WATERFORD.

CALEDONIA CO. The west part of Waterford is watered by the Passumpsic, and the north border by Moose River. Here is a water power and some manufactures. A part of the town borders on Fifteen Mile Falls, in Connecticut River. The banks of that river are steep at this place, and form but little intervale. The uplands are rough and stony, but good for sheep.

The settlement of the town was commenced in 1787. The Rev. Asa Carpenter was ordained over the Congregational Church in 1798 ; dismissed in 1816.

Boundaries. North-east by Concord, south-east by Connecticut River, which separates it from Lyman, N. H., south-west by Barnet, and north-west by St. Johnsbury.

Productions of the Soil. Wheat, 2,750 bushels ; Indian corn, 5,022 bushels ; potatoes, 64,265 bushels ; hay, 5,015 tons ; maple sugar, 2,905 pounds ; wool, 12,032 pounds.

Distances. Eighteen miles south-east from Danville, and forty-eight north-east from Montpelier.

The Connecticut River Railroad passes through the town.

WATERVILLE.

LAMOILLE CO. Waterville is environed by mountains, and is itself mountainous. It is watered by a branch of Lamoille River.

There are many good mill privileges in this town, and some fine land on the borders of its streams.

The settlement commenced here about the year 1789.

Boundaries. North by Bakersfield, east by Belvidere and Johnson, south by Cambridge, and west by Fletcher.

Productions of the Soil. Wheat, 697 bushels ; Indian corn, 11,04 bushels ; potatoes, 23,054 bushels ; hay, 1,319 tons ; maple sugar, 11,020 pounds ; wool, 3,116 pounds.

Distances. Twelve miles north-west from Hydepark, and thirty-nine miles north-west from Montpelier.

WEATHERSFIELD.

WINDSOR CO. This town lies on the west side of Connecticut River, at the " Bow," so called from a bend in the river. It contains large tracts of rich meadow land, and the uplands are of a good quality.

William Jarvis, Esq., for many years a resident here, owns a large and superior farm, and has greatly benefited this section of country, by the introduction of new modes of agriculture, and more valuable breeds of stock. The agricultural products of Weathersfield are very valuable.

This town is large, and contains a number of pleasant villages. It is watered by several ponds, and by Black River, which gives it a water power, and which is applied to manufacturing operations to some extent. In common with all the towns on Connecticut River, Weathersfield has its share of delightful scenery ; and there is no better place to find it, in all its richness, than on the *Ascutney*, at the north part of the town.

Perkinsville, situated in the south-western part of the town, derives its name from a *Mr. Perkins*, a capitalist from Boston, who, in 1830, purchased a small woollen factory, which he greatly enlarged, thus giving an impulse to the business of the village, and attracting the attention of other capitalists to improve the favorable advantages afforded by the Rapids in Black River to engage in the same enterprise.

Boundaries. North by Windsor, east by Connecticut River, which separates it from Claremont, N. H., south by Springfield, and west by Cavendish and Baltimore.

First Settlers. The early settlers of this town emigrated principally from Connecticut.

First Ministers. The Rev. James Treadway, of the Congregational order, the first minister, was settled by the town in 1779, and continued their pastor till 1783. Rev. Dan Foster was settled in 1787, and dismissed in 1799. Rev. James Converse was ordained February 10, 1802, and remained their pastor until his death, January 7th, 1839.

Productions of the Soil. Wheat, 532 bushels; Indian corn, 14,204 bushels; potatoes, 58,498 bushels; hay, 5,921 tons; maple sugar, 9,185 pounds; wool, 30,120 pounds.

Distances. Seventy miles south by east from Montpelier, and about ten below Windsor.

The Sullivan railroad passes on the opposite side of the river.

WELLS.

RUTLAND Co. A part of this township is level, and a part mountainous. The soil is generally good, and productive of grain, and of pasturage for sheep.

The principal stream in the town issues from Wells or St. Augustine Lake or Pond, a beautiful sheet of water, partly in Poultney, five miles in length, and covering 2,000 acres. At the outlet of this pond is a snug village, with some water power machinery.

Boundaries. North by Poultney and a part of Middletown, east by a part of Middletown and Tinmouth, south by Pawlet, and west by Hampton, New York.

First Settler. The settlement was commenced by Ogden Mallary, about the year 1768.

There are various denominations of Christians in this town, a number of handsome meeting-houses, and an Episcopal Church.

Productions of the Soil. Wheat, 742 bushels; Indian corn, 4,275 bushels; potatoes, 16,360 bushels; hay, 2,261 tons; maple sugar, 6,200 pounds; wool, 8,752 pounds.

Distances. Sixty-five miles south south-west from Montpelier, and thirteen south-west from Rutland.

WENLOCK.

ESSEX Co. This mountain town gives rise to a principal branch of Nulhegan River. The lands here are too elevated for cultivation.

The town was chartered in 1761.

Boundaries. Northerly by Lewis and Avery's Gore, easterly by Brunswick, southerly by Ferdinand and Brighton, and westerly by Morgan.

Productions of the Soil. Wheat, 60 bushels; Indian corn, 12 bushels; potatoes, 950 bushels; hay, 76 tons; maple sugar, 1,200 pounds; wool, 65 pounds.

Distances. Thirty miles north-west from Guildhall, and seventy-three north-east from Montpelier.

WEST FAIRLEE.

ORANGE Co. West Fairlee is watered by Ompomponoosuc River, and by a part of Fairlee Pond. The surface is rough and mountainous, but capable of sustaining a considerable number of cattle.

West Fairlee was chartered, in connection with Fairlee, in 1761.

Boundaries. North by Bradford, east by Fairlee, south by Thetford, and west by Vershire.

Productions of the Soil. Wheat, 821 bushels; Indian corn, 3,758 bushels; potatoes, 29,641 bushels; hay, 2,775 tons; maple sugar, 12,622 pounds; wool, 10,525 pounds.

Distances. Twenty-eight miles south-east from Montpelier, and twelve east by south from Chelsea.

The Connecticut River Railroad passes near the town.

WESTFIELD.

ORLEANS Co. A number of the branches of Missisco River meet in this town, and afford a good water power. A part of the surface of Westfield is mountainous, and in the town is the pass in the Green Mountains called Hazen's Notch.

Boundaries. North by Jay, east by Troy, south by Lowell, and west by Montgomery.

First Settlers. The settlement of Westfield was commenced about the year 1790, by Jesse Olds, a Mr. Hobbs, and others.

There are in this town a variety of religious denominations.

Productions of the Soil. Wheat, 917 bushels; Indian corn, 958 bushels; potatoes, 19,190 bushels; hay, 1,221 tons; maple sugar, 11,375 pounds; wool, 3,711 pounds.

Distances. Ten miles north-west from Irasburgh, and forty-four miles north from Montpelier.

WESTFORD.

CHITTENDEN Co. Westford was settled soon after the revolutionary war, by Hezekiah Parmelee and others.

The town is well watered by Brown's River, a branch of the Lamoille. The surface is rough, and the soil good for grazing.

The Rev. Simeon Parmelee was settled in Sept. 1809 over the Congregational Church, and continued many years.

Boundaries. North by Fairfax, east by Underhill, south by Essex, and west by Milton.

Productions of the Soil. Wheat, 1,617 bushels; Indian corn, 4,780 bushels; potatoes, 45,317 bushels; hay, 4,456 tons; maple sugar, 21,885 pounds; wool, 13,636 pounds.

Distances. Thirteen miles north north-east from Burlington, and thirty-five north-west from Montpelier.

WEST HAVEN.

RUTLAND Co. West Haven was set off from Fair Haven in 1792. It is well watered by Hubbardston and Poultney Rivers, and Cogman's Creek, on the former of which are handsome falls and mill sites. The soil is productive of grain and grass; there is much limestone and clay in West Haven.

The site of the village is pleasant; it is a place of some trade, navigation, and manufactures.

Boundaries. North by Benson, east by Fair Haven, south by Poultney River, which separates it from Whitehall, New York, and west by Lake Champlain.

First Settlers.—See Fair Haven.

First Ministers. The Rev. Ebenezer Hibbard was installed over the Congregational Church in 1822, and dismissed in 1829.

Productions of the Soil. Wheat, 1,196 bushels; Indian corn, 2,458 bushels; potatoes, 7,895 bushels; hay, 2,578 tons; maple sugar, 340 pounds; wool, 16,153 pounds.

Distances. Nineteen miles west from Rutland.

WEST WINDSOR.

WINDSOR Co. The western part of the beautiful town of Windsor was set off in the year 1848, and called by the above name.

The act creating this a new town is in common form, but a better name might have been selected.

WESTMINSTER.

WINDHAM Co. The surface and soil of Westminster are favorable for agriculture, and various articles of produce are annually sent to market.

The principal and oldest village is delightfully situated in the East Parish, on the bank of Connecticut River. The main street, which is perfectly level, crosses a table of land about one mile in diameter, considerably elevated above the river, and also above the large and fertile meadows by which it is approached on the north and south; and the whole is enclosed by a semi-circle of hills, which touch the river about two miles above and below the town. It is this barrier which, while it contributes to the natural beauty of the place, has, by turning the water course in another direction, deprived it of all those facilities of access and of water power, which have so much contributed to the rapid growth of some of the neighboring villages.

Boundaries. North by Rockingham, east by Connecticut River, which separates it from Walpole, N. H., south by Putney, and west by Brookline and Athens.

First Settlers. The earliest permanent settlers came from Northfield, in Massachusetts, and from Ashford and Middletown, in Connecticut, about 1741, and were soon followed by others from the same States. The pleasant situation of the town, and its proximity to the fort maintained by the New Hampshire government, in what is now called Walpole, caused the settlement to proceed with considerable rapidity, and it was, at an early period, one of the principal towns west of the Connecticut. A jail formerly stood in this place, and a court house, in which were held some of the earliest courts of justice; and when Vermont subsequently set up an independent jurisdiction, several sessions of the legislature were also held here. It was here that the famous massacre of the 13th of March, 1775 took place, and that the first regular measures were adopted to resist by force the government of New York. And after the erection of the county of Windham, the courts were held alternately at Westminster and Marlborough, for many years, until they were removed to Newfane.

First Ministers. A Congregational Church was organized here, and Rev. Jesse Goodel settled in 1767, who left in 1769. Rev. Joseph Bullen, from 1774 to 1785. Rev. Sylvester Sage, from 1790 to 1838, with the exception of a settlement at Braintree, Mass., in the years 1807, 8, and 9.

Productions of the Soil. Wheat, 1,893 bushels; Indian corn, 12,498 bushels; potatoes, 30,267 bushels; hay, 4,307 tons; maple sugar, 28,670 pounds; wool, 31,382 pounds.

Distances. Eighty-two miles south from Montpelier, and thirteen north-east from Newfane.

This town lies a little below Bellows Falls, and is in the vicinity of two railroads.

WESTMORE.

ORLEANS Co. Westmore contains Willoughby's Lake, a handsome sheet of water, surrounded by Mounts Hor, Pico, and other elevations. This lake is about six miles in length, and one and a half in width. Branches of Barton, Clyde, and Passumpsic Rivers rise in this and other ponds in the town.

Westmore appears to be too high for the habitation of many people or cattle.

The settlement commenced here about the year 1800; it was abandoned during the war of 1812, but resumed on the return of peace.

Boundaries. Northerly by Brighton and Charleston, easterly by Newark, southerly by Sutton, and westerly by Brownington.

Productions of the Soil. Wheat, 308 bushels; Indian corn, 55 bushels; potatoes, 2,350 bushels; hay, 92 tons; maple sugar, 48 pounds; wool, 114 pounds.

Distances. Twelve miles east from Irasburgh, and fifty-two north-east from Montpelier.

WESTON.

WINDSOR Co. West River passes through this town, and on its banks are some good lands, some manufactures, and two pleasant villages. It was set off from Andover in 1790, and organized as a town in 1800.

A union meeting-house was completed here in 1817.

Boundaries. North by Mount Holly and Ludlow, east by Andover, south by Londonderry, and west by Mount Tabor and Landgrove.

Productions of the Soil. Wheat, 1,159 bushels; Indian corn, 631 bushels; potatoes, 33,555 bushels; hay, 2,776 tons; maple sugar, 13,455 pounds; wool, 6,858 pounds.

Distances. Sixty-six miles south by west from Montpelier, and twenty-two south-west from Windsor.

The Southern Railroad passes near this town.

WEYBRIDGE.

ADDISON Co. Weybridge is watered by Otter Creek, which affords it good mill sites. Lemonfair River, a sluggish stream, also waters it. Some parts of the town are mountainous, but the soil is generally good; the basis being limestone, it yields good crops.

Boundaries. North and east by Otter Creek, which separates it from New Haven and Middlebury, south by Cornwall, and west by Bridport and Addison.

First Settlers. The settlement was commenced about the beginning of the revolutionary war, by David Stow and John Sanford, but the settlers were soon after dispersed, or made prisoners by the enemy. The settlement was recommenced on the return of peace. The first settlers were mostly from Massachusetts.

First Minister. A Congregational Church was organized in 1794. Rev. Jonathan Hovey was settled over it, from 1806 to 1816.

Productions of the Soil. Wheat, 717 bushels; Indian corn, 4,808 bushels; potatoes, 14,215 bushels; hay, 2,776 tons; maple sugar, 896 pounds; wool, 28,989 pounds.

Distances. Thirty miles south by east from Burlington. It adjoins Middlebury, through which the Southern Railroad passes.

WHEELOCK.

CALEDONIA Co. There is some good land in this town, but a great part of it is mountainous or hilly, and fit only for pasturage. The streams flow north-west into the Lamoille, and south-east into the Passumpsic.

This town was granted, in 1785, to the Charity School at Dartmouth College, and named in honor of John Wheelock, who was, at that time president of that institution.

The first settlers were Joseph Page, Abraham Morrill, and Dudley Swasey, in 1790.

Boundaries. North by Sheffield, east by Lyndon, south by Danville, and west by Greensborough.

Productions of the Soil. Wheat, 1,967 bushels; Indian corn, 1,100 bushels; potatoes, 57,520 bushels; hay, 3,334 tons; maple sugar, 32,160 pounds; wool, 8,287 pounds.

Distances. Forty-four miles northeast from Montpelier, ten miles north from Danville, and ten miles northwest from St. Johnsbury.

Wheelock lies five miles from Lyndon, through which a railroad passes.

WHITING.

ADDISON Co. Otter Creek waters the eastern border of the town, but affords no mill privileges.

Otter Creek, till lately, afforded no valuable fish. In the spring of 1819, Mr. Levi Walker, of Whiting, proposed to the inhabitants of this and the neighboring towns along the creek to transfer fish from the lake into the creek, above Middlebury Falls. The plan was carried into execution, and the fish have since multiplied exceedingly. In 1823, not less than 500 pounds of excellent pickerel were taken from the creek, in the distance of two miles.

Along the eastern part of the town, near Otter Creek, is a swamp, which covers 2 or 3,000 acres. It affords an abundance of excellent cedar, pine, ash, &c.

The soil is generally of the marly kind, and produces good grass and grain. In 1810, Mr. Samuel H. Remmele had a field of five acres of wheat, which averaged fifty bushels to the acre; and Mr. Benajah Justin for several years raised an annual crop of corn, which averaged 100 bushels to the acre.

Boundaries. North by Cornwall, east by Otter Creek, which separates it from Leicester and Salisbury, south by Sudbury, and west by Orwell and Shoreham.

First Settlers. John Wilson erected the first house in Whiting, in 1772, and in June, 1773, a family by the name of Bolster moved into it. In 1774, Mr. Wilson's and several other families moved here. During the revolution the settlement was abandoned, but was recommenced, immediately upon its close, by those persons who had been driven off, and by others. Among the first settlers were a Mr. Marshall, Gideon Walker, Joseph Williams, Daniel Washburn, Joel Foster, Samuel Beach, Ezra Allen, Jehiel Hull, Henry Wiswell, and Benjamin Andrus.

First Ministers. Elder David Rathbun was ordained over the Baptist Church, in June, 1800, and continued three or four years. After this, the Rev. John Ransom preached here about two years. In Jan. 1810, the Rev. Justin Parsons was settled over the Congregational Church, and continued about three years.

Productions of the Soil. Wheat, 1,232 bushels; Indian corn, 2,255 bushels; potatoes, 7,150 bushels ; hay, 2,837 tons ; maple sugar, 1,590 lbs. ; wool, 27,168 pounds.

Distances. Forty-miles south-west from Montpelier, and ten south from Middlebury.

The Southern Railroad passes in this vicinity.

WHITINGHAM.

WINDHAM CO. Deerfield River runs through the whole length of this town, along the western part, fertilizing some handsome tracts of meadow. There are many other smaller streams in different parts. There are two natural ponds. *Sawdawda* Pond is so called from an Indian of that name, who formerly lived near it, and was afterwards supposed to have been drowned in going down Deerfield River. This pond has been gradually decreas-

ing for fifty years past, by land forming over the water, which, to the extent of seventy or eighty acres, rises and falls with the waters of the pond.

The surface of Whitingham is uneven, but the soil is generally good, and is timbered with maple, beech, birch, ash, spruce, and hemlock.

A mineral spring was discovered here in 1822, which was analyzed by Dr. Wilson, and found to contain the following ingredients, viz. : Muriate of lime, carbonate of lime, muriate of magnesia, carbonate and per-oxyde of iron, alumina, with an acid trace. It is said to be a specific for cutaneous eruptions, scrofulous humors, dropsy, gravel, chronic ulcers, liver complaint, and a variety of other diseases.

The western part of the town abounds with limestone, which is burnt extensively into lime, and transported to various places.

Boundaries. North by Wilmington, east by Halifax, south by Heath and Rowe, Mass., and west by Readsborough.

First Settlers. The settlement was commenced in 1770, by a Mr. Bratlin and Silas Hamlinton. In 1773, Messrs. Angel, Gustin, Nelson, Lamphire, and Pike, emigrants from Massachusetts and Connecticut, moved their families here.

There have been several instances of longevity. Mr. Benjamin Cook died here in 1832, aged one hundred and six years. His health and strength held out remarkably, and he celebrated his hundredth birth-day by making a pair of shoes without spectacles. Many of the first settlers of this town had numerous families of children. Mr. Pike had twenty-eight children ; ten by his first wife, and eighteen by two others.

There are the usual number of religious denominations in the town.

Productions of the Soil. Wheat, 1,154 bushels; Indian corn, 3,270 bushels; potatoes, 4,978 bushels ; hay, 4,999 tons ; maple sugar, 30,389 pounds ; wool, 6,809 pounds.

Distances. Seventeen miles west by south from Brattleborough, and eighteen east south-east from Bennington.

12*

WILLIAMSTOWN.

ORANGE Co. Williamstown lies on the height of land between Winooski and White Rivers, and contains no large streams. A brook, which here runs down a steep hill towards the west, divides naturally, and while one part runs to the north, forming Steven's Branch of Winooski River, the other runs to the south, forming the second branch of White River.

The turnpike from Royalton to Montpelier passes along these streams, and is known by the name of the *Gulf Road*, on account of the deep ravine through which it passes in this town, near the head of the second branch. The hills here, upon each side of the branch, are very high and abrupt, and approach so near each other, as hardly to leave space for a road between them. In this ravine a medicinal spring has recently been discovered, which is thought to be equal to that at Clarendon.

Williamstown is timbered principally with hard wood, and the soil is well adapted to the production of grass. There is a small but pleasant village near the centre of the town.

Boundaries. North by Barre, east by Washington, south by Brookfield, and west by Northfield.

First Settlers. The settlement of this town was commenced in June, 1784, by Hon. Elijah Paine, John Paine, John Smith, Joseph Crane, and Josiah Lyman. Penuel Deming moved his family here in February, 1785, and this was the first family in town. Hon. Cornelius Lynde moved here in 1786.

First Ministers. A Congregational Church was organized here in 1795, and its first minister was the Rev. Jesse Olds. He was succeeded by the Rev. Nathan Waldo, Benton Perley, Joel Davis, Andrew Royce, &c.

Productions of the Soil. Wheat, 3,712 bushels; Indian corn, 4,528 bushels; potatoes, 85,066 bushels; hay, 5,459 tons; maple sugar, 33,451 pounds; wool, 20,555 pounds.

Distances. Ten miles south-east from Montpelier, and about the same distance north-west from Chelsea. The Northern Railroad passes through the neighboring town of Northfield.

WILLISTON.

CHITTENDEN Co. This is an excellent farming town, of a rich soil, with an uneven surface, but not mountainous. It is very productive of all the varieties common to a northern climate. Its product of wool, in 1837, was 9,225 fleeces.

Williston is watered by Winooski River and some smaller streams, but its water power is small.

THOMAS CHITTENDEN was the father of this town. He came here in 1774. He was a member of the convention, which, in 1777, declared Vermont an independent State, and was active in procuring its admission into the Union. When the Vermont Constitution was established, in 1778, Mr. Chittenden was selected as a candidate for governor, to which office he was annually elected, with the exception of one year, till his death, in 1797. He was sixty-seven years of age.

Boundaries. North by Winooski River, which separates it from Essex, east by Jericho and Richmond, south by St. George, and west by Muddy Brook, which separates it from Burlington.

First Minister. Rev. Aaron Collins was settled over the Congregational Church in 1800; dismissed in 1803.

Productions of the Soil. Wheat, 2,726 bushels; Indian corn, 7,526 bushels; potatoes, 42,529 bushels; hay, 4,926 tons; maple sugar, 13,167 pounds; wool, 23,138 pounds.

Distances. Twenty-seven miles west north-west from Montpelier.

This town adjoins Burlington, and is easy of access to lake and railroad transportation.

WILMINGTON.

WINDHAM Co. The east and west branches of Deerfield River unite in this town, which, with the waters of Beaver and Cold Brooks, and of Ray's Pond, a large and beautiful sheet of water, a valuable mill power is produced. There are some fine tracts of land in the town, and a considerable portion that is rough and hard to till. There are a number of mills of various kinds in the town, and a pleasant and thriving village.

Wilmington was settled before the revolutionary war, but increased but slowly until the peace.

Boundaries. North by Dover and a part of Somerset, east by Marlborough, south by Whitingham, and west by Searsburgh.

First Ministers. The Congregational Church was organized here in 1780, and has had the following ministers: Rev. Winslow Packard, from July 3, 1781, to October 12, 1784 ; Rev. Jonas Hatch, from March 7, 1787, to February 18, 1791 ; Rev. E. Fairbanks, from September 11, 1793, to January 3, 1800, &c.

Productions of the Soil. Wheat, 1,152 bushels ; Indian corn, 1,618 bushels ; potatoes, 66,110 bushels ; hay, 4,991 tons ; maple sugar, 81,159 pounds ; wool, 5,419 pounds.

Distances. Seventeen miles east from Bennington, and fourteen south-west from Newfane.

WINDHAM COUNTY.

NEWFANE is the shire town. This county is bounded north by Windsor County, east by Connecticut River, south by the State of Massachusetts, and west by the County of Bennington. For some years it bore the name of Cumberland.

The surface of the county is much broken by hills and valleys ; the western part is very elevated, and contains a part of the Green Mountain range. The geological character of the county is primitive. Immense quantities of granite is found in all parts of the county, both in quarries and boulders, most of which is of fine grain and very handsome. It also contains gneiss, hornblende, serpentine, primitive limestone, and mica, talcose, chlorite, and argellite slates.

The soil of the county is various ; from the rich and alluvial meadows on the Connecticut, to the cold and rugged lands on the sides of the mountains. The general character of the soil may be considered as tolerable for grain, and excellent for grazing.

Windham County is finely watered by Williams', Saxton's, and West Rivers, with their branches, and by numerous other streams. These waters give the county a great hydraulic power, which is rapidly coming into use for manufacturing purposes.—See *Tables.*

COURTS IN WINDHAM COUNTY.

The *Supreme Court* sits at Newfane, on the third Tuesday after the fourth Tuesday in January ; and the *County Court* on the second Tuesday in April and September.

WINDHAM.

WINDHAM Co. Branches of West, Williams', and Saxton's Rivers give this town a good water power. The surface of the town is elevated; the soil, though strong, is better adapted for grazing than tillage.

Windham was formerly a part of Londonderry.

The actynolite, embedded in talc, is found in this town, in slender four-sided prisms of a leek green color. The crystals vary in size; some are six inches in length and an inch in breadth. These crystals are abundant. Chlorite, garnets, serpentine, and steatite, are also found.

There is in this town a beautiful pond.

Boundaries. North by Andover, east by Grafton, south by Jamaica, and west by Londonderry.

First Settlers. Edward Aiken, James McCormick, and John Woodburn.

First Minister. Rev. John Lawton was settled over the Congregational Church, in 1809.

Productions of the Soil. Wheat, 1,378 bushels; Indian corn, 1,434 bushels; potatoes, 36,083 bushels; hay, 2,723 tons; wool, 11,722 pounds.

Distances. Thirty miles north-east from Bennington, and twenty-five south-west from Windsor.

WINDSOR COUNTY.

WOODSTOCK is the county town. This county is bounded north by the county of Orange, east by Connecticut River, south by Windham County, and west by Rutland and a part of Addison Counties.

Windsor County is watered by White, Queechy, Black, West, and Williams' Rivers, and by other excellent mill streams. The surface of the county is uneven, and in some parts mountainous, but generally it is too elevated to admit of cultivation. The soil produces fine crops of grain, hay, vegetables, and fruits; the lands are peculiarly adapted for grazing.

The beautiful Connecticut, which washes its whole eastern boundary, gives to this county large tracts of alluvial meadow land, and affords it a navigable channel to the sea board, for its surplus productions and for its wants from abroad.

The hydraulic power of Windsor County is very large, and its local position is such as to induce men of enterprise and capital to embark in manufacturing operations, which are annually increasing, with fair prospects of success.—See *Tables.*

COURTS IN WINDSOR COUNTY.

The *Supreme Court* sits at Woodstock, the fourth Tuesday next following the fourth Tuesday of January, and the *County Court* on the last Tuesday of November, in each year.

The *United States Circuit* and *District Courts* meet annually, on the 21st and 27th of May, at Windsor.

WINDSOR.

WINDSOR Co. The surface of this delightful town is uneven, but there are but few parts of it unfit for cultivation. It contains large tracts of alluvial meadow, and the uplands are generally fertile. Mill Brook waters the south part of the town, and furnishes it with mill sites.

The manufactures of Windsor are numerous and valuable. The agricultural interests are also valuable; and many neat cattle, horses, and productions of the dairy, are annually transported to its various markets.

This town has become the centre of an important commerce, both from the river and a fertile interior country. The favorable position of Windsor, as a place of trade, was early discovered; and it has been fortunate in possessing a succession of men, who, by their enterprise and wealth, have rendered it one of the most flourishing towns on Connecticut River. The manufactures of Windsor are considerable.

The village of Windsor is on elevated ground, on the bank of the river; it is compactly, and somewhat irregularly built, but very beautiful. There are but few villages in our country which make a more delightful appearance. It contains a great number of handsome dwelling-houses and stores. Some of the private houses, churches, and other public buildings, are in a style of superior elegance. This is the site of the Vermont State Prison. The streets are wide, and beautifully shaded.

The scenery around Windsor is highly picturesque; from the highlands across the river, in Cornish, which is united to Windsor by a bridge, or on the Ascutney, at the south part of the town, some of the best landscapes in our country are presented to view.

For the purpose of affording the village the advantages of water power, in 1835 a stone dam was constructed across Mill Brook, half a mile from its mouth. It is 360 feet in length, fifty-six in breadth at the base, twelve at the top, and forty-two in height, forming a reservoir of water nearly one mile in length, with a surface of 100 acres, having an available fall of sixty feet in the distance of one third of a mile. The dam is built on the arc of a circle, over which, in flood time, the water flows in an unbroken sheet, 102 feet in length, forming one of the most beautiful cascades in the country.

A new epoch has opened to Windsor, by the opening of a railroad from Boston through it, and to the fertile and extensive country beyond it. Instead of the old process of conveying passengers and property by teams, stages, and river craft, the "Iron Horse" comes along two or three times a day, carrying in his train a burthen of 200 tons, or more, at the rate of twenty-five miles an hour; smoking his pipe, the while, with as much composure as a Mohawk River Dutchman. The site of Windsor is such as will continue to command a large share of the trade of this section of country.—See *Public Buildings*.

Boundaries. North by Hartland, easterly by Connecticut River, which separates it from Cornish, N. H., south by Weathersfield, and westerly by Reading.

First Settlers. The first permanent settlement in the town was commenced by Capt. Steele Smith, who removed his family from Farmington, Ct., in August, 1764. At that time there was no road north of Charlestown, N. H. The next season, Major Elisha Hawley, Capt. Israel Curtis, Dea. Hez. Thompson, Dea. Thomas Cooper, and some others. came on and began improvements.

First Ministers. At an early period, two religious societies of the Congregational order were formed in Windsor; one in the east, and the other in the west parish of the town. About the year 1778, the Rev. Martin Tuller and the Rev. Pelatiah Chapin were ordained the first ministers over their respective churches in those parishes.

Productions of the Soil. Wheat, 2,864 bushels; Indian corn, 12,920 bushels; potatoes, 61,075 bushels; hay, 5,673 tons; maple sugar, 18,320 pounds; wool, 25,343 pounds.

Distances. Fifty-five miles south by

east from Montpelier, and eleven south-east from Woodstock.

The Central Railroad between this town and Hartford, united with the Sullivan Railroad in New Hampshire, was opened for travel on the 31st of January, 1849. The opening of these roads completes the line of railroad communication between Boston and Burlington, via Fitchburg. Ms., Keene and Walpole, N. H., and Windsor and Montpelier, Vt.

WINHALL.

BENNINGTON CO. This town was chartered in 1761, and its settlement commenced during the revolutionary war. The surface is rough, and the soil not very productive.

Winhall River rises in this town, and affords it a good water power. It passes through a part of Jamaica, and joins West River in Londonderry.

Boundaries. North by Peru, east by Jamaica and a part of Londonderry, south by Stratton, and west by Manchester.

First Minister. The Rev. B. Barrett was settled over the Congregational Church, in 1796.

Productions of the Soil. Wheat, 579 bushels; Indian corn, 564 bushels; potatoes, 17,388 bushels; hay, 1,466 tons; maple sugar, 11,000 pounds; wool, 1,590 pounds.

Distances. Thirty-three miles south-west from Windsor, and twenty-five miles north-east from Bennington.

WOLCOTT.

LAMOILLE CO. Wolcott is well watered by Lamoille River, and by Green and Wild Branch, its branches. "Fish Pond," in Wolcott, is a pretty piece of water, and bears an appropriate name. There is some good grain land in the town, but most of the lands are fit only for pasturage. There are some mills in the town.

Wolcott was chartered to Joshua Stanton and others, in 1781.

Boundaries. North by Craftsbury, east by Hardwick, south by Elmore, and west by Hydepark.

Productions of the Soil. Wheat, 1,733 bushels; Indian corn, 2,040 bushels; potatoes, 30,101 bushels; hay, 1,728 tons; maple sugar, 32,565 pounds; wool, 4,025 pounds.

Distances. Ten miles south-east from Hydepark, and thirty-seven north from Montpelier.

WOODBURY.

WASHINGTON CO. Woodbury was first settled in 1800. The town is watered by branches of Winooski and Lamoille Rivers, and probably contains a greater number of ponds than any other town in the State. The surface is rough, but the soil is good for grazing.

This town has a great variety of beautiful scenery, and nowhere can the sportsman, for fish or fowl, find a better resort.

Boundaries. North by Hardwick, east by Cabot, south by Calais, and west by Elmore.

Productions of the Soil. Wheat, 826 bushels; Indian corn, 1,748 bushels; potatoes, 5,935 bushels; hay, 1,437 tons; maple sugar, 18,695 pounds; wool, 2,586 pounds.

Distances. Fifteen miles north by east from Montpelier.

WOODFORD.

BENNINGTON CO. Woodford contains several large ponds, from which issue branches of Woloomsack and Deerfield Rivers. There is a good deal of wild scenery on the road, in crossing the mountains from Bennington through Woodford and Searsburgh. The gurgling of the streams down the mountain sides allays, in a great degree, the fatigue of the journey. The greater part of this town is too elevated and broken for cultivation. It is a good location for the sportsman; for fish and fowl are abundant, and the deer, the bear, and other wild animals, roam with almost undisputed sway.

The town began to be settled immediately after the revolutionary war.

Boundaries. North by Glastenbury,

east by Searsburgh and a part of Readsborough, south by Stamford, and west by Bennington.

Productions of the Soil. Buckwheat, 27 bushels; Indian corn, 40 bushels; potatoes, 1,900 bushels; hay, 193 tons; maple sugar, 515 pounds; wool, 350 pounds.

Distances. Seven miles east from Bennington, on the road to Brattleborough.

WOODSTOCK.

WINDSOR CO. This is the shire town of the county. Woodstock is well watered by Queechy River and its branches.

The soil of the town is generally very fertile, with a pleasant surface of hills and vales. The agricultural productions are large and valuable.

"Woodstock Green," so called, is a beautiful village. It is the seat of a flourishing country trade, and contains many very handsome buildings. The court house, planned and built under the supervision of Ammi B. Young, Esq., a native architect of great promise, and the architect of the custom house in Boston, is one of the most chaste and classical structures in New England.

The South Village is neat and pleasant; it is about five miles from the "Green."

Woodstock is a delightful place of residence, and its growth in commerce and manufactures is such, as to warrant the construction of a branch railroad to the Central Railroad at Windsor.

Boundaries. North by Pomfret, east by Hartland, south by Reading, and west by Bridgewater.

First Settlers. The settlement of this town was commenced by Mr. Jas. Sanderson, who moved his family here about the year 1768. He was soon joined by other settlers, and in 1773 the town was organized.

First Minister. Rev. George Daman was ordained over the Congregational Church, in 1782.

Manufactures. Woodstock is a place of important manufactures, as much so as any town in the State. The articles manufactured are numerous; among which are scythes, axes, clothiers' shears, and other edged tools; also carding machines, jacks, and all other articles used in woollen factories. A large amount of these articles is annually made, and transported to various parts of the country.

Productions of the Soil. Wheat, 4,671 bushels; Indian corn, 15,141 bushels; potatoes, 82,584 bushels; hay, 8,374 tons; maple sugar, 32,072 pounds; wool, 39,072 pounds.

Distances. Forty-six miles south from Montpelier, and eleven northwest from Windsor.

WORCESTER.

WASHINGTON CO. A branch of Winooski River gives this town a good water power, which is used for various purposes. Much of this township is mountainous; but there is some good land along the stream, and the highlands afford good pasturage for cattle.

Boundaries. North by Elmore, east by Calais, south by Middlesex, and west by Stowe.

First Settlers. The settlement was commenced in 1797, by George Martin and John Ridlan, emigrants from Kennebec, Me. The town was organized March 3, 1803.

First Ministers. A Congregational Church was gathered here, in 1804. There are also societies of Freewill Baptists and Methodists.

Productions of the Soil. Wheat, 883 bushels; Indian corn, 1,386 bushels; potatoes, 3,305 bushels; hay, 415 tons; wool, 267 pounds.

Distances. Eight miles north from Montpelier, and thirty-one east from Burlington.

The great Northern Railroad, which passes through Montpelier and its neighboring town of Middlesex, gives the citizens of this and the towns in its vicinity an easy access for transportation to all parts of the country.

GORES OF LAND.

There are in this State, certain tracts of land, denominated " Gores," which are thus described by Mr. Thompson, in his Gazetteer of the State.

AIKIN'S GORE, called also Virgin Hall, a small tract of only 930 acres, granted February 25, 1782, to Edward Aikin, and lying upon the Green Mountains between Winhall and Landgrove.

AVERY'S GORES. A considerable number of tracts of land situated in different sections of the State were granted to Samuel Avery in 1791, and received the name of Avery's Gores. Several of these have since been annexed to townships.

BENTON'S GORE is a tract of 5000 acres, lying in the south-western part of Windsor County, now forming the westerly part of Weston, granted to Samuel Benton and twenty-three associates, October 26, 1781.

BUEL'S GORE, a tract of 4273 acres lying between Avery's Gore, in Chittenden County, and Starksborough. A part of it has been annexed to Huntington, the remaining part containing eighteen inhabitants in 1840.

COVENTRY GORE, a tract of 2000 acres of land belonged to Coventry, (now Orleans,) lying in Orleans County, a few miles to the south-west of that town. It is bounded north by Newport, east by Irasburgh, south by Lowell, and west by Troy, and contained ten inhabitants in 1840.

GOSHEN GORES. There are two gores of this name, and both in Caledonia Co. The largest contains 7,339 acres, and is bounded north by Wheelock, east by Danville, south by Walden, and west by Greensborough. The first permanent settlement was made here in 1802, by Elihu Sabin, and his daughter Mary was the first child born. In the north-east corner of the gore is a pond covering about eighty acres. It is watered by a branch of the Lamoille Ri-

ver. *Statistics of* 1840 —Horses, 27; cattle, 180; sheep, 429; swine, 100; wheat, bush. 265; barley, 100; oats, 1,420; Indian corn, 56; potatoes, 7,920; hay, tons, 559; sugar, pounds, 7,760; wool, 912. Population, 143. The other gore of this name is situated in the south-west corner of Caledonia County, and contains 2,828 acres. It is bounded north by Marshfield and a part of Harris' Gore, east by Harris' Gore, south by Orange, and west by Plainfield. Gunner's Branch passes through the south part of this gore. Population, 44.

HARRIS' GORE, a tract of land containing 6,020 acres, lying in the south-west corner of Caledonia County, is bounded north-west by Marshfield and Goshen Gore, north-east by Groton, and south-west by Orange. It was granted February 25, 1781, and chartered to Edward Harris, October 30, 1801. It is mountainous, and contained, in 1840, only sixteen inhabitants. Gunner's Branch originates in this gore, and unites with Stevens' Branch in Barre.

WARNER'S GORE, a tract of 2,000 acres of land, lying in the north-western part of Essex County, is bounded north by Norton, east by Warren's Gore, south by Morgan, and west by Holland. It was granted October 20, 1787. It contains no streams of consequence, and is uninhabited.

WARREN GORE, an uninhabited tract of 6,380 acres, lying in the north-western part of Essex County, and belonging to Warren, is bounded north by Norton, east by Avery's Gore, south by Morgan, and west by Warner's Gore. On the line between this gore and Norton is a considerable pond, the waters of which flow to the north into Masuippi River in Canada.

POPULATION TABLE

ALPHABETICALLY ARRANGED BY TOWNS.

TOWNS.	1791.	1800.	1810.	1820.	1830.	1840.
Addison, ...	401	734	1,100	1,210	1,306	1,229
Albany, ...		12	101	253	683	920
Alburgh, ...	446	750	1,106	1,172	1,239	1,344
Andover, ...		622	957	1,000	975	878
Arlington, ...	991	1,597	1,463	1,354	1,207	1,035
Athens, ...	450	459	478	507	415	378
Averill, ...					1	11
Bakersfield, ...	13	222	812	945	1,087	1,258
Baltimore, ...	275	174	207	204	179	155
Barnard, ...	673	1,236	1,648	1,691	1,881	1,774
Barnet, ...	477	858	1,301	1,488	1,764	2,030
Barre, ...	76	919	1,669	1,955	2,012	2,126
Barton, ...		128	447	372	726	892
Belvidere, ...		217	198	185	207
Bennington, ...	2,377	2,243	2,524	2,485	3,419	3,429
Benson, ...	658	1,159	1,561	1,481	1,493	1,403
Berkshire, ...		172	918	831	1,308	1,818
Berlin, ...	134	684	1,067	1,455	1,664	1,598
Bethel, ...	473	913	1,041	1,318	1,667	1,886
Bloomfield, ...		27	144	132	150	179
Bolton, ...	88	219	249	306	452	470
Bradford, ...	654	1,064	1,302	1,411	1,507	1,655
Bradlyvale, ...					21	350
Braintree, ...	221	531	850	1,009	1,209	1,332
Brandon, ...	637	1,076	1,475	1,395	1,946	2,194
Brattleborough, ...	1,589	1,867	1,891	2,017	2,141	2,623
Bridgewater, ...	293	781	1,125	1,125	1,311	1,363
Bridport, ...	449	1,124	1,520	1,511	1,774	1,480
Brighton, ...					105	157
Bristol, ...	211	665	1,179	1,051	1,274	1,233
Brookfield, ...	421	988	1,384	1,507	1,677	1,789
Brookline, ...		472	431	391	376	328
Brownington, ...		65	236	265	412	486
Brunswick, ...	66	86	143	124	160	130
Burke, ...		108	460	541	866	997
Burlington, ...	332	815	1,690	2,111	3,226	4,271
Cabot, ...	122	349	886	1,032	1,304	1,440
Calais, ...	45	443	841	1,111	1,539	1,079
Cambridge, ...	359	733	990	1,176	1,613	1,790
Canaan, ...	19	74	332	227	373	378
Castleton, ...	800	1,039	1,420	1,541	1,783	1,769
Cavendish, ...	491	921	1,295	1,551	1,498	1,427

TOWNS.	1791.	1800.	1810.	1820.	1830.	1840.
Charleston, ...			56	90	564	731
Charlotte, ...	635	1,231	1,679	1,526	1,702	1,620
Chelsea, ...	239	897	1,327	1,462	1,958	1,959
Chester, ...	981	1,878	2,370	2,493	2,320	2,305
Chittenden, ...	159	327	446	528	610	644
Clarendon, ...	1,478	1,789	1,797	1,712	1,585	1,549
Colchester, ...	137	347	657	960	1,489	1,739
Concord, ...	49	322	677	806	1,031	1,024
Corinth, ...	578	1,410	1,876	1,907	1,953	1,970
Cornwall, ...	826	1,163	1,270	1,120	1,264	1,163
Coventry, ...		7	178	282	729	796
Craftsbury, ...	18	229	566	605	982	1,151
Danby, ...	1,206	1,487	1,730	1,607	1,362	1,379
Danville, ...	574	1,514	2,240	2,300	2,631	2,633
Derby, ...		178	714	925	1,469	1,681
Dorset, ...	958	1,286	1,294	1,359	1,507	1,432
Dover, ...			859	829	831	729
Dummerston, ...	1,501	1,692	1,704	1,658	1,592	1,263
Duxbury, ...	39	153	326	440	652	820
East Haven, ...						79
East Montpelier, . . .						
Eden, ...		29	224	201	461	702
Elmore, ...	12	45	157	157	442	476
Enosburgh, ...		143	704	932	1,560	2,022
Essex, ...	354	729	957	1,089	1,664	1,824
Fairfax, ...	354	787	1,301	1,359	1,729	1,919
Fairfield, ...	129	901	1,618	1,573	2,270	2,448
Fair Haven, ...	375	411	645	714	675	633
Fairlee, ...	232	386	983	1,143	656	644
Fayston, ...		18	149	253	458	635
Ferdinand, ...						
Ferrisburgh, ...	481	956	1,647	1,581	1,822	1,755
Fletcher, ...	47	200	382	497	793	1,014
Franklin, ...	46	280	714	631	1,129	1,410
Georgia, ...	340	1,068	1,760	1,703	1,897	2,106
Glastenbury, ...	34	48	76	48	52	53
Glover, ...		36	387	549	902	1,119
Goshen, ...		4	86	290	555	621
Grafton, ...	561	1,149	1,365	1,482	1,439	1,326
Granby, ...		69	120	49	97	105
Grand Isle, ...	337	1,289	623	898	648	724
Granville, ...	101	185	324	328	403	545
Greensborough, . . .	19	280	566	625	784	883
Groton, ...	45	248	449	595	836	928
Guildhall, ...	158	296	544	529	481	470
Guilford, ...	2,432	2,256	1,872	1,862	1,760	1,525
Halifax, ...	1,309	1,600	1,758	1,567	1,562	1,399
Hancock, ...	56	149	311	442	472	455
Hardwick, ...	3	260	735	867	1,216	1,354
Hartford, ...	988	1,494	1,881	2,010	2,044	2,194
Hartland, ...	1,652	1,960	2,352	2,553	2,503	2,341 .
Highgate, ...	103	437	1,374	1,250	2,038	2,292
Hinesburgh, ...	454	933	1,238	1,332	1,669	1,682

Towns.	1791.	1800.	1810.	1820.	1830.	1840.
Holland,			128	100	422	605
Hubbardton,	404	641	724	810	865	719
Huntington,	167	405	514	732	929	914
Hydepark,	43	110	261	373	823	1,080
Ira,	312	473	519	498	442	430
Irasburgh,		15	292	432	860	971
Isle la Motte,	47	135	338	312		435
Jamaica,	263	582	996	1,313	1,553	1,586
Jay,				52	196	308
Jericho,	381	728	1,185	1,219	1,654	1,684
Johnson,	93	255	494	778	1,079	1,410
Kirby,		20	311	312	401	520
Landgrove,	31	147	299	341	355	345
Leicester,	343	522	609	548	638	602
Lemington,	31	52	132	139	183	124
Lewis,						
Lincoln,		97	255	278	639	770
Londonderry,	362	330	637	958	1,302	1,216
Lowell,			40	139	314	431
Ludlow,	179	410	877	1,144	1,227	1,363
Lunenburgh,	119	393	714	856	1,054	1,130
Lyndon,	59	542	1,090	1,296	1,822	1,753
Maidstone,	125	152	177	166	236	271
Manchester,	1,276	1,397	1,502	1,508	1,525	1,590
Mansfield,		12	38	60	279	223
Marlborough,	629	1,087	1,245	1,296	1,218	1,027
Marshfield,		172	513	710	1,271	1,156
Mendon,	34	39	111	174	432	545
Middlebury,	395	1,263	2,138	2,535	3,468	3,161
Middlesex,	60	262	401	726	1,156	1,279
Middletown,	699	1,066	1,207	1,039	919	1,057
Milton,	282	786	1,548	1,746	2,100	2,136
Monkton,	450	880	1,248	1,152	1,384	1,310
Montgomery,		36	237	293	460	548
Montpelier,	113	890	1,877	2,308	2,985	3,725
Moretown,	24	191	405	593	806	1,120
Morgan,			135	116	231	422
Morristown,	10	144	550	726	1,315	1,502
Mount Holley,		668	922	1,157	1,318	1,356
Mount Tabor,	165	153	209	222	210	226
Newark,		8	88	154	257	360
Newbury,	873	1,304	1,363	1,623	2,225	2,579
Newfane,	660	1,000	1,276	1,506	1,441	1,043
New Haven,	723	1,135	1,688	1,566	1,834	1,503
Newport,		50	28	52	284	591
Northfield,	40	204	426	690	1,412	2,013
North Hero,	125	324	552	503	638	716
Norton,						
Norwich,	1,158	1,486	1,812	1,985	2,316	2,218
Orange,		348	686	751	1,016	984
Orwell,	778	1,376	1,849	1,730	1,598	1,504
Panton,	220	363	529	548	605	670
Pawlet,	1,458	1,938	2,233	2,155	1,965	1,748

TOWNS.	1791.	1800.	1810.	1820.	1830.	1840.
Peacham, ...	365	873	1,301	1,294	1,351	1,443
Peru, ...	71	130	239	314	455	578
Pittsfield, ...	49	164	338	453	505	615
Pittsford, ...	850	1,413	1,936	1,916	2,005	1,927
Plainfield, ...		256	543	660	874	880
Plymouth, ...	106	497	834	1,112	1,237	1,417
Pomfret, ...	710	1,106	1,433	1,635	1,867	1,774
Poultney, ...	1,121	1,694	1,905	1,955	1,909	1,880
Pownal, ...	1,746	1,692	1,655	1,812	1,835	1,613
Putney, ...	1,848	1,574	1,607	1,547	1,510	1,382
Randolph, ...	892	1,841	2,255	2,487	2,743	2,678
Reading, ...	747	1,120	1,565	1,603	1,409	1,363
Readsborough, ...	64	234	410	530	662	767
Richford, ...		13	440	440	704	914
Richmond, ...		718	935	1,014	1,109	1,054
Ripton, ...				42	278	357
Rochester, ...	215	524	911	1,148	1,392	1,396
Rockingham, ...	1,235	1,684	1,954	2,155	2,272	2,330
Roxbury, ...	14	113	361	512	737	784
Royalton, ...	748	1,501	1,753	1,816	1,893	1,917
Rupert, ...	1,033	1.648	1,630	1,332	1,318	1,091
Rutland, ...	1,407	2125	2,379	2,369	2,753	2,708
Ryegate, ...	187	406	812	994	1,119	1,222
Salem, ...		16	58	80	230	299
Salisbury, ...	446	644	709	721	907	942
Sandgate, ...	773	1,020	1,187	1,185	933	777
Searsborough, ...				9	40	120
Shaftsbury, ...	1,999	1,895	1,973	2,022	2,143	1,835
Sharon, ...	569	1,158	1,363	1,431	1,459	1,371
Sheffield, ...		170	388	581	720	821
Shelburne, ...	389	723	987	936	1,123	1,089
Sheldon, ...	110	408	883	927	1,427	1,734
Sherburne, ...	32	90	116	154	452	498
Shoreham, ...	721	1,447	2,033	1,881	2,137	1,675
Shrewsbury, ...	383	748	990	1,149	1,289	1,218
Somerset, ...	111	130	199	173	245	262
South Hero, ...	337	1,289	826	842	717	664
Springfield, ...	1,097	2,032	2,556	2,702	2,749	2,625
St. Albans, ...	256	901	1,609	1,636	2,395	2,702
Stamford, ...	272	383	378	490	563	662
Starksborough, ...	40	359	726	914	1,342	1,263
Sterling, ...		9	122	181	183	193
St. George, ...	57	65	28	120	135	121
St. Johnsbury, ...	143	663	1,334	1,404	1,592	1,887
Stockbridge, ...	100	432	700	964	1,333	1,419
Stow, ...		316	650	957	1,570	1,371
Strafford, ...	845	1,642	1,805	1,921	1,935	1,761
Stratton, ...	95	271	265	272	312	341
Sudbury, ...	258	521	754	809	812	796
Sunderland, ...	414	557	576	496	463	437
Sutton, ...		144	433	697	1,005	1,068
Swanton, ...	74	858	1,657	1,607	2,158	2,313
Thetford, ...	862	1,478	1,785	1,915	2,113	2,065

Towns.	1791.	1800.	1810.	1820.	1830.	1840.
Tinmouth, ...	935	973	1,001	1,069	1,049	781
Topsham, ...	162	344	814	1,020	1,384	1,745
Townshend, ...	676	1,083	1,115	1,406	1,386	1,345
Troy, ...			281	227	608	856
Tunbridge, ...	487	1,324	1,640	2,003	1,920	1,811
Underhill, ...	65	212	490	633	1,052	1,441
Vergennes, ...	201	516	835	817	999	1,017
Vernon, ...	482	480	521	627	681	705
Vershire, ...	439	1,031	1,311	1,290	1,260	1,998
Victory, ...					53	140
Waitsfield, ...	61	473	647	935	958	1,048
Walden, ...	43	153	455	580	827	913
Wallingford, ...	536	912	1,386	1,570	1,740	1,608
Waltham, ...	201	247	244	264	301	283
Wardsborough, . . .	753	1,484	1,159	1,016	1,148	1,102
Warren, ...		58	229	320	766	943
Washington, ...	72	500	1,040	1,160	1,374	1,359
Waterbury, ...	93	644	966	1,269	1,650	1,192
Waterford, ...	63	565	1,289	1,247	1,358	1,388
Waterville, ...	15	51	193	273	488	610
Weathersfield, . . .	1,146	1,944	2,115	2,301	2,213	2,002
Wells, ...	622	978	1,040	986	880	740
Wenlock, ...					24	28
West Fairlee, . . .	463	391	983	1,143	841	824
Westfield, ...		16	149	225	353	370
Westford, ...	63	648	1,107	1,025	1,290	1,352
Westhaven, ...	545	430	679	684	724	774
Westminster, ...	1,601	1,942	1,925	1,974	1,737	1,546
Westmore, ...					32	122
Weston, ...		17	629	890	972	1,032
West Windsor, . . .						
Weybridge, ...	175	502	750	714	850	797
Wheelock, ...	33	568	964	906	834	881
Whiting, ...	250	404	565	609	653	660
Whitingham, ...	442	868	1,248	1,097	1,477	1,391
Williamstown, . . .	146	839	1,353	1,481	1,487	1,620
Williston, ...	471	836	1,185	1,246	1,608	1,554
Wilmington, ...	645	1,011	1,193	1,369	1,367	1,296
Windham, ...		429	782	931	847	757
Windsor, ...	1,542	2,211	2,757	2,956	3,134	2,744
Winhall, ...	155	212	429	428	571	576
Wolcott, ...	32	47	124	123	492	824
Woodbury, ...		23	254	432	824	1,092
Woodford, ...	60	138	254	212	395	487
Woodstock, ...	1,605	2,132	2,672	2,610	3,044	3,315
Worcester, ...		25	41	44	432	587

RECAPITULATION BY COUNTIES.

COUNTIES.	1791.	1800.	1810.	1820.	1830.	1840.
ADDISON, ...	6,489	13,417	19,993	20,469	24,940	23,569
BENNINGTON, . .	12,254	14,617	15,892	16,125	17,470	16,879
CHITTENDEN, . . .	3,918	9,551	14,646	15,995	21,496	22,978
CALEDONIA, . . .	2,047	7,566	14,966	16,669	20,967	21,891
ESSEX, ...	567	1,479	3,087	3,334	3,981	4,226
FRANKLIN, . . .	1,472	6,534	14,411	14,886	20,977	24,532
GRAND ISLE, . . .	1,155	2,498	3,445	3,527	3,696	3,883
LAMOILLE, . . .	564	1,751	4,021	4,903	8,965	10,388
ORANGE, ...	7,334	16,318	21,724	24,169	27,285	27,873
ORLEANS, . . .	34	1,054	4,512	5,396	10,889	13,634
RUTLAND, . . .	15,565	23,813	29,487	29,975	31,295	30,701
WASHINGTON, . .	699	5,342	9,382	13,611	19,383	23,506
WINDHAM, . . .	17,693	23,581	26,760	28,457	28,748	27,431
WINDSOR, . . .	15,748	26,944	34,877	38,233	40,623	40,359
Total, ...	85,539	154,465	217,204	235,749	280,715	291,850

CLASSIFICATION

OF THE POPULATION OF VERMONT.

Number of white Males, .	146,378	Learned professions, . .	1,563
" " Females,	144,840	Pensioners, . . .	1,320
Colored persons, { Males, .	364	Deaf and dumb, . .	137
{ Females, .	366	Blind, ...	103
Males over 100 years of age,	15	Insane and idiots,	
Females, " " .	7	At public charge, . .	148
Males between 90 and 100, .	84	At private charge, . .	263
Females, " " " .	100	Universities or colleges, . .	3
Engaged in		Students in universities or colleges,	233
Mining, ...	77	Academies and grammar schools,	46
Agriculture, . . .	73,150	Students in academies and gram-	
Commerce, . . .	1,303	mar schools, . . .	4,113
Manufactures and Trades,	13,174	Primary and common schools,	2,402
Navigating the Ocean, .	41	Scholars in primary schools,	97,518
Navigating canals, lakes and		White persons over 20 years of	
rivers, ...	146	age who cannot read and write,	2,270

MOUNTAINS.

ASCUTNEY MOUNTAIN is situated partly in Windsor and partly in Weathersfield, being crossed by the line between those townships. It is an immense mass of granite, producing but little timber, or vegetation of any kind, particularly on the southern portion of the mountain. The name of this mountain is undoubtedly of Indian origin, but writers are not agreed with regard to its signification. Dr. Dwight says that it signifies the *three brothers*, and that it was given in allusion to its three summits. Kendall tells us that the true Indian name is *Cas-cad-nac*, and that it means a peaked mountain with steep sides.

From the summit of this mountain, the prospect is extensive and beautiful, and richly repays the labor of climbing its rugged ascent. The Connecticut, which is easily traced, winding its way through the rich and highly cultivated meadows, adds much to the interest and charm of the scenery.

CAMEL'S HUMP, next to the Chin, in Mansfield, is the most elevated summit of the Green Mountains. It is situated in the eastern part of Huntington, near the west line of Duxbury. It lies seventeen miles west of Montpelier, twenty-five north-easterly from Middlebury, and twenty southeast from Burlington. The summit is conspicuous from the whole valley of Lake Champlain, and the prospect which it commands is hardly surpassed in extent and beauty. The summit is hardly accessible, except from the north. It is usually ascended by way of Duxbury, where carriages can approach within about three miles of the summit. The remainder of the way can be passed on foot, without difficulty, excepting about half a mile, which is very steep and rugged. The

rocks which compose the mountain are wholly of mica slate, and the Hump is nearly destitute of soil or vegetation, only a few mosses, stinted shrubs, and alpine plants, being met with. This mountain is often erroneously called *Camel's Rump*.

CHIN, the name given to the north peak of Mansfield Mountain, in the township of Mansfield. This is the highest summit in the State, being, according to Captain Partridge, 4,279 feet, and according to E. F. Johnson, Esq., 4,359 feet above tide water.

GREEN MOUNTAINS. The celebrated range which gives name to the State, extends quite through it from south to north, keeping nearly a middle course between Connecticut River on the east and Lake Champlain on the west. From the line of Massachusetts to the southern part of Washington County, this range continues lofty, and unbroken through by any considerable streams; dividing the counties of Windham, Windsor, and Orange, from the counties of Bennington, Rutland, and Addison. In this part of the State, the communication between the eastern and western sides of the mountain was formerly difficult, and the phrase, *going over the mountain*, denoted an arduous business. But on account of the great improvement of the roads, more particularly in their more judicious location near the streams, the difficulty of crossing the mountain has nearly vanished.

In the southern part of Washington County, the Green Mountains separate into two ranges. The highest of these ranges, bearing a little east of north, continues along the eastern boundaries of the counties of Chittenden and Franklin, and through the county of Lamoille to Canada line; while the other range strikes off much more to the east, through the southern and eastern parts of Washington county, the western part of Caledonia County, and the north-western part of Essex County, to Canada. This last is called the *height of lands*, and it divides the waters, which fall into Connecticut River, in the north part of the State, from those which fall into Lake Champlain and Lake Memphremagog. This branch of the Green Mountains, though it nowhere rises so high as many points of the western branch, is much more uniformly elevated; yet the acclivity is so gentle as to admit of easy roads over it in various places. The western range, having been broken through by the rivers Winooski, Lamoille, and Missisco, is divided into several sections, these rivers having opened passages for good roads along their banks, while the intervening portions are so high and steep as not to admit of roads being made over them, with the exception of that portion lying between the Lamoille and Missisco. This part of the Green Mountains presents some of the most lofty summits in the State; particularly the Nose and Chin, in Mansfield, and Camel's Hump, in Huntington. The sides, and, in most cases, the summits of the mountains in Vermont, are covered with evergreens; such as spruce, hemlock, and fir. On this account the French, being the first civilized people who visited this part of the world, early gave to them the name of *Verd Mont*, or Green Mountain; and when the inhabitants of the New Hampshire Grants assumed the powers of government, in 1777, they adopted this name, contracted by the omission of the letter *d*, for the name of the new State.

HAZEN'S NOTCH, a remarkable notch in the mountain between Lowell and Montgomery, through which Hazen's Road passed.

KILLINGTON PEAK is a summit of the Green Mountains, in the south part of Sherburne. It is the most northerly of the two similar peaks situated near each other. The south peak is the highest; is in Shrewsbury, and is called *Shrewsbury Peak*.

MANSFIELD MOUNTAINS extend through the town of Mansfield, from north to south. They belong to the Green Mountain range, and the *Nose* and *Chin*, so called, from their resemblance to the face of a man lying on his back, exhibit some of the loftiest summits in the State.

MOUNT INDEPENDENCE lies in the north-west corner of the township of Orwell, and about two miles south-east of Ticonderoga Fort. It is an inconsiderable mountain, and worthy of notice only on account of the fortifications formerly erected upon it, and its connection with the early history of our country.

MOUNT NEBO, an eminence in Middlebury, resting on a base of about two miles by one, and rising gradually 439 feet above the level of Otter Creek. Upon its southern declivity the north-east part of the village rests. It affords some of the best arable land in the township, and is cultivated to its summit, where it exhibits to view Lake Champlain. It is a place of much resort to those who love to take an extended view of natural scenery; see "Alps on Alps arise;" and gaze at the mountains, which stretch off to a great distance north and south, both in New York and Vermont. This eminence is sometimes called *Chipman's Hill*.

MOUNT TOM, a considerable eminence in Woodstock.

STERLING PEAK.—See *Sterling*.

RIVERS, CREEKS, BROOKS, &c.

BARTON RIVER is formed in the township of Barton. One of the head branches of this river originates in Glover, from the fountains of *Runaway* Pond, and runs northerly into Barton; the other rises from two small ponds, on the line between Sutton and Sheffield, and after passing through Belle Pond, unites with the stream from Glover. Their united waters take a northerly direction, and, just before they reach the north line of Barton, receive Willoughby's River, a considerable stream which arises from a large pond of the same name in Westmore, and runs westerly eight or nine miles, through the south part of Brownington and north part of Barton. From Barton, Barton River continues a north course, passing through the north-east corner of Irasburgh and eastern part of Orleans, into Memphremagog Lake. This river waters about 160 square miles.

BATTENKILL RIVER. This river is about forty-five miles in length. It rises in Dorset, and passing Manchester, Sunderland, and Arlington, it receives Roaring Brook, and other tributaries, in Vermont; it then passes into the State of New York, and falls into the Hudson, three miles below Fort Miller, and about thirty-five miles north from Albany, N. Y.

BLACK RIVERS. Black River, in *Windsor County*, is thirty-five miles in length. It rises in Plymouth, passes Ludlow, Cavendish, and Weathersfield, and falls into the Connecticut at Springfield. This river passes through many natural ponds, and affords a great number of mill sites.

Black River, in *Orleans County*, is about thirty miles in length. It rises in some ponds in Craftsbury, and passing through Albany, Irasburg, and Coventry, it falls into Memphremagog Lake, at Salem.

BLACK CREEK.—See *Fairfield*.

BROAD BROOK, a small mill stream, which rises in the eastern part of Barnard, runs across the south-eastern corner of Royalton, and falls into White River in Sharon.

BROWN'S RIVER originates among the Mansfield Mountains, runs westerly through the south part of Underhill, and north part of Jericho, into Essex, and thence northerly through Westford, and empties into Lamoille River in Fairfax. Its length is about twenty miles, and it derives its name from a family by the name of Brown, which settled upon its banks in Jericho.

CASTLETON RIVER originates in Pittsford, runs south into Rutland, thence west, through Ira, Castleton, and Fair Haven, into Poultney River. In Castleton, it receives the waters of Lake Bombazine, and another considerable mill stream from the north. The road from Rutland to Whitehall, through Castleton village, passes along this river for a considerable part of the distance. Length of the stream about twenty miles.

CLYDE RIVER has its source in Pitkin's and Knowlton's Ponds, in the north-east part of Brighton, and runs a north-westerly course through Brighton, Charleston, Salem, and Derby, to Lake Memphremagog. Excepting a few short rapids, this is a dead, still river, until it comes within three miles of Lake Memphremagog. This stream runs through Round Pond, in Charleston, and through Salem Lake, a beautiful sheet of water, near two miles in length and one in width, lying partly in Salem and partly in Derby. It waters about 150 square miles.

CONNECTICUT RIVER. This beautiful River, the *Quonektacut* of the Indians, and the pride of the Yankees, has its sources in New Hampshire and the mountainous tracts in Lower Canada. Its name in the Indian language is said to signify *Long River*, or, as some render it, *River of Pines.* Its general course is north and south. After forming the boundary line between New Hampshire and Vermont, it crosses the western part of Massachusetts, passes the State of Connecticut, nearly in its centre, and, after a fall of 1,600 feet, from its head, north of latitude 45°, it falls into Long Island Sound, in latitude 41° 16'. The breadth of this river, at its entrance into Vermont, is about 150 feet, and in its course of sixty miles it increases to about 390 feet. In Massachusetts and Connecticut, its breadth may be estimated from 450 to 1,050 feet. It is navigable to Hartford, forty-five miles, for vessels of considerable burthen, and to Middletown, thirty miles from the sea, for vessels drawing twelve feet of water. By means of canals, and other improvements, it has been made navigable for boats to Fifteen Mile Falls, nearly 250 miles above Hartford.

The most considerable rapids in this river are Bellows' Falls, the Falls of Queechy, just below the mouth of Waterqueechy River; the White River Falls, below Hanover, and the Fifteen Mile Falls, in New Hampshire and Vermont ;—the Falls at Montague and South Hadley, in Mass., and the Falls at Enfield, in Ct., where it meets the tide water. The perpendicular height of the falls, which have been overcome by dams and locks, between Springfield, in Mass., and Hanover, in N. H., a distance of 130 miles, is 240 feet. Bars of sand and gravel extend across this river in various places, over which boats with difficulty pass in low water.

The most important tributaries to the Connecticut, in New Hampshire, are Upper and Lower Amonoosuck, Israel's, John's, Mascomy, Sugar, and Ashuelot Rivers; in Vermont, Nulhegan, Passumpsic, Wells, Wait's, Ompomponoosuck, White, Waterqueechy, Black, Williams, Sexton's, and West Rivers ; in Massachusetts, Miller's, Deerfield, Agawam, Chickopee, and Westfield Rivers; and the Farmington, in Connecticut.

The intervales are generally spread upon one or both sides of the river, nearly on a level with its banks, and extending from half a mile to five miles in breadth; but its borders are in some places high, rocky, and precipitous. In the spring it overflows its banks, and, through its winding course of nearly 400 miles, forms and fertilizes a vast tract of rich meadow. In point of length, utility, and beauty, this river forms a distinguished feature of New England.

Large quantities of shad are taken in this river, but the salmon, which formerly were very plenty, have entirely disappeared. Connecticut River passes through a basin, or valley, of about 12,000 square miles ; it is decorated, on each side, with towns and villages of superior beauty, and presents to the eye a wonderful variety of enchanting scenery.

DEERFIELD RIVER. This beautiful and important Indian stream joins the Connecticut, between Greenfield and Deerfield. It rises in the high grounds of Windham County, near Stratton, Dover, and Somerset, Vermont; and proceeding in a south-easterly course, it passes through Monroe, Florida, Rowe, Charlemont, Hawley, Buckland, Shelburne, and Conway. The most important tributaries to this stream are *Cold* River; a river from Heath and Coleraine ; one from Leyden, via Greenfield ; and a river from Conway. Its whole length is about fifty miles, In some places Deerfield River is rapid, and its banks very precipitous. Its passage through the mountains is very curious and romantic.

DOG RIVER is formed in Northfield, by the union of several streams from

Roxbury, Brookfield, &c., and taking a northerly course, through Berlin, falls into Winooski River, three quarters of a mile below the village of Montpelier. Its length is about sixteen miles, and it waters about eighty square miles.

FERRAND RIVER. This river heads in Avery's and Warner's Gores, runs nearly south, through the corners of Morgan and Wenlock, and unites with Clyde River in Brighton.

GRASSY BROOK.—See *Brookline*.

GREEN RIVER. There are two small streams of this name. One rises in Eden, passes through the corner of Hydepark, and falls into the Lamoille, in Wolcott. The other originates in Marlboro', and after running through a part of Halifax and Guilford, passes off into Massachusetts.

HOOSIC RIVER is formed in Pownal, and runs north-westerly into the township of Hoosic, N. Y., where it receives the River Walloomscoik from Shaftsbury and Bennington, and, taking a westerly course, falls into the Hudson, near Stillwater. Its whole length is about forty miles, and it receives the waters from 182 square miles in Vermont.

HUBBARDTON RIVER. This river rises from several small ponds in Sudbury, runs south-westerly through Gregory's Pond, in Hubbardton, through Benson, and falls into the head of East Bay, in West Haven. In its course it affords several very good mill privileges. Its length is about twenty miles.

HUNTINGTON RIVER rises in Lincoln, runs through Starksborough and Huntington, and joins Winooski River in Richmond. This is a very rapid stream, with a gravel or stony bottom, especially after it arrives within two or three miles of the Winooski. Its length is about twenty miles.

INDIAN RIVER. This is a small stream which rises in Rupert, runs through the corner of Pawlet, and unites with Pawlet River in Granville, N. Y. Another small stream of this name rises in Essex, and falls into Colchester Bay, in Colchester.

LAMOILLE RIVER formerly originated from a pond in the south-east corner of Glover.—See *Glover*. It is now formed by the union of several streams in Greensborough, and, after running south-westerly into Hardwick, pursues a north-westerly course till it falls into Lake Champlain, in the north-west corner of Colchester. This river is joined in Hardwick by a considerable stream, which issues from Caspian Lake, in Greensborough, in Wolcott by Green River, from Hydepark, in Johnson by Little North Branch, in Cambridge by Great North Branch, and in Fairfax by Brown's River.

The current of the River Lamoille is, in general, slow and gentle above Cambridge. Between this township and the lake are a number of considerable falls. Along this river are some very beautiful and fertile tracts of intervale. It is not quite so large as the Winooski and Missisco. It is said to have been discovered by Champlain, in 1609, and called by him *la mouette*, the French for mew, or gull, a species of water fowl, which were very numerous about the mouth of this stream. In Charlevoix's map of the discoveries in North America, published in 1774, it is called *la riviere a la Mouelle*, probably a mistake of the engraver, in not crossing the t's. Thus to the mere carelessness of a French engraver we are indebted for the smooth, melodious, sounding name of *Lamoille*.

LAPLOT RIVER. This stream rises in the south-eastern part of Hinesburgh, and, running north-westerly through a corner of Charlotte, and through Shelburne, falls into the head of Shelburne Bay. It is a small stream, about fifteen miles in length, and affords several mill sites.

Respecting the origin of the name of this stream, tradition has handed down the following stories. In the fall of 1775 a party of Indians was discovered, making their way up Shelburne Bay, in their bark canoes. From the head of the bay they proceeded about 100 rods up this stream, and landed on the west side ; and, having drawn their canoes on shore, and concealed them among the bushes, they proceeded cautiously forward, for the purpose of surprising and plundering the settlement, which was about half a mile distant. Their motions having been watched, and the alarm spread among the settlers, the men were mustered, to the number of ten, and a consultation was held, with regard to the course to be pursued. Concluding that the Indians, if vigorously attacked, would make a precipitate retreat to their canoes, it was agreed that three of their number should proceed to their place of landing, and disable their canoes, by cutting slits through the bark in various places, and then conceal themselves near by, and await the result ; while the other seven should make a furious and tumultuous assault upon the enemy, who had already commenced their work of plunder. The plot succeeded beyond their most sanguine expectations. The onset of the seven, favored by the approach of night, was made with so much show and spirit, as to lead the Indians to suppose that they were assailed by a force far superior to their own, and that their only chance of escape consisted in a hasty retreat to their canoes. They accordingly betook themselves to flight, and, being closely pursued, when they reached their landing place, they seized their canoes, hurried them into the stream, and leaped on board with the utmost precipitation. But what was their surprise, when they found their canoes were disabled, and were all filling with water ! In this forlorn condition they were attacked by the three men who had lain concealed on the bank, and the pursuing party soon coming to their aid, the Indians were all shot, while struggling to keep themselves afloat, or sunk to rise no more—not an individual being allowed to escape, to tell to their kin-

dred the tale of woe. This well contrived and successful stratagem, gave name to *Laplot* (*the plot*) *River.* So says tradition. Another, and more probable account of the origin of this name is, that, during the colonial wars and before any settlements were made in these parts, an ambush was formed near the mouth of this stream, for an English scouting party which was expected that way ; but the scout getting information of the plot, managed to surprise and defeat the liers-in-wait, and to slaughter the greater part of their number, and hence the name *La Plot.* But these traditions to the contrary notwithstanding, this river undoubtedly took its name from the point in the west part of Shelburne, called, on the early French maps, *Pointe au Platre,* or Plaster Point. It was formerly often written *La Platte.*

LEECH'S STREAM proceeds from a small pond in the north part of Averill, and runs about north-east across the west part of Canaan, and falls into Leech's Pond, which is about two miles wide and three long, and lies about half in Canada and half in Vermont. From this pond the stream runs nearly east about three miles, then southeast into Connecticut River. Its mouth is nearly two rods wide.

LEMONFAIR RIVER is a branch of Otter Creek, which rises in Whiting and Orwell, runs through the eastern part of Shoreham, across the southeast corner of Bridport, and joins Otter Creek in Weybridge. There are some mill sites near the head of this river, but it is, in general, a very sluggish, muddy stream. The following is the account given of the name of this stream.

As some of the early settlers were coming into this part of the country, they arrived at this muddy stream, and seeing the difficulty of crossing it, an old woman of the company exclaimed, " *It is a lam-en-ta-ble affair,*" and this exclamation, contracted into *Lemonfair,* became ever afterwards the name of the stream.

LEWIS CREEK rises near the north line of Bristol, runs north through the western part of Starksborough, and eastern part of Monkton, into Hinesburgh, thence westerly, through the south part of Hinesburgh, and the south-east corner of Charlotte, and falls into Lake Champlain in Ferrisburgh, a short distance north of the mouth of Little Otter Creek. The mill privileges on this stream are numerous, and many of them excellent.

LITTLE OTTER CREEK rises in Monkton and New Haven, and falls into Lake Champlain in Ferrisburgh, three miles north of the mouth of Otter Creek. This stream, towards its mouth, is wide and sluggish, and runs through a tract of low, marshy ground. It affords but few mill privileges.

LOCUST CREEK is a small mill stream which rises in Barnard, and falls into White River in Bethel. It is in general a rapid stream, and affords several good mill sites.

MAD RIVER, a rapid stream which rises in the highlands south of Warren, and, after passing through Waitsfield, falls into Winooski River at Moretown.

MERRITT'S, or *Joe's River.*—See *Joe's Pond.*

MIDDLEBURY RIVER rises in Hancock, passes through Ripton, and directing its course westerly, mingles its waters, in the south part of Middlebury, with those of Otter Creek. The turnpike from Vergennes to Bethel is, for a considerable distance, built on, or near, one of the banks of this stream, which presents to the eye of the traveller a number of highly romantic prospects. A large proportion of the land contiguous to this stream, after it leaves the mountain, is alluvial, and there are some small patches of alluvial land among the mountains. The length of this stream is about fourteen miles, and it affords several mill privileges.

14

MILES' RIVER rises near the west corner of Lunenburgh, and, pursuing a southerly direction into Concord, where it receives the stream from Miles' Pond, which is a considerable body of water, bends its course easterly, and falls into Connecticut River by a mouth seven or eight yards wide.

MILL BROOK.—See *Windsor.*

MILLER'S RIVER rises in Sheffield, runs through a part of Wheelock, and falls into the Passumpsic near the centre of Lyndon. It is, generally, a rapid stream, and affords some good mill privileges, particularly in Wheelock, where there is a considerable fall.

MISSISCO RIVER rises in Lowell, and, pursuing a north-easterly course through a part of Westfield and Troy, crosses the north line of the State into Potton, in Canada, where it receives a large stream from the north-east. After running several miles in Canada, it returns into Vermont about a mile west from the north-east corner of Richford. Thence it runs south-westerly through the corner of Berkshire, where it receives Trout River, into Enosburgh. It then takes a westerly course through Sheldon, into Highgate, where it bends to the south into Swanton, and, after performing a circuit of several miles in that town, returns into Highgate, and, running north-westerly, falls into Missisco Bay, near Canada line. There are several falls and rapids in this stream, but the current is, generally, moderate, and the river wide and shallow. It affords a considerable number of valuable sites for mills, and the alluvial flats along its margin are extensive, and very fertile. Besides those abovementioned, Black Creek and Taylor's Branch are its most considerable tributaries. The length of this river, including its windings, is about seventy-five miles, and it receives the waters from about 582 square miles in Vermont. This river is navigable for vessels of fifty tons burthen, six miles, to Swanton Falls, at which place is an hydraulic power of great value.

MOOSE RIVER is an eastern branch of the Passumpsic, and rises in Granby and East Haven. Taking a southwesterly course through Victory, Bradleyvale, Concord, and a part of St. Johnsbury, it falls into the Passumpsic opposite to St. Johnsbury Plain. It is generally a rapid stream, except through Bradleyvale and a part of Concord, where it is sluggish through flat land. Length twenty-four miles.

MUDDY BROOK. This stream divides Williston from Burlington, and falls into Winooski River.

NEAL'S BROOK rises near the north corner of Lunenburgh, in several branches, and, running south, falls into a pond of the same name, which is about a mile long and half a mile wide, and lies near the centre of Lunenburgh. It then continues its course south, meets a westerly branch, and, after running about half a mile further, falls into Connecticut River, by a mouth nearly two rods wide. On this stream are several mills, and other machinery.

NULHEGAN RIVER rises partly in Averill and partly in Wenlock. The North Branch runs a southerly course through Averill, Lewis, and a part of Bloomfield, the West branch runs an easterly course through Wenlock, and a part of Brunswick. They unite in Bloomfield, and, taking a south-easterly course, fall into Connecticut River a little above the north-east corner of Brunswick. This river is generally rapid, except that part of the West Branch that runs through Wenlock and Brunswick, which is very still and deep, and bordered by alder meadows. Through this and Clyde River, which runs a north-west course into Lake Memphremagog, the Indians formerly had their navigation from said lake to Connecticut River. They had a carrying place of about two miles, from the head of one river to that of the other, and several other carrying places by the falls and rapids in these streams. This river waters about 120 square miles, and is about three rods wide at its mouth.

OMPOMPANOOSUCK RIVER rises in the north-western part of Vershire, and runs easterly into West Fairlee. It then takes a south-easterly course into Thetford, where it receives a considerable stream from Fairlee Lake, which is a large body of water, lying partly in Fairlee and partly in Thetford. Continuing a south-easterly course through the township, the Ompompanoosuck mingles its waters with Connecticut River in the north-eastern part of Norwich. In the south part of Thetford, it receives a considerable mill stream from the west, which originates in the western part of Tunbridge and in Strafford. The whole length of this river is about twenty miles, and it affords a number of valuable mill privileges. The name, which is Indian, is said to signify a stream where many onions are found.

OTTA QUECHEE RIVER, (called also Water Quechee and Queechee River,) rises in Sherburne, runs nearly east through the south part of Bridgewater, thence east north-east through Woodstock, into the south part of Hartford, and thence south-east, through the north-east corner of Hartland, into Connecticut River, about two miles above Quechee Falls. In Bridgewater it receives two considerable branches, namely, North Branch, which rises in the north part of this township, from the north, and South Branch, which rises in Plymouth, from the south, both considerable mill streams. In Woodstock, it receives two other branches, of considerable size ; one rising in the north-east corner of Bridgewater, and south-east corner of Barnard, falls into Quechee River from the north, just below the north village in Woodstock ; the other rising in the south part of Woodstock, passes through both the villages in that town, and empties into it from the south, just above the mouth of the last mentioned stream. Both these streams afford excellent mill sites.

Quechee River, in its course, receives numerous other tributaries of less note. It is a clear and lively stream, with a gravel or stony bottom. This stream is about thirty-five miles in length, and waters about 212 square miles. The name of this stream is of Indian origin, and is said to signify quick whirling motion, and was probably given, on account of appearances exhibited at the falls near its mouth.

OTTER CREEK is the longest stream in Vermont. It originates in Mount Tabor, Peru, and Dorset, within a few rods of the head of the Battenkill. In Dorset it turns suddenly towards the north, and returns into Mount Tabor, running nearly north through the western part of this township and Wallingford, and through the central part of Clarendon into Rutland; it then takes a north-westerly course through Pittsford and Brandon; between Leicester and Salisbury on the east, and Whiting and Cornwall on the west; through the western part of Middlebury; between New Haven and Weybridge; through the north-east corner of Addison; between Waltham and Panton; and through Vergennes and Ferrisburgh, into Lake Champlain. From the south-west, it receives in Ferrisburgh a large creek which originates in Bridport; in Weybridge, Lemonfair River, from Orwell and Shoreham; in Rutland, Little West River, or Furnace Brook, from Tinmouth; and in Mount Tabor, Mill River, from Danby. From the east, it receives New Haven River in New Haven, Middlebury River in Middlebury, Leicester River in Leicester, Furnace River in Pittsford, East Creek in Rutland, and Cold River and Mill River in Clarendon, all of which are considerable mill streams.

Otter Creek, above Middlebury, is a very still stream, and its waters deep, affording very few mill privileges. From Middlebury to Pittsford, a distance of twenty-five miles, it is navigable for boats. At Middlebury, Weybridge, and Vergennes, are falls in the creek, which afford excellent sites for mills, and on which are some of the

finest manufacturing establishments in the State. From Vergennes to the mouth, a distance of eight miles, the creek is navigable for the largest vessels on the lake.

The alluvial flats along this stream are very extensive, and are inferior to none in the State. Its whole length is about ninety miles, and it waters about 900 square miles. Otter Creek was named by the French *Riviere aux Loutres*, the River of Otters, long before any settlements were made by the English in this State.

PASSUMPSIC RIVER has its source in a pond on the easterly line of Westmore, and, running a southerly course through Newark, passes into the west corner of East Haven; thence it pursues nearly a south course through Burke, Lyndon, St. Johnsbury, Waterford, and Barnet, and falls into the Connecticut a mile below the foot of the Fifteen Mile Falls. From its source till it approaches near the centre of Lyndon, it is a swift stream. It then meanders through a rich tract of intervale till it approaches the south line, where there is a high fall. The greatest part of the way through St. Johnsbury it is swift, but in a few places it runs slow, through excellent intervale land; and through Waterford and Barnet it runs slow, through rich, flat land, though there are some large falls in Barnet. It is generally deep, and it is between four and six rods wide below St. Johnsbury Plain.

It receives several large branches in Lyndon, two in St. Johnsbury, and one in Barnet. Its length is about thirty-four miles. The name of this stream is said to be derived from the Indian phrase, *Bas-soom-suc*, signifying a stream, where there is much medicine.

PAWLET RIVER is a small stream which rises in Dorset, runs northwesterly across the north-east corner of Rupert, diagonally across the township of Pawlet, and unites with Wood Creek, in the State of New York, two or three miles above its mouth. This stream affords a number of eligible mill sites in Vermont.

PHILADELPHIA RIVER is a small stream which rises in the south part of Goshen, runs south-west through Chittenden, and unites with East Creek in Pittsford.

PIKE RIVER.—See *Berkshire.*

PLATT, or *Plott River.*—See *Laplot.*

POULTNEY RIVER rises in Tinmouth, and runs a westerly course, through Middletown and Poultney. On arriving at the west line of Poultney, it begins to form the boundary between Vermont and New York, and, running between Fair Haven and West Haven, on the north, and Hampton, N. Y., on the south, falls into the head of East Bay, which is an arm of Lake Champlain. From Fair Haven it receives Castleton River, and from West Haven, Hubbardton River. The whole length of Poultney River is about twenty-five miles, and it affords a number of excellent mill sites.

A remarkable change took place in this stream in 1783. A little above its junction with East Bay, a ridge of land crosses in a northerly direction. The river running a northwesterly course, on meeting the ridge, turned suddenly towards the north-east, and, after keeping that course about half a mile, turned westerly, rushing down a steep ledge of rocks, and forming a number of fine mill privileges. The river had, for some years, been observed to be making encroachments upon the ridge, at the place where it turned to the north-east; and in May, 1783, during a violent freshet, the river broke through the ridge, and, meeting with no rocks, it cut a channel 100 feet deep, lowering the bed of the river for some distance above, and carrying immense quantities of earth into East Bay. The bay, which was before navigable for vessels of forty tons burthen, was so completely filled, for several miles, that a canoe could with difficulty pass at low water, and the navigation much obstructed at Fiddler's Elbow, a narrow place in the lake, near South Bay. The obstructions have since been mostly removed by the force of the current.

QUEECHEE RIVER.—See *Otta Queechee.*

ROCK RIVER. This river rises in Franklin, and runs through Highgate into Missisco Bay.

SAXTON'S RIVER is formed in Grafton, by the union of several streams from Windham, and running an easterly course about ten miles, through the south part of Rockingham, falls into Connecticut River in the north-east corner of Westminster, about one mile below Bellows' Falls. It derives its name from a Mr. Saxton, who unluckily fell into it while crossing it on a log, for the purpose of surveying the line between Rockingham and Westminster, but was not drowned.

STEVENS' BRANCH.—See *Barre.*

STEVENS' RIVER. This excellent mill stream rises in Peacham and Ryegate. It received its name in compliment to Capt. Phineas Stevens, the brave defender of Charlestown, N. H. The waters of this river are remarkably clear, and its banks luxuriant and romantic. It meanders about fifteen miles, and in its course through Barnet it receives Harvey's Lake, a pellucid sheet of water, covering an area of 300 acres. This beautiful river mingles its crystal waters with those of the Connecticut, at Barnet, by a leap of 100 feet, in the distance of ten rods, as it were in joy to meet a sister stream on its passage to the bosom of the ocean.

TROUT RIVER. This river is formed in Montgomery, by several branches; it runs in a north-west direction, and falls into the Missisco on the border of Enosburgh and Berkshire. This is a good mill stream, and, with its tributaries, fertilizes considerable tracts of country.

WAIT'S RIVER. The main branch of this river rises in Harris' Gore, and runs south-easterly along the west line of Topsham. Another branch, called Jail Branch, rises in Washington, and running north-easterly, joins the main branch in the south-west part of Topsham. Another stream rises from several heads in the north part of Topsham, and, running southerly unites with the main stream, near the north-east corner of Corinth. Another stream called the South Branch, rises near the middle of Washington, and pursuing a south-easterly course, joins the river at Bradford.

Wait's River, and all its branches, are lively streams, and afford a number of very good mill privileges. In Bradford, where this river is crossed by the main road leading up the Connecticut, is a fall, which furnishes a number of fine mill sites. This river is said to have derived its name from a Captain Wait, belonging to Major Rogers' Rangers, who killed a deer near its mouth, on the return from St. Francis, in 1759, which was probably the means of saving the lives of several of that famishing party.

WALLOOMSCOIK RIVER is a small stream which is formed in Bennington, by the union of several branches which rise in Glastenbury, Woodford, and Pownal. It takes a north-western direction, leaves the State near the north-west corner of Bennington, and unites with Hoosic River nearly on the line between Washington and Rensalaer Counties, N. Y.

Between this stream and Hoosic River was fought the Bennington battle. On the Walloomscoik and its branches are many good mill privileges and some fine meadows.

WATERBURY RIVER rises in Morristown, and runs south through the western part of Stowe and Waterbury, into Winooski River. In Stowe it receives one considerable tributary from the east, which rises in Worcester, and two from the west, which rise in Mansfield. It also receives several tributaries from the west in Waterbury, which

originate in Bolton. The whole length of the stream is about sixteen miles, and it affords a number of good mill privileges.

WATER QUECHEE RIVER.—See Otta Quechee.

WELLS RIVER has its source in Kettle Pond, which lies at the north-west corner of Groton, and a part of it in Marshfield. It runs nearly south-east about two miles, and falls into Long Pond in Groton, which is about two miles long and 100 rods wide. From this pond it continues its south-easterly course half a mile, and falls into another pond, which is about half a mile long and a quarter of a mile wide. It then runs a mile and a half, and meets the South Branch, which rises near the south-west corner of the town, and runs nearly east to its junction with the main stream; it then runs east south-east about a mile, and receives the North Branch, which has its source near the north-east corner of the town. Continuing the same course, it passes through the north-west part of Ryegate into Newbury, and running near the line between Newbury and Ryegate about four miles, falls into Connecticut River about half a mile south of the north-east corner of Newbury.

This is generally a rapid stream, furnishing many excellent mill privileges, on which mills are erected.

WEST RIVER. This river is also called Wantasticook. It rises in Weston, and runs south into Londonderry. Near the south line of this township it receives Winhall River from Winhall. It then takes a south-easterly course through Jamaica, Townshend, Newfane, and Dummerston, and unites with Connecticut River in the north-east part of Brattleborough. In Jamaica, it receives from the west Bald Mountain Branch, which rises in Stratton, and another large branch from Wardsborough; and from the east, Meadow Branch, which rises in Windham. In Newfane, it receives South Branch and Smith's Branch. This stream affords but few mill privileges, but there are a great number on its branches. Along its banks are some fine tracts of intervale. This river receives the waters from about 440 square miles.

WHETSTONE BROOK is a small mill stream which rises in Marlborough, and runs nearly east through Brattleborough into Connecticut River. It affords a considerable number of good mill privileges.

WHITE CREEK is formed in Rupert, by the union of a number of small branches, and, taking a south-westerly course, unites with the Battenkill in Washington County, N. Y.

WHITE RIVER rises in Granville, and running a south-easterly course through the north-east corner of Hancock, the south-west part of Rochester, and the north-east corner of Pittsfield, enters Stockbridge. It then turns to the north-east, and, after running through the south-east corner of Bethel, into Royalton, bears to the south-east, through Sharon and Hartford, and falls into Connecticut River about five miles above the mouth of Otta Quechee River. From Granville this river runs slowly through a narrow tract of intervale, till it arrives at the eastern part of Stockbridge, after which the current is very rapid, till it reaches Bethel Village. From Bethel to its mouth the channel of the river is from sixteen to eighteen rods in width, and the current generally rapid, and the water shallow.

On account of its proximity to Otta Quechee River, White River receives no large tributaries from the south. Broad Brook and Locust Creek are the most important. From the north it receives three large branches, called the first, the second, and the third branch. The *First Branch* rises in Washington, near the head branches of Wait's and Winooski River, and, running through Chelsea and Tunbridge, unites with White River in the eastern part of Royalton. The *Second Branch* rises in Williamstown, in con-

junction with Stevens' Branch of Winooski River, and, running southerly through Brookfield and Randolph, enters White River a little west of the centre of Royalton. This stream runs with a gentle current through a narrow tract of fine intervale. The *Third Branch* originates in Roxbury, runs through the corner of Granville, through Braintree and the corner of Randolph, and joins White River at Bethel Village. Each of these streams is about twenty miles in length, and on each are several very good mill privileges, particularly on the latter, in Bethel Village. White River is the largest stream in Vermont on the east side of the mountains. Its length is about fifty-five miles, and it waters about 680 square miles. This stream was known by the name of White River, long before any settlements were made in Vermont.

WILD BRANCH. This stream rises in Eden, runs through the western part of Craftsbury, and unites with the River Lamoille in Wolcott.

WILLIAMS' RIVER is formed in Chester, by the union of three considerable branches, which originate in small streams in the townships of Ludlow, Andover, Windham, and Grafton. These three branches unite about a mile and a half to the south-east of the two villages in Chester, and their united waters, after running fifteen miles in a south-easterly direction, fall into Connecticut River in Rockingham, three miles above Bellows' Falls. Along this river is some fine intervale, and it affords several good mill privileges. Williams' River derives its name from the celebrated Rev. John Williams, who was taken by the Indians, at Deerfield, Mass., in 1704, and who, at the mouth of this stream, preached a sermon to his fellow captives.

WILLOUGHBY RIVER issues from Willoughby Lake, in Westmore, runs through the south part of Browningon, and unites with Barton River in the north part of Barton.

WINHALL RIVER is a small mill stream which is collected in Winhall, and, after running easterly through the corner of Jamaica, unites with West River in the south part of Londonderry.

WINOOSKI RIVER, called also Onion River, is formed in Cabot by the union of several small streams, and, taking a southerly course, enters Marshfield, where it receives a large tributary from Peacham and Cabot.

On this stream is a remarkable cataract, where the water falls about 500 feet in the distance of thirty rods. Through Marshfield the river continues a southerly course into Plainfield, where it bends to the south-west, and crosses the corner of the township into Montpelier. Here it receives Kingbury Branch, from Calais. After crossing the south-east corner of Montpelier, the river takes a north-westerly course, which it continues until it falls into Lake Champlain, between Colchester and Burlington, five miles north of Burlington Village.

Its most considerable tributaries are Dog River and Stevens' Branch, in Berlin, North Branch, at Montpelier Village, Mad River, in Moretown, Waterbury River, in Waterbury, Huntington River, in Richmond, and Muddy Brook, between Williston and Burlington.

The alluvial flats along this river are narrow, till the river has passed through the western range of the Green Mountains, when they become much more extensive. In Bolton, where it passes the range, the mountains approach very near the river.

The channels which have been worn in the rocks by this river are a great curiosity. One of these, between Middlesex and Moretown, is about eighty rods in length, sixty feet in width, and thirty feet deep; the rock appearing like a wall on each side. Another of these channels is between Waterbury and Duxbury, four miles below Waterbury Village. Its depth is about 100 feet, and the rocks on the south side are perpendicular. The rocks have here fallen into the chasm, and formed a *natural bridge*, which is crossed by footmen at low water.

Among the rocks here are also several curious caverns. Holes, also, of cylindrical form, are here worn into the solid rocks, several feet in depth. This chasm is but a few steps from the turnpike leading from Montpelier to Burlington, and is worthy the attention of the curious traveller. A third channel of this kind is between Burlington and Colchester, about three-fourths of a mile above Winooski Lower Falls. The channel here is about forty rods in length, seventy feet in width, and sixty-five feet deep. Across the channel a bridge has been thrown, which is perfectly secure from floods. There is abundant evidence, both here and at the natural bridge above mentioned, that there formerly existed a large pond at each place, whose waters were drained off by the wearing down of the channels.

In Winooski River are several falls, which afford excellent sites for mills. This river is one of the largest in the State, being about seventy miles in length, and watering 970 square miles.

That part of the great Northern Railroad, which lies between Montpelier and Burlington, passes almost the whole distance along the banks of this most enchanting stream. People generally love to travel as fast as the fiery courser can carry them; but on this route it is far different, for in almost every mile the traveller wishes to stop, to gaze and admire.

LAKES AND PONDS.

BELLE POND, called also Belle Water Pond, is three miles long, and one and a half wide, situated in the south-eastern part of Barton. It derives its name from the clearness of its water.

BOMBAZINE LAKE.—See *Castleton.*

CASPIAN LAKE.—See *Greensborough.*

CHAMPLAIN LAKE. This lake commences at Whitehall, at the junction of Wood Creek with East Bay. A mile or two north of this it receives the waters of South Bay, which projects to the south-west. From Whitehall to the south part of Orwell, the average width of the lake is about half a mile. At Sholes Landing about one mile south of Mount Independence, the lake is not more than forty rods wide, and between Mount Independence and Ticonderoga, only eighty rods. The widest place, in the lake against Orwell, is about two miles, and its average width about one mile. The distance from Whitehall to Ticonderoga, N. Y. is about twenty miles.

The fortress of this name is now a heap of ruins. It was built by the French, in 1756, on a point of land formed by the junction of Lake George Creek with Lake Champlain, and was two miles north-west from Mount Independence, and opposite the north-west corner of Orwell. Ticonderoga is derived from the Indian and signifies noisy. The French called the fort Carillon. It was a place of great strength, both by nature and art. On three sides it was surrounded by water, and about half the other was occupied by a deep swamp, while the line was completed by the erection of a breastwork nine feet high on the only assailable ground. In 1758, Gen. Abercrombie, with a British army, was defeated in an attempt upon this fortress with the loss of 1941 men, but it was the next year surrendered to Gen. Amherst. It was surprised by Col. Allen, May 10, 1775,

at the commencement of the revolution, and retained till 1777, when it was evacuated on the approach of Gen. Burgoyne. Near this place is one of the richest localities of minerals in the United States, and is a most interesting spot to the man of science. " Within the limits of four or five acres are found massive and crystalized garnet, several varieties of coccolite, augite, white and green, crystalized and massive, very beautiful adularia and common feldspar, tabular spar, hornblend, calcareous spar containing brucite, and elegant crystals of silico calcareous oxyde of titanium."

From Ticonderoga to Crown Point, N. Y., a distance of twelve or fourteen miles, the width of the lake continues from one to two miles. *Crown Point Fortress* is now in ruins and is opposite to the south part of Addison. It was built by the French, in 1731, on a point of land between West Bay and the lake, and was called Fort St. Frederick. In 1759, it was surrendered to the British troops under Gen. Amherst, and was held by the British till May 10, 1775, when it was taken by Col. Seth Warner, on the same day that Ticonderoga surrendered to Allen. It again fell into the hands of the British, in 1776, who kept possession of it till after the capture of Burgoyne in 1777. This fortress is in lat. 44° 3′ and in long. 73° 29′ west from Greenwich. It is nearly a regular pentagon, the longest curtain being ninety, and the shortest about seventy-five yards in length. The ramparts are about twenty-five feet in thickness, and riveted with masonry throughout. The ditch is blasted out of the solid rock. There are two demilunes and some small detached outworks. An arched passage led from the interior of the works to the lake, and a well about ninety feet in depth was sunk in one of the bastions.

The fort erected by the French in 1731, was a smaller work, and nearer the water. The present fort was commenced by the English, in 1759, and according to Dr. Dwight, cost about two millions of pounds sterling. The whole peninsula being of solid rock, covered with a thin layer of earth, the works cannot be assailed by regular approaches, and both in construction and position, the fortress is among the strongest in North America. It has been long dismantled, and is now quite dilapidated, but its form and dimensions are still easily traced and measured.

From Crown Point to Split Rock, a distance of about nineteen miles, the width of the lake will average about three miles and a half. The width from Thompson's Point to Split Rock, in the town of Essex, N. Y., is only three quarters of a mile. Split Rock is a considerable curiosity. A light house is erected here. At McNeil's Ferry, between Charlotte and Essex, N. Y., a few miles further north, the width of the lake wants twenty rods of three miles.

From this place the lake spreads as it flows north, and at Burlington from the bottom of Burlington Bay to that of Douglas' Bay is nine miles and three quarters wide. Upon Juniper Island at the entrance of Burlington Bay from the south, a light house has been erected, and a few miles to the north-west of this bay the steamboat Phœnix was consumed by fire on the morning of the 5th of September, 1819, and much property and several lives lost.

Between Juniper Island and Pottier's Point, a large rock rises above the water, called Rock Dunder, and to the south-west of Juniper lie four small islands called the *Four Brothers*. They were named on Charlevoix map the isles of the Four Winds. The bay opposite Burlington, called Douglas' Bay, was called by the French *Corlar*, and the island lying a little to the north, called Schuyler's Island, they called *Isle aux Chapon*. The greatest expanse of water is between the Four Brothers and Grand Isle, but the greatest width from east to west shore is further north across the islands, where the distance is about fourteen miles.

Cumberland Bay, on the head of which stands Plattsburgh, N. Y., is about twenty-two miles from Burlington. This bay is celebrated for the signal victory of the American squadron, under Commodore McDonough, over the British fleet, on the 11th of September, 1814.

The peninsula lying north of Cumberland Bay called Cumberland Head, was called by the French *Cape Scoumouton*. On this point is a light house. From South Hero to the 45th degree of lat. the breadth of the lake including the islands is from nine to twelve miles. Where the lake leaves the State on the west side of Alburgh, its width is less than two miles. The lake extends into Canada twenty-four miles to St. Johns, where the River Richelieu commences and conveys the waters to the St. Lawrence. The Richelieu is about sixty miles long, and joins the St. Lawrence near the upper end of Lake St. Peters, and about forty-five miles below Montreal. The navigation of the Richelieu is interrupted by the Chambly Rapids, but the lake is connected with the St. Lawrence at Montreal, by a railroad eighteen miles in length, leading from St. Johns to Laprairie.

Lake Champlain lies between this State and the State of New York, and more than half of it within the limits of Vermont. It extends in a straight line from south to north, 102 miles along the western boundary, from Whitehall to the 45th degree of latitude, and thence about twenty-four miles to St. Johns in Canada, affording an easy communication with that province and with New York. The length of this lake from south to north, measured in a straight line from one extremity to the other, and supposing it to terminate northerly at St. Johns, is 126 miles. Its width varies from one fourth of a mile to thirteen miles, and the mean width is about four and a half miles. This would give an area of 567 square miles, two thirds of which lie within the limits of Vermont. The waters, which this lake receives from Vermont, are drained, by rivers and other streams, from 4088 miles of its territory. Its depth is generally sufficient for the navigation of the largest vessels. It received its present name from Samuel Champlain, a French nobleman, who discovered it in the spring of 1609, and who died at Quebec in 1635, and was not drowned in its waters, as has been often said.

One of the names given to this lake by the aborigines is said to have been *Caniaderi-Guarunte*, signifying the mouth or door of the country. If so, it was very appropriate, as it forms the gate-way between the country on the St. Lawrence and that on the Hudson. The name of this lake in the Abenāqui tongue was *Petawâ-bouque*, signifying alternate land and water, in allusion to the numerous islands and projecting points of land along the lake. Previous to the settlement of the country by Europeans, this lake had long been the thorough-fare between hostile and powerful Indian tribes, and its shores the scene of many a mortal conflict. And after the settlement, it continued the same in reference to the French and English colonies, and subsequently in reference to the English in Canada and the United States. In consequence of this peculiarity of its location, the name of Lake Champlain stands connected with some of the most interesting events in the annals of our country; and the transactions associated with the names of Ticonderoga, and Crown Point, and Plattsburgh, and many other places, united with the variety and beauty of the scenery, the neatness and accommodation of the steamboats, and the unrivalled excellency of their commanders, render a tour through this lake one of the most interesting and agreeable to the enlightened traveller.

DUNMORE LAKE is about four miles long and three fourths of a mile wide. It is situated partly in Leicester and partly in Salisbury, and discharges into Otter Creek by what is called Leicester River. Trout weighing twenty-five pounds have been taken out of this lake. It is sometimes called Trout Pond.

ELLIGO POND lies partly in Greensborough and partly in Craftsbury. It is about two miles long and half a mile wide, and has two outlets, one to the north and the other to the south. The northern outlet constitutes one of the head branches of Black River; the southern, after passing through Little Elligo Pond, communicates with the River Lamoille in Hardwick. The scenery about Elligo Pond is romantic and beautiful. The eastern bank presents abrupt, and, in some places, perpendicular rocks of considerable height, while the western rises gradually, and is covered with a luxuriant growth of forest trees, which contrast finely with the naked cliffs of the opposite shore.

Near the centre of the pond are two small islands. This pond is a favorite resort for the sportsman and the admirer of nature in her own simplicity. Its waters abound with fine trout, and its banks with a plenty of game. It was formerly a favorite hunting ground of the St. Francis Indians, to whom the northern part of Vermont once belonged. These Indians called this pond *Elligo Scootlon*, and hence it is now sometimes, but improperly, called *Elligo Scotland*.

FAIRLEE LAKE.—See *Fairlee.*

HOSMER'S PONDS.—See *Craftsbury.*

JOE'S POND.—See *Danville.*

KNOWLTON LAKE. A considerable body of water, nearly on the line between Brighton and Wenlock, from which issues the principle head branch of Clyde River.

LONG, OR RUNAWAY POND.—See *Glover.*

MEMPHREMAGOG LAKE, is thirty miles in length, and two or three miles wide. It lies mostly in Canada, only seven or eight miles of the south end extending into Vermont. It is situated about half way between Connecticut River and Lake Champlain, and that part within this State lies between the towns of Derby and Newport. A bay extends south into Orleans. These waters cover about fifteen square miles in Vermont, and receives from this State, Clyde, Barton and Black River.

The waters of this lake are discharged to the north by what is called Magog Outlet, into the River St. Francis, and through that into St. Peters Lake, about fifteen miles below the mouth of the River Richelieu.

Upon the west side of a small uninhabited island situated at the mouth of Fitch's Bay, and about two miles north of Canada line, is a considerable quarry of novaculite known by the name of the " Magog Oil Stone." The vein of novaculite is from two to eight feet wide where it has been quarried, and the length of the quarry is several hundred feet. It is situated beneath a cliff, and, at the top, is interspersed with quartz. The vein of novaculite runs parallel with the cliff and lake shore, and is so low that it is usually overflowed by the rising of the lake in spring and autumn. Large quantities of the " Magog Oil Stone " have been prepared for use and vended in various parts of the United States.

The Indian words from which the name of this lake was derived, were *Mem-plow-bouque*, signifying a large expanse of water. On the east side of this lake the country is beautiful, with an easy, rich soil; on the west it is broken, and less productive.

MOLLY'S POND.—See *Cabot*.

SEYMOUR LAKE.—See *Morgan*.

WILLOUGHBY'S LAKE.—See *West-more*.

WATERFALLS.

BELLOWS' FALLS.—See *Rockingham*.

FIFTEEN MILE FALLS.—See *Lunenburgh*.

MCINDOES FALLS, a considerable fall in Connecticut River at the head of boat navigation on that stream, and opposite the south-east corner of Barnet.

WINOOSKI FALLS.—See *Winooski River*.

BAYS, HARBORS, CAPES, POINTS OF LAND, ETC.

ALLEN'S POINT. This is the southern extremity of Grand Isle, in the township of South Hero. It takes its name from Mr. Allen, one of the early settlers.

BASIN HARBOR.—See *Ferrisburgh*.

BELAMAQUEEN BAY. A small bay jutting into the town of Ferrisburgh from Lake Champlain.

BURLINGTON BAY. A large open bay lying west of Burlington Village, between Appletree Point on the north and Pottier's Point on the south, and embracing the entrance into Shelburne Bay.

CHIMNEY POINT is in Addison opposite to Crown Point and is the most westerly land in Vermont. It was upon this point that the first settlement was made in the western part of Vermont by the French in 1731, and here they erected a stone wind mill, which was garrisoned during the colonial wars, and hence it has sometimes been called Windmill Point, but this name is now confined to a point in Alburgh.

MCQUAM BAY. A large open bay in the western part of Swanton.

MISSISCO BAY is a large arm of Lake Champlain, which extends into Canada between Swanton and Highgate on the east, and Alburgh on the west. Its width from east to west, on Canada line, is about five miles, and it extends four or five miles into Canada. This bay covers an area of about thirty-five square miles.

POTTIER'S POINT. This point is situated on the west side of Shelburne, two miles, 182 rods from the south wharf in Burlington. It took its name from John Pottier, the first settler upon it. It is often called Shelburne Point.

SHARPSHIN POINT. A high, rocky point situated on the north side of Burlington Bay, one mile and 217 rods from the south wharf in Burlington.

SHELBURNE BAY.—See *Shelburne.*

SOUTH BAY. There are two bays of this name, one at the south end of Lake Champlain near Whitehall, and the other at the south end of Lake Memphremagog between Salem and Newport.

WINDMILL POINT.—See *Alburgh.*

STATISTICAL TABLES.

The following Tables, with the preceding Tables of Population; comprise a large amount of valuable information relating to each county and town in the State.

These statistics are presented in tabular form, and will be found exceedingly easy of reference. The relative value of every town and county in the State may be seen almost at a glance. They are derived from the most authentic sources.

COUNTY TABLE.

This Table contains the number of towns in each county in the State with the date of incorporation of the counties; the number of horses, cattle, sheep and swine; also the quantity of some of the most important articles of production in each county, with the area in square miles, and the distance of the shire towns from Boston, the capital of New England.

COUNTIES.	Date of Incorpor'n.	Number of Towns.	Shire Towns.	Latitude of Shire Towns.	Distance of Sh. towns fr. Boston.	Number of Horses.	Number of Cattle.
Addison, . .	1785	22	Middlebury,	44°	173	5,425	39,718
Bennington, .	1779	17	{ Bennington & Manchester,	42° 51' } 43° 10' }	120	3,397	16,879
Caledonia .	1792	18	Danville,	44° 26'	180	5,852	32,668
Chittenden, .	1787	15	Burlington,	44° 27'	206	4,231	24,142
Essex, . . .	1792	17	Guildhall,	44° 32'	238	1,207	6,837
Franklin, . .	1792	14	St. Albans,	44° 49'	225	4,427	26,965
Grand Isle, .	1802	5	North Hero,	44° 51'	225	1,161	5,463
Lamoille, . .	1835	12	Hydepark,	44° 37'	187	2,597	16,555
Orange, . .	1781	17	Chelsea,	40°	140	6,674	36,853
Orleans, . .	1792	19	Irasburgh,	44° 48'	205	3,464	18,299
Rutland, . .	1781	26	Rutland,	43° 37'	140	6,200	40,023
Washington, .	1810	17	MONTPELIER	44° 17'	160	4,360	25,415
Windham, .	1779	23	Newfane,	42° 58'	102	4,969	42,661
Windsor, . .	1781	23	Woodstock,	43° 36'	116	8,440	51,863

15

COUNTY TABLE—Continued.

Counties.	Number of Sheep.	Number of Swine.	Bushels of Grain.	Bushels of Potatoes.	Tons of Hay.	Pounds of Sugar.	Pounds of Wool.	Area of Counties.
Addison, . .	261,010	14,305	287,321	440,079	111,120	132,013	676,969	677
Bennington, .	104,721	9,906	264,324	564,279	42,907	180,986	223,674	612
Caledonia, .	100,886	18,991	472,987	1,066,848	67,077	665,397	183,198	640
Chittenden, .	110,774	25,310	324,838	522,792	56,357	177,343	215,019	485
Essex, . . .	14,188	3,639	83,185	235,180	13,167	99,385	23,605	620
Franklin, . .	87,385	8,935	229,262	709,396	61,263	400,775	225,802	549
Grand Isle, .	27,451	3,179	99,051	76,408	8,593	34,478	57,546	83
Lamoille, . .	40,921	7,287	123,124	472,563	29,616	295,476	85,595	431
Orange, . .	156,053	22,516	483,328	1,055,379	73,004	420,639	311,674	615
Orleans, . .	46,669	9,750	220,956	596,855	37,291	507,446	107,580	689
Rutland, . .	271,727	15,563	398,743	642,108	103,737	396,804	653,819	904
Washington, .	110,872	12,150	340,369	698,745	55,100	451,348	159,724	571
Windham, .	114,336	29,435	397,498	743,366	70,398	423,400	222,260	782
Windsor, . .	234,826	22,834	627,252	1,072,753	107,109	462,444	552,770	893

GRAND LIST FOR 1848,

AS REPORTED BY THE STATE AVERAGING COMMITTEE.

We now present a copy of the GRAND LIST, which embraces the amount and value of every species of property in all the towns and counties in the State, subject to taxation. Property of every description in Vermont is liable to taxation, except articles of indispensable necessity.

"Where the revenue of a country is raised, as in Vermont, by a direct tax upon the real and personal property of the citizens, the first object undoubtedly should be to ascertain what each individual really owns, that the share of the public burthen, thrown upon each, may be in proportion to his ability to bear it; but this is found, in practice, to be an object of very difficult attainment. By most of the former listing laws, a large share of the taxable property, has been entered by name, with a fixed valuation. But this produced great inequality, on account of the great difference in the value of property of the same kind, depending upon quality and location. Another provision of the old listing laws required a person, who had purchased property on credit, and given his note for it, to pay taxes on that property, while the holder of the note was taxed for it as money at interest, thus taxing the same property twice, and throwing an unjust and heavy burden upon the man in debt. The present listing law of 1841, was designed to correct these evils, by requiring all rateable property to be appraised at its cash value, and by allowing the debts due from a person, over and above the amount due to him, to be deducted from the appraised value of his personal property."

GRAND LIST FOR 1848.

ADDISON COUNTY.

Towns.	Polls at $2. (Dolls.)	Real Estate Acres.	Real Estate Appraisal. (Dolls. / Cts.)	Personal Estate Appraisal. (Dolls. / Cts.)	Attorney's, Phy-sicians and Sur-geon's assess'ts. (Dolls.)	1 per cent. of real & personal estate with polls and as-sessments of At-torneys, &c. (Dolls. / Cts.)	Deduct for Militia equipped. (Dolls.)	Balance is the List for State Taxes. (Dolls. / Cts.)
Addison,	314	23,864	508,179	44,255 25	10	5,848 14		5,848 14
Bridport,	384	24,473	459,579 50	70,933	20	5,709 13		5,709 13
Bristol,	510	18,420	210,364	53,486	25	3,173 50		3,173 50
Cornwall,	312	17,035	296,414	40,854	9	3,693 68		3,693 68
Ferrisburgh,	440	27,272	589,468	76,319	20	7,117 87		7,117 87
Goshen,	146	17,794	61,480	6,003 09		820 83		820 83
Granville,	198	9,254	68,540	10,574 74		989 15	2	987 15
Hancock,	144	19,000	47,824	13,982 94		762 07		762 07
Leicester,	232	11,749	122,084	18,807 07		1,640 91		1,640 91
Lincoln,	412	16,068	82,279	16,579	7	1,407 58		1,407 58
Middlebury,	956	20,782	590,161 24	141,125 99	93	8,361 87	137 40	8,224 47
Monkton,	386	19,252	259,452	39,010	15	3,385 62		3,385 62
New Haven,	400	23,772	476,254	98,210	55	6,199 64		6,199 64
Orwell,	358	24,725	523,889 04	203,246 09	25	7,654 36	4	7,650 36
Panton,	164	9,158	184,452 02	18,755 18	3	2,199 07		2,199 07
Ripton,	180	30,947	68,255 05	2,841		890 96	4	886 96
Salisbury,	314	16,497	197,619	21,094	5	2,506 13	8	2,498 13
Shoreham,	410	25,593	514,551	112,153	10	6,687 04		6,687 04
Starksboro',	496	21,904	114,136 92	34,125 26	9	1,987 62	12 41	1,975 21
Vergennes,	444	-,160	247,095	136,648	20	4,301 43	26	4,275 43
Waltham,	118	5,276	103,208	8,848		1,238 56	66	1,172 56
Weybridge,	230	10,031	219,899 61	29,389 13		2,722 89	2	2,720 89
Whiting,	198	7,659	152,793	13,064	3	1,859 57		1,859 57
Total,	7,746	421,383	6,097,977 38	1,210,284 14	329	81,157 62	261 81	80,895 81

GRAND LIST FOR 1848—Continued.

BENNINGTON COUNTY.

Towns.	Dolls.	Acres.	Dolls. Cts.	Dolls. Cts.	Dolls.	Dolls. Cts.	Dolls.	Dolls. Cts.
Arlington,	460	20,462	267,101	93,531	9	4,075 32		4,075 32
Bennington,	1,216	22,913	758,958	128,222	154	10,241 80	38	10,203 80
Dorset,	476	22,806	275,847	34,700	7	3,588 47	20	3,568 47
Glastenbury,	22	24,209	14,984		1	172 84		172 84
Landgrove,	104	5,253	33,839	10,124 76	1	544 64		528 64
Manchester,	642	24,028	358,440	102,287 14	57	5,306 27	16	5,298 27
Peru,	186	18,551	61,691	10,647		909 38	8	909 38
Pownal,	540	23,002	330,169	53,879	10	4,390 48		4,390 48
Readsboro',	248	23,729	68,629	8,635	1 50	1,022 14		1,022 14
Rupert,	370	24,251	289,650	79,047 85		4,056 98		4,056 98
Sandgate,	258	22,666	120,481	20,219 82	4	1,669 01		1,669 01
Searsburgh,*	78	9,982	16,843	3,750		283 93		283 93
Shaftsbury,	524	23,410	456,556	41,016	10	5,509 72		5,509 72
Stamford,*	300	26,652	106,052	18,591 51		1,546 44		1,546 44
Sunderland,	190	22,178	71,289 71	11,269 55		1,015 59		1,015 59
Winhall,	236	24,505	84,675	12,400	1	1,207 75	4	1,203 75
Woodford,	180	26,707	74,169	775		929 44		929 44
Total,	6,080	365,304	3,389,373 71	629,095 63	255 50	46,458 20	86	46,384 20

* Not represented.

CALEDONIA COUNTY.

Towns.	Dolls.	Acres.	Dolls. Cts.	Dolls. Cts.	Dolls.	Dolls. Cts.	Dolls.	Dolls. Cts.
Barnet,	714	24,586	350,243	82,096	15	5,052 39	18	5,034 39
Burke,	392	19,191	170,391 50	28,595 25	18	2,399 87	132	2,267 87
Cabot,	476	21,444	220,436	57,789	11	3,269 25	92 95	3,176 30
Danville,	862	34,784	486,400 28	96,321 93	26	6,715 22	210 00	6,505 22
Groton,	316	23,807	111,034	30,648 50	6	1,738 83		1,738 83

GRAND LIST FOR 1848—Continued.

CALEDONIA COUNTY—Continued.

Towns.	Dolls.	Acres.	Dolls. Cts.	Dolls. Cts.	Dolls.	Dolls. Cts.	Dolls.	Dolls. Cts.
Hardwick,	516	21,717	264,493	71,377	13	3,887 70	108	3,779 70
Kirby,	166	13,481	89,382	2,047 46		1,180 29		1,180 29
Lyndon,	666	22,861	350,775	73,580	39	4,948 55	28	4,920 55
Newark,	144	21,690	50,763	3,821		689 84	15 30	674 54
Peacham,*	450	26,866	253,316	176,625	15	4,764 41	108	4,656 41
Ryegate,	374	31,304	228,775	36,222	5	3,028 97		3,028 97
Sheffield,	240	20,531	104,193 08	13,525		1,417 18	40	1,377 18
St. Johnsbury,	822	20,882	391,663	166,494	7	6,410 57	72	6,338 57
Sutton,	396	20,628	144,974	24,205 47	8	2,095 79	128	1,967 79
Walden,	320	21,119	141,729	28,117		2,018 46	40	1,978 46
Waterford,	452	23,531	241,526	72,281	7	3,597 07		3,597 07
Wheelock,	280			15,817	1	439 17	96	343 17
Total,	7,586	367,952	3,600,093 86	989,562 61	171	53,653 56	1,088 25	52,565 31

CHITTENDEN COUNTY.

Towns.	Dolls.	Acres.	Dolls. Cts.	Dolls. Cts.	Dolls.	Dolls. Cts.	Dolls.	Dolls. Cts.
Bolton,	176	25,744	76,515 84	3,453		975 69	8	967 69
Burlington,	2,008	14,327	1,219,407 12	520,037	106	19,508 44	108	19,400 44
Charlotte,	382	23,400	475,209 72	80,420	5	5,943 29	16	5,927 29
Colchester,	618	21,403	406,107	50,442	13	5,196 49		5,196 49
Essex,	618	22,040	299,903 58	69,339		4,310 43	22	4,288 43
Hinesburgh,	440	20,849	352,335 96	82,080	23	4,807 16		4,807 16
Huntington,	370	20,056	136,520 64	16,117	3	1,899 38	114	1,785 38
Jericho,	582	20,284	354,731 40	77,988	23	4,932 19	44	4,888 19
Milton,	680	28,013	417,806 35	88,643 02	46	5,790 49		5,790 49
Richmond,	372	17,718	250,334 28	42,142	10	3,306 76		3,306 76

15*

GRAND LIST FOR 1848—CONTINUED.

CHITTENDEN COUNTY—CONTINUED.

TOWNS.	Dolls.	Acres.	Dolls. Cts.	Dolls. Cts.	Dolls.	Dolls. Cts.	Dolls.	Dolls. Cts.
Shelburne,	330	13,940	293,751 36	86,252	13	4,143 03		4,143 03
St. George,	56	2,190	24,038 64	8,216		378 54		378 54
Underhill,	566	36,299	167,240 16	19,101	5	2,434 41	60	2,374 41
Westford,	474	21,164	201,498 84	26,843	6	2,763 42		2,768 42
Williston,	420	18,269	318,591 52	82,792	12	4,445 84		4,445 84
Total,	8,092	305,596	4,993,992 41	1,253,865 02	265	70,835 56	372	70,463 56

ESSEX COUNTY.

TOWNS.	Dolls.	Acres.	Dolls. Cts.	Dolls. Cts.	Dolls.	Dolls. Cts.	Dolls.	Dolls. Cts.
Bloomfield,	96	21,278	31,923 29	4,410 66		459 35		459 35
Brighton,	76	19,695	24,608 23	342 50		325 51		325 51
Brunswick,	36	12,839	38,078 91	8,523		502 02		502 02
Canaan,	148	17,469	60,742 05	11,143 25	2	868 85		868 85
Concord,	392	23,663	131,546 40	44,205 48	2	2,151 52		2,151 52
East Haven,	40	20,106	23,222 80	693		279 16		279 16
Granby,	36	21,700	17,812 50	1,449 53		228 62		228 62
Guildhall,	184	18,481	78,869	8,898	17	1,078 67		1,078 67
Lemington,*	50	19,688	23,127 44	4,402 22		325 30		325 30
Lunenburgh,	370	25,643	118,149 60	12,506	7	1,683 56		1,683 56
Maidstone,	84	17,704	42,401 35	7,700 30		585 01		585 01
Victory,	50	22,885	22,469 40	375		278 44		278 44
Total,	1,562	241,151	612,951 60	104,648 94	28	8,766 01		8,766 01

GRAND LIST FOR 1848—Continued.

FRANKLIN COUNTY.

Towns.	Dolls.	Acres.	Dolls.	Cts.	Dolls.	Cts.	Dolls.	Dolls.	Cts.	Dolls.	Dolls.	Cts.
Bakersfield,*	416	22,675	211,650		39,386		23	2,949	36		2,949	36
Berkshire,*	570	22,967	227,235		40,661		23	3,271	96	4	3,267	96
Enosburgh,	560	25,005	249,798		23,473	82		3,292	72		3,292	72
Fairfax,	654	21,47–	244,397		50,772	75	29	3,634	70		3,634	70
Fairfield,	610	26,17–	289,500		38,100		40	3,926		300	3,626	
Fletcher,	348	20,615	154,550	68	22,298			2,116	49		2,116	49
Franklin,*	468	20,429	184,963	80	24,854		8	2,574	18		2,574	18
Georgia,	592	22,385	318,739	75	58,897		6	4,374	37		4,374	37
Highgate,*	788	27,811	346,497	18	28,816		6	4,547	07		4,547	07
Montgomery,	310	20,963	78,797		18,577		1	1,284	74		1,284	74
Richford,	318	20,542	81,611	84	12,602		10	1,270	14		1,270	14
Sheldon,	458	22,105	250,721		56,400		13	3,542	21		3,542	21
Swanton,*	714	23,010	321,091		42,955		24	4,378	46		4,378	46
St. Albans,	750	24,014	534,961		237,777		86	8,563	38		8,563	38
Total,	7,556	320,174	3,494,513	25	695,563	57	269	49,725	78	304	49,421	78

GRAND ISLE COUNTY.

Towns.	Dolls.	Acres.	Dolls.	Cts.	Dolls.	Cts.	Dolls.	Dolls.	Cts.	Dolls.	Dolls.	Cts.
Alburgh,	404	14,660	203,123		19,743		42	2,674	66	49 70	2,624	96
Grand Isle,	200	9,507	164,004		24,063			2,080	67		2,080	67
Isle La Mott,	130	4,454	57,094		2,086	75	10	721	81	10	711	81
North Hero,	224	1,237	119,343	51	13,481	92	11	1,562	25		1,562	25
South Hero,	196	8,635	156,337		27,250	43		2,042	88		2,042	88
Total,	1,154	38,553	699,902	51	86,625	10	63	9,082	27	59 70	9,022	57

GRAND LIST FOR 1848—Continued.

LAMOILLE COUNTY.

Towns.	Dolls.	Acres.	Dolls. Cts.	Dolls. Cts.	Dolls.	Dolls. Cts.	Dolls.	Dolls. Cts.
Belvidere,	86	1,915	29,550 85	2,198	14	403 49		403 49
Cambridge,	648	31,128	335,340 54	97,170	1	4,987 11		4,987 11
Eden,	228	30,382	81,057 75	11,481 25		1,154 39	12	1,142 39
Elmore,	182	19,230	74,848 25	5,834		988 82		988 82
Hydepark,	450	22,356	179,323 23	11,512 75	10	2,358 36	172	2,186 36
Johnson,	452	20,032	143,749	36,051		2,260	8	2,252
Mansfield,	80	13,958	33,665	665		423 30		423 30
Morristown,	520	21,536	251,314 20	62,038 50	14	3,667 53	4	3,663 53
Sterling,*	86	12,546	25,257	8,029 15		418 86		418 86
Stowe,	576	21,508	255,324 50	67,486 50	27	3,831 11		3,831 11
Waterville,	210	9,923	81,617 91	13,728 79	3	1,166 47		1,166 47
Wolcott,	344	18,883	122,547	13,589	4	1,709 36		1,709 36
Total,	3,862	222,397	1,613,595 23	329,783 94	73	23,368 80	196	23,172 80

ORANGE COUNTY.

Towns.	Dolls.	Acres.	Dolls. Cts.	Dolls. Cts.	Dolls.	Dolls. Cts.	Dolls.	Dolls. Cts.
Bradford,	644	17,794	356,163 70	93,478	13	5,173 42	114	5,059 42
Braintree,	490	21,369	217,511 28	30,082	6	2,971 93	48	2,923 93
Brookfield,*	624	24,205	333,708 67	67,046	19	4,650 55	48	4,602 55
Chelsea,*	686	23,096	351,994 72	107,996	32	5,317 91	136	5,181 91
Corinth,	698	27,969	426,404 55	78,807	17	5,767 12	444	5,323 12
Fairlee,	184	11,433	154,158	22,585 09		1,951 43		1,951 43
Newbury,	980	36,911	570,503 61	78,147	14	7,480 51	64	7,416 51
Orange,	336	19,778	165,096 64	29,052		2,277 49	220	2,057 49
Randolph,*	1,004	27,543	617,989 70	195,077	49	9,183 67	44	9,139 67
Strafford,*	586	24,538	365,778 75	115,595	11	5,410 74	16	5,394 74

GRAND LIST FOR 1848—Continued.

ORANGE COUNTY—Continued.

Towns.	Dolls.	Acres.	Dolls.	Cts.	Dolls.	Cts.	Dolls.	Dolls.	Cts.	Dolls.	Dolls.	Cts.
Thetford,	704	23,980	401,548	61	82,074	84	27	5,567	23	4	5,563	23
Topsham,	614	27,551	279,016	70	57,663		15	3,995	80	188	3,807	80
Tunbridge,	670	25,901	376,394	96	48,352		12	4,929	47	104 58	4,824	89
Vershire,*	400	20,985	226,282	76	37,812		7	3,047	95	112	2,935	95
Washington,	510	20,841	222,169	97	26,929	25	6	3,006	99	16 82	2,990	17
West Fairlee,	250	13,207	132,749	49	13,509	77		1,712	59	172	1,540	59
Williamstown,	544	22,901	317,489	26	53,947	10	12	4,270	36		4,270	36
Total,	9,944	390,002	5,514,961	37	1,138,153	05	240	76,715	37	1,731 40	74,983	76

ORLEANS COUNTY.

Towns.	Dolls.	Acres.	Dolls.	Cts.	Dolls.	Cts.	Dolls.	Dolls.	Cts.	Dolls.	Dolls.	Cts.
Albany,	360	15,609	96,715		17,187	10	3	1,502	02	8	1,494	02
Barton,	340	20,163	136,113	59	47,622		14	2,191	36	2	2,189	36
Brownington,	180	15,636	63,559		12,492		5	945	51		945	51
Charleston,	316	20,736	93,179	50	11,216	16	3	1,362	97		1,362	97
Coventry,	306	16,978	99,009		36,128		4	1,661	37		1,661	37
Craftsbury,	440	21,839	179,573		30,490		12	2,552	63	92	2,460	63
Derby,	576	19,248	260,419		54,054	04	20 50	3,741	23	84	3,657	23
Glover,	426	20,800	156,694		31,134	19		2,304	28	100	2,204	28
Greensboro',	354	20,726	142,686		38,032		5 50	2,166	68	41 04	2,125	64
Holland,	180	18,183	54,424		7,305			797	29	8	789	29
Irasburgh,	336	19,911	107,756		57,522		15	2,003	78		2,003	78
Jay,	108	16,000	27,695		1,346			398	41	16	382	41
Lowell,	204	39,166	68,679	50	5,560			946	40		946	40
Morgan,	148	16,975	44,100		4,298			631	98		631	98
Newport,	218	23,081	65,991		6,829		1	947	30	12	935	20

GRAND LIST FOR 1848—Continued.

ORLEANS COUNTY—Continued.

Towns.	Dolls.	Acres.	Dolls. Cts.	Dolls. Cts.	Dolls.	Dolls. Cts.	Dolls.	Dolls. Cts.
Salem,	112	9,346	31,877	3,146 56		462 24	2	460 24
Troy,*	366	22,719	132,967	35,704	29	2,081 71		2,081 71
Westfield,	170	20,131	59,372	5,111	1	815 83		815 83
Westmore,	40	20,295	22,722			267 22	2	265 22
Total,	5,180	377,572	1,843,531 59	405,177 05	113 00	27,780 11	367 04	27,413 07

RUTLAND COUNTY.

Towns.	Dolls.	Acres.	Dolls. Cts.	Dolls. Cts.	Dolls.	Dolls. Cts.	Dolls.	Dolls. Cts.
Benson,	450	23,410	379,442	52,803	10	4,782 45		4,782 45
Brandon,	622	22,589	463,980	161,126	62	6,935 06		6,935 06
Castleton,	722	21,582	446,561	97,586	38	6,201 47	58	6,143 47
Chittenden,	218	35,303	120,799	17,508		1,601 07		1,601 07
Clarendon,	478	21,177	467,475	59,293	13	5,758 68	112	5,646 68
Danby,	570	22,295	372,370	68,438	22	5,000 08	4	4,996 08
Fairhaven,	238	9,683	147,078	46,441 75	10	2,183		2,183
Hubbardton,	244	15,307	152,535 40	33,470		2,104 05		2,104 05
Ira,	126	9,455	106,216	28,287		1,471 03		1,471 03
Mendon,	168	20,999	83,322	4,245		1,039 67		1,039 67
Middletown,	358	13,073	194,024	36,165	18 50	2,678 39	4	2,678 39
Mount Holly,	504	27,634	254,074 75	33,183	9	3,385 58		3,385 58
Mount Tabor,	86	21,690	61,325	1,639		715 64		715 64
Pawlet,	582	24,220	546,527	57,809	11	6,636 36	72	6,564 36
Pittsfield,	190	11,746	66,278	10,355	4	960 33		960 33
Pittsford,	636	26,163	573,559	80,136	37	7,209 95	8	7,201 95
Poultney,	718	23,243	497,111	109,855	45	6,832 96		6,832 96
Rutland,	914	28,409	826,853 60	280,224	170	12,154 78	16	12,138 78
Sherburne,	200	24,747	68,000	6,000		940		940

GRAND LIST FOR 1848—Continued.

RUTLAND COUNTY—Continued.

Towns.	Dolls.	Acres.	Dolls.	Cts.	Dolls.	Cts.	Dolls.	Dolls.	Cts.	Dolls.	Dolls.	Cts.
Shrewsbury,	418	26,569	288,585		90,341		6	4,213	26		4,213	26
Sudbury,	264	11,719	173,480		15,110			2,149	90		2,149	90
Tinmouth,	204	15,893	217,703		26,024		30	2,671	27	8	2,663	27
Wallingford,	600	24,281	427,813		258,314		45	7,506	27		7,506	27
Wells,	266	11,770	146,836	85	18,368	60	16	1,934	05		1,934	05
West Haven,	228	14,363	161,156		20,179		6	2,047	35		2,047	35
Total,	10,004	507,320	7,243,104	64	1,612,910	35	552 50	99,116	65	282	98,834	65

WASHINGTON COUNTY.

Towns.	Dolls.	Acres.	Dolls.	Cts.	Dolls.	Cts.	Dolls.	Dolls.	Cts.	Dolls.	Dolls.	Cts.
Barre,	750	19,346	450,517		110,107		13	6,369	24	32	6,337	24
Berlin,	478	20,996	309,940		38,255		4	3,963	95		3,963	95
Calais,	538	20,857	281,772		38,263	77	5	3,753	36	168	3,585	36
Duxbury,	298	23,420	114,453		13,820			1,580	73	53	1,527	73
Fayston,	176	20,522	65,741		4,382	05		877	23	92	785	23
Marshfield,	384	22,755	187,257		20,016			2,456	53	28	2,428	53
Middlesex,	420	22,192	226,222		21,672		10	2,914	94		2,914	94
MONTPELIER,	1,186	21,801	803,641		256,291		65	11,850	32	138	11,712	32
Moretown,	396	21,485	146,284		18,760		6	2,052	44	8	2,044	44
Northfield,	878	23,817	330,959		54,319		33	4,803	78	136	4,667	78
Plainfield,	298	9,262	148,501		27,371		11	2,067	72	168	1,899	72
Roxbury,	286	20,923	105,583		18,857	90		1,530	41	80	1,450	41
Waitsfield,	316	14,520	187,724		48,080	58		2,685	05	100	2,585	05
Warren,	342	21,403	109,261	55	10,419	33	11	1,540	81		1,540	81
Waterbury,	606	21,426	382,801		63,222		2	5,091	23	8	5,083	23
Woodbury,	314	21,400	84,744		9,000		25	1,251	44	18	1,233	44
Worcester,	222	22,723	79,227	77	4,297			1,057	25		1,057	25
Total,	7,894	348,848	4,018,608	32	758,133	63	185	55,846	43	1,029	54,817	43

GRAND LIST FOR 1848—Continued.

WINDHAM COUNTY.

Towns.	Dolls.	Acres.	Dolls. Cts.	Dolls. Cts.	Dolls.	Dolls. Cts.	Dolls.	Dolls. Cts.
Athens,	144	7,923	77,594 10	16,676		1,086 70	52	1,034 70
Brattleboro',	1,118	20,006	739,556	261,195	82	11,207 50	240	10,967 50
Brookline,	100	6,539	68,051 35	9,763 45		878 15	30	848 15
Dover,	288	16,268	143,271 40	43,923	1	2,160 94		2,160 94
Dummerston,	388	18,276	233,885 25	29,509	6	3,027 94		3,027 94
Grafton,	474	22,549	246,577 25	46,892	5	3,413 69	200	3,213 69
Guilford,	540	23,336	367,139 85	71,229	2	4,925 69		4,921 69
Halifax,	422	23,997	200,420 36	27,212	10	2,708 32	4	2,708 32
Jamaica,	506	26,047	226,812 50	40,054	6	3,180 67		3,172 67
Londonderry,	456	18,045	170,923 15	26,433	16	2,445 56	8	2,239 56
Marlboro',	334	23,014	210,445 57	33,654	5	2,780	206	2,780
Newfane,	470	22,957	328,333 30	72,462	26	4,503 95		4,503 95
Putney,	460	16,147	335,901 95	61,732	15	4,451 34		4,451 34
Rockingham,	880	24,772	593,235 10	141,244	43	8,267 79	132	8,135 79
Somerset,	122	21,097	59,864 25	5,772		778 36		778 36
Stratton,*	128	23,855	44,541 70	5,543 25		628 85		628 85
Townshend,	514	25,510	310,048 89	74,449	11	4,369 98		4,359 75
Vernon,	240	11,520	189,104 15	40,564	30	2,566 64	10 23	2,566 64
Wardsboro',	406	17,106	195,175 60	34,622	9	2,712 98		2,712 98
Westminster,	520	24,357	411,706 25	106,505	14	5,716 11	28	5,638 11
Whitingham,	518	22,987	216,820 40	42,331	13	3,122 52		3,122 52
Wilmington,	550	26,554	297,671 10	64,482	18	4,189 53	4	4,185 53
Windham,	264	14,943	136,447 55	27,872 93	1	1,908 20	80 75	1,827 45
Total,	9,842	457,605	5,803,527 02	1,284,119 63	313	81,031 41	994 98	80,036 43

GRAND LIST FOR 1848—Continued.

WINDSOR COUNTY.

Towns.	Dolls.	Acres.	Dolls. Cts.	Dolls. Cts.	Dolls.	Dolls. Cts.	Dolls.	Dolls. Cts.
Andover,	252	15,986	140,332	28,252		1,937 84	24	1,913 84
Baltimore,	46	2,866	36,093	9,111 75		498 05		498 05
Barnard,	588	26,712	291,986	40,489 10		3,922 75	164	3,758 75
Bethel,*	630	24,627	342,268	67,594 29		4,757 62	12	4,745 62
Bridgewater,	504	23,520	189,639	47,086 18		2,889 25		2,889 25
Cavendish,	624	24,097	387,837 50	152,687 79	9	6,038 25		6,038 25
Chester,*	786	34,787	510,669	139,900	26	7,317 69		7,317 69
Hartford,	730	25,273	481,239	84,335 57	12	6,397 75	32	6,365 75
Hartland,	810	26,761	543,336 64	146,708	18	7,728 45		7,728 45
Ludlow,	590	18,393	301,151	54,318	16	4,160 69	80	4,080 69
Norwich,*	658	23,892	408,216 50	54,357	10	5,293 74	4	5,289 74
Plymouth,	436	26,656	236,078	41,089	4	3,211 67		3,211 67
Pomfret,	608	22,201	287,389	83,293	5	4,319 82		4,319 82
Reading,	468	24,470	285,711	52,722	6	3,858 33	44	3,814 33
Rochester,	542	21,272	217,017	54,507 78	32	3,289 25	4	3,285 25
Royalton,	580	23,993	366,313	86,731	28	5,138 44	8	5,130 44
Sharon,	468	21,076	253,824 70	40,405	2	3,412 30	137 98	3,274 32
Springfield,	968	28,462	604,210	135,830 80	22	8,390 41	74	8,316 41
Stockbridge,	474	24,145	212,750	22,664 25	9	2,837 14	56	2,781 14
Weathersfield,	600	25,790	474,153 48	146,574	6	6,813 27		6,813 27
Weston,	356	18,957	172,500	37,950	4	2,464 50	24	2,440 50
Windsor,	990	25,172	649,690 80	112,061 70	32	8,639 53		8,639 53
Woodstock,	1,154	25,320	701,431	197,219	115	10,255 50	100	10,155 50
Total,	13,862	534,428	8,093,835 62	1,835,886 64	413	113,572 24	763 98	112,808 26

16

GRAND LIST FOR 1848—Concluded.

AGGREGATE BY COUNTIES, CHRONOLOGICALLY ARRANGED.

Counties.	Polls at $2. Dolls.	Real Estate. Acres.	Appraisal. Dolls. Cts.	Personal Estate. Appraisal. Dolls. Cts.	Attorney's, Physicians and Surgeon's assess'ts. Dolls.	1 per cent. of real & personal estate with polls and assessments of Attorney's, &c. Dolls. Cts.	Deduct for Militia equipped. Dolls.	Balance is the List for State Taxes. Dolls. Cts.
Bennington,	6,030	365,304	3,389,373 71	629,095 63	255 50	46,470 20	86	46,384 20
Windham,	9,842	457,605	5,803,527 02	1,284,119 63	313	81,031 41	994 98	80,036 43
Windsor,	13,862	534,424	8,093,835 62	1,835,886 64	413	113,572 24	763 98	112,808 26
Rutland,	10,004	507,320	7,243,104 64	1,612,910 35	552 50	99,116 65	282	98,834 65
Addison,	7,746	420,383	6,097,977 38	1,210,284 14	329	81,157 62	261 81	80,895 81
Orange,	9,944	390,002	5,514,961 37	1,138,153 05	240	76,715 16	1,731 40	74,983 76
Chittenden,	8,092	305,596	4,993,992 41	1,253,865 02	265	70,835 56	372	70,463 56
Washington,	7,894	348,848	4,018,608 32	758,133 61	185	55,846 43	1,029	54,817 43
Caledonia,	7,586	367,952	3,600,093 86	989,562 61	171	53,653 56	1,088 25	52,565 31
Franklin,	7,556	320,174	3,494,513 25	695,563 57	269	49,725 78	304	49,421 78
Orleans,	5,180	377,572	1,843,531 59	405,177 05	113	27,780 11	367 04	27,413 07
Lamoille,	3,862	222,397	1,613,595 23	329,783 94	73	23,368 80	196	23,172 80
Essex,	1,562	241,151	612,951 60	104,648 94	28	8,766 01		8,766 01
Grand Isle,	1,154	38,553	699,902 48	86,625 10	63	9,082 27	59 70	9,022 57
Total,	100,314	4,897,285	57,019,968 44	12,333,809 30	3,270 00	797,121 80	7,536 16	789,585 64

POST VILLAGES.

Although most of the towns in Vermont have post offices of their own names, yet many have within their limits one or more post offices in villages bearing the name of some favored patron, or having one of the cardinal points of the compass attached to it. Post villages not having the name of the town in which they are situated connected with theirs, are difficult to find. For instance :—A stranger wishes to go to *Perkinsville*. He finds, perchance, by the Post Office Book, that the flourishing manufacturing village of Perkinsville is in the State of Vermont, and in the county of Windsor ; but not one person in fifty, at a distance of twenty miles from it, can tell in what direction it lies, or that it is located in the beautiful town of Weathersfield.

It is impossible for us to insert the names and locations of all the post offices as soon as they are established. The last edition of the Post Office Book was published at Washington, in 1846.

Alburgh, West.
—— Springs.
Arlington, West.
Barnard, East.
Burtonville, Rockingham.
Bellows' Falls, ——.
Barre, South.
Bennington, North.
Berkshire, East.
—— West.
Bethel, East.
Bradford, *Centre*.
Braintree, West.
Brattleboro', West.
Brookfield, East.
Brownsville, Windsor.
Calais, East.
Cambridgeport, Rockingham.
Charleston, East.
—— West
Chimney Point, Addison.
Chipman's Point, Orwell.
Clarendon East.
—— *Springs*.
Corinth, East.
Corners, Weathersfield.
Craftsbury, South.
Cuttingsville, Shrewsbury.
Danby Four Corners, Danby.
Danville, North.

Derby, West.
—— *Line*.
Dorset, South.
—— East.
—— North.
Dummerston, East.
—— West.
East Mills, New Haven.
Enosburgh, West.
—— *Falls*.
Factory Point, Manchester.
Fairfax, North.
Fairfield, East.
Fayetteville, Newfane.
Felchville, Reading.
Ferrisburgh, North.
Gaysville, Stockbridge.
Greenbush. Weathersfield.
Halifax, West.
—— South.
Hardwick, South.
—— North.
Hartford, West.
Hartland, North.
Highgate, East.
—— *Springs*.
Hydeville, Castleton,
Houghtonville, Grafton.
Jacksonville, Whittingham.
Jeffersonville, Cambridge.

Jericho, *Centre.*
Lower Waterford.
Lyndon, *Centre.*
Mechanicsville, Mount Holly.
McIndoe's Falls, Barnet.
Middlebury, East.
Milton, West.
Montpelier, East.
———— North.
Newbury, South.
Orwell, *Centre.*
Passumsic, Barnet.
Perkinsville, Weathersfield.
Post Mills, Thetford.
Poultney, East.
———— West.
Proctersville, Cavendish.
Quechee Village, Hartford.
Randolph, East.
———— West.
Reading, South.
Roxbury, East.
Rutland, West.
St. Johnsbury, East.
St. Johnsbury, *Centre.*
Saxe's Mills, Highgate.

Saxton River, Rockingham.
Shaftsbury, South.
Sheldon, East.
Simondsville, Andover.
Snow's Store, Pomfret.
Springfield, North.
Strafford, South.
Swanton, West.
———— *Centre.*
———— *Falls.*
Taftsville, Hartland.
Topsham, West.
Townshend, West.
Troy, North.
— *Furnace.*
Tyson Furnace, Plymouth.
Union Village, Thetford.
Walden, South.
Wallingford, South.
Wardsboro', North.
———— West.
Waterford, Lower.
Wells River, Newbury.
Westminster, West.
Winooski, Colchester.
Woodstock, South.

NAME OF THE STATE.

Although this fourteenth State was not admitted into the Union until after the revolutionary contest was over, yet she vigorously resisted British oppression. A range of mountains covered with spruce, hemlock, and other evergreens, divides this State nearly in its centre; hence its name; and hence the epithet " Green Mountain Boys," celebrated for their bravery in the war of independence.—See *Mountains.*

BOUNDARIES AND EXTENT.

This State is bounded north by Lower Canada, east by Connecticut River, south by Massachusetts, and west by New York. Situated between 42° 44′ and 45° north latitude, and 73° 16′ and 71° 20′ west longitude.

Vermont is divided into fourteen counties, to wit: Bennington, Windham, Rutland, Windsor, Addison, Orange, Chittenden, Washington, Caledonia, Franklin, Orleans, Lamoille, Essex, and Grand Isle.—See *Population* and *Statistical Tables.*

GENERAL DESCRIPTION OF THE STATE.

See *Counties, Towns, Mountains, Rivers, &c.*

GOVERNMENT AND JUDICIARY.

The government of Vermont consists of three parts; the legislative, the executive, and the judicial.

The Supreme Legislature consists of a Senate and House of representatives, chosen annually by the freemen of the State, on the first Tuesday of September. The Senate consists of thirty members; each county being entitled to at least one, and the remainder to be apportioned according to population. The House of Representatives is composed of one member from each town. The senators are to be thirty years of age; and the lieutenant-governor is *ex officio* president of the Senate.

The body so chosen is called THE GENERAL ASSEMBLY OF THE STATE OF VERMONT. The *General Assembly* meets annually, on the second Tuesday of October. They have power to choose their own officers, to meet on their own adjournments, to terminate their sessions at pleasure; to enact laws, grant charters, to impeach state criminals, &c. And, in conjunction with the council, they annually elect the justices of the Supreme, County, and Probate Courts; also the sheriffs, high bailiffs, justices of the peace, &c.; and, when occasion requires, they elect majors and brigadier-generals. The General Assembly have full and ample legislative powers, but they cannot change the constitution.

The supreme executive power of the State shall be exercised by the governor, or, in case of his absence or disability, by the lieutenant-governor; who shall have all the powers and perform all the duties vested in, and enjoined upon the governor and council, by the eleventh and twenty-seventh sections of the second chapter [part the second] of the constitution, as at present established, excepting that he shall not sit as a judge in case of impeachment, nor grant reprieve, or pardon, in any such case; nor shall he command the forces of the State in person in time of war, or insurrection, unless by the advice and consent of the senate; and no longer than they shall approve thereof. The governor may have a secretary of civil and military affairs, to be by him appointed during pleasure, whose services he may at all times command; and for whose compensation provision shall be made by law.

The General Assembly, in joint meeting with the governor and council, annually elect the judges, justices of the peace, sheriffs, high bailiffs, &c.

The lieutenant-governor is lieutenant-general of the forces.

16*

The judicial power is vested in a Supreme Court and Court of Chancery, a County Court in each county, consisting of one of the justices of the Supreme Court, and two assistant justices; a Probate Court in each district; and justices of the peace, who have a limited criminal and civil jurisdiction.

The judges of probate appoint their own registers, and the sheriffs and high bailiffs appoint their own deputies.

The several town clerks are registers of deeds of conveyance of lands in their respective towns; and if there be no town clerk, the deeds shall be recorded in the county clerk's office.

A council of thirteen censors is chosen by the people once in seven years, on the last Wednesday of March, and meets on the first Wednesday of June following. Their duties are, to inquire if the constitution has been violated; if the legislature, &c., have performed their duty; if the taxes have been justly levied and collected; and if the laws have been obeyed. They may pass public censures; order impeachments; recommend the repeal of laws; propose amendments in the constitution, and call conventions to act on them. Their power expires in one year after their election.

SUCCESSION OF GOVERNORS.

Thomas Chittenden, 1791—1796. Isaac Tichenor, 1797—1806. Israel Smith, 1807. Isaac Tichenor, 1808. Jonas Galusha, 1809—1812. M. Chittenden, 1813, 1814. Jonas Galusha, 1815—1819. Richard Skinner, 1820—1822. C. P. Van Ness, 1823—1825. Ezra Butler, 1826, 1827. Samuel C. Crafts, 1828—1830. William A. Palmer, 1831—1835, Silas H. Jenison, 1836—1840. Charles Paine, 1841—1843. John Mattocks, 1844. William Slade, 1845, 1846. Horace Eaton, 1847.

SUCCESSION OF CHIEF JUSTICES.

Samuel Knight, 1791—1793. Isaac Tichenor, 1794, 1795. Nathaniel Chipman, 1796. Israel Smith, 1797. Enoch Woodbridge, 1798—1800. Jonathan Robinson, 1801—1806. Royal Tyler, 1807—1812. Nathaniel Chipman, 1813, 1814. Asa Aldis, 1815. Richard Skinner, 1816. Dudley Chase, 1817—1820. C. P. Van Ness, 1821, 1822. Richard Skinner, 1823—1828. Samuel Prentiss, 1829. Titus Hutchinson, 1830—1833. Charles K. Williams, 1834—1846. Stephen Royce, 1847.

State House, Montpelier, Vermont.

CONGRESSIONAL DISTRICTS.

No. 1.—Windham, Bennington, and Rutland Counties.
No. 2.—Windsor and Orange Counties.
No. 3.—Addison, Chittenden, Franklin, and Grand Isle Counties.
No. 4.—Washington, Caledonia, Essex, Orleans, and Lamoille Counties.

STATE SENATORIAL DISTRICTS.

By *Counties.*

PUBLIC BUILDINGS.

STATE HOUSE. — We take pleasure in presenting to the public a well executed engraving of the Vermont State House, at Montpelier; designed by A. B. YOUNG, Esq., a native of New England, and executed under his immediate superintendence.

The engraving represents a south-east front view of the building, which stands on an elevated site, about 325 feet from State street, on which it fronts, and is alike beautiful in design and execution. The yard and grounds pertaining to it are large and spacious, and, in the manner they are laid out, give great importance to the building. Through the whole design, a chaste architectural character is preserved, which, combined with the convenient arrangement of the interior and the stability of its construction, renders this edifice equal, in every respect, to any in New England, and probably to any in the United States. The building is in the form of a cross, showing in front a centre, 72 feet wide, and two wings, each 39 feet, making the whole length 150 feet. The centre, including the portico, is 100 feet deep; the wings are 50 feet deep. The six columns of the portico are 6 feet in diameter at their base, and 36 feet high, supporting an entablature of classic proportions. The dome rises 36 feet above the ridge, making the whole height from the ground 100 feet. The order of architecture used is the Grecian Doric, and is made to conform to the peculiar arrangement necessary in this building. The walls, columns, cornices, &c., are of dark Barre granite, wrought in a superior manner; the dome and roofs are covered with copper.

In the interior, the lower story contains an Entrance Hall, rooms for the Secretary of State, Treasurer, Auditor, and numerous committee rooms. The second, or principal story, contains a vestibule, and stairways, a Representatives Hall, 57 by 67 feet, with a lobby and galleries for spectators; a Senate Chamber, 30 by 44 feet, with lobby and gallery; a Governor's Room, 24 by 20 feet, with an ante-room, and a room for his Secretary adjoining; a Library Room, 18 by 36 feet; rooms for the several officers of the Senate and House of Representatives, and several committee rooms. The cost of this building, including all expenses, was about $132,100; of which the inhabitants of Montpelier paid $15,000.

At the first session of the Legislature of Vermont, within this building, in October, 1838, the following resolution was unanimously adopted:

" Resolved, by the General Assembly of the State of Vermont, that the thanks of this Legislature be presented to AMMI B. YOUNG, Esq., as a testimonial of their approbation of the taste, ability, fidelity, and perseverance, which he has manifested in the design and execution of the new capitol of this State; which will abide as a lasting monument of the talents and taste of Mr. YOUNG as an architect."

STATE PRISON. — The Vermont State Prison is located at Windsor. The first building for this purpose was commenced in 1808, and nearly completed in 1809. A second building for this purpose was erected in 1830. This building for the solitary confinement of prisoners, and other buildings located in a spacious yard, are well adapted for the purposes designed. The whole expenditures for these buildings was estimated at $47,000. In this prison, September 1, 1848, there were 52 prisoners in confinement; 51 males and 1 female. This prison is well conducted, and its finances are in a prosperous state.

ASYLUM FOR THE INSANE. — In the fall of 1834, Mrs. Anna Marsh, widow of the late Dr. Perly Marsh, of Hinsdale, New Hampshire, left by will $10,000 to found an Asylum for the Insane on the bank of the Connecticut, somewhere in Windham County, Vermont; and in October of that year the Hon. Samuel Clark and John Holbrook, Epaphri Seymour and John C. Holbrook, Esqrs., were incorporated as trustees of said institution, by an act of the legislature. In 1835, the legislature appropriated $10,000 in aid of the benevolent designs of the institution, and have since appropriated $6,000 more.

In 1836, the trustees decided upon its location in Brattleborough, on the place formerly occupied by Joseph Fessenden, Esq., situated at a short distance, in a north-westerly direction from the east village. The old mansion was at first enlarged and opened in December, 1836, for the reception of patients, with whom it became crowded in the course of about seven months; and in 1838 another more spacious building was erected, adapted especially to the objects of the institution.

The following is a report of the trustees of this Institution, for the year 1848:

" It is nearly twelve years since the Institution was first opened. Thirteen hundred and twenty-three patients have been admitted, ten hundred and eleven discharged, and three hundred and twelve now remain. Of those discharged, five hundred and ninety-two have recovered.

"Three hundred and four were remaining at the commencement of the past year. One hundred and fifty-six have been admitted, one hundred and forty-eight discharged, and three hundred and twelve remain in the Institution.

"It has been a year of great prosperity. No serious accident nor epidemic disease has occurred, and the patients have enjoyed a good degree of health.

"It was found by sad inconvenience, that the centre building, and especially those parts of it which were appropriated for cooking, washing, and the laundry, were altogether too small. This year we are making a large addition to the main building, without injuring its symmetry or proportions. Additions are also making to those parts devoted to the accommodation of patients. They will probably be finished in a few weeks. We hope to receive funds from donations and other sources sufficient to defray the expenses of their erection, without being obliged to call on the State for its aid.

"One hundred and fifty-eight patients have received their share of the State appropriation for the benefit of the insane poor. There were one hundred and twenty remaining at the commencement of the year, thirty-eight have been admitted, and forty discharged, leaving one hundred and eighteen in the Institution. Of those discharged, eighteen were recovered.

"When it is considered that nearly all this class continue at home as long as they remain quiet, and that few are sent by the towns except those who are very troublesome, the care of such must be unusually great. Many are sent whose insanity is accompanied by some fatal disease, such as consumption and like disorders, to be taken care of in the last few months, and sometimes the last few weeks of their lives. These latter cases should not be sent to the Asylum, as the design of the Institution is for the restoration of the insane, and not merely a hospital of the sick. They, however, have received all that kindness and attention which they so much required.

"For the purpose of giving more exercise in the open air to such of our male patients as would be benefitted by agricultural pursuits, forty-five acres of cultivated land have been purchased the past year. The farm connected with the Institution is yearly increasing in the richness of its soil, and in the quantity of its products. The employment that is hereby given to our male patients is of great benefit in promoting their restoration.

"The price of labor, and of provisions of every kind, has been so great the past year, that the trustees were apprehensive for the result. By reference to the table of expenditure and income of the Institution, we are gratified to learn the latter exceeds the former by $319 41, which is nearly equal to the bad debts for the same time.

"In conclusion, the trustees would express their public commendation of the neatness, good order, and the kind and judicious management which has pervaded every part of the Institution, and recommend it to the continued patronage of the State, as worthy of their protection and care."

Terms of Admission. To those of this State, two dollars per week for the first six months, and one dollar and seventy-five cents per week afterwards.

For those from other States, two dollars per week, or one hundred dollars per year, if the patient remain such a length of time.

When the insanity is connected with epilepsy or paralysis, the terms are two dollars and fifty cents per week.

No charge is made for damages in any case.

Applications may be made to Dr. W. H. Rockwell, or to either of the Trustees.

BANKS.

	Incorporated.	Capital.		Incorporated.	Capital.
Bank of Brattleboro',	1821	$100,000	Bank of Orleans,	1832	$60,000
Bank of Burlington,	1818	150,000	Farmers' Bank, Orwell,	1833	100,000
Bank of Rutland,	1824	100,000	Farmers' and Mechanics' Bank, Burlington,	1834	150,000
Bank of Caledonia,	1825	100,000			
Bank of St. Albans,	1825	100,000			
Bank of Vergennes,	1826	100,000	Bank of Montpelier,	1840	75,000
Bank of Orange Co.,	1827	100,000	Bank of Poultney,	1840	100,000
Bank of Woodstock,	1831	100,000	Black River Bank,		40,000
Bank of Middlebury,	1831	100,000	Vermont B'k, Montpelier,	1848	100,000
Bank of Bellows' Falls,	1831	100,000			
Bank of Manchester,	1832	100,000	Brandon Bank, Brandon,	1848	50,000
Bank of Newbury,	1832	100,000			

MUTUAL FIRE INSURANCE COMPANIES.

The Bennington County Mutual Fire Insurance Office is located at Arlington; the Orange County Office in Chelsea; the Rutland and Addison County Office in Brandon; the Windham County Office in Newfane; and the Windsor County Office at Woodstock.

The Office of the VERMONT Fire Insurance Company is located at Montpelier. This Office insures about ten millions value of property. The annual losses are about twenty-nine thousand dollars.

AGRICULTURE AND MANUFACTURES.

There is, perhaps, no section of country in the world where the agricultural and manufacturing interests are more closely united than in Vermont. In this State are found a surface and soil every way adapted to the growth of all the necessaries and luxuries proper for the use of man, and an hydraulic power sufficient to turn every manufacturing wheel in Europe. Let waving grain fields and verdant pastures take the place of the immense forests, which now spread over nearly three fourths of the surface of the State ; and let the delightful streams which everywhere rush in crystal torrents down the mountains and through the valleys, be appropriated to the manufacture of those articles which now are supplied, in a great degree, by the labor of foreign paupers, and at a loss to the country of vast sums, which good policy requires should be kept at home, to reward the labors and industrial habits of the people, and to place the independence of the country on a more sure foundation.

Vermont possesses ores and minerals of much value, and in great variety and abundance ; and its beautiful white and variegated marble forms the basis of its hills. This marble, which was formerly transported to our seaports at the slow pace of twenty miles a *day*, can now pass to the ocean at the rate of twenty miles an *hour*. So far as Vermont is concerned, her forests laugh at all revenue laws on *sugar*.

In an address delivered by Henry Stevens, Esq., of Barnet, at the Annual Fair before the Agricultural Society of Orange County. held at Chelsea, September 27, 1848, much good sense and sound judgment was displayed, in regard to the internal policy of the State with respect to manufactures.

We give a few of Mr. Stevens' remarks, and would cheerfully copy the whole address, did our limits permit :

" Vermont was termed an agricultural State. Our territory is limited and mountainous. Only about one-fifth of the territory of Vermont is yet cleared of the forest. Yet I claim that when we take into consideration the number of acres of improved land, its appraised value, number of inhabitants employed in agriculture, amount of production, we far surpass any other State in the American Union. I refer you to the census of 1840, and to our annual Grand List." * * *

" The agricultural productions of industry of Vermont, by pursuing a proper policy, might with ease be doubled in ten years. Our young men must clear one million of acres of our forest lands and bring it under cultivation. In so doing, all matters considered, our products of industry would be more than doubled." * * *

" It has long since become a proverb, that Vermont is the back bone — the hip — the shoulder — the kidney and pluck of New England. Vermont has pursued a policy materially different from that of any other State. So much so, that it has become a proverb that Liberty delights to dwell among her mountains — the Star that never sets." * * *

" As a people, we have from the time our fathers declared the New Hampshire Grants a free and independent State — 15th January, 1777 — pursued this policy. It was the pursuing of this policy that enabled our fathers to meet the expenses of the revolutionary war — to redeem the then paper issues at par ; and ours was the only State that ever did redeem their paper issues even at a discount of forty dollars for one. Not a single bill of purchase of woollen blankets or woollen garments, out of the State, for our brave soldiers during the revolutionary war, has yet been discovered." * * *

"I admit, gentlemen, in honor of your fathers, that they cleared the land, sowed, planted, and harvested the crops. Who but your mothers manufactured the flax and wool into cloth — by hand cards, linen, and woollen wheels, and hand looms ? It then became a proverb in Vermont, that the woman who manufactured for her own household, and one piece of goods for sale, did more to retain the solid coin in the State, than all the political financiers." * * *

"From the census of 1810, we learn that there was manufactured in this State 1,207,976 yards of woollen cloth, 1,859,931 yards of linen cloth, 131,326 yards of cotton cloth, 191,426 yards of mixed cloth. There was in this State 14,801 looms, weaving on an average 240 yards each, or 3,552,240 yards. Spinning wheels, 67,756, spinning on an average 70 skeins each, or 4,742,920 skeins." * * *

"The county of Orange, at that time, produced 91,100 pounds of wool — made 93,707 yards of woollen cloth, and 40,810 yards of mixed cloth — of linen cloth 125,763 yards, and of cotton cloth 15,857 yards — in the whole 276,237 yards." * * *

"Had we sufficient machinery of the most perfect kind in the State, we could compete with any portions of our country. The manufacturing of our wool for our own supply, would more than treble the value of our wool in the hands of the citizens of this State. It would offer an opportunity for those of our citizens who are now abroad, employed in the manufacturing business, to return with the skill they have become masters of, and greatly to the interest of the State. To multiply our flocks for no other purpose but to exchange their fleeces for the manufactured article on the sea-board, is a policy which, if pursued, will bring poverty to the door of every husbandman." * * *

"I have to say, that as an individual I have become satisfied that there is a manifest impropriety in boasting of our liberty, of the independence of our State or country, so long as we exchange the raw material for the manufactured articles which we are capable of manufacturing ourselves." * * *

"It is impossible for a farmer — a freeman of Vermont, to speak of our liberties, of our independence, as being only upon parchment, until our laws give full employment to the artizan, mechanic, and manufacturer, in converting the raw material, that we as farmers create, into necessary manufactured articles equal to a full supply — then, and not till then, can we talk of our liberties, of our independence, as being a reality." * * *

"An agricultural community or commonwealth, dependent upon sister States, or foreign governments, for food and necessary clothing, are in a measure slaves." * * *

In the descriptions of towns and Statistical Tables in this volume will be found limited, though as full accounts of the products of the soil and manufactures of the State, as can at present be given.

COMMERCE AND NAVIGATION.

All the commerce connected with navigation belonging to this State, is found on Lake Champlain. Burlington is the principal port in Vermont.

In the year ending the 30th of June, 1847, there were 268 vessels cleared in Vermont; tonnage, 72,064; crews, 7,672 men and 7 boys. Total amount of American tonnage on the Lake, in Vermont, 2,560 tons. Total amount of imports in Vermont, 239,641 tons. Total amount of American and foreign produce exported from Vermont, $514,298. All the exports and imports were in American vessels. The total tonnage of the Lake, including that of New York, was 7,305 tons.

LIGHT HOUSES.

See *Lake Champlain.*

FINANCES.

By the Treasurer's Report on State Finances, dated September 1, 1848, it appears that " The standing of the State finances, at this date, are as follows :

Balance in the Treasury,	$3,659 40
Taxes not collected,	34,215 03
Notes and interest due the State, on account of the late School Fund,	6,746 30
	$44,618 73

The State is indebted to the Safety Fund Banks,		$35,883 22
Interest on same,		2,152 98
Salaries falling due October 1, 1848 :—		
Judges Supreme Court,	$3,281 08	
Other officers,	1,108 33	3,281 08
Due counties, for money received from pedler's licenses, under present law,		1,790 00
Due Bank of Brattleboro', loan to pay annual appropriation to the Asylum,		5,000 00
		$48.107 28

17

COMMON SCHOOLS.

By the Report of the State Commissioner on Common Schools, it appears that, in 1848, there were in Vermont 2,616 school districts, with about thirty-seven scholars in each district between the ages of four and eighteen years; that the cost for teaching amounted to about fifty dollars annually for each district, and about the same sum for other expenses.

This gives schoolage to about 100,000 youth of both sexes, at an annual cost of not less than two hundred and sixty thousand dollars.

COLLEGES.

MIDDLEBURY COLLEGE. — Middlebury College was incorporated in 1800. It is pleasantly situated, on ground elevated 342 feet above Lake Champlain, and is a respectable seminary. The funds of the College are not large, having been formed solely from individual grants. There are two college buildings, one of wood, three stories high, containing a chapel and twenty rooms for students; the other, a spacious edifice of stone, 108 feet by 40, four stories high, containing 48 rooms for students. The college library contains about 8,000 volumes;—students about 50; whole number that has been graduated, 862. The philosophical apparatus is tolerably complete. The board of trustees, styled "The President and Fellows of Middlebury College," is not limited as to number. The executive government is composed of a president, five professors, and one tutor. The commencement is held on the third Wednesday in August. Vacations: — From commencement, four weeks; from last Wednesday in November, one week; from second Wednesday in February, two weeks; and from third Wednesday in May, two weeks.

Succession of Presidents.

Accessus.		Exitus.
1800, ... Rev. JEREMIAH ATWATER, D. D., ...		1809.
1810, ... Rev. HENRY DAVIS, D. D., ...		1817.
1818, ... Rev. JOSHUA BATES, D. D., ...		1840.
1841, ... Rev. BENJAMIN LABAREE, D. D., ...		

UNIVERSITY OF VERMONT. — The University of Vermont was incorporated and established at Burlington, in 1791, but it did not go into operation till 1800. It is finely situated on the east side of the village, a mile distant from Lake Champlain, on ground elevated 245 feet above the surface of the water, and commands an extensive and delightful prospect, embracing a view of the lake, with the high mountains beyond on the west, and the Green Mountains on the east. A large college edifice of brick, which was completed in 1801, was consumed by fire in 1824; since which time three brick edifices have been erected, two of them containing rooms for students, the other containing a chapel, and other public rooms. Its officers are, a president, a professor of intellectual and moral philosophy, a professor of mathematics and natural philosophy, a professor of the learned languages, and a tutor.

Commencement on the third Wednesday in August. Vacations:— From commencement, four weeks, and from the first Wednesday in January, eight weeks. Alumni, 1848, 460. Present number of students, about 120.

Succession of Presidents.

Accessus.		Exitus.
1800, ...	Rev. DANIEL C. SAUNDERS, D. D., ...	1814.
1816, ...	Rev. SAMUEL AUSTIN, D. D., ...	1821.
1822, ...	Rev. DANIEL HASKELL, M. A., ...	1824.
1824, ...	Rev. WILLARD PRESTON, M. A., ...	1826.
1826, ...	Rev. JAMES MARSH, D. D., ...	1833.
1834, ...	Rev. JOHN WHEELER, D. D., ...	

PROBATE COURTS.

The State of Vermont contains fourteen counties. Each county comprises one or more probate districts. The Judges of Probate are appointed annually by the Legislature; they hold their courts at such times and places, within their districts, as seems to them most proper. The Registers of Probate reside in their own districts, and are appointed by the respective District Judges.

The following are the names of the Probate Districts within the State:—

ADDISON CO.— Addison and New Haven Districts.
BENNINGTON CO — Bennington and Manchester Districts.
CALEDONIA CO. — Caledonia District.
CHITTENDEN CO. — Chittenden District.
ESSEX CO. — Essex District.
FRANKLIN CO.— Franklin District.
GRAND ISLE CO.— Grand Isle District.
LAMOILLE CO. — Lamoille District.
ORANGE CO. — Randolph and Bradford Districts.
ORLEANS CO. — Orleans District.
RUTLAND CO.— Rutland and Fair Haven Districts.
WASHINGTON CO.— Washington District.
WINDHAM CO.—Marlboro' and Westminster Districts.
WINDSOR CO — Windsor and Hartford Districts.

RAILROADS.

THE public spirit of the "Green Mountain Boys" will not suffer any State in the union to rival them in its patronage to the MONARCH CARRIER, in its successful efforts in cutting the ties of distance between oceans and inland countries.

Besides the Passumpsic, Central, Northern, Southern, and Connecticut River Railroads, and others, the following have recently been chartered.

WOODSTOCK RAILROAD. — Incorporated 1847. From Woodstock to some point on the Central Railroad. About twelve miles.

BLACK RIVER RAILROAD. — Incorporated 1847. From Perkinsville, in Weathersfield, through Springfield, down Connecticut River, to meet the Sullivan Railroad in New Hampshire.

RUTLAND AND WASHINGTON RAILROAD. — Incorporated 1847. From Rutland, through the towns of Ira, Castleton, and Fair Haven, or Poultney, to some point on the west side of the State, to meet the Saratoga and Washington Railroad in the State of New York.

UNION RAILROAD. — Incorporated 1847. From Montpelier, through Barre, to some point in the town of Bradford, as said Company may designate; also through the said town of Barre, thence through the Gulf, so called, in Williamstown, to some point in the town of Royalton, as said Company may designate, or either of said routes.

CONNECTICUT RIVER, BRATTLEBORO', AND FITCHBURG RAILROAD. — Incorporated 1847.

RUTLAND AND WHITEHALL RAILROAD. — Incorporated 1848. This road branches off at or near Castleton, and passes to Whitehall, N. Y.

DANVILLE AND PASSUMPSIC RAILROAD. — Incorporated 1848. From Danville Green to meet the Connecticut and Passumpsic River Railroads, in the town of Barnet.

VERMONT VALLEY RAILROAD. — Incorporated 1848. From Brattleboro' to Bellows' Falls, to connect with the Rutland and Burlington Railroad, and with the Sullivan, in New Hampshire. In case the Sullivan Railroad Co. refuse this connection, this railroad is permitted to pass up the west side of Connecticut River, to meet the Central Railroad at Windsor.

ATLANTIC AND ST. LAWRENCE RAILROAD. — Incorporated 1848. This Railroad is permitted to pass through this State to the boundary of Canada, there to connect with the St. Lawrence and Atlantic Railroad to Montreal.

MILITIA.

With the exceptions mentioned below, the militia of Vermont consists of all the able-bodied white male citizens of the State, between the age of eighteen and forty-five years. The exemptions from military service embrace ministers of the gospel, commissioned officers who have been honorably discharged, and such as may be so discharged after having served as commissioned officers for a period of five years, members of fire companies, to the number of twenty to each engine, faculties and students of colleges and academies, judges of the supreme, county, and probate courts, county clerks, registers of probate, sheriffs, deputy sheriffs, high bailiffs, and constables, Quakers, physicians, stated school-masters, ferrymen, and millers.

The whole military force of the State, according to the return of the adjutant and inspector general for 1840, was 26,304, including officers and private soldiers. This force, of which the governor is commander in chief, is divided into three divisions, with a major general to each division. Each division is divided into three brigades, with a brigadier general to each. Each brigade is divided into from two to four regiments, and each regiment is designed to consist of ten companies, of 100 men in each. Each company is commanded by a captain and two lieutenants; each regiment by a colonel, lieutenant-colonel, and major; each brigade by a brigadier general, a brigade inspector, a quartermaster, and one aid-de-camp; each division by a major general, a division inspector, a quartermaster, and two aids-de-camp; and the whole by the governor, as captain general, an adjutant and inspector general, a quartermaster general, and two aids-de-camp. The adjutant and inspector general, and the quartermaster general, are appointed by the governor. The major generals and brigadier generals are appointed by the legislature; the colonels, lieutenant colonels, and majors, are elected by the captains and lieutenants of their respective regiments; and the captains, lieutenants, and non-commissioned officers of each company, are elected by their respective companies. The militia of the State is at present divided into *three* divisions, *nine* brigades, *twenty-eight* regiments, including a rifle regiment, and *two hundred and ninety* companies. The regiments are numbered in regular progression from one up to twenty-eight.

On the first Tuesday of June in each year, every company is called together for the purpose of inspection, drill, and discipline, and a return, of the name and equipments of each individual, made to the clerk of the town to which the company belongs; and once in three years, between the 5th of September and the 3d of October, the militia of the State may be assembled, for review, inspection, and discipline, by regiment, or separate battalion, as the commandant of brigade shall direct. The commissioned and non-commissioned officers and musicians of each regiment are required to rendezvous two days annually, in their uniforms, for the purpose of training and improvement in military discipline. The poll of each person belonging to the militia, who is returned fully equipped, is exempted from all taxes, except the highway tax; and each officer, non-commissioned officer, and musician, is paid one dollar per day, and the adjutant and inspector-general three dollars per day, for attendance at regimental drill.

The militia of Vermont, or Green Mountain Boys, as they have been more commonly denominated, have always been proverbial for their intrepidity and valor. During the revolutionary war they acted, in proportion to their numbers, a very conspicuous and important part; as the fields of Hubbardton and

17*

Bennington, and the surrender of Burgoyne, bear witness. And when our country was invaded during the last war with Great Britain, their previous reputation was fully sustained by the promptness and bravery with which they met the enemy at Plattsburgh, on the memorable 11th of September, 1814.

CLIMATE AND INDIAN SUMMER.

We copy from Mr. Thompson the following sensible remarks on the climate of Vermont: —

"It has been said, though we do not vouch for its truth, that it was a maxim with the aborigines of this country, which had been handed down from time immemorial, that there would be thirty smoky days both in the spring and autumn of each year; and their reliance upon the occurrence of that number in autumn was such, that they had no fears of winter setting in till the number was completed. This phenomenon occurred between the middle of October and the middle of December, but principally in November; and it being usually attended by an almost perfect calm, and a high temperature during the day, our ancestors, perhaps in allusion to the above maxim, gave it the name of *Indian Summer*. But it appears that, from the commencement of the settlement of the country, the Indian Summers have gradually become more and more irregular, and less strikingly marked in their character, until they have almost ceased to be noticed. Now upon the hypothesis advanced in the preceding articles, this is precisely what we should expect. When our ancestors arrived in this country, the whole continent was covered with one uninterrupted luxuriant mantle of vegetation, and the amount of leaves, and other vegetable productions, which were then exposed to spontaneous dissolution upon the surface of the ground, would be much greater than after the forests were cut down and the lands cultivated. Every portion of the country being equally shielded by the forest, the heat. though less intense, on account of the immense evaporation and other concurring causes, would be more uniformly distributed, and the changes of wind and weather would be less frequent, than after portions of the forest had been removed, and the atmosphere, over those portions, subjected to sudden expansions from the influence of the sun upon the exposed surface of the ground. It is very generally believed that our winds are more variable, our weather more subject to sudden changes, our annual amount of snow less, and our mean annual temperature higher, than when the settlement of the country was commenced. And causes, which would produce these changes, would, we believe, be sufficient to destroy, in a great measure, the peculiar features of our Indian Summers. The variableness of the winds, occasioned by cutting down large portions of the forests, would of itself be sufficient to scatter and precipitate those brooding oceans of smoke, and prevent the long continuance of those seasons of dark and solemn stillness, which were, in ages that are past, the unerring harbingers of long and dreary winters and deluges of snow."

CAVES.

There are a number of caves in Vermont worthy the inspection of the curious, many of which are described under the towns where they exist. Those of Clarendon, Danby, and Plymouth, are the largest; the two former may be found in pages 49 and 53, the latter is thus described by Mr. Thompson:

" The Plymouth caves are situated at the base of a considerable mountain, on the south-west side of Black River, and about fifty rods from that stream. They are excavations among the lime rock, which have evidently been made by running water. The principal cave was discovered about the 1st of July, 1818, and on the 10th of that month was thoroughly explored. The passage into this cavern is nearly perpendicular, about the size of a common well, and ten feet in depth. This leads into the first room, which is of an oval form, thirty feet long, twenty feet wide, and its greatest height about fifteen feet. It appears as if partly filled up with loose stones, which had been thrown in at the mouth of the cave. From this to the second room is a broad sloping passage. This room is a little more than half as large as the first. The bottom of it is the lowest part of the cave, being about twenty-five feet below the surface of the ground, and is composed principally of loose sand, while the bottoms of all the other rooms are chiefly rocks and stones. The passage into the third room is four feet wide and five high, and the room is fourteen feet long, eight wide, and seven high. The fourth room is thirty feet long, twelve wide, and eighteen high; and the rocks, which form the sides, incline towards each other, and meet at the top like the ridge of a house. The fifth room, very much resembling an oven in shape, is ten feet long, seven wide, and four high, and the passage into it from the third room is barely sufficient to admit a person to crawl in. At the top of this room is a conical hole, ten inches across at the base, and extending two feet into the rock. From the north side of the second room are two openings, leading to the sixth and seventh, which are connected together, and each about fifteen feet long, seven wide, and five high. From the seventh room is a narrow passage, which extends northerly fifteen or sixteen feet into the rocks, and there appears to terminate. When discovered, the roof and sides of this cavern were beautifully ornamented with stalactites, and the bottom with corresponding stalagmites, but most of these have been rudely broken off and carried away by the numerous visiters. The temperature, both in winter and summer, varies little from $44\frac{1}{2}°$, which is about the mean temperature of the climate of Vermont in that latitude. A few rods to the westward of this cavern there is said to be another, which is about two thirds as large."

CONSTITUTION OF VERMONT

ADOPTED BY THE CONVENTION HOLDEN AT WINDSOR, JULY 4TH, 1793.

CHAPTER I.

ARTICLE 1.

That all men are born equally free and independent, and have certain natural, inherent, and unalienable rights, amongst which are enjoying and defending life and liberty, acquiring, possessing, and protecting property, and pursuing and obtaining happiness and safety : therefore, no male person born in this country, or brought from over sea, ought to be holden by law to serve any person as a servant, slave, or apprentice, after he arrives to the age of twenty-one years, nor female, in like manner, after she arrives to the age of eighteen years, unless they are bound by their own consent, after they arrive to such age, or bound by the law for the payment of debts, damages, fines, costs, or the like.

ARTICLE 2.

That private property ought to be subservient to public uses when necessity requires it ; nevertheless, when any person's property is taken for the use of the public, the owner ought to receive an equivalent in money.

ARTICLE 3.

That all men have a natural and unalienable right to worship Almighty God according to the dictates of their own consciences and understandings, as in their opinion shall be regulated by the Word of God : and that no man ought to, or of right can, be compelled to attend, any religious worship, or erect or support any place of worship, or maintain any minister, contrary to the dictates of his conscience ; nor can any man be justly deprived or abridged of any civil right as a citizen, on account of his religious sentiments or peculiar mode of religious worship ; and that no authority can or ought to be vested in, or assumed by, any power whatever, that shall in any case interfere with, or in any manner control, the rights of conscience in the free exercise of religious worship. Nevertheless, every sect or denomination of Christians ought to observe the Sabbath, or Lord's Day, and keep up some sort of religious worship, which to them shall seem most agreeable to the revealed will

ARTICLE 4.

Every person within this State ought to find a certain remedy, by having recourse to the laws, for all injuries or wrongs which he may receive in his person, property, or character : he ought to obtain right and justice freely, and without being obliged to purchase it ; completely, and without any denial ; promptly, and without delay ; conformably to the law.

ARTICLE 5.

That the people of this State, by their legal representatives, have the sole inherent, and exclusive right of governing and regulating the internal police of the same.

ARTICLE 6.

That all power being originally inherent in, and consequently derived from. the people, therefore, all officers of government, whether legislative or executive, are their trustees and servants, and at all times, in a legal way, accountable to them.

ARTICLE 7.

That government is, or ought to be, instituted for the common benefit, protection, and security of the people, nation, or community, and not for the particular emolument or advantage of any single man, family, or set of men, who are a part only of that community ; and that the community hath an indubitable, unalienable, and indefeasible right to reform or alter government, in such manner as shall be, by that community, judged most conducive to the public weal.

ARTICLE 8.

That all elections ought to be free and without corruption, and that all freemen, having a sufficient evidence, common interest with, and attachment to the community, have a right to elect officers, and be elected into office, agreeably to the regulations made in this constitution.

ARTICLE 9.

That every member of society hath a right to be protected in the enjoyment of life, liberty, and property, and therefore is bound to contribute his proportion towards the expense of that protection, and yield his personal service, when necessary, or an equivalent thereto ; but no part of any person's property can be justly taken from him, or applied to public uses, without his consent, or that of the representative body of freemen ; nor can any man, who is conscientiously scrupulous of bearing arms, be justly compelled thereto, if he will pay such equivalent ; nor are the people bound by any law but such as they have in like manner assented to, for their common good ; and previous to any law being made to raise a tax, the purpose for which it is to be raised ought to appear evident to the legislature to be of more service to the community than the money would be if not collected.

ARTICLE 10.

That, in all prosecutions for criminal offences, a person hath a right to be heard by himself and his counsel ; to demand the cause and nature of his accusation; to be confronted with tne witnesses; to call for evidence in his favor, and a speedy public trial, by an impartial jury of his country; without the unanimous consent of which jury, he cannot be found guilty; nor can he be compelled to give evidence against himself; nor can any person be justly deprived of his liberty, except by the laws of the land, or the judgment of his peers.

ARTICLE 11.

That the people have a right to hold themselves, their houses, papers, and possessions, free from search or seizure; and, therefore, warrants without oath or affirmation first made, affording sufficient foundation for them, and whereby any officer or messenger may be commanded or required to search suspected places; or to seize any person or persons, his, her, or their property, not particularly described, are contrary to that right, and ought not to be granted.

ARTICLE 12.

That when an issue in fact, proper for the cognizance of a jury, is joined in a court of law, the parties have a right to trial by jury, which ought to be held sacred.

ARTICLE 13.

That the people have a right to a freedom of speech, and of writing and publishing their sentiments, concerning the transactions of government, and therefore the freedom of the press ought not to be restrained.

ARTICLE 14.

The freedom of deliberation, speech, and debate, in the legislature, is so essential to the rights of the people, that it cannot be the foundation of any accusation, or prosecution, action, or complaint, in any other court or place whatsoever.

ARTICLE 15.

The power of suspending laws, or the execution of laws, ought never to be exercised but by the legislature, or by authority derived from it, to be exercised in such particular cases as this constitution, or the legislature, shall provide for.

ARTICLE 16.

That the people have a right to bear arms for the defence of themselves and the State; and, as standing armies in time of peace are dangerous to liberty, they ought not to be kept up; and that the military should be kept under strict subordination to, and governed by, the civil power.

ARTICLE 17.

That no person in this State can, in any case, be subjected to law martial, or to any penalties or pains by virtue of that law, except those employed in the army, and the militia in actual service.

Article 18.

The frequent recurrence to fundamental principles, and firm adherence to justice, moderation, temperance, industry, and frugality, are absolutely necessary to preserve the blessings of liberty, and keep government free ; the people ought, therefore, to pay particular attention to these points, in the choice of officers and representatives, and have a right, in a legal way, to exact a due and constant regard to them, from their legislators and magistrates, in making and executing such laws as are necessary for the good government of the State.

Article 19.

That all people have a natural and inherent right to emigrate from one State to another that will receive them.

Article 20.

That the people have a right to assemble together to consult for their common good : to instruct their representatives : and apply to the legislature for redress of grievances by address, petition, or remonstrance.

Article 21.

That no person shall be liable to be transported out of this State for trial of any offence committed within the same.

CHAPTER II.

Plan or Form of Government.

§ 1. The Commonwealth or State of Vermont shall be governed hereafter by a governor or lieutenant-governor, council, and an assembly of the representatives of the same, in manner and form following :

§ 2. The supreme legislative power shall be vested in a house of representatives of the freemen of the Commonwealth or State of Vermont.

§ 3. The supreme executive power shall be vested in a governor, or, in his absence, a lieutenant governor, and council.

§ 4. Courts of justice shall be maintained in every county in this State, and also in new counties, when formed, which courts shall be open for the trial of all causes proper for their cognizance ; and justice shall be therein impartially administered, without corruption or unnecessary delay. The judges of the supreme court shall be justices of the peace throughout the State ; and the several judges of the county courts, in their respective counties, by virtue of their office, except in the trial of such causes as may be appealed to the county court.

§ 5. A future legislature may, when they shall conceive the same to be expedient and necessary, erect a court of chancery, with such powers as are usually exercised by that court, or as shall appear for the interest of the Commonwealth: Provided they do not constitute themselves the judges of the said court.

§ 6. The legislative, executive, and judiciary departments shall be separate and distinct, so that neither exercise the powers properly belonging to the other.

§ 7. In order that the freemen of this State might enjoy the benefit of election, as equally as may be, each town within this State, that consists or may consist of eighty taxable inhabitants within one septenary, or seven years next after the establishing this constitution, may hold elections therein, and choose each two representatives; and each other inhabited town in this State may, in like manner, choose each one representative to represent them in general assembly, during the said septenary or seven years; and after that, each inhabited town may, in like manner, hold such election, and choose each one representative, forever thereafter.

§ 8. The house of representatives of the freemen of this State shall consist of persons most noted for wisdom and virtue, to be chosen by ballot, by the freemen of every town in this State, respectively, on the first Tuesday in September annually forever.

§ 9. The representatives so chosen, a majority of whom shall constitute a quorum for transacting any other business than raising a State tax, for which two thirds of the members elected shall be present, shall meet on the second Thursday of the succeeding October, and shall be styled *The General Assembly of the State of Vermont:* they shall have power to choose their speaker, secretary of state, their clerk, and other necessary officers of the house — sit on their own adjournments — prepare bills, and enact them into laws — judge of the elections and qualifications of their own members: they may expel members, but not for causes known to their own constituents antecedent to their own elections: they may administer oaths and affirmations in matters depending before them, redress grievances, impeach State criminals, grant charters of incorporation, constitute towns, boroughs, cities, and counties; they may, annually, on their first session after their election, in conjunction with the council, or oftener if need be, elect judges of the supreme and several county and probate courts, sheriffs, and justices of the peace; and also with the council may elect major generals and brigadier generals, from time to time, as often as there shall be occasion; and they shall have all other powers necessary for the legislature of a free and sovereign State: but they shall have no power to add to, alter, abolish, or infringe any part of this constitution.

§ 10. The supreme executive council of this State shall consist of a governor, lieutenant governor, and twelve persons, chosen in the following manner, viz.: The freemen of each town shall, on the day of the election, for choosing representatives to attend the general assembly, bring in their votes for governor, with his name fairly written, to the constable, who shall seal them up, and write on them, *votes for the governor*, and deliver them to the representatives chosen to attend the general assembly; and at the opening of the general assembly, there shall be a committee appointed out of the council and assembly, who, after being duly sworn to the faithful discharge of their trust, shall proceed to receive, sort, and count the votes for the governor, and declare the person who has the major part of the votes to be governor for the year ensuing. And if there be no choice made, then the council and general assembly, by their joint ballot, shall make choice of a governor. The lieutenant governor and treasurer shall be chosen in the manner above directed. And each freeman shall give in twelve votes, for twelve councillors, in the same manner, and the twelve highest in nomination shall serve for the ensuing year as councillors.

§ 11. The governor, and, in his absence, the lieutenant governor, with the council, a major part of whom, including the governor, or lieutenant governor, shall be a quorum to transact business, shall have power to commission all officers, and also to appoint officers, except where provision is, or shall be otherwise made by law, or this frame of government; and shall supply every vacancy in any office, occasioned by death, or otherwise, until the office can be filled in the manner directed by law or this constitution.

They are to correspond with other States, transact business with officers of government, civil and military, and to prepare such business as may appear to them necessary to lay before the general assembly. They shall sit as judges to hear and determine on impeachments, taking to their assistance, for advice only, the judges of the supreme court. And shall have power to grant pardons, and remit fines, in all cases whatsoever, except in treason and murder; in which they shall have power to grant reprieves, but not to pardon, until after the end of the next session of the assembly; and except in cases of impeachment, in which there shall be no remission or mitigation of punishment, but by act of legislation.

They are also to take care that the laws be faithfully executed. They are to expedite the execution of such measures as may be resolved upon by the general assembly. And they may draw upon the treasury for such sums as may be appropriated by the house of representatives. They may also lay embargoes, or prohibit the exportation of any commodity, for any time not exceeding thirty days, in the recess of the house only. They may grant such licenses as shall be directed by law: and shall have power to call together the general assembly, when necessary, before the day to which they shall stand adjourned. The governor shall be captain general and commander in chief of the forces of the State, but shall not command in person, except advised thereto by the council, and then only so long as they shall approve thereof. And the lieutenant governor shall, in virtue of his office, be lieutenant general of all the forces of the State. The governor, or lieutenant governor, and the council, shall meet at the time and place with the general assembly; the lieutenant governor shall, during the presence of the commander in chief, vote and act as one of the council: and the governor, and, in his absence, the lieutenant governor, shall, by virtue of their offices, preside in council, and have a casting, but no other vote. Every member of the council shall be a justice of the peace, for the whole State, by virtue of his office. The governor and council shall have a secretary, and keep fair books of their

18

proceedings, wherein any councillor may enter his dissent, with his reason to support it; and the governor may appoint a secretary for himself and his council.

§ 12. The representatives, having met and chosen their speaker and clerk, shall, each of them, before they proceed to business, take and subscribe, as well the oath or affirmation of allegiance hereinafter directed, except where they shall produce certificates of their having heretofore taken and subscribed the same, as the following oath or affirmation, viz. :

" You ———, do solemnly swear (or affirm) that, as a member of this assembly, you will not propose or assent to any bill, vote, or resolution, which shall appear to you injurious to the people, nor do or consent to any act or thing whatsoever, that shall have a tendency to lessen or abridge their rights and privileges, as declared by the constitution of this State; but will, in all things, conduct yourself as a faithful, honest representative, and guardian of the people, according to the best of your judgment and abilities : (*in case of an oath*) so help you God. (*And in case of an affirmation*) under the pains and penalties of perjury."

§ 13. The doors of the house in which the general assembly of this Commonwealth shall sit, shall be open for the admission of all persons who behave decently, except only when the welfare of the State may require them to be shut.

§ 14. The votes and proceedings of the general assembly shall be printed, when one third of the members think it necessary, as soon as convenient after the end of each session, with the yeas and nays on any question, when required by any member, except where the vote shall be taken by ballot, in which case every member shall have a right to insert the reasons of his vote upon the minutes.

§ 15. The style of the laws of this State, in future to be passed, shall be : *It is hereby enacted by the General Assembly of the State of Vermont.*

§ 16. To the end that laws, before they are enacted, may be more maturely considered, and the inconvenience of hasty determinations, as much as possible, prevented, all bills which originate in the assembly shall be laid before the governor and council, for their revision and concurrence, or proposals of amendment; who shall return the same to the assembly, with their proposals of amendment, if any, in writing; and if the same are not agreed to by the assembly, it shall be in the power of the governor and council to suspend the passing of such bill until the next session of the legislature : Provided, that if the governor and council shall neglect or refuse to return any such bill to the assembly, with written proposals of amendment, within five days, or before the rising of the legislature, the same shall become a law.

§ 17. No money shall be drawn out of the treasury, unless first appropriated by act of legislation.

§ 18. No person shall be elected a representative until he has resided two years in this State; the last of which shall be in the town for which he is elected.

§ 19. No member of the council or house of representatives shall, directly or indirectly, receive any fee or reward to bring forward or advocate any bill, petition, or other business to be transacted in the legislature; or advocate any cause, as counsel, in either house of legislation, except when employed in behalf of the State.

§ 20. No person ought, in any case, or in any time, to be declared guilty of treason or felony by the legislature.

§ 21. Every man of the full age of twenty-one years, having resided in this State for the space of one whole year next before the election of representatives, and is of a quiet and peaceable behavior, and will take the following oath or affirmation, shall be entitled to all the privileges of a freeman of this State :

"You solemnly swear (or affirm) that whenever you give your vote of suffrage touching any matter that concerns the State of Vermont, you will do it so as in your conscience you shall judge will most conduce to the best good of the same, as established by the constitution, without fear or favor of any man."

§ 22. The inhabitants of this State shall be trained and armed for its defence, under such regulations, restrictions, and exceptions, as congress, agreeably to the constitution of the United States, and the legislature of this State, shall direct. The several companies of militia shall, as often as vacancies happen, elect their captain and other officers, and the captains and subalterns shall nominate and recommend the field officers of their respective regiments, who shall appoint their staff officers.

§ 23. All commissions shall be in the name of the freemen of the State of Vermont, sealed with the State seal, signed by the governor, and in his absence the lieutenant governor, and attested by the secretary, which seal shall be kept by the governor.

§ 24. Every officer of state, whether judicial or executive, shall be liable to be impeached by the general assembly, either when in office or after his resignation or removal, for mal-administration. All impeachments shall be before the governor, or lieutenant governor, and council, who shall hear and determine the same, and may award costs; and no trial or impeachment shall be a bar to a prosecution at law.

§ 25. As every freeman, to preserve his independence, if without a sufficient estate, ought to have some profession, calling, trade, or farm, whereby he may honestly subsist, there can be no necessity for, nor use in, establishing offices of profit, the usual effects of which are dependence and servility, unbecoming freemen, in the possessors or expectants, and faction, contention, and discord, among the people. But, if any man is called into public service, to the prejudice of his private affairs, he has a right to a reasonable compensation ; and whenever an office, through increase of fees, or otherwise, becomes so profitable as to occasion many to apply for it, the profits ought to be lessened by the legislature. And if any officer shall wittingly and wilfully take greater fees than the law allows him, it shall ever after disqualify him from holding any office in this State, until he shall be restored by act of legislation.

§ 26. No person in this State shall be capable of holding or exercising more than one of the following offices at the same time, viz. : Governor, lieutenant governor, judge of the supreme court, treasurer of the State, member of the council, member of the general assembly, surveyor general, or sheriff. Nor shall any person, holding any office of profit or trust under the authority of congress, be eligible to any appointment in the legislature, or of holding any executive or judiciary office under this State.

§ 27. The treasurer of the State shall, before the governor and council, give sufficient security to the secretary of the State, in behalf of the general assembly ; and each high sheriff, before the first judge of the county court to the treasurer of their respective counties, previous to their respectively entering upon the execution of their offices, in such manner, and in sums, as shall be directed by the legislature.

§ 28. The treasurer's accounts shall be annually audited, and a fair statement thereof laid before the general assembly at their session in October.

§ 29. Every officer, whether judicial, executive, or military, in authority under this State, before he enters upon the execution of his office, shall take and subscribe the following oath or affirmation of allegiance to this State, unless he shall produce evidence that he has before taken the same ; and also the following oath or affirmation of office, except military officers, and such as shall be exempted by the legislature :

The oath or affirmation of office.

" You do solemnly swear (or affirm) that you will be true and faithful to the State of Vermont, and that you will not, directly or indirectly, do any act or thing injurious to the constitution or government thereof, as established by convention : (*If an oath*) so help you God. (*If an affirmation*) under the pains and penalties of perjury.

The oath or affirmation of office.

' You ———, do solemnly swear (or affirm) that you will faithfully execute the office of ——— for the ——— of ——— ; and will therein do equal right and justice to all men, to the best of your judgment and abilities, according to law : (*If an oath*) so help you God. (*If an affirmation*) under the pains and penalties of perjury.' "

§ 30. No person shall be eligible to the office of governor or lieutenant governor until he shall have resided in this State four years next preceding the day of his election.

§ 31. Trials of issues, proper for the cognizance of a jury, in the supreme and county courts, shall be by jury, except where parties otherwise agree ; and great care ought to be taken to prevent corruption or partiality in the choice and return or appointment of juries.

§ 32. All prosecutions shall commence, *by the authority of the State of Vermont ;* all indictments shall conclude with these words : *against the peace and dignity of the State.* And all fines shall be proportioned to the offences.

§ 33. The person of a debtor, where there is not strong presumption of fraud, shall not be continued in prison after delivering up and assigning over, *bona fide*, all his estate, real and personal, in possession, reversion, or remainder, for the use of his creditors, in such manner as shall be hereafter regulated by law. And all prisoners, unless in execution or committed for capital offences, when the proof is evident or presumption great, shall be bailable by sufficient sureties; nor shall excessive bail be exacted for bailable offences.

§ 34. All elections, whether by the people or the legislature, shall be free and voluntary; and any elector, who shall receive any gift or reward for his vote, in meat, drink, moneys, or otherwise, shall forfeit his right to elect at that time, and suffer such other penalty as the law shall direct; and any person who shall, directly or indirectly, give, promise, or bestow any such rewards, to be elected, shall thereby be rendered incapable to serve for the ensuing year, and be subject to such further punishment as a future legislature shall direct.

§ 35. All deeds and conveyances of land shall be recorded in the town clerk's office, in their respective towns; and for want thereof, in the county clerk's office of the same county.

§ 36. The legislature shall regulate entails in such manner as to prevent perpetuities.

§ 37. To deter more effectually from the commission of crimes, by continued visible punishments of long duration, and to make sanguinary punishments less necessary, means ought to be provided for punishing by hard labor those who shall be convicted of crimes not capital, whereby the criminal shall be employed for the benefit of the public, or for the reparation of injuries done to private persons : and all persons, at proper times, ought to be permitted to see them at their labor.

§ 38. The estates of such persons as may destroy their own lives shall not for that offence be forfeited, but descend or ascend in the same manner as if such persons had died in a natural way. Nor shall any article, which shall accidentally occasion the death of any person, be henceforth deemed a deodand, or in any wise forfeited, on account of such misfortune.

§ 39. Every person of good character, who comes to settle in this State, having first taken an oath or affirmation of allegiance to the same, may purchase, or by other just means acquire, hold, and transfer land, or other real estate; and, after one year's residence, shall be deemed a free denizen thereof, and entitled to all rights of a natural born subject of this State, except that he shall not be capable of being elected governor, lieutenant governor, treasurer, councillor, or representative in assembly, until after two years' residence.

§ 40. The inhabitants of this State shall have liberty, in seasonable times, to hunt and fowl on the lands they hold, and on other lands not enclosed; and in like manner to fish in all boatable and other waters, not private property, under proper regulations, to be hereafter made and provided by the general assembly.

§ 41. Laws for the encouragement of virtue and prevention of vice and immorality, ought to be constantly kept in force, and duly executed; and a competent number of schools ought to be maintained in each town, for the con-

18*

venient instruction of youth ; and one or more grammar schools to be incorporated, and properly supported, in each county in this State. And all religious societies or bodies of men, that may be hereafter united or incorporated for the advancement of religion and learning, or for other pious and charitable purposes, shall be encouraged and protected in the enjoyment of the privileges, immunities, and estates, which they in justice ought to enjoy, under such regulations as the general assembly of this State shall direct.

§ 42. The declaration of the political rights and privileges of the inhabitants of this State, is hereby declared to be a part of the constitution of this Commonwealth, and ought not to be violated on any pretence whatsoever.

§ 43. In order that the freedom of this Commonwealth may be preserved inviolate forever, there shall be chosen, by ballot, by the freemen of this State, on the last Wednesday in March, in the year one thousand seven hundred and ninety-nine, and on the last Wednesday in March, in every seven years thereafter, thirteen persons, who shall be chosen in the same manner the council is chosen, except they shall not be out of the council or general assembly, to be called the council of censors ; who shall meet together on the first Wednesday in June next ensuing their election, the majority of whom shall be a quorum in every case, except as to calling a convention, in which, two thirds of the whole number elected shall agree, and whose duty it shall be to inquire whether the constitution has been preserved inviolate in every part during the last septenary, including the year of their service, and whether the legislative and executive branches of government have performed their duty, as guardians of the people, or assumed to themselves, or exercised other or greater powers than they are entitled to by the constitution : They are also to inquire, whether the public taxes have been justly laid and collected in all parts of this Commonwealth ; in what manner the public moneys have been disposed of ; and whether the laws have been duly executed. For these purposes they shall have power to send for persons, papers, and records : they shall have authority to pass public censures, to order impeachments, and to recommend to the legislature the repealing such laws as shall appear to them to have been passed contrary to the principles of the constitution : These powers they shall continue to have for and during the space of one year from the day of their election, and no longer. The said council of censors shall also have power to call a convention, to meet within two years after their sitting, if there appears to them an absolute necessity of amending any article of this constitution, which may be defective : explaining such as may be thought not clearly expressed : and of adding such as are necessary for the preservation of the rights and happiness of the people : but the articles to be amended, and the amendments proposed, and such articles as are proposed to be added or abolished, shall be promulgated at least six months before the day appointed for the election of such convention, for the previous consideration of the people, that they may have an opportunity of instructing their delegates on the subject.

By order of Convention, July 9, 1793.

THOMAS CHITTENDEN, *President.*

Attest, LEWIS R. MORRIS, *Secretary.*

NOTE.

BENNINGTON BATTLE. — From an able address delivered before the Legislature at Montpelier, October 20th, 1848, by the Rev. James D. Butler, of Wells River, on the battle of Bennington, we make a few extracts, which show the great importance of this battle to the interests of the country, and pay a just tribute to its heroes:

"The results of this victory can scarcely be overrated. It was much to cut off from Burgoyne's army, in a single day, one sixth of its numbers, or more than a thousand of killed, wounded, and prisoners, — to capture their arms, artillery, and baggage, — to annihilate a detachment to the leader of which Burgoyne's words were: 'Always bear in mind that your corps is too valuable to let any considerable loss be *hazarded.*' The moral effect of this success was heightened by various particulars. At Bennington, militia with scarcely a bayonet, — for the first time, I believe, — stormed intrenchments, — at Bunker Hill they had only defended them. Here, raw troops, many of whom had never seen a cannon, stormed a battery, ground to powder a corps composed of Frazer's marksmen, or 'chosen men from all the regiments,' and German dragoons, veterans of the seven years' war, — 'the best I had of that nation,' says Burgoyne, or, as described by a Hessian, 'men of tried valor and enterprise.' Moreover here was a victory gained by a beaten army over a successful one, — by one often beaten over one often successful. How could it fail to inspirit and inspire ? True it was a single star, but it was the first star which arose in a firmament hitherto the blackness of darkness. Henceforth Burgoyne's honeymoon was over, and Hessian forces were less dreaded than Hessian flies.

"Let us further consider the results of this action. It was exactly what had been Washington's heart's desire, or rather it was twice as much as he had dared to hope, onward from the loss of Ticonderoga, for on the 22d of July he wrote to Schuyler: 'Could we be so happy as to cut off one of his detachments, supposing it should not exceed four, five, or six hundred men, it would inspirit the people and do away much of their present anxiety. In such an event they would lose sight of past misfortunes, fly to arms, and afford every aid in their power.'

" The revolution wrought in Burgoyne's feelings is betrayed by the contrast between his letters just before and just after the expedition. In the former he writes to the leader of the corps sent against Vermont: 'Mount your dragoons, send me thirteen hundred horses, seize Bennington, cross the mountains to Rockingham and Brattleborough, try the affections of the country, take hostages, meet me a fortnight hence in Albany.' Four days *after* the battle he writes to England : ' The Hampshire Grants in particular, a country unpeopled and almost unknown in the last war, now abounds in the most active and rebellious race of the continent, and hangs like a gathering storm upon my left.' Burgoyne was far from overrating the influence of Stark's success. Within three days thereafter, Schuyler wrote to Stark : ' The signal victory you have gained, and the severe loss the enemy have received, cannot fail of producing the most salutary results.' Within a week, a handbill was issued at Boston containing an account of Stark's triumph; the news was there proclaimed by criers, and rung out from all the bells. Clinton wrote : ' Since the affair at Bennington, not an Indian has been heard of; the scalp-ing has ceased ; indeed I do not apprehend any great danger from the future operations of Mr. Burgoyne.' Washington, writing Putnam, was high in hope that New England, following the great stroke struck by Stark, would entirely crush Burgoyne ; and a rumor that Burgoyne *was* crushed, raised the siege of Fort Stanwix and broke his right wing. All this was within one week after Baum and Breymann were discomfited. In one day more a rumor was rife in New Hampshire that Burgoyne had been taken at Stillwater :

> ' As the sun
> Ere he be risen, sometimes paints his image
> In the atmosphere, the shadows of great events
> Precede the events, and in to-day already walks to-morrow.'

" Three weeks before the Hessian overthrow, Governeur Morris wrote from Schuyler's camp : ' If a body of 3,000 men can be formed somewhere upon the New Hampshire Grants ; if General Washington can spare a reinforce-ment of 1,500 good troops ; if the governor discharge all of the militia in the highlands ; if he be put at the head of one third of the New York militia, and two hundred good riflemen sent into Tryon County, we may laugh at Messrs. Howe and Burgoyne.' None of the consummations wished for by these *ifs* came to pass, yet the day of Bennington, by enabling us to laugh at Burgoyne, accomplished what Morris had most at heart. That nothing less than this was among the many-sided utilities of that great day, is attested by many witnesses. It is the testimony of the Baroness Riedesel, then in the British camp, whose words are : ' This unfortunate event [Baum and Brey-mann's discomfiture] paralyzed at once our operations.' It is the testimony of contemporary journals, in which we read of the victories at Bennington, as ' sowing the seed of all the laurels that Gates reaped during the cam-paign.' It is the testimony of Jefferson, who declares them ' the first link in the chain of successes which issued in the surrender of Saratoga.'

" Students of our State history will always behold in this first success, the lone star which lit the way to the attacks under Warner and Herrick, at Lake George landing, and thus to the capture of the vessels in which Burgoyne might have escaped to Canada. Previous to these operations, the achieve-ments of Stark emboldened Green Mountain rangers to infest or break up Burgoyne's communications with his depots of provisions, and thus for a whole month threw him into a chloroform stupefaction. That enterprising general was rearing an arch of conquest huge enough to darken all our land. The repulse on the banks of the Walloomscoik, plucked out the crowning keystone from that well-nigh finished arch, so that the whole structure cracked, crumbled by piecemeal, tottered, and fell, a wreck of ruin, never to rise again. In two months to a day, from that first reverse, Burgoyne's motto: '*This army must never retreat,*' was strangely interpreted, for we behold

> ' The destroyer desolate,
> The victor overthrown.'

'One more such stroke,' said Washington, on hearing the tidings, 'one more such stroke, and we shall have no great cause for anxiety as to the future designs of Britain.'"

The Rev. gentleman in his address gave the following interesting account of an interview with one of the veterans of this battle:

"Ascertaining that a veteran of Bennington was still living some eight miles from my house in Wells River, I paid him a visit about a week ago. His name is Thomas Mellen, and though upwards of ninety-two years of age, he is so far from being bald or bowed down, that you would think him in the Indian Summer of life. His dress was all of grey homespun, and he sat on a couch, the covering of which was sheepskins with the wool on. I will repeat his statements, as far as possible in his own words:

" ' I enlisted,' said he, 'at Francestown, New Hampshire, in Colonel Stickney's regiment, and Captain Clark's company, as soon as I learned that Stark would accept the command of the State troops. Six or seven others from the same town joined the army at the same time. We marched forthwith to Number Four, and stayed there a week. Meantime I received a horn of powder, and run two or three hundred bullets. I had brought my own gun. Then my company was sent on to Manchester. Soon after I went with a hundred others under Colonel Emerson, down the valley of Otter Creek. On this excursion, we lived like lords on pigs and chickens in the houses of tories who had fled. When we returned to Manchester, bringing two hogsheads of West India rum, we heard that the Hessians were on their way to invade Vermont. Late in the afternoon of rainy Friday, we were ordered off for Bennington, in spite of rain, mud, and darkness. We pushed on all night, each making the best progress he could. About daybreak, I, with Lieutenant Miltimore, came near Bennington, and slept a little while on a hay-mow. When the barn-yard fowls waked us, we went for bread and milk to the sign of the Wolf, and then hurried three miles west to Stark's main body.

" ' Stark and Warner rode up near the enemy to reconnoitre, were fired at with the cannon, and came galloping back. Stark rode with shoulders bent forward, and cried out to his men : " Those rascals know that I am an officer ; don't you see they honor me with a big gun as a salute ? " We were marched round and round a circular hill till we were tired. Stark said it was to amuse the Germans. All the while a cannonade was kept up upon us from their breastwork. It hurt nobody, and it lessened our fear of the great guns.

After a while I was sent, with twelve others, to lie in ambush on a knoll a little north, and watch for tories on their way to join Baum. Presently we saw six coming towards us, who, mistaking us for tories, came too near us to escape. We disarmed them and sent them, under a guard of three, to Stark. While I sat on the hillock, I espied one Indian whom I thought I could kill, and more than once cocked my gun, but the orders were not to fire. He was cooking his dinner, and now and then shot at some of our people.

" 'Between two and three o'clock the battle began. The Germans fired by platoons, and were soon hidden by smoke. Our men fired each on his own hook, aiming wherever they saw a flash. Few on our side had either bayonets or cartridges. At last I stole away from my post, and ran down to the battle. The first time I fired I put three balls into my gun. Before I had time to fire many rounds, our men rushed over the breastwork, but I and many others chased straggling Hessians in the woods. We pursued till we met Breymann with eight hundred fresh troops and larger cannon, which opened a fire of grape shot. Some of the grape shot riddled a Virginia fence near me, one struck a small white oak tree behind which I stood. Though it hit higher than my head, I fled from the tree, thinking it might be aimed at again. We skirmishers ran back, till we met a large body of Stark's men, then faced about. I soon started for a brook I saw a few rods behind, for I had drank nothing all day, and should have died with thirst had I not *chewed a bullet* all the time. I had not gone a rod when I was stopped by an officer, sword in hand, and ready to cut me down as a runaway. On my complaining of thirst, he handed me his canteen, which was full of rum. I drank and forgot my thirst.

" 'But the enemy outflanked us, and I said to a comrade: " We must run or they will have us." He said : " I will have one more fire first." At that moment a major on a black horse rode along behind us, shouting : " Fight on, boys ; reinforcements close by." While he was yet speaking, a grape shot went through his horse's head, and knocked out two teeth. It bled a good deal, but the major kept his seat, and spurred on to encourage others. In five minutes we saw Warner's men hurrying to help us. They opened right and left of us, and half of them attacked each flank of the enemy, and beat back those who were just closing around us. Stark's men now took heart and stood their ground. My gun-barrel was by this time too hot to hold, so I seized the musket of a dead Hessian, in which my bullets went down easier than in my own. Right in front were the cannon, and seeing an officer on horseback waving his sword to the artillerymen, I fired at him twice. His horse fell. He cut the traces of an artillery horse, mounted him, and rode off. I afterwards heard that that officer was Major Skeene.

" 'Soon the Germans ran; and we followed. Many of them threw down their guns on the ground, or offered them to us, or kneeled, some in puddles of water. One said to me: *"Wir sind ein, bruder !"* I pushed him behind me and rushed on. All those near me did so. The enemy beat a parley, minded to give up, but our men did not understand it. I came to one wounded man, flat on the ground, crying *water*, or *quarter*. I snatched his sword out of his scabbard, and, while I ran on and fired, carried it in my mouth, thinking I might need it. The Germans fled by the road, and in a wood each side of it. Many of their scabbards caught in the brush, and held the fugitives till we seized them. We chased them till dark. Colonel Johnston, of Haverhill, wanted to chase them all night. Had we done so, we might have mastered them all, for they stopped within three miles of the battle-field. But Stark, saying he would run no risk of spoiling a good day's work, ordered a halt and return to quarters.

" ' I was coming back, when ordered by Stark himself, who knew me, as I had been one of his body guard in Canada, to help draw off a field piece. I told him I was worn out. His answer was : " Don't seem to disobey ; take hold, and if you can't hold out, slip away in the dark." Before we had dragged the gun far, Warner rode near us. Some one, pointing to a dead man by the wayside, said to him : " Your brother is killed." " Is it Jesse ? " asked Warner; and when the answer was, Yes, he jumped off his horse, stooped, and gazed in the dead man's face, and then rode away without saying a word. On my way back I got the belt of the Hessian, whose sword I had taken in the pursuit. I also found a barber's pack, but was obliged to give up all my findings till the booty was divided. To the best of my remembrance, my share was four dollars and some odd cents. One tory, with his left eye shot out, was led by me mounted on a horse who had also lost his left eye. It seems cruel now — it did not then.

" ' My company lay down and slept in a cornfield near where we had fought; each man having *a hill of corn for a pillow*. When I waked next morning, I was so beaten out that I could not get up till I had rolled about a good while. After breakfast I went to see them bury the dead. I saw thirteen tories, mostly shot through the head, buried in one hole. Not more than a rod from where I fought, we found Captain McClary dead, and stripped naked. We scraped a hole with sticks, and just covered him with earth. We saw many of the wounded who had lain out all night. Afterwards we went to Bennington and saw the prisoners paraded. They were drawn up in one long line ; the British foremost, then the Waldechers, next the Indians, and hindmost the tories.'

" The old man from whose lips I wrote down the foregoing narrative has been a teetotaler for several years, though he was long an inebriate. When I surprised him in his sequestered abode, I found him busy with a book in large print, entitled ' The Consolations of Religion.' "

The Address, from which we make the above extract, was on the occasion of the receipt of four pieces of cannon taken at this celebrated battle. The eloquent orator thus speaks of those trophies of war:

" Two years ago, addressing the Vermont Historical Society in this capital, I was constrained to say : ' The cannon taken at Bennington, in defence of our frontier, lie unclaimed at Washington.' I have lived to see a better day,— to behold in my native State, yea in this place of honor, — as trophies, those death-dealing engines, which my grandsire, now in his grave, jeoparded his life to wrest from his country's invaders. These trophies are ours by many titles. Ours, for Vermont blood shed in this battle, at Hubbardton, and else-where, — ours, for expenses not reimbursed us by the United States as were those of other States, — ours, for their profaning our territory with their hos-tile balls, — ours, for supplies furnished Stark's brigade, — ours, for the supe-rior skill of Warner and Herrick, who, alone of all the colonels, were named by Stark as his most efficient colleagues.

"Where are the two six-pounders? Who can tell? New Hampshire should have them, — she would have them this day, could she boast an antiquarian like him who has ferreted out these our cannon, a senator and a representa-tive like those who have pressed our claim upon Congress, — had they but a Stevens, an Upham, and a Collamer.

"When I remember that Stark's donation to Vermont, the Hessian gun and bayonet, the broadsword, brass-barrelled drum, and grenadier's cap, were not hung up for monuments as in Massachusetts, but vilely thrown away, I am glad Congress have kept these trophies so long, lest they should have been minted into cents, or beaten into brass kettles, by some grovelling utilitarian. If we lose these relics, may we be vouchsafed no more! Some of you have marked how Massachusetts delights to honor the revolutionary trophy cannon, which are among her perpetual possessions, by enshrining them in the sky-climbing chamber of the Bunker Hill Monument. Others of you may have observed, that England glorifies with similar spoils the chief places of con-course in London. Let us, actuated by a congenial feeling, resolve that the time-honored relics so long lost, but now in the midst of us, shall go no more out from these walls, of which we have more reason to be proud than of any other edifice in our highland homes; or that if they go hence, it shall be to grace a monument erected on the spot where the Hessian battery was formed, as the niche they were ordained to fill. Let them rouse an interest in our *history*, as the Swiss bone-houses and the tablets in German churches engraved with names of those who died for their father-land, rouse an interest in their history. Let them cause us to shudder at the curses of WAR, till we shall study the things which make for peace, and know war only by its trophies. Let them fill us with the same resolution to preserve our rich inheritance which they were witnesses that our fathers showed in acquiring it. Let them open our eyes to look upon all things, as Stark more than once spoke of his victory: 'As given by the divine BEING who overpowers and rules all things, — or as given by the God of armies, who was pleased to make him, his offi-cers, and men, instruments in checking the progress of the British forces.' Then shall our mountains still be the holy land of freedom, and all our battle-fields remain that hallowed ground which speaks of nations saved."

E N D .

ABBOTT, James 92 Mr 68
ABERCROMBIE, Gen 164
ADAMS, Daniel 28 James 111
   Martin 111
AIKEN, Edward 140 144 John 51
ALDIS, Asa 186
ALEXANDER, John 32
ALLEN, 16 Col 16 164 Ebenezer
   93 101 Ethan 14 15 34 73 117
   Ezra 137 Ira 50 77 Ithamer 129
   Justus 35 Lamberton 66 Mr
   167
ALLYN, Abner 45
ALLYNE, Abner 25 Jonathan 25
AMHERST, Gen 24 128 164
AMY, Micah 68
ANDREWS, Andrew 73
ANDROS, 9
ANDRUS, Benjamin 137 Eldad 51
ANGEL, 137
ARMAND, John 51
ARMS, John 32
ARNOLD, 16 97 Jonathan 111
ASHLEY, Elisha 87 Enoch 87
   Thomas 101
ASHMUN, 16
ATHERTON, Joseph 22
ATWATER, Jeremiah 194
AUSTIN, Samuel 195
AVERY, Samuel 144
AYERS, 31
AYRES, David 36
Abenaki Indians 8
Acton 65
Addison 19 34 93 97 136 145 159
   164 167 171 183
Addison County 19 33 35 47 51 61
   65 66 69 79 80 85 87 93 95–97
   104 107 112 115 118 126 129
   130 136 140 150 151 169–171
   182 184 187 195

Addison County Mutual Fire
   Insurance Company 190
Addison District 195
Adirondack Indians 8
Aiken's Gore 144
Albany 20 25 52 65 75 81 111 145
   153 177 212
Alburgh 20 66 72 122 145 165 168
   175
Alburgh Springs 183
Alburgh West 183
Alder Brook 59
Algonkin Indians 8
Allen's Point 167
Amherst 27
Andover 21 46 82 135 140 145 162
   181 184
Appletree Point 167
Arlington 21 42 113 121 145 153
   172 190
Arlington West 183
Ascot 94
Ascutney Mountain 151
Ascutney River 141
Ashley's Pond 116
Asylum for the Insane 188
Athens 21 36 65 124 135 145 180
Atlantic & Saint Lawrence Rail-
   road 196
Averill 22 42 80 94 145 156 158
Avery's Gore 22 25 35 74 80 81
   88 94 104 133 144 155
Ayers' Brook 30 31
Ayres' Brook 106
BABCOCK, Solomon 50
BAKER, Joseph 22 Mrs Remem-
   ber 50 Remember 21 50
BALDWIN, 123 Benjamin 30 55
   Mr 61 Truman 46
BALL, Joseph 50 Levi 50
BALLARD, Joseph 60

BANKER, Joseph 84
BARBER, 27 Job 28
BARKER, Barnabas 111 Joseph
31 Mrs Joseph 31
BARLOW, Hubbard 60 William
98
BARNARD, Samuel 88
BARNET, John 85
BARRETT, B 142
BARTHOLOMEW, Eleazer 43
BARTLET, Joshua 118
BARTON, Simeon 98
BASCOM, Samuel 114
BASIER, Joseph 22
BASS, Hiram 31 Samuel 31
BATCHELDER, Joseph 100
Moulton 100
BATES, Joshua 194
BAUM, 212 214
BAYLEY, Frye 92 Jacob 92
BEACH, Aaron 48 Samuel 137
BEADEN, Smithfield 60
BEALS, Isaac 49
BEARDSLEY, Evans 116
BECKWITH, Amos 37 121 122
BEEBE, Lewis 98
BELKNAP, 14
BELLOWS, John 70
BENT, David 91
BENTLEY, James Jr 51 Samuel
61 Thomas 51
BENTON, Samuel 144
BETHEL, 28
BIDWELL, George 118
BIGELOW, Henry 86 Joel 106
BINGHAM, Silas L 93
BINNEY, Col 120
BIRD, Col 43
BISCO, 21
BISHOP, Enos 35 John 87
BLAKE, Ephraim 112
BLANCHARD, William 76
BLISS, Enos 31 96 Joshua 41
BLOCK, Adrian 12
BLODGET, Asa 51 Samuel 51
BLOOD, Caleb 114 Isaac 107
BOARDMAN, Mr 50
BOGUE, Publius Virgil 64 Rev
Mr 90
BOIES, William 123
BOLSTER, 137

BOND, Asa 46
BOWE, Daniel 99 Jacob 99
BOWMAN, Joseph 23
BRADFORD, E G 129 130
BRADLEY, Andrew 60 Elisha 74
Mr 121 Stephen R 88
BRAINARD, Elijah 103
BRATLIN, Mr 137
BRATTLE, Col 32
BREYMANN, 212 214
BRIDGMAN, John 63
BRIGHAM, Joel 22
BRISTOL, Mr 113
BROCK, Walter 24
BROTHER JONATHAN 72
BROWN, 153 Edmund 51 Isaac
57 Joseph 35 Mr 77 Mrs 77
BROWNSON, Amos 104 Asa 104
Joel 104 Mr 121
BRUCE, James 39
BUEL, Ephraim 43
BULL, Crispin 53 Johnny 72
BULLEN, Joseph 135
BURGE, Caleb 68
BURGOYNE, 16 34 124 198 211-
213 Gen 164
BURNHAM, Barnabas 87
BURREL, Henry 54
BURT, Asahel 78
BURTON, Asa 123 Simon 21
BUTLER, Ezra 186 James D 211
BUTTS, Joseph 70
Bakersfield 22 58 60 62 132 145
175
Bald Mountain 113 127
Bald Mountain Branch 161
Baldwin Creek 35
Ball Mountain Mfg Company 76
Baltimore 22 47 117 133 145 181
Barnard 22 28 33 101 107 118 145
153 157 158 181
Barnard East 183
Barnet 23 53 54 98 109 132 145
159 160 167 172 184 191 196
Barre 24 28 89 95 96 100 138 144
145 160 179 196
Barre South 183
Barrington 25
Barton 25 37 65 75 114 145 153
162 164 177
Barton River 25 52 64 65 75 96

Barton River (continued)
    114 121 135 153 162 167
Basin Harbor 61 167
Battenkill River 21 55 83 107 113
    121 153 159 162
Beaver Brook 138
Belamaqueen Bay 167
Belle Pond 25 153 164
Belle Water Pond 164
Bellows Falls 22 83 105 106 135
    154 160 162 167 183 196
Bellows Falls Bank 190
Bellows Falls Village 106
Belvidere 25 57 75 78 81 132 145
    176
Belvidere Mountain 57
Bennington 11 17 21 22 26 33 42
    55 62-64 69 77 79 81 83 84 86
    90 94 98 101 102 104 107 113
    114 116 118 121 124 129 130
    137 139 140 142 143 145 155
    161 169 172 198 211-213 215
Bennington Battle of 211
Bennington County 21 26 55 64 79
    83 98 101 104 107 113 117 121
    139 142 150 151 169 170 172
    182 184 187 195
Bennington County Mutual Fire
    Insurance Company 190
Bennington District 195
Bennington North 183
Benson 27 60 74 96 97 121 134
    145 155 178
Benton's Gore 144
Benton's Meadow 111
Berbe's Pond 73
Berkshire 27 28 58 63 104 145
    157 160 175
Berkshire East 183
Berkshire West 183
Berlin 24 28 89 145 155 163 179
Bethel 22 23 31 103 105 107 118
    119 145 157 162 181
Bethel East 183
Bethel Village 162
Bird's Mountain 42
Black Creek 22 59 62 115 153 157
Black Mountain 56
Black River 20 43 52 64 67 75 81
    96 100 103 107 117 132 133
    140 153 154 166 167 199

Black River Bank 190
Black River Falls 43 117
Black River Railroad 196
Black's Pond 74
Bloody Brook 94
Bloomfield 29 31 80 145 158 174
Bolton 29 56 74 77 104 131 132
    145 161 163 173
Bombazine Lake 164
Borough 42
Boston & Montreal Railroad 54 79
Bradford 25 29 30 51 61 92 94 133
    145 161 176 196
Bradford Academy 30
Bradford Centre 183
Bradford District 195
Bradleyvale 30 50 78 110 127 145
    158
Braintree 30 36 66 103 105 106
    145 162 176
Braintree West 183
Brandon 18 31 48 65 79 99 121
    145 159 178 190
Brandon Bank 190
Brattleborough 9 32 37 55 56 64
    68 83 93 102 104 113 116 118
    121 124 126 130 137 143 145
    161 162 180 188 196 211
Brattleborough Bank 190 193
Brattleborough West 183
Brewster's River 41 42
Bridgewater 23 33 100 103 115
    143 145 158 181
Bridgman's Fort 126
Bridport 20 33 51 116 136 145 156
    159 171
Brighton 35 44 45 56 61 91 133
    135 145 153 155 166 174
Bristol 35 80 85 87 93 105 118
    145 157 171
Bristol Pond 35
Broad Brook 22 68 153 162
Brookfield 30 36 46 103 106 138
    145 155 162 176
Brookfield East 183
Brookline 22 36 56 102 124 135
    145 155 180
Brown's River 59 77 125 134 153
    155
Brownington 37 45 52 75 112 135
    145 153 162 177

Brownsville 183
Brunswick 21 29 37 83 133 145
   158 174
Buck Mountain 129
Buckland 154
Buel's Gore 74 118 144
Bunker Hill 23
Burke 37 56 78 82 91 121 127 145
   159 172
Burlington & Montreal Railroad
   64 87 110
Burlington 18 22 28 29 37 38 39
   46 47 49–51 58–61 63 66 71 73
   74 76 78 80 85 87 93 94 95 99
   104 106 109 110 114 115 117
   122 126 129 132 134 136 138
   142 143 145 151 158 163 165
   169 173 190 193 194
Burlington Bank 190
Burlington Bay 38 165 167 168
Burlington Company 38
Burlington Village 163 167
Burnside Mountain 68
Burtonville 183
Butler Meadow 111
CAHOON, Daniel 82
CALDWELL, William 81
CARD, 102
CARPENTER, Asa 132 Jonathan
   28
CASE, Lyman 52
CAZIER, Mathias 43
CHAFFEY, Daniel 73
CHAMBERLAIN, Jacob Bailey 92
   Jason 69 John 104 123 Joshua
   104 Richard 92 Samuel 104
   123 Thomas 92 123
CHAMBERS, Henry 97
CHAMPLAIN, 155 Samuel 11 166
CHANDLER, John 47 Thomas 47
   Thomas Jr 47
CHAPIN, Lewis 77 Pelatiel 141
   Sylvanus 34
CHAPMAN, Edmund 39
CHARLES II King of ---- 13
CHARLEVOIX, 11
CHARTER, John 97
CHASE, Calvin Y 51 Dudley 28
   186
CHEEDLE, John 101 William 23
CHENEY, Joseph 87

CHILSON, Jos 62
CHIPMAN, 34 John 85 Mr 121
   Nathaniel 186
CHITTENDEN, Bethuel 115 M
   186 Noah 42 Thomas 16 138
   186 210
CLAFLIN, Daniel 70 Ebenezer 70
CLAP, Joshua 88 Reuben 88
CLARK, Capt 213 Isaac 75 John
   91 Mr 113 Samuel 39 188
CLEVELAND, Aaron 31 Oliver 60
CLINTON, 212 Gov 14
COBB, S 52 T 52
COFFEIN, John 44
COLBURN, Zerah 39
COLBY, Ezekiel 51 Henry 51
COLDEN, 8 Lieut-Gov 13
COLE, Mr 113 Simeon 111
COLLAMER, 216
COLLINS, Aaron 138 John 39
   Samuel 53
COLUMBUS, 9
CONANT, Samuel 65
CONVERSE, James 133
COOK, Benjamin 137 Elkanah 49
   Samuel 65
COOLEY, Benjamin 99 Gideon 99
COOPER, Thomas 141
COWAL, Joseph 73
CRAFTS, Ebenezer 52 Samuel C
   186
CRANE, Joseph 138
CROSBY, Aaron 56
CROSS, Mrs Shubal 36 Shubal 36
CROWLY, Abraham 91
CROWN, John 124
CULVER, Nathaniel 74
CURTIS, 102 Asahel 81 Israel
   141
CUSHMAN, Rufus 60
CUTLER, Amos 31 Mr 67 Nathan
   53
Cabot 39 53 54 67 75 84 98 128
   142 145 163 167 172
Cabot Plains 39
Cadysville 90
Calais 39 40 41 84 89 142 143
   163 179
Calais East 183
Caledonia Bank 190
Caledonia County 23 30 37 39 41

Caledonia County (continued)
53 58 67 70 78 79 82 91 95 96
98 109 110 114 121 128 130
132 136 144 150 152 169 170
172 173 182 184 187 195
Caledonia District 195
Cambridge 41 62 75 78 118 125
132 145 155 176 183
Cambridge Port 106
Cambridgeport 183
Camel's Hump 74
Camel's Hump Mountain 151 152
Camel's Rump Mountain 151
Canaan 22 42 80 145 156 174
Caniaderi-Guarunte Lake 166
Cape Scoumouton 165
Cas-cad-nac Mountain 151
Caspian Lake 67 155 164
Castleton 27 42 74 75 101 145
153 164 178 183 196
Castleton River 43 60 75 108 153
160
Catbow Branch 82
Cavendish 22 43 47 81 133 145
153 181 184
Central Railroad 142 143 196
Centre Village 42 103 110
Chambly Rapids 165
Charity School 136
Charlemont 154
Charleston 35 37 90 112 135 146
153 177
Charleston East 183
Charleston West 183
Charlestown 10 23 24 40 44 71
Charlotte 45 62 73 87 114 146 155
157 165 173
Checker-Berry 86
Chelsea 30 31 36 46 51 61 92 95
96 103 120 123-125 127 131
134 138 146 162 169 176 190
191
Chelsea Academy 46
Chester 21 22 44 46 47 65 81 117
146 162 181
Chimney Point 167 183
Chin Mountain 151 152
Chipman's Hill 85 152
Chipman's Point 183
Chittenden 31 48 65 84 99 108
146 160 178

Chittenden County 19 29 37 45 47
49 59 62 72 74 76 79 86 104
110 114 125 130 134 138 144
150 151 169 170 173 174 182
184 187 195
Chittenden District 195
Clarendon 48 74 75 90 109 116
123 129 138 146 159 178 199
Clarendon Cave 49
Clarendon East 183
Clarendon Springs 48 183
Clear Pond 74
Clyde River 35 44 45 54 58 73 89
90 112 135 153 155 158 166
167
Coatacook River 94
Cogman's Creek 134
Colchester 38 39 49 50 59 77 86
146 155 163 173 184
Colchester Bay 155
Colchester Point 50
Cold Branch 95
Cold Brook 138
Cold River 48 108 116 154 159
Cole's Pond 128
Coleraine 154
Colt's Pond 36
Concord 30 50 82 92 110 127 132
146 157 158 174
Connecticut River 9 10 12 13 22-
24 26 29 30 32 37 39 41 42 50
53 55 56 58 61 68 70 71 73 78
80 82 83 91 92 94 95 102 103
105 106 109 112 112 117 122
125 126 132 133 134 135 139-
141 151-154 156-162 166 167
188 196
Connecticut River Railroad 24 51
56 61 68 71 72 92 95 98 102
106 109 117 120 123-125 127
132 134 196
Connecticut River, Brattleborough
& Fitchburg Railroad 196
Conway 154
Coossuck Indians 7
Corinth 28 50 51 96 123 127 131
146 161 176
Corinth East 183
Corners 183
Cornish 141
Cornwall 34 51 85 112 116 136

Cornwall (continued)
137 146 159 171
Coventry 52 144 146 153 177
Coventry Gore 75 81 93 144
Cow Mountain 68
Craftsbury 20 52 57 67 75 142 146
153 162 166 177
Craftsbury Academy 52
Craftsbury South 183
Crooked Brook 59
Crown Point 10 16 19 20 34 109
165–167
Crown Point Fortress 164
Culloden Battle of 126
Cumberland Bay 165
Cumberland County 14 139
Cumberland Head 165
Cuttingsville 183
DAMAN, George 143 Ebenezer 78
DANA, Nathan 74
DARLING, Levi 70
DAVIS, Experience 103 Henry 194
Jacob 40 89 Joel 138 John
Preston 84 Parley 40 41 89
DE LAET, 12
DEBELINE, M 23
DEMING, Penuel 138
DEWEY, Jedediah 27 Noah 29 61
Thomas 87 Zebadiah 87
DIBBLE, Charles 28
DILSE, Peter 29
DODDRIDGE, 16
DODGE, Ebenezer 84
DOOLITTLE, Ephraim 116 Mr
113
DORMAN, Eben H 59 122
DOUGLASS, William 51
DUDLEY, Rev Mr 124
DUMMER, Lieut–Gov 9
DUNHAM, 102
DURFEE, Mr 27
DURKEE, Bartholomew 101 John
118 Mrs Bartholomew 101
DWIGHT, Dr 151 165 Joseph 25
DYER, Ebenezer 92
Danby 53 55 91 98 123 146 159
178 183 199
Danby Four Corners 183
Danville & Passumpsic Railroad
196

Danville 23 24 37 39 41 53 68 70
79 82 91 98 109 111 112 114
122 128 132 136 144 146 166
169 172
Danville Green 196
Danville North 183
Danville Village 54
Dartmouth College 94 136
Dead Creek 41
Deerfield 154
Deerfield River 55 64 104 116 120
137 138 142 154
Derby 54 73 90 93 112 146 153
154 166 177
Derby Line 54 183
Derby West 183
Desert Mountain 55
Devil's Den 30
Dog River 28 93 106 154 163
Dorset 53 55 83 98 107 146 153
159 172
Dorset East 183
Dorset North 183
Dorset South 183
Douglas' Bay 165
Dover 55 83 92 116 129 139 180
Dummer Meadows 32
Dummerston 32 36 56 71 83 92
102 146 161 180
Dummerston East 183
Dummerston West 183
Dun's Den 69
Dunmore Lake 166
Dutchman's Point 94
Dutton's Village 43
Duttonsville 44
Duxbury 56 61 74 89 131 146 151
163 179
Duxbury Branch 56
EARL, Joseph 53
EASTMAN, Calvin 35 Cyprian 35
Jonathan 35 Mr 59 107 120
Tilton 103
EATON, Horace 186 Samuel 78
EDSON, Jesse 69
ELIOT, Edmund 73
ELIPHAZ, Mr 73
ELKINS, Jonathan 98
ELMORE, Aaron 84 Jesse 57
Martin 57

EMERSON, Col 213
EVANS, William 103
EVARTS, Mr 121
EVEREST, Zadock 20
East Bay 43 155 160 164
East Berkshire 28
East Charleston 45
East Creek 48 96 99 108 159 160
East Haven 35 37 56 61 65 91 127
    146 158 159 174
East Mills 183
East Montpelier 56 146
East Mountain 118
East Parish 108 109 134
East Poultney 101
East Village 32 51 110 111
Echo Pond 45 90
Eden 20 25 52 57 75 81 146 155
    162 176
Eligo-sigo 52
Elligo Pond 52 67 166
Elligo Scotland 166
Elligo Scootlon 166
Elmore 57 90 142 143 146 176
Elmore Mountain 57
Emerson's Branch 69
Enosburgh 22 27 58 88 115 146
    157 160 175
Enosburgh Falls 183
Enosburgh West 183
Equinox Mountain 55 83 113
Essex 49 59 62 77 134 138 146
    153 155 173
Essex County 22 29 35 37 41 42
    50 56 58 61 65 68 80 82 94 96
    127 133 144 150 152 169 170
    174 182 184 187 195
Essex District 195
Etechemin Indians 8
FAIRBANKS, E 111 139 T 111
FAIRFIELD, William 98
FARNSWORTH, John 52
FARNUM, Samuel 123
FARRAND, William 63
FARRAR, Joseph 57 Thomas 56
FARRIER, Thomas 109
FASSET, Amos 42 John Jr 42
FASSETT, Amos 58
FAY, John 62
FENTON, Jacob 95
FERGUSON, John 118

FERRIS, Peter 97
FESSENDEN, Joseph 188
FISHER, Amos 65 Ephraim 97
    William 97
FISK, Ebenezer 127
FITCH, Ichabod 76 Jabez 75 John
    54
FLETCHER, James 33 Jesse 82
    Josiah 82 Samuel 124
FLINT, Mrs Silas 31 Silas 31
FOLLETT, Martin D 58
FOOT, Nathan 51
FOSTER, Dan 133 Joel 137
    Jonathan 22
FOWLER, Barnet 23 Jacob 28 51
    Joanthan 23
FRAZER, 211
FREEMAN, Seth 100 Thomas 23
    William 23
FRENCH, Elijah 31 Justus W 25
FRIZZLE, Joel 89
FRY, John 50
FULLER, Cyrus M 55 Stephen
    127
Factory Point 183
Fair Haven 27 43 60 134 146 153
    160 178 196
Fair Haven District 195
Fairfax 59 60 62 63 134 146 153
    155 175
Fairfax North 183
Fairfield 22 59 62 115 122 146
    153 175
Fairfield East 183
Fairfield River 59 62
Fairlee 30 61 122 133 146 166
    176
Fairlee Lake 158 166
Fairlee Pond 61 133
Farmer's River 94
Farmers' & Mechanics' Bank 190
Farmers' Bank 190
Farrand's River 89
Fay's Brook 127
Fayetteville 183
Fayston 56 61 74 80 127 130 146
    179
Felchville 103 183
Ferdinand 35 56 61 65 83 133 146
Ferrand River 155
Ferren's River 35

Ferrisburgh 45 61 87 93 97 126 129 146 157 159 167 171
Ferrisburgh North 183
Fiddler's Elbow 160
Fifteen Mile Falls 23 132 154 159 167
First Branch 162
Fish Pond 121 142
Fitch's Bay 167
Fletcher 22 41 42 59 60 62 132 146 175
Florida 154
Flower Branch 53
Fordway Mountain 57
Fort Dummer 32 126
Fort Miller 153
Fort Saint Frederick 10 164
Fort Saint John 16
Fort Stanwix 212
Fort Ticonderoga 16 34 51 152
Four Brothers Islands 165
Franklin 27 63 72 115 146 160 175
Franklin County 22 27 47 58 59 62 63 72 79 87 96 104 109 115 122 150 151 169 170 175 182 184 187 195
Franklin District 195
Fresh River 12
Furnace Brook 48 99 123 159
Furnace River 159
GAGE, George 55
GALUSHA, Capt 114 Jonas 113 186
GARDNER, 102
GARVIN, Ephraim 75
GAY, Bunker 69 127
GEORGE II King of ---- 11
GIBBS, Mr 110
GILBERT, Thomas 44
GILLET, Daniel C 46
GIRLEY, Royal 69
GODARD, Samuel 50
GOLDSBURY, John 25
GOODALL, David 69
GOODEL, Jesse 135
GOODHUE, Josiah 102
GOODRICH, Allen 27 William 28
GOODWILLIE, David 24 109
GORDON, Alexander 66
GRAVES, Increase 34

GREEN, Henry 129 Joseph 91 Mr 110
GREENLEAF, Stephen 32
GREGORY, Daniel 50
GRISWOLD, 129 Benjmain 35 John 98
GROSS, Thomas 71
GROUT, Theophilus 78
GUILDER, Andrew 63
GUSTIN, 137
Gaysville 183
George's Pond 74
Georgia 59 63 86 110 146 175
German Spa waters 48
Glastenbury 64 113 116 121 142 146 161 172
Gloucester County 14
Glover 20 25 64 67 114 146 153 155 166 177
Gookin's Falls 108
Goshen 31 48 54 65 70 79 95 99 105 112 146 160 171
Goshen Gore 67 100 128 144
Governor's Farm 32
Grafton 22 47 65 106 124 140 146 160 162 180 183
Granby 56 61 65 68 82 127 146 158 174
Grand Isle 66 117 146 165 167 175
Grand Isle County 20 58 66 76 94 116 150 169 170 175 182 184 187 195
Grand Isle District 195
Granville 31 66 70 105 196 130 146 162 171
Grassy Brook 36 155
Great Brook 99 100
Great Falls 44 82 86 90
Great Hosmer Pond 20 52
Great Meadows 102
Great Narrows 118
Great North Branch 155
Great Notch 35
Great Oxbow 91
Great Pond 74
Great Round Mountain 32
Green Branch 142
Green Hill 129
Green Mountain Boys 48 109 184 196 197 212

Green Mountains 29 35 39 41 48 69 74 79 83 84 91 95 96 98 112 113 116 118 121 129 130 134 139 144 151 152 163 194 195

Green River 21 57 68 69 74 83 155

Greenbush 183

Greenfield 154

Greensborough 52 53 64 65 67 70 136 144 146 155 164 166 177

Greenwich 164

Gregory's Pond 73 155

Grog Harbor 62

Groton 67 95 98 109 144 146 161 172

Guildhall 22 29 35 37 42 50 56 58 65 68 80 82 83 127 133 146 169 174

Guilford 32 68 69 126 146 155 180

Gulf Road 138

Gulf The 196

Gunner's Branch 144

HACKET, Mr 121

HALE, Enoch 105

HALL, Daniel 23 Elijah 23 Enoch 68 76 Jacob 23 Samuel K 50 Sarah 23 William 65

HAMLINTON, Silas 137

HARMON, Calvin 52 Daniel W 52 Reuben 107

HARRINGTON, Antipas 78 Mr 86

HARRIS, Edward 144

HARVEY, Alexander 24

HARWOOD, Eleazar 27 Peter 27

HASKELL, Daniel 39 195

HASKINS, Joseph 60

HATCH, Jonas 139

HATHAWAY, Shadrach 97

HAVENS, Robert 107 114

HAWKINS, Mr 33

HAWKS, Col 44

HAWLEY, Elisha 141 Gideon 62 Jehiel 21 Josiah 21

HAYNES, Gov 12 Lemuel 109

HAZELTON, Betsey 92

HAZEN, William 66

HAZLETON, John 92 124

HEATH, Jonathan 39 Phinehas 28

HENRY IV King of France 11

HERRICK, 212 216 Samuel 117

HEWETT, Aaron 100

HIBBARD, Ebenezer 134 Ithamer 101

HICKOK, Elizabeth 74 Mrs Uriah 74 Uriah 74

HILLIKER, John 122

HINKLEY, Mr 65

HINMAN, Timothy 54

HOBART, James 28

HOBBS, Mr 134

HODGKINS, Thomas 99

HOLBROOK, John 188 John C 188

HOLLY, Jas 104

HOLT, Stephen 99

HOOKER, Mr 12

HOPKINS, David Jr 112 Ebenezer 99

HOPKINSON, David 68

HOSFORD, 123

HOSMER, John 30 Mr 67

HOTTON, Ebenezer 47

HOUSE, John 28 Stephen 58

HOVEY, Joanthan 136

HOWARD, Benjamin 76 Caleb 76 Mr 36 William 76

HOWE, Mr 212 Reuben 68 Simeon 68

HOXSIE, Gideon 87

HUBBARD, Samuel 63

HUDSON, Brazilla 28

HUGH, John 42

HULL, Jehiel 137

HUNTER, Henry 49

HUNTINGTON, Amos 114 Christopher 106

HURLBUT, Salmon 105

HUTCHINSON, Elisha 101 Titus 186

HYDE, Ebenezer 76 Jedediah 75

Hadley Mountain 57

Halifax 68 69 137 146 155 180

Halifax South 183

Halifax West 183

Hall's Brook 29

Hall's Pond 50

Hampton 101

Hancock 65 66 69 70 105 146 157 162 171

Hardwick 27 67 70 128 142 146 155 166 173

Hardwick North 183

Hardwick South 183
Harriman's Brook 91
Harris' Gore 67 68 84 95 144 161
Hartford 12 70-72 95 101 142 146
    154 158 162 181 184
Hartford District 195
Hartford West 183
Hartland 25 71 141 143 146 158
    181 184
Hartland North 183
Harvey's Lake 160
Harvey's Pond 23
Hawk's Mountain 22 44
Hawley 154
Haystack Mountain 97
Hazen's Notch 134 152
Hazen's Road 70
Heath 154
Heights of Abraham 48
Highgate 63 72 115 122 146 157
    160 168 175 184
Highgate East 183
Highgate Springs 183
Hill's Brooks 91
Hinesburgh 45 72-74 87 110 118
    146 155 157 173
Hinkley Brook 65
Hinkum Pond 121
Hinman's Pond 54
Hinsdale 69 126
Hinsdale's Fort 126
Hiram's Pond 128
Hog Island 72
Hog's Back Mountain 35 86 87
    118 119
Holden 24
Holland 54 73 90 94 144 147 177
Hoosack River 117
Hoosic 26
Hoosic Forts 27
Hoosic River 27 101 155 161
Hosmer's Ponds 166
Houghtonville 183
Howland's Pond 74
Hubbardston River 134
Hubbardton 16 17 27 43 73 99 114
    121 147 155 178 197
Hubbardton Battle of 216
Hubbardton Pond 121
Hubbardton River 155 160
Hubbell's Falls 59 77

Hudson River 26 153 155
Huntington 29 56 61 73 74 104
    118 144 147 151 152 155 173
Huntington River 104 118 155 163
Hydepark 25 42 57 74 75 78 79 90
    118 119 132 142 147 155 169
    176
Hydeville 183
IDE, Ichabod 47 John 52
INDIAN Sawdawda 137
IRISH, William 87
ISHAM, Joshua 110
IVES, Amos 91 Ebenezer 91
    Jonah 91
Indian Creek 49
Indian River 59 97 155
Ira 43 49 75 86 99 101 108 109
    123 147 153 178 196
Ira Brook 48
Irasburgh 20 25 37 45 52-54 65 67
    73 75 76 81 90 93 96 112 125
    134 135 144 147 153 169 177
Iron Horse 33 72 89 141
Iroquois Indians 7
Isle La Motte 76 147 175
Isles of the Four Winds 165
JACKSON, Abraham 129 William
    55
JAMES, John 68
JAMES King of ---- 14
JARVIS, William 132
JEFFERSON, 212
JENISON, Silas H 186
JENNIE, Prince 100
JENNINGS, James 41
JOHNS, Benjamin 49 Jehiel 74
JOHNSON, E F 151 Eden 35
    Edward 47 Isiah 47 James 111
    John 29 Thomas 92
JOHNSTON, Col 215
JONES, Asa 33 Deacon 33 John
    129 Miss 33
JOSLIN, Josiah 78
JUNE, David 31
JUSTIN, Benajah 136
Jacksonville 183
Jail Branch 24 95 161
Jamaica 76 80 120 124 129 140
    142 147 161 163 180
Jay 76 104 125 134 147 177
Jay Peak 57

Jay's Park 76
Jefferson 130
Jeffersonville 183
Jericho 59 76 77 104 125 138 147
   153 173
Jericho Centre 184
Jo and Molly's Pond 39
Joe's Brook 54 128
Joe's Pond 53 90 166
Joe's River 157
Johnson 25 42 57 59 75 78 118
   132 147 155 176
Juniper 165
Juniper Island 38 165
KEAD, Peter 82
KEELER, Aaron 57 75
KELLOGG, Gardner 30 Horace
   118
KENEDY, John 29 Robert 29
KENT, Dan 27 Elisha 107 Jacob
   92 chancellor 14
KEYES, Elias 118
KIMBALL, Asa 25 John 25
KING, Reuben 66 Salmon 67
KINGSBURY, Ebenezer 77
KINGSLEY, Phinehas 72
KINNEY, Bradford 100 Jonathan
   100
KINSLEY, Stephen 42
KNIGHT, Samuel 186 Simeon 106
Keeler's Pond 74
Kettle Pond 67 161
Killington Peak 115 116 152
Kingbury Branch 163
Kingsbury Branch 88
Kingston 105
Kirby 30 37 50 78 82 110 111 127
   147 173
Knowlton Lake 35 166
Knowlton's Pond 153
Knox Mountain 95
LABAREE, Benjamin 194
LACY, Isaac 55
LAMB, Aaron 33 Dana 35
LAMPHIRE, 137
LATHERBEE, Benjamin 65
LAWRENCE, 77 Isaac 73 Mrs
   Isaac 73 Stephen 39
LAWTON, John 140
LEACH, Jonathan 78
LEAVENWORTH, Nathan 72

LEAVITT, Seth 130
LEE, Chancey 121 Col 43
LELAND, Luther 54
LEWIS, Jonathan 78
LIDEUS, Col 49
LOGAN, 115
LORD, Jos 111 Samuel 130
LOW, Mr 50
LULL, Mrs Timothy 71 Timothy
   71
LUTHER, 9
LYMAN, Elijah 36 Gershom C 84
   John 36 Joseph 84 Josiah 138
LYNDE, Cornelius 138
LYON, Asa 66 James 125 Mat-
   thew 60
La Platt River 114
La Platte 156
Lake Beautiful 67
Lake Bombazine 42 60 73 153
Lake Champlain 8 10 12 16 18–21
   27 34 35 37 38 43–45 47 49 57
   61–63 66 76 78 86 96 97 109
   110 114–117 122 126 134 151
   152 155 157 159 160 163–168
   193 194
Lake Dunmore 79 112
Lake George 27 212
Lake George Creek 164
Lamoille County 25 41 57 62 74
   78 79 83 90 96 118 119 130
   132 142 150 152 169 170 176
   182 184 187 195
Lamoille District 195
Lamoille River 25 41 42 47 49 52
   57 59 62–64 67 70 74 78 79 86
   128 132 134 136 142 144 153
   155 162 166
Lamoilleville 70
Landgrove 79 80 98 136 144 147
   172
Langdon 37
Laplot River 45 72 155 156 160
Laprairie 165
Lee's Brook 77
Leech's Pond 156
Leech's Stream 156
Leeds Pond 42
Leicester 31 65 79 112 137 147
   159 166 171
Leicester River 65 69 79 112 159

227

Leicester River (continued)
166
Lemington 22 29 42 80 147 174
Lemonfair River 51 96 115 136
156 159
Lenoxville 94
Lewis 22 29 80 133 147 158
Lewis Creek 45 61 72 87 118 157
Leyden 154
Lincoln 35 61 80 118 130 147 155
171
Little Elligo Pond 166
Little Falls 82
Little Hosmer Pond 52
Little North Branch 88 155
Little Otter Creek 61 87 93 157
Little Pond 67 68
Little River 77
Little Round Mountain 32
Little West River 48 159
Locust Creek 22 157 162
Logan's Point 115
Londonderry 76 79 80 136 140 142
147 161 163 180
Long Pond 40 64 161 166
Long River 154
Lowell 20 25 57 75 81 88 125 134
144 147 152 157 177
Lower Falls 50
Lower Waterford 184
Ludlow 21 44 46 47 81 81 91 100
135 147 153 162 181
Ludlow Mountain 91
Ludlow Pond 81
Lull's Brook 71
Lunenburgh 50 68 82 127 147 157
158 167 174
Lutterloh 20
Lyman 23
Lyndon 45 78 82 111 121 136 147
157 159 173
Lyndon Centre 184
M'Connel's Falls 78
M'INTOSH, Donald 126
MALLARY, Ogden 133
MAN, Charles 47
MANLEY, John 55
MANN, Robert 123
MANNING, Joel 21
MANSFIELD, Amos 87

MARSH, Anna 188 Isaac 84
James 131 195 Joseph 52 Mrs
James 131 Perly 188
MARSHALL, Mr 137
MARTIN, Caleb 36 George 99 14
Peter 75
MATTISON, 113
MATTOCKS, John 186
MAY, James 25
MCCLARY, Capt 215
MCCORMICK, James 140
MCDANIEL, John 75
MCDONOUGH, 126 Commodore
165
MCEWEN, George 73 James F
34
MCFAIRLAIN, Jesse 104
MCGAFFEY, Andrew 45 Mrs 45
MCKEITH, Thomas 123
MCLAIN, Mr 50
MCNEAL, John 123
MCNEIL, John 45
MEACHAM, Hine 73 Jacob 73
John 60 William 60
MEAD, Stephen 99 Thomas 86
MEIGS, Mr 110
MELLEN, Thomas 213
MENDALL, Amos 33 Lucy 33
Mrs Amos 33
MERRILL, John 37 T A 85
MESSENGER, Mr 77
MILLER, Samuel 61
MILTIMORE, Lieut 213
MOGOON, Alexander 54
MONROE, President 120
MONTAGUE, Samuel 42
MONTS, Sieur de 11
MOORE, Fairbank 32 Harry 30
James 29 John 100 Jonah 36
Mrs Fairbank 32 Paul 116
Samuel 46 Thomas 46 Thomas
Porter 46
MORGAN, 102 Asaph 59 Thomas
86
MORRILL, Abraham 136 Mr 110
MORRIS, Gov 212 Lewis R 117
210
MORSE, Daniel 131 John 131
Josiah 111 Mr 68
MORSMAN, 120

MUDGE, John 100
MURRAY, Eber 97
Mad River 19 56 61 80 89 127 130
  157 163
Magog Oil Stone 167
Magog Outlet 167
Maidstone 37 61 65 68 82 147 174
Maidstone Lake 83
Mallet's Bay 49 50
Mallet's Creek 49
Manchester 26 27 55 74 83 85 113
  121 142 147 153 169 172 183
  213
Manchester Bank 190
Manchester District 195
Mansfield 29 83 118 119 125 131
  147 151 152 161 176
Mansfield Mountain 119 151-153
Markhum Mountain 21
Marlborough 32 55 56 69 83 92
  135 139 147 155 162 180
Marlborough District 195
Marsh Pond 73
Marshfield 39 40 84 89 98 100
  144 147 161 163 179
Masuippi River 94 144
McIndoe's Falls 23 167 184
McNeil's Ferry 165
McQuam Bay 168
Mead's Falls 109
Mead's Pond 57
Meadow Branch 161
Mechanicsville 184
Medical College 18
Medway 84
Memphremagog Lake 25 37 52 54
  57 64 93 96 112 114 152 153
  158 166 168
Mendon 48 84 108 109 115 116
  147 178
Merrimac River 9
Merritt's River 54 157
Metcalf Pond 41 59 62
Micmac Indians 8
Middlebury 19 20 31 36 46 51 62
  65 66 70 80 85 87 97 99 105
  112 113 116 118 126 129 136
  137 147 151 152 157 159 169
  171
Middlebury Bank 190
Middlebury College 18 194

Middlebury East 184
Middlebury Falls 51 136
Middlebury River 69 85 93 104
  112 157 159
Middlesex 40 85 86 89 131 143
  147 163 179
Middlesex Narrows 88
Middletown 75 86 101 123 133
  147 154 160 178
Miles' Pond 50 157
Miles' River 157
Mill Brook 21 30 77 127 141 157
Mill River 20 31 48 53 90 116 128
  159
Miller's River 157
Milton 49 63 86 117 134 147 173
Milton West 184
Minehead 29 37
Missisco Bay 21 63 72 157 160
  168
Missisco River 22 27 41 58 59 62
  63 72 81 87 93 96 104 115 122
  124 125 134 152 155 157 160
Mohawk Indians 7 8
Mohawk River Dutchman 141
Molly's Pond 167
Monadnock of Vermont the 80
Monarch Carrier 75 111 196
Monkton 35 45 62 72 73 87 118
  147 157 171
Monkton Pond 87
Monroe 39 154
Montgomery 58 81 87 88 104 134
  147 152 160 175
Montpelier 20-25 27-33 35-37
  39-76 78-101 103-107 109 110
  112-138 142 143 147 151 155
  163 169 179 187 188 190 196
  211
Montpelier Bank 190
Montpelier East 184
Montpelier North 184
Montpelier Village 88 163
Moon Brook 108
Moose River 30 50 56 58 110 127
  132 158
Moretown 28 30 56 86 89 127 131
  147 157 163 179
Morgan 45 73 89 112 133 144 147
  155 167 177
Morristown 57 75 90 118 119 131

Morristown (continued) 147 161 176
Morrisville 90
Morse's Pond 23
Mount Holly 48 82 90 91 100 116 129 135 147 178 184
Mount Hor 135
Mount Independence 96 97 152 164
Mount Nebo 152
Mount Norris 57
Mount Pico 135
Mount Pisgah 116
Mount Tabor 53 55 91 98 129 136 147 159 178
Mount Tom 100 152
Mount Zion 73
Mud Pond 74
Muddy Brook 138 158 163
Mussey Brook 108
NASH, Timothy 68
NEAL, Benjamin 20
NELSON, 137
NEWMAN, David 127
NEWTON, John 23 Marshal 116
NICHOLS, Ammi 31 Isaac 31 James 21
NILES, Henry 69
NOBLE, 27 102 Calvin 46
NORRIS, 70 Samuel 51
NORTON, William 75
NOYES, Oliver 75
NUTTING, David 28 John 51
NYE, Jonathan 110
Neal's Branch 82
Neal's Brook 158
Neal's Pond 82 158
New Haven 35 62 85 93 129 136 147 157 159 171 183
New Haven District 195
New Haven River 35 80 159
New Salem 70
Newark 35 37 56 91 121 135 147 159 173
Newburn 24
Newbury 29 30 51 67 71 91 92 100 109 123-125 147 161 176 184
Newbury Bank 190
Newbury South 184
Newbury Stream Mfg Company 92

Newfane 22 33 36 37 55 56 65 69 76 83 84 92 102 106 124 127 129 130 135 139 147 161 169 180 183 190
Newport 52 54 75 93 112 144 147 166 168 177
Newton Academy 116
Norfolk 42
North Branch 41 51 158 161 163
North Hero 20 21 66 94 110 116 117 122 147 169 175
North Pond 57
North River 12 69
North Village 103
Northern Railroad 25 29 31 36 46 56 59 62 66 71 72 74 78 86 87 89 94 95 101 103-105 107 114 119 125 128 132 138 143 163 196
Northern Yeomen 26
Northfield 28 46 93 106 107 127 128 138 147 154 179
Northfield Mfg Company 93
Norton 22 73 94 144 147
Norton Pond 73 94
Norwich 71 94 106 114 122 147 158 181
Norwich Plain 94
Norwich University 95
Nose Mountain 152
Nulhegan River 22 29 35 37 58 80 133 154 158
OAKES, Seth 22
OGDEN, John C 29
OLDS, Jesse 134 138 Mr 77
OLMSTEAD, James 57 Seth 57
OLMSTED, Moses 99
ORDWAY, Moses 125
OSBORN, Benjamin 123 129
OSMORE, Mr 68
OWEN, Edward 99 Leonard 87
Ompompanoosuc River 94 95 119 122 127 133 154 158
Onion River 50 98 130 163
Onion River Pond 98
Orange 24 95 100 123 131 144 147 176
Orange County 19 29 30 36 41 46 50 60 91 95 102 109 119 122 123 125 127 130 131 133 138

Orange County (continued)
140 150 151 169 170 176 177
182 184 187 192 195
Orange County Agricultural Socie-
ty 191
Orange County Bank 190
Orange County Mutual Fire Insurance Company 190
Orleans 37 52 75 93 112 144 153
166
Orleans Bank 190
Orleans County 25 37 41 44 52-54
58 62 64 67 73 75 76 79 81 89
93 96 112 124 134 144 150 153
169 170 177 178 182 184 187
195
Orleans District 195
Orleans Iron Company 125
Orwell 27 96 97 116 121 137 147
152 156 159 164 171 183 190
Orwell Centre 184
Otta Quechee Mill Company 33
Otta Quechee River 33 71 158
160-162
Otter Creek 19 20 31 44 48 51 53
55 61 69 74 79 85 90 91 93 97
99 107-109 112 121 123 126
128 129 136 137 152 156 157
159 166 213
PACKARD, Winslow 139
PADDOCK, Robert 25
PAGE, David 68 Joseph 136 Mr
68 Mrs 68 Phinehas 78 Porter
70 Samuel 68
PAIGE, Nathaniel 23
PAINE, Charles 186 Elijah 94
138 John 138
PAINTER, Gamaliel 84
PALMER, Aaron 25 Thomas 29
William A 186
PANGBORN, John 97
PARK, John 103 Jonathan 92
PARKER, Elder 91 James 58 125
Jeremiah 80 Ralph 65 Thomas
H 57
PARMELEE, Hezekiah 134
Reuben 73 Simeon 134
PARSONS, Justin 118 137 Justus
99 Silas 121
PARTRIDGE, Capt 151
PATCH, 120

PATTERSON, Jas 80
PAYNE, John 28 36 Noah 36
PEARSALL, Thomas 30
PECK, John 104 Thomas 21 123
PECKHAM, Samuel 63
PERCIVAL, Orin 45
PERHAM, Jonathan 22
PERKINS, Mr 132 Nathaniel 128
Theodore 100
PERLEY, Benton 138
PETERS, John 30
PHELPS, E 97
PHILIPS, Paul D 54
PHIPPS, William 102
PIERCE, Jonathan 36 Jotham 52
PIKE, 137
PINGREY, Nathaniel 91
PITKIN, Calvin 84 Martin 84
PLUMER, 34
PLYMPTON, Oliver 98
POMROY, Rufus 113
POTTER, Andrew 110 Lyman 95
POTTIER, 115 John 168
POWELL, Felix 55 99
POWERS, Peter 92
PRATT, Abijah 22 Samuel 27
Timothy 27
PRENTISS, Samuel 186
PRESTON, Willard 195
PRINGLE, William 109
PUTNAM, 212 Edward 65 Mr 86
Paawlet 53 155
Palches Pond 90
Panton 20 62 97 126 129 147 159
171
Paris 24
Parker's Gore 84
Parkerstown 48 84
Parmelee's River 59
Passumpsic Railroad 196
Passumpsic River 23 24 30 35 37
41 54 56 58 64 82 91 110 114
121 132 135 136 154 157-159
Passumpsic River Railroad 196
Passumsic 184
Paul's Stream 37 61 82 83
Pawlet 97 107 133 147 159 178
Pawlet River 53 55 97 107 155
159
Peacham 23 39 54 68 84 98 148
160 163 173

Peal's Pond 116
Pension Pond 45
People's Academy 90
Perkinsville 132 183 184 196
Peru 55 79 91 98 142 148 159 172
Petawa-bouque Lake 166
Philadelphia River 48 65 99 160
Philips Academy 54
Phoenix Mill Co 106
Pike River 20 27 63 160
Pine Brook 127
Pitkin's Pond 35 153
Pittsfield 48 65 99 105 118 148
    162 178
Pittsford 31 43 48 74 99 109 112
    148 153 159 160 178
Plain The 39 110 111
Plainfield 24 84 89 95 99 144 148
    163 179
Plaster Point 156
Platt River 160
Plattsburgh 38 39 48 64 166
Plott River 160
Plymouth 33 44 81 91 100 103
    116 148 153 158 181 184 199
Plymouth Cave 100
Plymouth Pond 81 103
Podunk Pond 119
Pomfret 71 100 101 114 143 148
    181 184
Pond Brook 72 87
Post Mills 184
Pottier's Point 115 165 167 168
Poultney 43 60 75 86 101 133 148
    160 178 196
Poultney Bank 190
Poultney East 184
Poultney River 43 60 86 101 134
    153 160
Poultney West 184
Pownal 26 27 101 117 148 155
    161 172
Prichard Mountain 72
Proctersville 184
Proctorsville 44
Providence 35
Putney 36 56 92 102 135 148 180
QUAIL JOHN 123
Quaker Hill 30
Queche Village 184
Quechee Falls 71 154 158

Quechee River 70 71 100 101 103
    158 160
Quechee Village 70 71
Queechy River 107 115 140 143
RANSOM, John 33 137
RATENBURGH, Thomas V 118
RATHBUN, David 137
REED, Abner 33 Simeon 82
REMINGTON, Jairus 102 Zadock
    43
REMMELE, Samuel H 136
REYNOLDS, Mr 120
RICE, Abner 69 Elder 30 Micah
    69 Randal 49 Elisha 99
RICHARDS, Mr 34 Mrs 34
RICHARDSON, 34 Staunton 94
RIDLAN, John 143
RIEDESEL, Baroness 212
ROBBINS, Zenas 70
ROBERTS, Eli 34
ROBINS, Aaron 31 George 31
ROBINSON, Amos 93 94 Ezekiel
    94 Jonathan 186 Leonard 27
    Moses 62 Samuel 26 27
    Samuel Jr 27
ROCKWELL, W H 190
ROGERS, James 80 Major 24
    Samuel 25 Timothy 62
ROOD, Mr 77
ROOT, Benajah 109
ROSBROOK, Eleazar 68 James
    68
ROSE, Samuel 83
ROYCE, Andrew 138 Elihu M 28
    Stephen 28 186
RUSSELL, Noadiah 44 Thomas
    29
Randolph 28 30 31 36 102 125 148
    162 176
Randolph District 195
Randolph East 184
Randolph West 184
Random 35
Ray's Pond 138
Reading 44 100 103 141 143 148
    181 183
Reading Centre Village 103
Reading South 184
Readsborough 104 113 137 143
    148 172
Red Mountain 21 113

Reedsborough 117
Richelieu River 165 167
Richford 27 58 76 87 104 148 157
    175
Richmond 29 73 74 77 104 138
    148 155 163 173
Ripton 65 66 70 85 104 148 157
    171
River of Pines 154
Roaring Branch 21 121
Roaring Brook 29 153
Rocher River 63
Rochester 28 65 66 69 70 99 105
    148 162 181
Rock Dunder 165
Rock River 63 72 160
Rockingham 47 65 105 106 117
    135 148 160 162 167 180 183
    184 211
Rockingham Village 106
Ross' Pond 23
Round Island 24
Round Pond 73 153
Rowell's Ledge 30
Roxbury 30 31 36 66 106 130 148
    155 162 179
Roxbury East 184
Royalton 23 28 104 107 114 125
    138 148 153 162 181 196
Royalton Village 107
Runaway Pond 67 153 166
Rupert 55 98 107 113 148 155 159
    162 172
Rutland & Burlington Railroad 44
    196
Rutland & Washington Railroad 196
Rutland & Whitehall Railroad 196
Rutland 27 43 48 49 53 60 74 75
    84 86 91 97-99 101 107 108
    113 115 116 121 123 129 133
    134 148 153 159 169 178 196
Rutland Bank 190
Rutland County 19 26 27 31 42 48
    53 60 73 75 81 84 86 90 91 97
    99 101 107 108 115 116 121
    123 128 133 134 140 150 151
    169 170 178 179 182 184 187
    195
Rutland County Mutual Fire
    Insurance Company 190
Rutland District 195

Rutland Village 108
Rutland West 184
Ryegate 23 68 92 109 148 160 161
    173
SABIN, Elihu 144 Gideon 70 Mary
    144 Mrs Gideon 70
SAFFORD, Silas 60
SAGE, Sylvester 135
SALISBURY, William 128
SANBURNE, Ebenezer 28
SANDERS, Daniel C 126 David 63
SANDERSON, Jas 143
SANFORD, John 136
SARGEANT, David 32 David Jr
    32 Jabez 47 John 32 Silas 42
    Thomas 32
SAUNDERS, Daniel C 195
SAWYER, N P 75 Truman 75
SAXTON, Frederick 39 Jonathan
    62 Mr 160
SCHUYLER, 211 212
SCOTT, Aaron 51 Oliver 107
    Walter 122
SEARLE, John 107
SEARLS, William 21
SEAVEY, Joseph 45
SEELYE, 102
SERGEANT, Nahum 103
SEYMOUR, Epaphri 188
SHAFTER, James 22
SHAW, Isaiah 33
SHELDON, Cephas 33 Elisha 115
    Samuel B 115
SHEPARD, Aaron 67 Ashbel 53
    67 Horace 67 Mrs Aaron 67
    Mrs Ashbel 67 William Scott
    67
SHERMAN, Jonathan 24 25
SILL, Elijah 55
SKEELES, Thomas 112
SKEELS, Thomas 75
SKEENE, Major 214
SKINNER, Richard 186 Samuel 36
SLADE, William 186
SLAFTER, John 95
SLEEPER, Samuel 30 92
SMALLEY, Benjamin 85
SMILEY, Robinson 117
SMITH, 34 Benjamin 28 Calvin
    24 Ebenezer 95 Elisha 43
    Israel 186 James 44 John 138

233

SMITH (continued)
  Mr 59 Samuel 54 Steele 141
SOPER, Joseph 53
SOUTHGATES, Mr 33
SPAFFORD, Amos 97 Asa 59
  Broadstreet 59 John 42 Mrs
  John 42 Nathan 59
SPALDING, Timothy 97
SPEAR, Andrew 103 Jacob 31
  Samuel 31
SPENCER, Amasa 112 Gideon 84
  Hubbard 42 Seth 37
SPRING, Samuel 65
SQUIRE, Odle 97
STANTON, Joshua 142
STARK, 212-216 John 44
STAUNTON, Joshua 50
STEARNS, Amos 35 Ebenezer 87
  John 87
STEBBINS, Ebenezer 51
STEDMAN, Nathaniel 92
STEELE, George 73
STEPHEN, Ichabod G 91
STEVENS, 216 Enos 23 24 Henry
  23 191 John 35 Mr 112 Phi-
  neas 23 160 Roger 99 Samuel
  23 24 Willard 23
STEWART, Samuel 35
STICKNEY, Col 213
STINSON, Robert 29
STOCKWELL, Abel 83
STODDARD, John 76
STONE, Moses 40 Philip 34
STOREY, Amos 112 Mrs Amos
  112
STOW, David 136
STREETER, Benjamin 50
STRONG, Benajah 71 Elijah 71
  John 20 Noah 31 Solomon 71
SUMNER, Clement 123 David H
  71
SWASEY, Dudley 136
SWEET, David 80
SWIFT, Job 20
Sacket's Brook 102
Saint Albans 22 28 58-60 62-64
  72 76 88 104 109 110 115 117
  122 148 169 175
Saint Albans Bank 190
Saint Augustine Lake 133
Saint Augustine Pond 133

Saint Francis 161
Saint Francis Indians 24 166
Saint Francis River 22 94 167
Saint George 73 110 114 138 148
  174
Saint James Church 21
Saint Johns 165
Saint Johnsbury 30 54 78 79 82
  110 111 132 136 148 158 159
  173
Saint Johnsbury Centre 184
Saint Johnsbury East 184
Saint Johnsbury Plain 158 159
Saint Lawrence 165
Saint Peters Lake 165 167
Salem 21 37 45 54 73 90 112 148
  153 154 168 178
Salem Lake 153
Salem Pond 54 73 112
Salisbury 51 65 79 84 112 137 148
  159 166 171
Sand Bar Bridge 86 117
Sandgate 83 107 113 148 172
Saratoga & Washington Railroad
  196
Sawdawda Pond 137
Saxe's Mills 184
Saxton's River 105 106 139 140
  160 184
Saxton's River Village 106
Schuyler's Island 165
Searsborough 148
Searsburgh 104 113 116 139 142
  143 172
Second Branch 162
Sexton's River 65 154
Seymour's Brook 41
Seymour's Lake 45 89 167
Shaftsbury 21 26 64 113 148 155
  172
Shaftsbury South 184
Sharon 22 95 101 107 114 120 148
  153 162 181
Sharpshin Point 168
Sheffield 25 65 114 121 136 148
  153 157 173
Shelburne 38 45 73 110 114 148
  154-156 168 174
Shelburne Bay 114 155 156 167 168
Shelburne Point 168
Sheldon 58-60 63 72 115 122 148

234

Sheldon (continued)
157 175
Sheldon East 184
Shepherd's Brook 127
Sherburne 33 84 115 118 148 152
158 178
Shetterack Mountain 113
Sholes Landing 96 164
Shoreham 34 51 97 115 137 148
156 159 171
Shrewsbury 48 49 84 90 91 100
116 119 148 152 179 183
Shrewsbury Peak 116 152
Simondsville 184
Skenesboro 77
Sleeper's Branch 54
Sleeper's River 54 110 111
Smith's Branch 161
Smithfield 60
Smithfield Pond 59
Snow's Store 184
Somerset 55 64 113 116 120 129
139 148 154 180
South Bay 52 112 160 164 168
South Branch 158 161
South Hero 66 86 116 117 148 165
167 175
South Mountain 35 53 55
South Reading 103
South Village 143
Southern Railroad 43 47–49 51 53
65 73 75 80 84 85 93 99 105
106 109 113 115 116 121 123
126 129 136 137 196
Split Rock 165
Spring Pond 31
Springfield 22 47 106 117 133 148
153 181 196
Springfield North 184
Spruce Mountain 53 113
Stamford 101 104 117 143 148 172
Starksborough 35 73 74 80 87 118
144 148 155 157 171
State House at Montpelier (illus)
187
State Prison 188
Sterling 42 78 90 118 148 152 176
Sterling Peak 118 152
Steven's Brook 59
Stevens' Branch 24 28 36 95 98
138 144 160 162 163

Stevens' Mills 23
Stevens' River 23 24 160
Stevensville 70
Stillwater 155 212
Stockbridge 23 28 99 115 118 148
162 181 183
Stockbridge Indians 84
Stone Bridge Brook 63
Stone's Brook 59 62
Stowe 83 90 119 131 143 148 161
176
Strafford 114 119 122 125 127 148
158 176
Strafford Copperas Works 119
Strafford South 184
Stratton 76 116 120 121 123 129
142 148 154 161 180
Street The 70
Sudbury 27 31 73 74 121 137 148
155 179
Sullivan Railroad 106 133 142 196
Sullivan Railroad Company 196
Sumner's Village 71
Sunderland 21 64 74 83 120 121
148 153 172
Sutherland's Falls 108
Sutton 37 82 91 114 121 135 148
153 173
Swanton 60 72 110 115 122 148
157 168 175
Swanton Centre 184
Swanton Falls 72 122 157 184
Swanton West 184
Swearing Hill 113
TABOR, Lemuel 124
TAPLIN, John 92
TAYLOR, Absalom 87 Mr 93
TENNEY, Samuel G 82
THOMPSON, Abel 62 104 David
61 Hez 141 Ignatius 101
James 101 Joseph 24 Lathrop
46 114 Mr 198 199 S 80
Samuel 124 William 61
THURBER, Joseph 28
THURSTON, Pearson 111
TICHENOR, Isaac 186
TOLMAN, Thomas 51
TOPLIFF, Mr 33
TOWLE, Bracket 51
TOWNER, 34
TREADWAY, James 133

TROUP, Joseph 51
TROWBRIDGE, William 74
TRUMBELL, Robert 53
TUBBS, Simon 39
TUFTS, James 129
TULLER, Martin 107 141
TUPPER, Absalom 62 Zuriel 62
TUTTLE, Amos 59 70 Hezekiah
   73
TWISS, Mrs Samuel 40 41
   Samuel 40
TYLER, Joseph 124 Royal 186
Taftsville 184
Taylor's Branch 157
Terrible Mountain 21
Thetford 61 94 95 120 122 133
   148 158 177 184
Third Branch 162
Thompson's Point 165
Thundering Brook 115
Tiney Pond 81
Tinmouth 48 49 53 75 86 108 123
   129 133 149 159 160 179
Topsham 51 68 92 95 123 149 161
   177
Topsham West 184
Townshend 22 36 76 92 124 129
   149 161 180
Townshend West 184
Trout Pond 166
Trout River 27 58 87 157 160
Troy 76 81 93 124 125 134 144
   149 157 178
Troy Furnace 184
Troy North 184
Tunbridge 46 103 107 120 125 149
   158 162 177
Turnersburgh 46
Tweed River 48 99 118
Twenty Miles Encampment the
   44
Twenty-mile Stream 43
Tyson Furnace 184
UNDERHILL, Abraham 55
UNDERWOOD, Amos 50
UPHAM, 216 James 88
UTLEY, Mrs William 79 Wil-
   liam 79
Underhill 42 59 77 125 134 149
   153 174
Union Railroad 196

Union Village 184
University of Vermont 194
VAIL, CAlvin 53 Luther 53 Micah
   53
VANCE, James 65
VANNESS, C P 186
Vergennes 34 61 62 73 93 97 104
   126 129 149 157 159 171
Vergennes Bank 190
Vermont Bank 190
Vermont Copperas Company 119
Vermont Mineral Factory Compa-
   ny 119
Vermont Mutual Fire Insurance
   Company 190
Vermont Southern Railroad 31
Vermont State Prison 141
Vermont Valley Railroad 196
Vernon 32 68 126 149 180
Vershire 46 51 120 127 133 149
   158 177
Victory 30 37 56 65 82 110 127
   149 158 174
Vineyard 76 117
Virgin Hill 144
Virgin Mountain 29
WAIT, Benjamin 76 Capt 161
   Gen 127 Joseph 37 Lynde 61
   Nathaniel 37
WALDEN, J 110
WALDO, Mr 113 Nathan 138
WALKER, Gideon 137 Jacob 90
   Levi 136 Mr 98
WALLIS, Ebenezer 21
WALTER, Ira 37 Lemuel 37
WARD, Mr 20 62
WARE, Avery 88
WARNER, 16 212 213 215 216
   Col 16 Jesse 215 Seth 14 164
   William 47
WARRENS, Mr 121
WASHBURN, Azel 107 Daniel
   137 Isaiah 115
WASHINGTON, Gen 211-213
WATERHOUSE, Abiel 112
WATERS, Ebenezer 30
WATSON, 102
WEARE, Meshech 16
WEBB, Derick 45 Mr 121
WEBSTER, Benjamin 39 Mr 67
WELD, John 103

WELLS, Samuel 32 52 William 33
WENTWORTH, Benning 26 Gov 13 14 Moses 57
WEST, Ebenezer 127 Francis 40
WHEELER, George 68 John 195 Joseph 60
WHEELOCK, Abijah 40 Asa 40 John 136 Lucinda 41 Mrs 40 41 Peter 40 41
WHELAN, John 31
WHITCOMB, Asa 23 118 Cyrus Jr 36 Lot 23
WHITE, Ebenezer 92 Jade 78 Joel 61 Noah 92
WHITELAW, J 45
WHITING, Samuel 47 106
WHITMORE, Mrs Thomas 83 Thomas 83
WHITNEY, James 82
WILCOX, Jacob 91 Nathan 90
WILLARD, John 82 Mr 59 Nathan 32
WILLIAMS, Charles K 186 Dr 13 14 Elisha 16 Henry 69 John 162 Joseph 96 137 William 24
WILLISTON, David H 125
WILLOUGHBY, Mr 113
WILMOT, Ezra 104
WILSON, Dr 137 James 30 John 137 Joseph 104 Mr 137
WINCHEL, Mr 59
WINSLOW, Jedediah 31
WISWELL, Henry 137
WOLF, 48
WOLFE, Gen 126
WOOD, Enos 94 Solomon 94
WOODARD, Mr 99
WOODBRIDGE, Enoch 186
WOODBURN, John 140
WOODBURY, Jesse 50 Jonathan 50
WOODS, Abel 116
WOODWARD, Joshua 99
WOOLAGE, Elijah 42 69
WOOLCUT, Elijah 45
WOOSTER, Benjamin 51 60
WORCESTER, John H 111 Leonard 98
WRIGHT, 102 Benoni 30 Moses 106

Wait's Branch 95
Wait's River 29 30 51 123 131 154 161 162
Waitsfield 61 89 127 130 149 157 179
Walcott 52
Walden 39 53 54 70 128 144 149 173
Walden South 184
Wallingford 48 49 90 91 123 128 149 159 179
Wallingford South 184
Walloomsack River 117
Walloomscoik Mill Co 26
Walloomscoik River 27 64 101 113 155 161 213
Walpole 106
Waltham 20 62 93 97 126 129 149 159 171
Wantasticook River 161
Wardsborough 55 76 92 116 120 124 129 149 161 180
Wardsborough North 184
Wardsborough West 184
Warm Brook 21
Warner's Gore 90 94 144 155
Warren 61 66 80 106 127 130 144 149 157 179
Warren's Gore 94 144
Washington 46 51 89 95 96 131 138 149 161 162 177 183 215
Washington County 19 24 28 39 41 47 56 61 79 84–86 88 89 93 95 99 106 127 130 131 142 143 150–152 169 170 179 182 184 187 195
Washington District 195
Water Cure Establisment 32
Water Quechee River 158 161
Waterbury 29 56 85 86 89 119 131 149 161 163 179
Waterbury River 119 131 161 163
Waterbury Village 163
Waterford 23 50 110 111 132 149 159 173
Waterford Lower 184
Waterqueechy River 154
Waterville 22 25 42 62 132 149 176
Weathersfield 22 44 103 117 132 141 149 151 153 181 183 184

237

Weathersfield (continued)
196
Wells 86 97 101 123 133 149 179
Wells River 67 68 91 109 154 161
184 211 213
Wells River Pond 67
Wenlock 35 37 61 80 90 133 149
155 158 166
West Bay 164
West Berkshire 28
West Branch 158
West Charleston 45
West Fairlee 61 127 133 149 158
177
West Haven 27 60 134 155 160
179
West Mountain 21 113
West Parish 108 109
West Poultney 101
West Randolph Academy 103
West River 32 36 55 56 79 80 83
92 108 124 129 135 139 140
142 154 161 163
West River Meadows 32
West Rutland 108
West Townsend Manufacturing
Company 124
West Village 32
West Windsor 134 149
Westfield 76 81 88 125 134 149
157 178
Westford 59 86 125 134 149 153
174
Westhaven 149
Westminster 22 36 94 102 105
106 134 135 149 160 180
Westminster District 195
Westminster West 184
Westmore 25 35 37 45 91 121 135
149 153 159 162 167 178
Weston 21 79 80 82 91 135 144
149 161 181
Weybridge 20 34 51 85 93 136
149 156 159 171
Wheeler Stream 37
Wheelock 53 54 67 82 114 136
144 149 157 173
Whetstone Brook 32 83 162
White Creek 162
White Mountains 39

White River 19 22 28 30 31 36 46
47 66 69 70 71 95 99 101 102
105–107 114 118 125 131 138
140 153 154 157 162
White River Falls 154
White River Iron Company 71
White River Village 70 71
White Rocks 129
White's Mills 43
Whitehall 38 39 43 77 153 164
165 168
Whiting 31 51 79 97 112 116 121
136 137 149 156 159 171
Whitingham 69 104 137 139 149
180 183
Wild Branch 52 57 142 162
Wildersburgh 24
Willard's Brook 42
Williams' River 46 47 65 105 139
140 154 162
Williamstown 24 28 36 40 46 131
138 149 162 177 196
Williston 38 49 59 77 104 110
138 149 158 163 174
Willoughby Lake 135 162 167
Willoughby River 37 153 162
Willoughby's Pond 153
Wilmington 55 83 113 116 137–
139 149 180
Wind-mill Point 20
Windham 21 46 65 76 80 124 140
149 160–162 180
Windham County 21 26 32 36 55
56 65 68 69 76 80 83 92 102
105 116 120 124 126 129 134
135 137–140 150 151 154 169
170 180 182 184 187 188 195
Windham County Mutual Fire
Insurance Company 190
Windmill Point 168
Windsor 18 21 22 23 29 32 33 36
37 44 47 69 71 72 81 82 95 98
100 101 103–105 107 114 116
119 127 128 133 136 140–143
149 151 157 181 183 188 196
200
Windsor County 19 21 22 28 33
43 46 70 71 81 82 94 95 100
103 105 107 114 117 118 132
134 135 139 140 141 143 144

Windsor County (continued)
150 151 153 169 170 181–184
187 195
Windsor County Mutual Fire
Insurance Company 190
Windsor District 195
Winhall 76 83 98 120 142 144 149
161 163 172
Winhall River 120 142 161 163
Winooski 184
Winooski City 38
Winooski Falls 73 167
Winooski Lower Falls 163
Winooski River 28 29 36 37 38 39
40 47 49 50 56 57 59 76 77 84–
86 88 89 95 98 99 100 104 106
127 128 130 131 138 142 143
152 155 157 158 161–163 167
Winooski Village 50
Winose River 24

Wolcott 57 67 70 75 142 149 155
162 176
Woloomsack River 142
Wood Creek 159 164
Woodard's Cave 69
Woodbury 40 57 70 142 149 179
Woodford 26 64 104 113 117 142
149 161 172
Woodstock 33 71 101 103 117 140
142 143 149 152 158 169 181
190 196
Woodstock Bank 190
Woodstock Green 143
Woodstock Railroad 196
Woodstock South 184
Worcester 40 57 86 119 131 143
149 161 179
Wright's Mountain 29
YOUNG, A B 88 187 Ammi B 143
188 Joab 120
Zack's Pond 74